SURRE ART

0181878443

D0323092

FABRICATIONS

Costume and the Female Body

AFI Film Readers
a series edited by
Edward Branigan and Charles Wolfe

Psychoanalysis and Cinema
E. Ann Kaplan, editor

The American Film Institute
P.O. Box 27999
2021 North Western Avenue
Los Angeles, California 90027

FABRICATIONS

Costume and the Female Body

EDITED BY

JANE GAINES
and **CHARLOTTE HERZOG**

ROUTLEDGE
New York • London

To our mothers

Nancy and Charlotte, Sr.

Published in 1990 by

Routledge
An imprint of Routledge, Chapman and Hall, Inc.
29 West 35 Street
New York, NY 10001

Published in Great Britain by

Routledge
11 New Fetter Lane
London EC4P 4EE

Library of Congress Cataloging-in-Publication Data

Fabrications : costume and the female body / edited by Jane M. Gaines
and Charlotte Herzog.
    p.   cm.—(AFI film readers)
  Bibliography: p.
  Contents: All the rage / Elizabeth Wilson — The female colossus /
Serafina K. Bathrick — Designing woman / Maureen Turim — Fig
Leaves in Hollywood / Jeanne Allen — Spectacular consumption /
Charlotte Herzog — Costume and narrative / Jane Gaines —
Handmaidens of glamour culture / Betsy Holdsworth Nielson — The
Carole Lombard in Macy's window / Charles Eckert — Masochism,
masquerade, and the erotic metamorphoses of Marlene Dietrich / Gaye
Studlar — Dance and social fantasy / Angela McRobbie — Working
(it) over / Laurie Schulze.
  ISBN 0-415-90061-1; ISBN 0-415-90062-X (pbk.)
  1. Costume—United States—History—20th century. 2. Body, Human–
–Social aspects. 3. Feminism and the arts. I. Gaines, Jane M.,
1943– . II. Herzog, Charlotte, 1946– . III. Series: AFI film
readers.
GT615.F33   1989
391'.00973—dc20   89-10277

British Library Cataloguing in Publication Data

Fabrications : costume and the female body. — (AFI Film
readers series)
  1. Women. Body. Psychosocial aspects
  I. Gaines, Jane M, *1946–*   II. Herzog, Charlotte,
1943–
  305.4
  ISBN 0-415-90061-1
       0-415-90062-X (pb)

Contents

Acknowledgments

The authors would like to thank the following people and institutions for their help in preparing this collection: Val Almendarez, Sam Gill, and Bob Kushman (Academy of Motion Picture Arts and Sciences Library); Edward Maeder (Los Angeles County Museum of Art Costume Department); Elizabeth Jackimowicz (Chicago Historical Society Costume Department); Films, Inc. and MGM/UA; Duke University Research Council; Renee Conley, Charles LeMaire, and David Chierichetti for their interviews; Milan and Shanta Herzog for their hospitality; Deborah Whitman and Jamie Hysjulien for help preparing the manuscript. Special thanks go to our colleagues in the field Richard Dyer, Bill Horrigan, Patricia Mellencamp, Eva Warth, Ellen Seiter, Joanne Yeck, and especially Bill Nichols who served as senior editor. Photographs by permission of Mary Evans Picture Library, British Film Institute Stills Archive, State Historical Society of Wisconsin, Academy of Motion Picture Arts and Sciences, Museum of Modern Art Stills Archive, and Bison Archive.

1

Introduction:
Fabricating the Female Body

Jane Gaines

> A good deal of the groomed beauty of the
> women in the glamour portraits comes from
> the fact that they are "made-up," in the
> immediate sense that cosmetics have been
> applied to their bodies in order to enhance
> their existing qualities. But they are also
> "made-up" in the sense that the images,
> rather than the women, are put together,
> constructed, even fabricated or falsified in the
> sense that we might say a story is made up if
> it is a fiction.—Annette Kuhn, *The Power of
> the Image*[1]

One of the most important contributions feminist film theory has made
to the larger field of feminist inquiry has been the argument that the image
of woman is a "construction." As this argument goes, the image is a
product of culture in several senses at once—as it has been industrially
manufactured, as it has been pieced together according to aesthetic rules
pertaining to lighting, gesture, and composition, and as it has been "prefab-
ricated" by men. The image of woman, as this argument continues, is
exactly what it is only because of the society which spawns it, and in
order to alter this image we have to reconstruct that society. This position
has been important as it has helped to clear up the confusion caused by
the success of the moving image at putting itself over as *the same as* the
reality to which it refers, and the work cut out for feminist film theorists
has been the continual rescue of this image which tends to dissolve into
a mist of naturalness—to hold it up for further scrutiny, and to make its
constructedness evident—to turn it inside out so that the stitching shows.
One can draw a useful analogy between the photographic representation
of woman and the everyday adornment of her body. Just as conventional
cinematic representation would seem to dissolve without a trace, leaving
the distillation "woman," costume delivers gender as self-evident or natural and then recedes as "clothing," leaving the connotation "femininity."
In popular discourse, there is often no distinction made between a woman
and her attire. She *is* what she wears. This continuity between woman and
dress works especially well to keep women in their traditional "place,"
especially during epochs when styles which accentuate the "natural" contours of woman's body are favored. Reviewing an exhibition of Cindy

1

Sherman's photography, Judith Williamson suggests how image and female identity get conflated, and how Sherman's "Film Stills" in particular demonstrate that the two could be forced apart:

> Sherman's pictures force upon the viewer that ellision of image and identity which women experience all the time: as if the sexy black dress made you *be* a femme fatale, whereas "femme fatale" is, precisely, an image; it needs a viewer to function at all.[2]

While this analogy between cinema and costume as representational systems—the comparison between two different mediators which construct "woman"—may be fruitful, the parallel also calls our attention to something significantly different about cinematic representation and woman's dress as self-representation. Although there has never been a colloquial manner of speaking about the constructedness of cinematic signifiers (indeed this exclusive insight has been cloistered in the academy), popular metaphors for describing dress have historically betrayed the suspicion that a fashion "look" is a calculated construction. When women speak about "making-up" the face and "getting-up" in fancy clothes, this manner of speaking itself suggests that dress and demeanor are complete fabrications *of women's own design*. But why have the practices of "making-up" and "getting-up" historically signaled female capitulation and acquiescence? And how does one distinguish "making-up" from "putting-on"?

Our point of departure in this collection is body *and* costume for several reasons. First, we wanted to highlight a continuity with the female body in feminist film theory since the majority of the articles here are informed by this theory. Second, what we have found is that we could not extricate one from the other. Significantly, as costume historian Anne Hollander tells us, the "unadorned self has more kinship with the *dressed* aspect than the undressed," thus the depiction of the art historical nude is generally derived from the current mode of dress.[3] Conversely, in this century, clothing conforms more closely to the body beneath than at any other time in history according to motion picture costume historian Edward Maeder.[4] But it is finally that body without clothing and clothing without body offer us untenable positions. While the clothingless sylph-like body (as opposed to the historically specified nude) is dangerously close to the mythic, archetypal, and essential, the ghostly garment is too corpse-like and is finally reminiscent of the empty space for woman produced by theories of culture derived from male models. As Roland Barthes says in his essay on the designer Erté, the body gives existence to the dress, "for it is impossible to conceive of a dress without a body . . . the empty garment, without head and limbs . . . is death, not the neutral absence of the body, but the body mutilated, decapitated."[5]

Feminist Theory and Costume Practice

This collection was conceived during one phase of feminist film theory and criticism and has finally come together in a different one, a time more hospitable to costume as a feminist area of investigation. I refer to different moments in feminism which could be characterized in relation to a moral stance which was strong in the beginning of the Second Wave of feminist politics and scholarship, but which has gradually eased into a less proscriptive position. Early in the Second Wave, beauty culture and feminism were seen as antithetical, or, as one feminist puts it, "Feminists are widely regarded as enemies of the family; we are also seen as enemies of the stiletto heel and the beauty parlor, in a word, as enemies of glamour. Hostility on the part of some women to feminism may have its origin here."[6] Following the contours of Simone de Beauvoir's thoughts about women and contemporary fashion, this negative position was based on two recurring charges against the culture of femininity. First, fashion is enslavement; women are bound by the drudgery of keeping up their appearance and by the impediments of the styles which prohibit them from acting in the world. Second, costume "may disguise the body, deform it, or follow its curves;" but ultimately "puts it on display."[7] Corollary to this is Beauvoir's understanding of female narcissism in which the looker is implicated since female display always depends, as she puts it, on attracting the attention of another. In Beauvoir's consideration of female adornment ritual in which young women learn to appraise themselves through the eyes of the male, there is a premonition of the theory of female representation as directed toward the male surveyor-owner. But this idea was introduced into the early 1970s, in conditions which produced the first feminist film criticism not via Beauvoir but by art historian John Berger, whose idea was then taken up by feminists and elaborated into a theory of gender and representation: men look at women and this is the visual organizing principle in oil painting, magazine advertising, and motion pictures.[8] Almost immediately, this insight was taken up and unfurled into an entire theory of voyeuristic looking, productively expanded by feminists to explain the allure of cinema, a moment I will return to shortly. There is a significant link between the notion of woman displayed by her dress and woman displayed by other representational systems. In addition, one might say that contemporary feminists have understood woman's inscription in the codes of contemporary representation because they themselves know too well what it is to be fitted up for representation. We are trained into clothes, and early become practiced in presentational postures, learning, in the age of mechanical reproduction, to carry the mirror's eye within the mind, as though one might at any moment be photographed. And this is a sense a woman in Western culture has learned, not only from feeling the constant surveillance of her public self, but also from studying the publicity images of other women—on screen certainly, but also in the pages of fashion magazines— *Elle, Seventeen, Vogue, Jackie, and Mademoiselle.*

In the same spirit as Beauvoir, feminists in the Second Wave originally explained the danger of fashion culture in terms of the patriarchy in league with capitalism. Femininity, in this analysis, was false consciousness. In one of the strongest statements against traditional feminine dress and adornment, Adrienne Rich puts *haute couture* and "feminine dress codes" in the same category as purdah, foot-binding, the veil, public sexual harrassment, and the threat of rape, all of which work in some way to physically confine and prohibit movement.[9] The first feminist fashion histories, then, were dictionaries of our bondage, and feminist historians whose analysis is subtle and complex in every other way, even assigned causality to beauty culture. For instance, a standard explanation for the demise of feminism in the 1920s is the observation that a new consumer culture "lured" a younger generation away from the movement. Rayna Rapp and Ellen Ross thus describe the "co- optation" of the flapper: "Sold on celluloid and male-oriented images of glamour, young women were no longer recruitable to what appeared as outmoded 'causes.' "[10]

The feminist movement position on beauty culture was locked into the same assumption which informed the early "images of woman" criticism in feminist film theory which used the notion of a real (unconstructed) woman to criticize consumer culture offerings.[11] Sheila Rowbotham, writing about the impossibility of the cosmetic ideal in one of her earlier works says, "Acting on the assumption that women regard themselves through men's eyes as objects of pleasure, advertising and the media project a haunting and un-real image of woman-hood."[12] For feminists, the the original challenge to "feminine" fashion culture, Hollywood star glamour, and glossy advertising imagery was the counter charge that actual women *did not look like* publicity images which simplified, selected, and falsified. The point also made in this earlier analysis—that whole segments of the female population of the world are "left out" of mainstream representation—has been well taken, especially as it has lead to an understanding of how ideology shapes an adjacent world that functions as "reality" for many people. Within feminist scholarship, the notion of systematic exclusion has led us to reconsider prostitutes in history, immigrant women as consumers, and Black beauty culture.[13] But neither the argument that "real women aren't like that," nor the charge that women have been left out, has made an impact on the culture industries. More importantly, blaming "manipulative" media has not helped our understanding of the way representation works ideologically. And suddenly, before we see the fulfillment of the later project, the more extreme contention of post-modernist theory—the idea that the image has swallowed reality whole—obliterates the problems endemic to comparisons between images and society. If the image now precedes the real, engulfs it and renders it obsolete as a point of comparison, do we any more need to show how representation is ideological?

Feminism, Film Theory, and Cultural Studies

Three developments have prepared the terrain in U.S. feminist film and television theory for the consideration of costume and body which goes beyond Rich's catalogue of oppressions. First, I would refer to the 1982 Barnard Conference and the ensuing pro-sex climate which had a catalyz-ing effect on feminist work already undergoing transformation.[14] Second, coincident with the aftermath of the Barnard Conference, feminist film theory as it had evolved over ten years time had reached what several U.S. critics called an "impasse," which, among other things, meant that the female spectator's gratification became more interesting than the male spectator's pathology.[15] Third, I would credit a phenomenon which might be called the Americanization of British Cultural Studies, perhaps formally introduced into this country at the Marxism and the Interpretation of Culture Conference held at the University of Illinois-Champaign-Urbana in July, 1984, but not theoretically absorbed into film studies until more recently.

The Feminist Movement and the Wild Place

The post-1982 pro-sex moment was produced by some brave movement feminists who spoke out about the discrepancy between their own experi-ence of sexual pleasure and the relatively pallid and politically cautious mode of intimate expression as well as public self-representation of female sexuality. And the bold imagination of the ways of "taking back" our pleasure, expressed, for instance, in the position of the "No More Nice Girls" action group reversed the taboos by refusing the notion of a woman's sexual "reputation."[16] What was produced was a much more risky and recalcitrant idea of women's potent pleasure, produced in the plural to suggest that it didn't stop with the body but that it spread to transform other "indulgences" into powers. This feminist movement pleasure was significantly different in both origin and flavor from the Barthesian "plea-sure of the text" which predated it, but the sudden simultaneity of the two notions meant that academic feminists could "have their cake and eat it too" with a respectable concept which also translated directly into their felt experiences as women.[17] As Annette Kuhn noted, *pleasure* had become a legitimate category of analysis.[18]

In a climate in which it was possible to confess a taste for pornography, it also became possible to declare an interest in and even to confess a serious passion for clothes. And in such a climate we found that we were not necessarily talking about a heterosexual passion as the conviction of the group "Lesbians for Lipstick" suggests.[19] If the idea was, to quote Cindy Patton, to dress to "repel male attraction," what were we to do with the femme in lesbian history who epitomized super femininity in her high heels and wasp-waisted dress which she wore in the job she held down to support her butch lover?[20] In an early lone voice of dissent, Carol Ascher questioned the representational strategy of the feminist anti-fashion dress. At the same time she gives us a rationale to live by in the late eighties when the pall of the AIDS epidemic threatens to shrivel those pleasures and to dry up the production of the signs of the pro-pleasure sensibility. First, says Ascher, the "genderless space" which the old feminist austerity strives for is impossible to achieve. Even long kinky hair and bare feet constitute a fashion construction, and plainness and naturalness in beauty draw on a romanticism that is highly ideological. Describing herself as a feminist who disappeared into inconspicuous clothing at one stage of her life because this guise helped her to write and speak out, Ascher reconsiders the significance of zero degree dressing, making one simple argument for not dismissing ornamentation: What if self-decoration gives women a sense of potency to act in the world? Talking back to a feminist moralism which she hears in her own head, Ascher says, ". . . the idea that clothing *ought to* yield a magical shift in one's feelings about oneself stems from an austere, prudish rationalism in which one does not allow oneself any comfort or pampering that goes beyond the logical 'necessity' into that unreasoned wild place where we all ultimately live."[21]

For feminist scholars, confronting our own moralism and replacing it with acceptance has meant an extention of the horizon of our research. Condemning cosmetics and romance-confession magazines, after all, means that we dismiss the women who buy them. Wearing high culture blinders, we are unable to appreciate the strength of the allure, the richness of the fantasy, and the quality of the compensation, especially if our analysis consists only of finding new ways to describe the predictable mechanisms of patriarchial culture. To signal the readjustment of the feminist position, we begin this collection with Elizabeth Wilson's "All the Rage," which captures the spirit of her recent *Adorned in Dreams: Fashion and Modernity,* perhaps the most important attempt to date to rewrite fashion history from a feminist point of view. Here, Wilson chides an earlier feminism for having been reductive and moralistic in its attitude toward fashion, and concludes: "The political subordination of women is an inappropriate point of departure if, as I believe, the most important thing about fashion is *not* that it oppresses women."[22]

The Body in Feminist Film Theory and Practice

Feminist film theory begins with the female body. Since this body has been understood as totally constructed by a patriarchial cinema, the first difficulty for feminist theorists has been to see if the connotations of sexuality it carries could be peeled off. But, given the way, as Monique Wittig says, the "category of sex sticks to the female body," this is as futile a project as trying to scrub the streets clean on our hands and knees.[23] Furthermore, the metaphors we use and the forms we imagine are already circumscribed within the terms of an erotic aesthetic which heterosexualizes the female body. Even the attempt to peel off the connotations is coded within male discourse, thus Mary Ann Doane has reminded us that the "gesture of stripping . . . is already the property of patriarchy."[24]

In this analysis, a female body that is not already the "property of the patriarchy" is impossible to construct anew and is not there to discover. This theory of the body has presented a much-discussed problem for the feminist filmmaker who would again photograph that impossible body carrying the layers of sexual connotation she cannot remove, and thus the ingenious theoretical solution for a time was to refuse to offer up the female body photographically, to *not show,* or to skirt the representation of that form. Such films as Chantel Ackerman's *News from Home* (1977), then, would be marked by the prominent absence of the body of her protagonist. From this position of refusal of the body it would be particularly difficult to introduce a serious study of screen costume or the fashion in body types. Also, through much of this discussion of "the body," it has been difficult to imagine the referent as anything other than an unclothed female form. In some ways, this explains the slightly prudish overtones of the past discussions, and the too easy confusion of cinema with pornography.

Cultural Studies and Women's Recalcitrance

To the theorization of women's pleasures, British cultural studies has contributed the important notion of *resistance,* which gives "pleasure" an edge and a bite, connecting it with a class analysis which allows it much broader political implications. The crucial concepts here were developed in response to the need to restore some modicum of power to people in history which earlier formulations of ideology did not afford them. Crucial here is Antonio Gramsci's notion of hegemony, the understanding that although people embrace the very tools of their oppression as their own, the effect of ideology is not settled once and for all, but is still in contest.[25] In the realm of meaning, above all, culture can be seized again and again by marginal groups, now understood as reinflecting signs already in circulation for their own political ends. Rediscovered in the work of Soviet linguist V.N. Volosinov would be the idea that consciousness is materially "embodied" in signs.[26] Taking Volosinov further, and crediting French Marxist Louis Althusser with the additional insight, Stuart Hall has recently reiterated that although "mental events" happen out of our reach "in the head," a materialist analysis of the contents of consciousness looks at the "registration" of ideas in social "practices," the all- encompassing term which allows us to analyze verbal language, bodily gesture, and cultural artifact as such registration.[27] Dick Hebdige's *Subculture: The Meaning of Style,* was the first of the studies following *Resistance Through Rituals* to apply this methodology evolving from the work of the Centre for Contemporary Cultural Studies to the phenomenon of outrageous body display and ornamentation-as-social-offense.[28] As Angela McRobbie quickly pointed out, however, subculture theory was derived exclusively from the study of working-class male cultures and young women were excluded from the picture, a particular irony since women (in recent history) have been seen as having superior mastery of the vocabularies of style.[29] Hebdige's "spectacular subcultures" expressed their opposition in ways both more public and more flagrant than the young working-class women McRobbie studied earlier. These women nevertheless could be seen as using clothes, make-up, and their budding "femaleness" to disrupt the middle-class ordering of the school. This early study is worth quoting because it anticipates a current development in feminist theory which sees domesticity and femininity as troublesome and potentially subversive as they come in contact with oppressive structures:

> . . . one way in which the girls combat the class-based and oppressive features of the school is to assert their "femaleness," to introduce into the classroom their sexuality and their physical maturity in such a way as to force the teachers to take notice. A class instinct then finds expression at the level of jettisonning the official ideology for girls in the school (neatness, diligence, appliance, femininity, passivity, etc.) and replacing it with a *more* feminine, even sexual one.[30]

What is significant here for feminist theory (and different from male subculture theory) is that the counter-ideology is produced with the most despised signs of "femaleness" and the accoutrements of "femininity." Sexual maturation—the functioning of the body which most nearly escapes culture—is deployed to turn the body itself into an instrument of disruption. What better site for disruption of the social order than the seeming scene of the origin of womens' oppression?

Feminist studies of anorexia provide a model of how we might forge a theory of the intersection of society and physiognomy based on the adaptive genius of women in history who displayed these apparently involuntary symptoms of the disorder. The feminist literature on anorexia suggests that however self-destructive and displaced the condition, the anorexic body which appears to confirm helplessness and weakness, is a profound statement of refusal and an implicit critique of social disorder. In her overview of this feminist work, Noelle Caskey has analyzed this woman's disease as a key to understanding the complex construction of the female body image in Western culture especially since we see in the characteristic "literal-mindedness" of the anorexic the full implications of the body/self/image/society nexus written out graphically. The anorexic, at once "supremely defiant" and "supremely obedient," registers precisely what is done to her: she sees her image as not herself, but rather as the projected composite wishes of others.[31] At the same time, she insists, as it would have been insisted so many times for her, that "the body" is synonymous with "the self." Caskey concludes:

> Anorexia is the cultivation of a specific image *as an image*—it is a purely artificial creation and that is why it is admired. Will alone produces it and maintains it against considerable physical odds.[32]

Whether we are talking about the Victorian or the contemporary anorexic, we are talking about a condition-as-outburst that uses the female body to sign a deeper trouble within the family. The study of female body-building, the healthy obverse of anorexia, may confirm the insights of women who are prone to eating disorders. In this collection, Laurie Schulze considers the ripped and striated body of the contemporary female body-builder as another significant outburst which "scandalizes" male culture. She enters totally uncharted cultural territory as she goes on to ask difficult questions about the ambivalent relationship between lesbian desire and the disengendered body of the professional weight-trainer. What makes this fully developed body so terrifying is the possibility that, taken to the very limits of biology, gender confusion becomes gender eradication.

But while we are in theoretical awe of the female body-builder who pushes the threshold of the physical beyond our current conceptions, we also have to ask what it means for women to "produce" either the deformed anorexic body or the reformed muscled body. Recent feminist considerations of the contemporary popularity of aerobics classes and nautilus training find that women still have an alienated relationship to the production of their own bodies. Although a woman may seem to be producing her own new image-body, Susan Willis argues, the nautilus body is really the product of the exercise machine which falsely positions her as worker-producer.[33] Aerobics training, concludes Margaret Morse, produces a body via a symbiotic relationship with a model, (the instructor). Thus the trainee does not "identify" with the production of her own new self, a condition which defines the "postmodern female subjectivity," says Morse.[34] These questions parallel larger issues which have to do with the position of woman in relation to industrial production as well as to cultural consumption. Two factors stand out here. First, the production/consumption split historically corresponds with the male and female spheres. Second, today in advanced capitalist societies, people increasingly see the significance of their lives in terms of consumption rather than production.[35] And it is here that feminism may need to undertake its second major revision of traditional Marxist theory following the first challenge mounted in the 1970s to a conception of social class which does not accommodate gender.

It is not as though the Marxist paradigm (which privileges production in such a way that consumption is left to itself), has not been subject to revision. Two of the earliest theorists of consumer culture used the changes in women's fashions as starting points in their analysis. Considering Thorstein Veblen together with Georg Simmel, as is seldom done, is occasion for asking why Veblen's formulation would have trickled down into common sense and Simmel's would have been nearly eclipsed during the same time period until his recent rediscovery as the "father of moder-nity."[36] For Veblen's extremely original identification of "conspicuous consumption" became the common sense "keeping up with the Joneses," picked up in middle-brow social criticism instead of his more devastating critique of the middle-class wife as slave who existed to display the wealth of her husband. We find in Simmel, Veblen's contemporary, a premonition of later Germans, the Frankfurt School critics, and in particular Walter Benjamin. One could say that the doubleness of consumer culture is to be found in Simmel's analysis of fashion configured as counter-tendency, as embodiment of community and exclusivity, difference and sameness, and change as well as stasis.[37]

Perhaps the most interesting question is why Veblen's *Theory of the Leisure Class* (1899) would stand alone for so long as the much-needed theory of consumer culture and that the Frankfurt School critics and their predecessor Simmel would be read selectively in a way that confirmed their negative diagnosis.[38] In the twentieth century, we can identify a series of shadings in the Left commentary on consumer culture from the end of World War II to the present. This shading is also a greying of a clear production-consumption distinction. Perhaps the clearest position to delineate, that of the Frankfurt School as associated with Theodor Adorno and Max Horkheimer's *The Culture Industry* (1944), theorized consumption from Marx's metaphor of the relation between the laborer and his production through the Lukácsian notion of *reification,* that exchange of places between persons and things (the commodity form) which colored the whole of capitalist society.[39] In *Society of the Spectacle,* first published in France in 1967, Guy Debord described the thorough look and dizzying rate of *reification,* exemplified by, among other things, the way a "style of dress emerges from a film."[40] Consumption, Henri Lefebvre would argue the same year, was a means of control.[41] In the mid-seventies, Stuart Ewen's history of advertising, *Captains of Consciousness,* updated the Frankfurt School premise and added the suggestion that consumption has bound the worker all the tighter to production since World War I, as consumerism has become a more elaborate version of the company store.[42] Shaded as a qualification of the Frankfurt School pessimism, however, is the more recent work on mass culture which insists on the utopian dimension in popular forms, best summed up in Fredric Jameson's often-quoted statement that mass culture can't hope to manipulate the public unless it holds out "some genuine shred of content as a fantasy bribe."[43]

Consumer Culture and the Glimmer of Utopia

Although a few theorists, such as Jameson, carried over the utopian dimension also found in the Frankfurt School dialectic in their work, this search for the "genuine shread of content" has only recently become the vogue in theoretical circles. Following Elizabeth Wilson's prodding, we might ask if contemporary theories of culture don't change in the same way that the fashion in clothing changes, with innovation speeded up by new communications technologies, and if re-reading earlier theorists is not unlike the way in which contemporary fashion plunders the fashion past, bringing back the leg-of-mutton sleeve, the padded shoulder, and the high Empire waist in remarkably different combinations. Suddenly, in their new English translation, the Frankfurt critics begin to sound dazzlingly current. But while some aspects of this work are still provocative, other aspects are interesting only for their nostalgia value as remnants of bygone attitudes, and this is no more true than in Kracauer, Adorno, Horkheimer, and Benjamin on women, cinema, and fashion in dress.

We have had some English translation previews of Siegfried Kracauer's journalistic writings from before his *Theory of Film* in recent issues of *New German Critique.*[44] Kracauer is disdainful of maids, salesclerks, and typists in "The Little Shop Girls Go to the Movies," saying that they "love, choose their wardrobe and commit suicide."[45] But he sees cinema-going as a hint of redemption through collective amusements, and in "The Cult of Distraction" is more approving of the way cinema would advise and set worldwide trends in "fashion, manners, and home design."[46] But Adorno and Horkheimer actually give the typist some credit for a resistance to the "pleasure industry," however "feeble" and fleeting that resistance:

> Of course, the starlet is meant to symbolize the typist in such a way that the splendid evening dress seems meant for the actress as distinct from the real girl. The girls in the audience not only feel that they could be on the screen, but realize the great gulf separating them from it.[47]

The culture industry's invitation to identify with the screen is a bogus offer, then, but the female viewer can accept it and reject it at once. What is crucial here is that rather than masking social class difference, the display of luxury in the cinema mise-en-scene *figures* social inequities. This "dual character" of luxury, as Adorno formulates it, was what Veblen, the "misogynist," did not see, for "Those features of luxury which Veblen designates as 'invidious,' revealing a bad will, do not only reproduce injustice; they also contain, in distorted form, the appeal to justice." For, involuntarily (and unknowingly), the conspicuous consumer reveals that "no individual happiness is possible which does not virtually imply that of society as a whole."[48] This "dialectic of luxury" then opens up consumer culture to be read as its opposite. The vision of plenitude for everyone seen in the personal ostentation which appears indifferent to the whole of society, is implied in personal display. The idea here is to read the utopian elements in the desires and longings expressed (however twistedly) in ostentation and pretentiousness.

Although there is a structural similarity between Adorno's reading of conspicuous consumption as an "appeal to justice" and Walter Benjamin's analysis of fashion as the "wish for change" despite social stasis, generally it is Benjamin, not Adorno, who is credited with theorizing the utopian dimension in mass culture. And in addition, since his prediction of the cultural artifact's loss of aura would be later understood as opening up a space for the knowledgeable subculture/audience (no longer intimidated by the authority of the text), Benjamin becomes associated with cultural studies and the interest in what real persons make of things.[49] While it is more difficult to find reference to the liberatory aspects of mass culture in the classic "Art in the Age of Mechanical Reproduction" essay, *Passagen-Werk,* Benjamin's unfinished, untranslated, and untranslatable commentary on the history of the Paris Arcades, elusively promises the fragments of a theory of fashion and social change.[50] Here the commodity (which in the contemporary period has been characterized in increasingly malevolent terms), is projected as the reverse, a "utopian wish-image."[51] Studying the remnants of the earliest consumer culture, the shells of commodities which seem to have lost both use-value and exchange-value, Benjamin looks at the relics of an earlier industrial age much as the authors of a number of the articles in this collection look at women's wear in earlier decades. Yes, we can see the lavish waste of the culture industries and women further bonded as workers and buyers to consumer culture's impossible body ideals. Can we also see a premonition of what revolution might "feel like" prefigured in the fresh consciousness proposed by the strikingly new season in styles, even the taste of victory in the culmination of a purchase? For in Benjamin, the commodity form is a clue to the dream-form in which the genuine aspirations (of the group acting collectivity) are stored. This, then, might provide us with the beginning of a theory of our ambivalence toward the alluring products of consumer culture, an ambivalence which Susan Buck-Morss provocatively suggests is signaled at the core in the fetish aspect of the commodity.[52]

There is also in Benjamin's work on the Arcades the inclination to read consumer culture as a dual system of meaning with the economic life of the commodity impinging upon its life as an object of cultural significance. The suggestion that there is a symmetry between production and consumption is not new, but the use of "production" taken over from industrial manufacture as a metaphor for signification has eroded the Leftist prohibition against stating outright that commodity consumption is the source of the worker's alienation. In Michel de Certeau we have now the full statement of this in the assertion that consumption is a different kind of production, and that in it we see the same alienation, but also the antagonistic relation of worker to capital.[53] In this shading, then, production and consumption become almost indistinguishable.

The relevance of this assertion to the articles in this collection appear more clearly in John Fiske's recent uses of de Certeau to explain the subversive uses of shopping. As Fiske's argument goes, the culture of the shopping mall is one of the vulnerable points of late capitalism and it is the place where workers can take back the power lost in the realm of production. It is here that unemployed youth and women engage in "tactical" raids on the exposed "belly" of capitalism. For women, Fiske suggests, oppositional shopping involves changing price tags, trying on clothes they never intend to purchase, and stealing them off the racks.[54] There are several points which give one pause here. First, there is still a need to consider the relation between the shopper and the saleswoman who might be part of a parallel women's culture which historically has both served and undermined the store system, as Susan Porter Benson has shown in her history of U.S. department store clerks' struggle to organize.[55] And then, we must figure into the other side of the equation the ways in which the merchandiser adds the cost of store theft as well as product failure to the price passed on to the consumer. And finally, Fiske's own theory is an example of the way in which ideology produces its antithesis in the same stroke. While the American marketing term for the consumer's weakest moment (where she is most susceptible to "impulse buying") is the "point of purchase," Fiske's Britishism, "point of purchase," theorizes the *strong* moment at which the consumer gets a meaningful grip on the object of culture.[56]

The coincidence of the appearance of the perfected institutions of capital and the opposition to them is dramatically demonstrated in the case of the first department stores in France and the construction of petty store theft as "kleptomania," a disease. The early explanations of such female theft in the mid- nineteenth century associated stealing with hysteria and consequently with sexual frustration.[57] But cases of the "disease" increased in direct proportion to the increase in size and number of the *grands magasins,* peaking around 1890.[58] Since, as one patient told her doctor, she only stole in the *grands magasins,* not the *petit* ones,[59] we might consider that the kleptomaniac, like the anorexic, was merely taking literally the magnanimous gesture of goods proffered for all. But here, as with Fiske's guerrilla shopper, we have to pause to ask if we want to consider the shoplifter as actively strategizing or rather involuntarily registering contradictions. In her article here on the representation of woman in nineteenth-century monumental statuary and lithography, Serafina Bathrick describes the double bind of a rapidly changing culture within which women's domestic arts were encouraged even though they represented a productive mode and a value system which undermined technological progress. What emerges from her description of the role of women in the Columbian Exposition is a portrait paralleling the case of the department store "kleptomaniac": patriarchy and capitalism working against each other and in seeming ignorance of how one undermined the other.

Bathrick's pre-history of cinema reminds us that motion picture technology only corresponds with one phase of the development of consumer culture, suggesting that we cannot theorize consumer culture if we read it only through what are sometimes identified as the pornographic features of postmodern culture. Jeanne Allen's earlier "The Film Viewer as Consumer" is one of the only attempts to place cinema-going within the historical context of the shift from theater to shopping mall.[60] It is also a significant corrective to the idea that the motion pictures produced consumer culture, as was sometimes implied in the early film histories often written without reference to parallel developments such as urbanization, the growth of railroads, the invention of plate glass, the development of the chain store, and, of course, the appearance of ready-wear garments. In her article in this collection, Allen goes on to read a historically specific ideology of consumption through Howard Hawks's *Fig Leaves* (1926), which for women in the 1920s was complexly tied to the issue of work outside the home as well as to extra-marital sexuality.

Allen's textual analysis of one film-commodity which is a narrative about clothes-commodities also gives us an opportunity to consider the increasing usage in contemporary theory of the term "consuming" as a synonym for "reading" (more often when the text to be read is a popular object than a high culture object). We might also consider the emergence in film and television studies of a notion of the consuming subject, now not only positioned as male or female but predicated as part of a consumer group, in terms of age, race, gender, and buying power. Mary Ann Doane has suggested that the female viewer addressed by the 1930s and 1940s woman's films was positioned in a way that complemented her role as consumer. In effect, says Doane, these films produce the desire for the "image/commodity" by conflating oppositions (subject-object, having-being, and being-appearing) and contributing to the very subject-object confusion which reproduces woman as object rather than subject.[61] As a way of further probing the screen/show window/consumer relation, Charlotte Herzog, in this collection, looks specifically at the reoccurrence of fashion show "numbers" in films from the 1920s through the 1950s as she considers how these sequences are constructed through editing to showcase the latest styles in women's clothing. If, as she says, the women watching in these films are constructed as shoppers, the men are constructed as consumer-voyeurs who have to learn like Adam Smith (Eve's husband in FIG LEAVES) not to oppose consumer culture but to align themselves with it as "sugar-daddies."

Raymond Williams, pondering the term "consumption," remarks that its use in relation to culture is a strange borrowing of a metaphor from the stomach and the furnace.[62] This is especially so when the concept applies to "durables" rather than "consumables." In reading, we don't exhaust or completely digest a book, nor do we, in wearing clothes, deplete the ornamental signifying value of them. Does "consuming" mean buying, having, or using? In some ways buying is the epitome of the bourgeois signifying act, since we all "buy in" to a degree, as we pay, even if we snub conventional use-values by turning safety-pins into nose-rings and shoes into hats. To what degree, however, would we want to see every act of consumption as an act of making-meaning or do we want to see every act of meaning as what Baudrillard refers to as a "sumptuary operation," an alienating labor?[63] Today, the analysis of culture as commodity may have lost its explanatory potency since we are left with so few examples of uncommodified relations. Who, other than anthropologists and people living in less complex cultures can distinguish *reification* from the commodity-exchange found in some form in all societies?[64]

Star Styles: The Essences of the Commodity Tie-up

Charles Eckert's "The Carole Lombard in Macy's Window" (1978), reprinted here, has become a minor classic in the field as the first critical history of the symbiotic relationship between Hollywood studios and consumer product industries in the 1930s. Eckert's suggestion that motion pictures "functioned as living display windows for all that they contained; windows that were occupied by marvelous mannequins and swathed in a fetish-inducing ambiance of music and emotion," is pertinent to film theory's concern with cinema realism as bourgeois aesthetic as well as to postmodern theory's analysis of the indistinguishability of fictional imagery and everyday life. For in the 1980s, we are seeing a return to some of the same publicity devices which Eckert identifies in the 1930s: motion picture product placement, product licensing, and commodity tie-up campaigns in both motion pictures and television. But how is the contemporary landscape, in which the the look-alike signs of popular film and television proliferate to produce Baudrillard's "simulacrum", different (if at all) from the manufactured spontaneity and the entrepreneurial enthusiasm of the earlier period which produced Eckert's Janet Gaynor "look-alike"?

Reception theory has also created renewed interest in Eckert's article because it offers an early profile of the spectator within the context of industry studies. It would remain for later feminist work such as Diane Waldman's important "From Midnight Shows to Marriage Vows: Women, Exploitation and Exhibition" to suggest what was at stake for women viewers to whom local theater promotions urged hegemonic interpretations of matinee features.[65] Although "The Carol Lombard in Macy's Window" does not offer the full ideological analysis of its companion pieces (Eckert's articles on *Marked Woman* [1938] and Shirley Temple),[66] it offers feminist theory a political paradigm. The star style, after all, is a direct and intimate link to the body and the consciousness of the female spectator.

However, it is probably best that we treat the cinema styles phenomenon as an emblem rather than as historical fact since the enormous success of the Modern Merchandising Bureau (which reputedly set up cinema shops in stores around the country) was really a figment of Bernard Waldman's public relations imagination. This is not to say that studios did not contract with manufacturers to produce ready-wear copies of costume designs featured in their films, or that they did not (through advertising agents such as the Modern Merchandising Bureau) publicize coming attractions by means of tie-up campaigns with manufacturers and retail stores such as Macy's. Waldman's agency did promote ready-wear copies for RKO of Bernard Newman's costumes in *Roberta* and Walter Plunkett's in *Mary of Scotland* in 1936. The following year as publicity for the rayon fabric produced by the American Viscose Corporation, MMB arranged a tie-up with United Artist's *Vogues* of 1938. Around the same time, Warner Brothers considered setting up its own company to license copies of Orry-Kelly's designs to manufacturers of hats and dresses who would then pay them a several cent royalty on every item sold. MGM executives drew up a plan for marketing Adrian's designs as ready-wear, but abandoned the idea and never finally authorized any reproduction of his designs for the mass market during his tenure at the studio. But the fashion tie-up phenomenon is really the story of sales pitch, hype, and piracy in the garment trade which was not to be outdone by the gimmicry, hyperbole, and good-natured fraud of motion picture exploitation in the 1930s. Publicists freely traded advertising favors for pre-release production stills from which fabric and garment manufacturers could loosely copy the styles they rushed to retailers before the release of a film. While some few tie-ups *were* the "official" copies their hang-tags said they were, the vast volume of shoes, hats, dresses, and accessories labeled "Worn in Hollywood" by Deanna Durbin, Ginger Rogers, or Sonja Heine, was essentially counterfeit merchandise.[67]

The critical metaphor "cultural production" takes on a new self-fulfilling dimension in the fashion tie-up where we see the culture industry "caught in the act" of a conspiracy which we would rather not acknowledge in our theory. In almost a caricature of empiricist accounts, it appears here that the motion picture industry really *did* produce the "effects" of its own popularity, reproducing itself as visually and materially continuous with the society it purported to "mirror." Not only did it manufacture the signs of its own success, but it sold these "effects" off the racks, taking a percentage of the gross sales of dresses, barrettes, hats, and slips. It is not surprising that the Payne Fund sociologists who studied the influence of the movies on young people in this period would single out cinema styles as direct and negative "effects" and mistake young women's consumer preferences for their sexual practices. (These women, "malleable to the touch of what is shown," would learn to use perfume on their ear lobes from Norma Talmadge who used this technique to induce her screen husband to kiss her ears.)[68] More importantly, the fashion tie-up prefigures the postmodern symptom of image-reality collusion: the real dress becomes the counterfeit to the movie fictional original. Pertinent to this, Angela McRobbie elsewhere describes postmodern popular culture in a way that looks forward to her study of the dance fantasies, reading practices, and consumption ideals of adolescent women included in this collection. The media versis society dichotomy in which reality is contrasted with its fictions, she says, does not help us to theorize postmodern society which is better understood as an interdependancy marked by continual "cross-referencing." She concludes that ". . . the sharp distinction between real life and fictional forms must give way to a deep intermingling. . ."[69]

What are then rendered untenable are the old relational metaphors of the original and its copy or reality and its "mirror image." These particular metaphors have been historically turned against women, who, as followers of fashion, have been constructed as "copycats," "imitators," and "dupes." Edgar Morin gives us a more comprehensive concept in his analysis of the "infinite mimetisms of appropriation" which describes the inextricability of the phenomenon of fandom and star merchandise. The mimetism is simultaneously the identification, the act of purchase, and the star-object itself. Neither is the star excluded in this circularity since "The star-object (merchandise) and the star-goddess (myth) are possible because the techniques of the movies excite and exalt a system of participations which affect the actor both in his performance and personality."[70]

Costume and Classical Hollywood Narrative

Motion picture fandom is not the only system of participations which has historically stimulated style consciousness. The novel has traditionally given its readers more in the way of costume detail than any other literary genre would attempt and given it in spite of the rule that such detail slowed down the narrative. In his overview of dress in the novel, costume historian James Laver compares writers in the novelistic tradition with Samuel Richardson, whose *Clarissa* (1748) he sees as a model of both accurate depiction and elaborate description of the styles of the period. Austen, Thackeray, and Dickens, among others, are faulted for inaccuracies and insufficient attention to their heroine's mode of dress.[71] The costume historian's comparison, of course, commits the error of insisting that verbal language reflect the reality it can only stand in for, but in his exercise correlating novelistic description with women's fashions in the eighteenth and nineteenth centuries he suggests the potential power of these evocations to produce fashion consciousness. Such novelistic realism actually inspired the earliest commodity tie-ups, such as the perfume and bonnets sold coincidentally with the appearance of Wilkie Collins's *The Woman in White* (1860) in serial form.[72] For the nineteenth century, then, the novel functioned as a "store window on the world."

What, then, is the connection between narrative form, naturalistic detail, consumerism, and the ideological production of female subjects? Consider, for instance, the millions of contemporary women who avidly read historical fiction. Janice Radway explains the mimesis in these books, effected by the build-up of minute detail, in terms of the connection the reader makes between herself and the heroine's experience. Naturalistic detail creates the impression of an earlier time period and establishes a world continuous with the reader's, and this continuity is instrumental in securing the ideological effect, the re-positioning of wife-subjects. And yet, what we might call the "consumer effect" is not necessarily coincidental with the ideological effect. Elaborate costume details which might be dismissed as "superfluous," says Radway, are finally a kind of "celebration of the reader's world of housewifely domesticity."[73] Extravagant costuming, justified as history, confirms a woman's concerns and interests by elevating them from ordinariness to the status of exquisite object. The elegant gown is an homage to woman's "preoccupations."

Costume in the classical realist cinema performs some of the same functions that lavish description performs in literary fiction. The accumulation of costume detail creates the necessary transparency which in turn encourages identification and involvement, and while the fictional space is purporting to be just like life, the narrative is flying in the face of the real. Both the fabulous gown on screen and the tale of the fabulist balance the extraordinary with the ordinary: fantasy is always revealed to us in some of the terms of the familiar.[74] In the most extravagant costume pictures such as *Mary of Scotland* (1936), *Marie Antoinette* (1938), *Cleopatra* (1934), *The Private Lives of Elizabeth and Essex* (1939), and *Forever Amber* (1947), then, spectacular fantasy is justified by means of history and authenticity, emphasized by studio promotion stories about years of research in Europe. Fantastic costs guarantee accuracy and exactitude at the same time that they insure marvelous splendor.[75] And yet, as I discuss in my article here on narrative and realism, for all of the extravagance, costume was perceived as a troublesome distraction which could divert the viewer's attention from the story itself.

While costuming created diverting fabrications, fictions for the eye, it also contributed to the requisite cinematic illusionism, the construction of which required the tireless labor of the ill-paid women employed in the big studio costume departments. There women were involved in the creation of the "seamless whole" of classical narrative in two contradictory ways: while on the one hand, you couldn't "cheat the camera," which meant that materials had to be flawless and sewing had to be perfect, on the other hand, creating the illusion meant "fooling the camera." The costume department was especially involved in creating the illusion of color and dimension. Before color processes, the spectrum was carefully faked with grey tones; black and white, the photographic troublemakers, were simulated with dark blue, and yellow or pink. Since early Technicolor could not reproduce some shades, red, in particular, had to be synthesized, and all colors had to be "tecked" or tested under lights before shooting. Betsy Nielsen's history of women costume workers in this volume gives the lie to cinematic self-effacement—the representation of exquisitely finished dream gowns as untouched by the hands of seamstresses, and neither lifted nor cleaned bythe women who were exploited before the establishment of a union. The traces of this toil had to be eradicated before the camera. This job of effacement, Nielsen tells us, was carried out in the perfect matching of dress to scene, often effected by making multiple copies of the same gown at different stages of wear and in the on-screen camouflage of a dress made over until it disintegrated.

Cinematic illusionism took its toll on the bodies of the actresses as it did the bodies of the seamstresses. One of the most successful fictions woven by Hollywood publicity is that costumes created by the studio departments were worn. Screen costumes, on the contrary, were not made to be worn, they were made to be photographed. These improbable clothes were often too heavy for actresses to wear without becoming exhausted or were too tight for them to sit in; hence they leaned against reclining stands called "costume boards" between takes and sometimes were even carried to their places on the set. But the labor of the seamstresses and the designers also points to something else. While these actresses' bodies were part of the material used to build the fantasy mise-en-scene, they also had their revenge, so to speak. From the point of view of the costume department, the greatest threat to the cinematic illusion was the "natural" body of the actress. To tell the story, that body had to be bound, thus designers devised tricks for reconstructing the star body. Kay Francis, too tall for most male leads, had her hems lengthened in back to effect a slouch; Greta Garbo's arms were relocated by "cheating" the seams up and using a Kimono sleeve.[76] When Edith Head began to design for Barbara Stanwyck, she realigned the star's body, de-emphasizing buttocks which were considered too low.[77] To the designer, who thought in terms of darts, eighth-of-an-inch tucks, and smoothness of line, breasts were an "engineering problem"[78] and weight changes were the ruin of a composition. The requirement of continuity met the most resistance from the actresses' bodies, however, in the case of pregnancy, when the designer worked against time to produce a perfectly proportioned denial of the most fully elaborated signs of femaleness.

Voyeurism and Fetishism

Feminist film theory begins with the female body and takes its inspiration directly from Marlene Dietrich's veils and feathers. I have argued earlier that the germ of Laura Mulvey's seminal "Visual Pleasure and Narrative Cinema" is the 1970 *Cahiers du Cinéma* collective text explicating *Morocco* (1930), Josef Von Sternberg's vehicle for Marlene Dietrich.[79] Therefore if the MOROCCO analysis is a forefather, Dietrich is a "foremother" of feminist film theory. This lineage becomes even more important in light of John Fletcher's recent reminder that Claire Johnston's analysis of Jean Peters's male masquerade in *Anne of the Indies* (1951), published almost coincidentally with "Visual Pleasure and Narrative Cinema" in 1975, also has its origins in the French psychoanalytic study of *Morocco*.[80] What this suggests is two lines of descent, the "visual pleasure" line based on the paradigm of voyeuristic looking to which I have already referred, and a second line based on the paradigm of "masquerade" which Fletcher describes as having been collapsed into the theory of the controlling male "look" via the concept of the phallic woman, theorized as a denial of "woman as woman" in Mulvey as well as in Johnston's 1973 "Woman's Cinema as Counter-Cinema."[81]

These two lines of descent produce contrasting theories of body and costume, just as they have already produced different theories of spectatorship. The model based on the thesis that spectator point of view in classical cinema is always male recapitulates the psychoanalytic account of the controlling look of voyeurism. The voyeuristic look has its companion formation in the phallic woman, the narcissistic male projection which magically turns her terrifying body into the comforting image of the male phallus. This phallic woman model, based on the Freudian oedipal, with its connotations of sadism and its its threat of castration, yields what we might call the "to-be-looked-at" costuming aesthetic, borrowing Mulvey's term.[82] This is a mode of costuming epitomized by show girl styles and what Charlotte Herzog discusses here as tactile, brazen, "girlie" fabrics, historically associated with broad forms of diversion and institutions of ill-repute: circus, revue, burlesque, vaudeville, saloon hall, and brothel. The classic example is Mae West's 1890s hour-glass shape with heavily beaded and feathered trimming. And does the black satin strapless sheath designed by Jean Louis for Rita Hayworth's "Put the Blame on Mame" number in *Gilda* (1946) exemplify the sadistic side of the "to-be-looked-at" aesthetic, with the screen image held in place by the male look just as the body of the actress was held in place in the dress by the designer's ingenious placement of stays?

But as soon as we propose a costume aesthetic "cut to the measure of desire," in Mulvey's terms, we encounter difficulties.[83] For as I suggest in my article on narrative codes, costume is a visually troublesome signifier which has to be made subservient to the story; thus it functions to feature the female body as spectacle at the same time that it is kept in check as "eye-catching" competition. The difficulty of adapting the pre-existing rhetoric of *haute couture* to the new language of American silent cinema is exemplified in the case of the French illustrator-costumer Erté, who was brought to Hollywood to design in the teens. Although he was hired as designer on several motion pictures, much of his work was never used.[84] Nevertheless, Erté's *Harper's Bazaar* covers during this period, which defined the two-dimensional flatness of the flapper, did set the parameters of the reigning style for those few designers who worked on a per picture basis during the 1920s. Even though it is agreed that Erté's silhouette was the model for the silent film costume design, his own work was too decoratively intricate and active, too complexly involved in its own system to work as the kind of emblematic restatement of character traits that would serve the dramatic needs of moving pictures. But also, since Erté saw women as completely decorative, the body always disappeared into the design. And here lies the dilemma. Although the "to-be-looked-at" aesthetic (hard surfaces, tight fits, glinty textures) may help to alleviate the threat of the female body by transmuting it into something else, the place of that body (and its substitutes) cannot not be usurped by a competing spectacle from which that body is totally missing.

In his essay on Erté's "Alphabet of Women" series, Barthes explains Erté's indifference to the female body as a consequence of his involvement with other languages. For the designer, woman has no meaning at all since his starting point is always the letter, and furthermore, Barthes goes on, "it is something of an illusion to believe that fashion is obsessed with the body . . ." It is, he says, "obsessed with the Letter."[85] But this idea of costume design for women as so engaged in its own logic that it is oblivious of the female body might prove to be an interruption or a frustration of voyeurism. What Erté's hieroglyphics suggest is not a language of the female form but motion picture aesthetics as a history of sartorial shapes, outlines, and silhouettes, an aesthetic created by doodling with the female body. This approach would give us the male designer-centered aesthetic of the silent period dominated by the flattened "S"-Curve of Erté's 1920s flapper, the 1930s as the perfectly matched pearl "O's" of Orry-Kelly's rounded-rump skirts seen in the Busby Berkeley musicals;[86] the heavy "V" of Adrian's 1940s suit, and the hour-glass of Christian Dior's silhouette, which Maureen Turim discusses in her article here on the 1950s.

Turim's "Designing Women: The Emergence of the New Sweetheart Line," reprinted in this collection, is a companion to her earlier "Gentlemen Consume Blondes," and indeed might be seen as filling out the intriguing reference in that article to the way the "hourglass figure, the lush, full body of Fifties fashion" sells the 1953 Howard Hawks film featuring Jane Russell and Marilyn Monroe. The fetishistic aesthetic is typified by the fragmentation and symbolic substitution we see in the replacement of "woman" for "diamonds" or "ermine fur," doubled in *Gentlemen Prefer Blondes* by the Monroe-Russell pairing. As Turim tells us in the "Addendum," her intention was to use the psychoanalytic notion of fetishism as the starting point for an analysis of a particular film, but this was not to suggest that fetishism should provide (in the way voyeurism has), the basis for a theorization of all cinematic form.[87] The foundation for such a theory based on fetishism is also laid out in the *Morocco* article, where the *Cahiers* editors describe Amy Jolly/Dietrich as interchangeable with "shoes" and "necklace." Furthermore, the image itself, analogous to the costume object, is also constituted as "mask, gauze, screen,"[88] and thus it is that out of the analysis of MOROCCO we have two kinds of looking: the "curious" voyeuristic look which requires a distance between the spectator and the screen and the fetishistic look which is more "captivated" than curious.[89]

Cinematic conventions that have encouraged fetishization have also lent themselves to the commoditization of the body, according to some critics. As Anne Friedberg describes this process, it is motion picture editing, the "metonomy of the body; a face, a hand, a leg, all cut up," that organizes the substitutional uses of star merchandise.[90] I would take this further to suggest that where film theory has emphasized the *standing in* aspect of the cinema, based on the "effect" of the world not there but created with shadows, it has missed the importance of the fetish object, clutched and hoarded. But also we might consider, following John Ellis's suggestion, how the logic of fetishism, if it is a substitution for looking, might finally "abolish" voyeurism.[91] What if the lavishly rendered texture of film costume awakens a tactile desire in the viewer which can only be satisfied by possession and collection? This possibility would seem to invoke the anthropological sense to the word *fetish* which Baudrillard reminds us was originally synonymous with *fabrication* or artifact. Whereas psychoanalysis trains us to think in terms of displacement, with its involuntary and compensatory connotations, the anthropological sense of fetish restores some power to the devotee who transforms and invests the sacred object. We might also recall how the *fetish* in history has been used to dismiss the ritual practices of the cultural other.[92] Cinematic fetishism, with its association with perverse practices, always seems to describe the fascination of everyone other than ourselves. One also thinks here of the dismissal of fans (the young girl collecting Lipographs or the gay male collecting Joan Crawford's costumes) who are really fabricators extraordinaire.

Turim's theory of fetishism yields the "gilded bondage" of the physically restricting and constraining "sweetheart style," the perfect metaphor for the limited social position of women in the 1950s. And yet, we have to ask again whether oppressive costume practices (and the fictional representations of them) translate directly into woman's oppression. The positions here have already been rehearsed in earlier feminist debates around the meaning of tight-lacing as both the ordinary Victorian mode of dress and as true fetish practice.[93] What could be said of the genuine perversion is that it holds a clue to the significance of the common practice. The waist-cinched "sweetheart" bride, the Victorian tight-lacer, the anorexic, and the romance novel reader all represent what was missed in the original notion of dominant culture: the muffled protests against oppression found in the very practices which seem to most graphically implement and spell out the patriarchial wish. And finally, feminist theory must be generous enough to accommodate another possibility—that the most constricting mode of dress might lead women to make erotic discoveries about their own bodies.[94]

Masquerade as Spectatorial and Critical Practice

Feminists have more recently turned to "masquerade" as a theoretical paradigm as a supplement to as well as a reaction against theories of voyeurism and fetishism which posit a generic male spectator. Most of these theories have circumvented the other line of descent from the *Morocco* analysis through the the the Johnston essay on female disguise in *Anne of the Indies,* "forgetting" that this early work, as John Fletcher now reminds us, was allied with *Cahiers du Cinéma's* notion of a progressive "ruptured" text and counter-cinema as a Brechtian thrust against the dominant, hinging on the capacity of masquerade to expose and critique.[95] Actually, Fletcher cites this 1975 article as occasion of the introduction of the concept of masquerade, but it is not as though Johnston's theorization of Dietrich's male dress in the 1973 article on counter-cinema didn't contain the suggestion, however quickly the fluid doubleness of masquerade hardened into the phallic woman. To quote her important statement again:

> This masquerade indicates the absence of man, an absence which is simultaneously negated and recuperated by man. The image of the woman becomes merely the trace of the exclusion and repression of Woman.[96]

The influence of this single formulation on the field has been enormous. Ironically, it was this phallic (not-male) woman paradigm in our own early feminist work which made it virtually impossible to theorize either woman in the audience or woman in the text. The return to the double-edged masquerade paradigm has provided the critical means for filling out women's spectatorial activity. Significantly, it has yielded more distinct variations than the voyeurism and the fetishism paradigms combined.

The masquerade metaphor has also yielded absolutely contradictory conclusions about the position of the female vis-à-vis the text. And yet all of these hypotheses depend upon the same thesis that women are capable of much more gender fluidity than men in their identification with screen characters, a thesis first posed by Tania Modleski in her consideration of female soap opera viewers.[97] I would contrast the two ends of the spectatorship spectrum in terms of the power this "oscillation" awards to the female spectator. At the one end, the notion of female spectatorship as transvestitism derived from Laura Mulvey's "Afterthoughts" on her visual pleasure article has been most fully elaborated in Mary Ann Doane's crucial essay, "Film and the Masquerade—Theorising the Female Spectator."[98] Here the theory of a thoroughly voyeuristic cinema only allows the female spectator to look from the vantage point of the male viewer. In order for her to assume the requisite voyeuristic distance, the woman puts on the sexual guise of the male, effecting a trans-sex identification. Significantly, for Doane, the visual pleasure derived from this positioning is a masochistic pleasure. I should note, however, that Doane draws a distinction in this essay between spectatorial transvestitism and masquerade with a deconstructive pose offering a radical possibility not available in trans-sex positioning. More recently, she has elaborated on her concept of masquerade in reference to the "double mimesis" of a femininity which knows it is excessive but uses its own overload parodically. As Stella Dallas's "performance" of mothering, especially in Barbara Stanwyck's interpretation of the role, the despised signs of femininity are "put on" again to the woman's own advantage.[99]

At the other end of the spectrum is the theorization of a lesbian spectatorship which claims full access to the screen image of the female body, relishing in particular the masquerade in which actresses are disguised as men. Lesbian readership as a possibility in feminist film criticism actually predates the theorization of transvestitism, coming to the new discipline as it did via the empirical accounts of lesbian reclamation of the classical male impersonation roles: Katherine Hepburn in *Sylvia Scarlett* (1935), Marlene Dietrich in *Morocco,* and Greta Garbo in *Queen Christina* (1933). This position was subsequently rediscovered and came to gain ground because it offered the clearest challenge to the model of patriarchial cinema as completely voyeuristic.[100]

More recently, the masquerade paradigm has been filled out at the liberatory end of the spectrum and many more critics are now considering the radical possibilities of what might be called spectatorial cross-dressing, a vision which takes its inspiration from the socially subversive meanings and increased options of sexual disguise. In this vein, Miriam Hansen has argued for employing a model of spectatorial flexibility to understand the complex appeal of Rudolph Valentino for viewers in the 1920s who appreciated his feminine positioning on the screen as in *Monsieur Beaucaire* (1923) in which he is as elaborately costumed as a female star would have been.[101] Gaylyn Studlar's essay in this collection on Dietrich and Von Sternberg is likewise motivated by an interest in developing paradigms which might better accommodate the female viewer. Working out her theory from the very narrow ledge of possibility available within psychoanalytic theory, she starts by replacing the Freudian notion of masochism (with all of its negative proscriptions for women), with an alternative from Gilles Deleuze, based on his re-reading of the literary works of Leopold von Sacher-Masoch. Deleuze's formulation of masochism depends on a pre-oedipal/oedipal distinction which replaces the mother left out of Freudian theory, explaining the punishment-fulfillment dialectic of masochism as related to a sense that one will never be reunited with the mother.[102] Studlar's analysis, then, offers us a third model of a psychoanalytic costume aesthetic, not out of the MOROCCO analysis, but out of Dietrich's image. Corroborating Studlar's findings, Ann Kaplan's discussion of *Blonde Venus* (1932) depends upon seeing the star actress as subverting the spectacle because of her awareness of the way in which she is being used.[103] Female-female bonding, in this analysis, is aligned with Dietrich's transvestitism, but Kaplan stops short of the strategic possibility suggested by Studlar—the masochist's impossible "wish to be both sexes at once," which gives us costume as a refuge and a site of gender confusion. However, as Chris Straayer cautions in "Redressing the 'Natural,' " cross-dressing is not automatically a radical stance since the device may be used to confirm the most conservative conviction that gender identity should correspond with biological body. For instance, such films as *Tootsie* (1985) and *Victor/Victoria* (1982), although a temporary tease for lesbian viewers, are finally reactionary in the way they reveal correct gender with a flourishing costume change confirming a "true" relationship between clothing and the gendered body beneath. But to leave the "true" gender ambiguous as in Straayer's examples of what she calls transgender casting (*The Year of Living Dangerously* [1983] and *Dorian Gray in the Mirror of the Boulevard Press* [1983]), is to offer a "radical unmasking of gender as culturally defined."[104]

In the last fifteen years, feminists have strived to effect a radical unmasking in their criticism as well as in their avant-garde media practice, but with much less dramatic results than is often achieved by the device of cross-dressing in narrative cinema. Counter-cinema, in both its critical and its practical embodiments has challenged but not undermined; it has needled patriarchial constructs, but failed to disturb them. The lesson in transgression we have from the transvestite as well as the female body-builder is that gender ambivalence is traumatically unsettling to the culture.[105] These counter practices of the body violate deeply felt premises. The sexual difference system around which societies are organized, after all, is guaranteed on a day-to-day basis by gendered dress, adornment, and body style. Even popular narrative representations of cross-dressing may provoke disorientation, discomfort, shock, and anger if the inverted world is not set right again and if the inversion is not excused by comic conventions. Can we learn something from this? Gayatri Spivak's idea that feminist literary critics could "fabricate strategic 'misreadings' " as counters to the preferred textual reading suggests one possibility.[106] Let us assume that the "correct" reading fits the text like the match up between the costume and the "correct" gender and that the maintenance of the socio-sexual order depends upon texts corresponding with proper readings. The "incorrect" reading left unrighted and undetected is then a deep structural trouble to the canonical body/society. What critic, however, dares to construct an elaborately formed, meticulously argued "wrong" reading, a textual mismatch? Spivak's suggestion takes its lesson from everywoman's secret knowledge and potency: the "useful and scrupulously fake reading" should replace the "passively active fake orgasm."[107] Or, who is to know?

If gender confusion and ambiguity is a female fabrication that is profoundly distressing to patriarchial culture, what, then, is the critical equivalent which can effect similar ideological erosion? As Annette Kuhn lays out the epistemology of critical cross-dressing, it is found in performance.[108] Here self:role as body:costume and gender: identity, each term in the pairing at odds with the other and in the relation of constant flux, with the advantage that, as we confuse the world, we are allowed to maintain our ambivalence for a little while longer.

2

All the Rage

Elizabeth Wilson

Strange that when so much else has changed there still exists such a strong hostility to fashion amongst so many radicals. No one objects to changing tastes in interior decoration; changing fashions in medicine, holidays, and food are hardly noticed as such, although none is devoid of the snobbery and competitiveness of which fashion is so often accused; and socialists feel no guilt for adding fashionable gadgets—videos for example—to their long list of worldly goods. Ideas and preoccupations at least of the academic left are highly sensitive to fashion; and although changing fashions in ideas are usually justified in terms of some higher truth, the justification often amounts to little more than the *Vogue* cry: "It's so Right for Now!"—The Austere Beauty of Habermas slashed with a Daring Touch of Baudrillard maybe.

Fashions in clothing are, of course, open to the objection that although we "need" clothes, we don't "need" fashion. Yet we never hear the argument that although we need food, we don't "need" pizzas, Peking Duck, or *nouvelle cuisine*. No one suggests that our dietary habits ought to be static, nor is there a movement for the reinstatement of "timeless" cooking. There must be, as Quentin Bell[1] has suggested, some moral quality about dress that makes us abnormally sensitive to its relationship to our ethical system.

Traditional left puritanism is part of the tradition of Fabian utilitarianism, a label I use to refer to the influence on socialists of the nineteenth-century scientific tradition for which rationality was the only reality. Marxism these days is frequently accused of an over-valuation of the positivistic scientific tradition; but it was stamped far more indelibly on mainstream Fabianism and the Fabians have had far more influence on the British left than Marxism ever did.

In the late nineteenth century, moralism in relation to dress expressed itself in an organized movement for dress reform (in which many individual Fabians, E. Nesbit, the children's writer, and George Bernard Shaw, for example, were involved). This movement attempted nothing less than the heroic project of the abolition of fashion.[2] It also expressed very specific ideals of beauty. A comfortable and *rational* style of dress would replace the "ugly" exaggerations of crinoline, corset, and bustle. Divided skirts were to be worn. Men's trousers, of which the reformers disapproved, were to be replaced by knickerbockers; and tightlacing by the "antique" waist modeled on ancient Greek proportions. Artistically minded reformers such as William Morris aimed for a pre-Raphaelite ideal of beauty in clothing which relied on medieval or early Renaissance taste in colors, styles, and materials (Figure 2.1). Japanese taste was also influential and contributed to the fashion for "off" colors (the "greenery yallery" satirized in Gilbert and Sullivan's comic opera *Patience*) which was also part of a reaction against the new and all too vivid aniline dyes of the 1860s and 1870s, when acid green, magenta, and electric blue were loosed upon the fashionable world.

Yet not only did the dress reformers fail to do away with changing modes; "aesthetic dress" as it was called eventually influenced mainstream fashion. The Edwardian "leg of mutton" sleeve, for example, was descended from the pre-Raphaelite fashion for full sleeves, itself a reaction against the tight sleeves and constricting sloping shoulders of the 1840s. In the early twentieth century tightlacing ceased to be a fashion style and became instead a sexual perversion.[3] Modernity arrived, with sports, bicycling, and motor-cars. (Figure 2.2). Sex, sunbathing, and psychoanalysis caused a reevaluation of the body.

In the nineteenth century fashion had come to be associated almost entirely with women's clothing, while men's clothes have since been perceived (inaccurately) as unchanging.[4] Fashion as a mania for change could therefore the more easily be interpreted either as evidence of women's inherent frivolity and flightiness; or—the other side of the coin—as evidence of women's subjection and oppression. As argued most influentially by Thorstein Veblen,[5] women's fashion was part of conspicuous consumption and reflected her status as property.

Not surprisingly, those of progressive views who believed in the emancipation of women and the possibility of their equality with men found such explanations congenial. Fashion was nothing else than women's bondage made visible. It was moreover *irrational;* it would, therefore, have no place in the socialist utopia, which was to be a wholly *rational* realm.

To a surprising extent Veblen's views are still accepted today, while contemporary feminists have too readily equated corsets with female

Figure 2.1 The Pre-Raphaelite ideal of beauty. *La Ghirlandata* by
Dante Gabriel Rossetti. Courtesy of The Medici Society Ltd., London.

bondage. But an alternative view has been put forward by those who argue
that the wearing of corsets expressed far more contradictory aspirations.[6]
Veblen's rationalism also does not stand up to closer investigation. His
continuing popularity today among radicals reflects their rejection of
consumer culture. Stuart and Elizabeth Ewen, for example, argue that
"rebellion fashions" can never be more than the *recuperation* of protest
and that "this desire for change would be more meaningfully pursued in
the realm of concerted social action."[7] Yet this ignores the extent to which

Figure 2.2 Sports and Daywear by Jean Patou, 1925. Courtesy of A.B.C., Paris.

fashion is one among many forms of aesthetic creativity which make possible the exploration of alternatives. Fashion is more than simply a displacement of protest; it is an art form and a symbolic system, and, "once literacy and a rich vocabulary of visual, aural and dramatic expressions exist, then society has a permanently available . . . resource in which all the tabooed, fantastic, possible and impossible dreams of humanity can be explored in blueprint."[8]

The idea of consumerist culture was first developed by Max Horkheimer and Theodor Adorno.[9] Leading members of the Frankfurt School of Marxists in the 1920s, they created a "critical theory" which brought the insights of psychoanalysis (amongst other things) to bear on the ideologies and the psychology first of capitalist and then of fascist society. Exiled, as Jews, to the USA, they witnessed there the first "mass" society at close quarters, and rejected with horror its mechanized pop culture, the culture industry as they termed it.

The Frankfurt tradition was an elitist one—mass culture, as they saw it, was false and sickening, and the only possibilities for a critical, oppositional protest lay in the realm of "high" art—modernist art. Contemporary feminists and researchers into popular culture have been more likely to reject this tradition in favor of a populism that tends to celebrate the pleasure to be found in popular forms.

This makes their dismissal of fashion even stranger. But, until recently, writers on pop culture have shown little interest in fashion (although some of them may be sharp dressers themselves). The only fashions that the left cultural commentators have really "seen" have been the oppositional fashions of postwar *male* (and mostly white) working class youth. These have been commented on[10] and understood largely in functionalist terms, as social ritual or symbolic protest. Many questions remain unanswered. Why is it that Britain or all western capitalist countries have been so especially rich in these styles? What has been their meaning for young women? Punk alone was a style equally for both sexes; for although Mod girls, teddy girls, and others did have special ways of dressing their styles were both distinct from and parasitical upon those of their boyfriends. (I remember girls' Mod suits being copied by C and A in 1964; severe tweed suits with longish straight skirts and Norfolk jackets.)

What do oppositional styles in general mean for women? Women have been so wholly identified with mainstream fashion that it is hard for them even to have oppositional styles. Sartorial excess and deviance readily equates with rebellion for men. It *can* signify revolt for young women—but even the bizarre can be fashionable, and attempts to outrage or, as often happens, to be overtly sexual or sexual in some different ways, may nevertheless remain within the stylistic boundaries of clothes that are still also expressing submissiveness to a boyfriend even if rebellion at home.

Today there is, of course, a style of oppositional dress associated with feminism. Just as the bourgeois feminist of the nineteenth century was caricatured in mannish clothing, so feminism today is popularly equated not only with masculinity but also with a rejection of all flamboyance, discomfort, and sexual objectification. And although the stereotype of the feminist in dungarees and Dr. Martens boots is in one way rather silly, it is accepted by some feminists themselves. Yet the clothes in question are neither functional nor comfortable. Dungarees and boiler suits were intended for men who do not have to undress when they go to the toilet. Symbolism and not utility has equated men's overalls with women's rights. Even dungarees and boiler suits, in any case, change with the times, and in the mid-1980s the ones with bell-bottoms are only to be found in jumbles sales and Oxfam shops.

To the extent that feminist style exists, its function is not to promote rational comfort but to announce the wearer's feminism in public. We live in an urban society in which fashion, or fashions, are one essential ingredient in the rituals of the cityscape. New definitions of the individual's social place and group affiliation are announced by means of clothes which become part of a performance. One's personality, beliefs, and even desires have to be stated. Clothes are the poster for one's act.

In the pre-industrial world, clothes were the badge of rank, profession, or trade. As classes fragment we revert, though now informally, to a state in which our clothes once more define us, no longer in terms of work but in terms of our play, our politics, our obsessions. Insofar as feminism evolves a style amongst these styles, it is joining the discourse, so to speak, rather than breaking with it, not transcending but capitulating. How could it be otherwise? This is how we use clothes now.

Yet fashion is more than a message, and the vulgarized view of it as a language or sign system[11] is only half, or less, of the story. The appeal of fashion is an ambiguous one, although for many of us, it is, whether we acknowledge it or not, extremely powerful. We produce images of ourselves that both somehow sum up some prevailing mood and at the same time try to halt the continual process of change of which fashion is itself such an important part; modern fashion always represents a snapshot of time, a passing mood and fleeting moment made permanent in the fixative of color, line, and surface.

Self-adornment links the biological body to aesthetics. The relationship of fashion to eroticism is both obvious and complex, but has perhaps been overemphasized in our sex-conscious culture at the expense of other and equally interesting relationships. Fashion and adornment, for example, seem to represent enduring efforts to change the biological given of one's body. Diets and aerobics can't simply be swept into the catch-all of consumerism, for many societies engage in different ways in the attempt radically to alter the stubbornly resistant human form, both male and female.

The relationship of fashion to art is also important. The fashions of the 1920s, for example, can't just be interpreted (as they usually boringly are) as expressive of women's emancipation and a new sexual freedom. That was all happening well before the first World War—Paul Poiret, the revolutionizing French designer, abandoned the corset in 1908 (Figure 2.3). More significant was the relationship of 1920s fashion to the artistic

Figure 2.3   The Revolutionary New Coats designed by Paul Poiret, illustrated by Paul Iribe, 1908. Courtesy of The Royal Pavilion, Art Gallery and Museums, Brighton.

movements of modernism and futurism. They imitated aspects of modernism in featuring abstract designs and in rendering the body as two-dimensional and flat as possible; they were futurist in suggesting speed and the clean lines of the machine. The great love affairs of black-and-white photography with fashion *was* the modernist sensibility (Figure 2.4).

Fashions of the 1920s were not, though, modernist in the thoroughgoing sense that Punk has been. For this questions its own activity and the actual

Figure 2.4 Black and White fashion photograph: Christian Dior evening dresses, photographed by Horst, 1948 (Paris collection, 1949). Courtesy of American *Vogue*.

terms of reference of fashion, as well as questioning traditional views about what is beautiful and chic.

Although however we might want to get away from the puritanism of the left in order to celebrate fashion as a legitimate and highly aesthetic pleasure, there are still problems about defending it. The attempt to understand ideologies at times falls over into an acceptance of any kind of hedonistic activity either simply because it is popular or because there can no longer be allowed to be *any* hierarchy of aesthetic values—*Dallas* becomes as important as *Madame Bovary* in this pseudo- democratization of culture. This call to hedonism can represent a flight from more threatening problems; and the recognition of pleasure and beauty as important forces in our lives—which emphatically they are—and as, therefore, a legitimate preoccupation of socialists, can easily degenerate into a kind of unreflective submersion and an irresponsibility that is actually the reverse side of the coin to moralism, an abdication of discrimination that is merely decadent.

Just as in the sphere of politics and social policy, reactionary proposals may sometimes be put forward as "left wing" or progressive simply because, for the left at least, they are *new,* so in the cultural field it may be chic to be crazy about the kitsch and glorify the trashy. An interest in fashion will then be merely a reaction against previous moralism. Perhaps, indeed, the pleasures of embracing what you formerly hated, whether in the erotic or the intellectual sphere are underestimated; it would certainly account for some strange couplings, conversions, and intellectual tergiversations.

Yet to ignore the importance of the seemingly superficial would be irresponsible, too. Fascism did after all eroticize the uniform, creating a fetishized idealization of the masculine body, a whole philosophy of domination, cruelty, and irrationalism made visible in the shape of the blonde Aryan, a male Valkyrie in gleaming black leather and knife-edged silhouette.

To the uniforms of fascism the left has opposed its bohemian styles. But whereas fascism orchestrated a great undertow of romanticism, mysticism, and paranoia to create a national movement that transcended boundaries of class, left bohemian styles—certainly in Britain—have remained class bound. For the most part the British left in opposition has expressed a merely middle-class rebelliousness, and, like socialist ideas, left-wing fashions have never become "hegemonic"; while when in power the left (here and elsewhere) has too often dressed with grim respectability, and in taking over the three-piece suit of the bourgeois businessman suggested a loss of revolutionary fervor and a submission to bureaucracy, capitalism, and all the dreary accoutrements of faceless power.

Male radical styles of the 1950s can still be seen today on some not so young socialists. The woolly tie (possibly red), the woolly shirt (possibly tan) and the crumpled tweeds and cords in autumnal rural tones were, when their wearers were young, the easily recognizable alternative to the cavalry twills and paisley cravats of the young conservatives of the 1950s. Then, there was, in addition, another smoother 1950s style: black shirts, white ties, and sunglasses worn indoors—a style associated with the Modern Jazz Quartet and a more hip, American approach to life. This

Figure 2.5 Oppositional modes meet post-punk urban chic: Lesbians in London, 1987. Photograph by Jean Fraser.

style is now being revived by the followers of big band jazz, so that audiences look like escapees from an existentialist novel—but, like all revivals, the style is inevitably worn with quotation marks.

Is the British left at present too fragmented to create even a unifying oppositional, let alone hegemonic style? What do discourse theorists wear? Should the followers of Foucault look like clones or leather freaks . . . or what? Just as sexual tastes may be ever more clearly as well as more minutely defined by dress, so perhaps theoretical tastes could be.

As it is, life in postmodern society becomes more and more like a fancy dress party. In Bloomingdale's you meet salesgirls dressed as Dresden shepherdesses to sell potpourri, as Botticelli's Primavera to sell plastic flowers, as Chinese princesses to promote the 1980 exhibition that celebrated the signing of the trade agreement with the People's Republic (even Maoism can be consumerized at Bloomingdale's).

At the other end of the spectrum, a group of anarchists at a British "Beyond the Fragments"[12] conference wore black t-shirts and jeans with holes in embarrassing places, plus lengths of fishing net, using their costume to dramatize their frequent protests at the too-orderly organization of the conference, as they saw it. (To other participants, the conference seemed in the best tradition of libertarian socialist chaos.) Or, at a women's meeting on sexuality, a group of anti-porn protesters were all dressed like the upper-class heroes of *Brideshead Revisited*—although the languid androgyny of their appearance hardly matched the savagery of their sentiments.

Underlying this often mysterious diversity is a division that is perhaps deeper and more interesting, more fundamental than the established divisions of "left" and "right." On the one hand there is a tradition of "authenticity," which tends to be associated with rural nostalgia (as with the hippies), ideas about one's "essential self" and which would find its expression in "timeless" dress—utopian styles, or dress reform. On the other hand is the "postmodern" sensibility, with its love of the city, and its insistence that we are socially constructed, but also construct ourselves. This emphasizes performance, bricolage, play, and walks a tightrope between pleasure and danger.

In fashion we often express our longing for the "authentic" and the "postmodern" simultaneously, attempting to have our cake and eat it, to be both simple and complex. We long for a leftie equivalent of the little black dress (maybe for a long time blue jeans *were* the little black dress of the counter culture). We want a garment that is totally different, and yet that will fix us forever and thereby negate the fluidity of personality. We long for a sartorial nirvana in which fashion—which expresses the change that is life—would be no more.

Traditionally western Christian culture has created a division between appearances and an inner and spiritual truth. Appearances, the immediate, sensual impact of life, are denigrated; only the spiritual is real. Yet the light and shade of change which plays across the surface of life *is* reality. Fashion in our culture is elaborate, fetishized, neurotic, because it goes against these dominant values, against the grain of the cultural norm, representing the return of the repressed and the profound importance of the superficial.

3

Fame, Flashdance, and Fantasies of Achievement

Angela McRobbie

At first the child sat numbed, tense. The
chills began going up and down her
spine. Her hands clenched. She could
feel the nails piercing the flesh of her
palms, but it didn't matter. Nothing
mattered only this—only loveliness
mattered . . . Yes, she would dance—
and nothing would stop her, nothing—
nothing in the world.[1] (*Dancing Star,* a
biography of Anna Pavlova)

Dance and Culture

It is surprising just how negligent sociology and cultural studies have been
of dance. As a leisure practice, a performance art and as a representational
form, dance continues to elude analysis. And while dance theory and
dance criticism are well-developed fields in their own right they do not
offer the kind of broader social and cultural analysis which is still needed.
It is in dance aesthetics that the most developed work has emerged, notably
that of Suzanne Langer who attempted in the 1950s to theorize modern
dance in terms of feeling, form, and the symbolic meaning of notation.[2]
Following from this Helen Thomas has argued for a sociology of dance
which includes an engagement with the internal dynamics of dance movement and which does not close them off in favor of a more socialized
account.[3]

Dance history is less adventurous than dance aesthetics and tends to be
either entirely empirical and anecdotal or else collapsed into the biographi-
cal details of great dancers. Some of this work is, of course, a useful
resource for the sociologist of dance. For example it is here that we find
the many accounts of the impact of Isadora Duncan's techniques; and the
descriptions of the network of artists, painters, and dancers (mostly Russian exiles), who came to live in Paris in the early years of the century,
and whose work was directly influenced by the ideas which resulted
from this cosmopolitan and bohemian mix (Figure 3.1). The immensely
interesting and anecdotal biography of Nijinsky written by his widow in
1933 with a postscript in the 1958 edition provides the sociologist of dance
with a fascinating glimpse of dance culture and its links with the high arts
in the early years of the century.[4]

39

Figure 3.1   Anna Pavlova (1885–1931) in her dressing room. Courtesy of New York Public Library of the Performing Arts.

The only piece of cultural studies analysis which intrudes into this sphere otherwise marked out by the dominance of taste and connoisseurship is Peter Wollen's recent essay.[5] Wollen argues that while the theorists of modernism are loath to admit it (since ballet has always been regarded as a less important art), the Russian Ballet directed by Diaghilev, choreographed by Fokine, and with stage sets (what he calls scenography) by Leon Bakst, was enormously influential in the uneasy lurch which was made in the early years of the century towards a modernist aesthetic. By documenting the central importance of Diaghilev, and the way in which his most popular ballet *Schéhérazade* looked to the Orient as a way of unsettling sexual and cultural mores, Wollen re-instates ballet as a crucial vehicle for the expression of radical ideas. The Russian Ballet was poised between the old and the new order and its decadence and excess accounted for what was an unfair marginalization in the writing of modernist history.[6]

Wollen's essay shows not just the importance of ballet in the broader sphere of the arts, but also the extent to which the boundaries which are used to demarcate aesthetic forms are frequently untenable. Diaghilev's *Schéhérazade* with Nijinsky as the athletic effeminate and androgynous centerpart, with the music of Rimsky-Korsakov and with lavishly colored, oriental sets by Bakst was on the cusp of the shift into modernism. What is more, this ballet and those that followed posited the dancer's body as unconfined, as more natural and modernist in its movements than had been the case before.

Most interesting perhaps is Wollen's comparison between the balletic body of 1912–13 and the ambiguously extravagant body which was part of punk style of the early 1980s. Considering these bodies, ". . . we can perhaps see a link between the Russian ballet and punk, the radical excess of the last years of the ancien régime and that of postmodern street culture, complete with its own scenography of bondage, aggressive display, and decorative redistribution of bodily exposure."[7] This analogy is important because it locates ballet outside the sterile terms of high culture, and instead posits it as something which has connections with the aesthetics of everyday life. The Russian ballet was in this context as prefigurative as punk was when it reverberated across British society in the late 1970s and early 1980s.

The really important feature about dance, however, (and the one most unlikely to be foregrounded in conventional dance writing), is that as an art and a representational form, as a performance and a spectacle, it has an extremely strong, almost symbiotic relationship with its public. For girls and young women, particularly for those not brought up in a cultural background which sees it as part of its duty to introduce young people to the fine arts, to painting, literature, classical music, and great drama, dance exists as both a practice and as a spectacle. It also comes to life as a set of magical childhood narratives. In each of these forms dance carries within it the possibility of some mysterious transformative power. Its art lies in its ability to create a fantasy of change, escape, or achievement for girls and young women who are surrounded by much more mundane and limiting leisure opportunities. Dance is also different from the other arts in that it is readily available to young girls as a legitimate passion, something they might be expected to want to do, unlike painting or classical music or even writing. It has a more interactive effect than the other high arts. The Royal Ballet speaks to the thousands of pre-teen and teenage girls who take ballet classes each week in the same way *Fame* (1981) and *Flashdance* (1983) speak to those children and teenagers who dream of going to stage school or who take disco dancing classes at school. Images of dance have the effect of making people want to do it too.

I stressed earlier that it was strange that dance had proved of so little interest to sociology and cultural studies. Strange because despite the absence of a sociological language which would embrace the formal dimensions of dance there is nonetheless a diversity of wider social questions and issues which are immediately raised by even the most superficial consideration of dance. Some of the most richly coded class practices in contemporary society can be observed in leisure and particularly in dance. The various contexts of social dancing tell us a great deal about the everyday lives and expectations of their participants. Dance marks out important moments in the lifecycle and it punctuates the more banal weekly cycle of labor and leisure, and what Ian Chambers has labeled the "freedom of Saturday night."[8]

Dance and Club Culture

> Dancing, where the explicit and implicit zones of socialized pleasures and individualized desires entwine in the momentary rediscovery of the "reason of the body" . . . is undoubtedly one of the main avenues along which pop's sense travels.[9]

A sociology of dance would have to step outside the field of performance and examine dance as a social activity, a sexual ritual, a form of self-expression, a kind of exercise, and a way of speaking through the body. Historians of working-class culture have acknowledged the place occupied by dance in leisure and the opportunities it has afforded for courtship, relaxation, and boisterous or even riotous behavior. Unfortunately in most cases the nature of the dance remains in the background, something enjoyed more by women than by men and therefore marginal to the real business of working-class life. This imbalance is slowly being redressed by American social historians like Elizabeth Ewen and Kathy Peiss who have attempted to chart the various histories of immigrant and working-women's leisure in the early years of the century.[10] However in this country it remains an unchartered ground coming through only in fleeting references in oral history or in collections like Sheila Rowbotham and Jean McCrindle's *Dutiful Daughters*.[11] Even here memories of dancing are always associated with pleasure and with loss, as though the rest of the woman's life can be measured against such moments. Social history generally has tended to be more concerned with the problem of the policing of the working class even in its leisure time. Robert Roberts makes a few telling comments about the social anxieties which came into play around the dance halls in the years following the end of the Great War.[12] These fears and anxieties hinged around the possible promiscuity of the working-class girls who flooded into the dance halls as many nights a week as they could and who also got dressed and wore make up for the occasion in a way which was seen as shocking and indicative of some immoral intent.

This strand continues right into the postwar years. Dance halls remain a key feature in working-class leisure and a focal point for the expression of concern about working-class youth. Outside the evangelical thrust of youth clubs and other forms of State provided or religiously controlled leisure, the dancehall or disco, run for profit by "uncaring" businessmen, exists as a site for the moral panics which have punctuated the force field of "youth" for many years. However, the target for the moral panic evolves not so much around dancing (though rock 'n' roll dancing and jiving were linked from the start with sexual license) but rather around the other activities accompanying dance; drinking, drug taking, or violence. Dancing is the least of the worries of the moral guardians. If the boys did more of it there would be less to worry about. Because of these social constraints and sexist sanctions girls are less of a problem and therefore remain largely in the shadows, dressed up, dancing, and immersed in the "reason of body."

The link between dance and youth culture is reflective of how a crucial element in subcultural activity was played down if not altogether ignored. Despite Phil Cohen's early cartography of subcultural components—argot, ritual, and style—dance has hardly merited any attention whatsoever.[13] With the notable exception of Dick Hebdige's description of the short sharp movements of the "pogo" dance and its articulation with all the other elements of punk style, and Ian Chambers's extensive documentation of the clubs and dancehalls which have provided the backdrop for urban youth culture and music in the postwar period, there has been little or nothing said about the various dances and movements which have been a constant feature of urban youth cultures.[14] A trivialized or feminized form? A ritual without resistance? A sequence of steps some steps removed from the active, creative core of youth cultural activity? Chambers mentions a range of dance styles by name: The Shake, the Jerk, the Northern Soul style of athletic, acrobatic dance, as well as the break dancing and "body popping" associated with black youth. He also makes connections between white youth culture dancing and the black music and dance from which it has continually borrowed. If, as Paul Gilroy has argued, black dance addresses the body in a different register from that of formal ballroom dancing or folk dance, if this urban soul dancing traverses the entire body surface, shifting the center of eroticism away from the narrowly genital and allowing instead a slow sensual spread, then the meaning of this hyper-eroticism must be seen in the broader context of racial discrimination and prejudice.[15]

Lurking behind the fears of the moral guardians, then, has also been the specter of racial difference and otherness, the hysterical anxieties about the black rejection of work and labor discipline, the assumptions of sexual license and drug abuse and the contaminating effect these might have on white youth. At the other end of the spectrum is the equally racist assumption about black ability in the sphere of entertainment, an ability which has of course its own material history, its own dynamics of necessity. Within this rhetoric of racial inferiority is also the debased positioning of black song and dance, and black-influenced forms, as lower arts, non-art, and even native art.

This has certain consequences for the remaining sections of this article, especially those dealing with two popular and contemporary dance narratives, *Fame* and *Flashdance*. In each case a narrative tension is set up around this divide (ballet/jazz, classical/pop) and in each case the contention is satisfactorily resolved within the framework of the story. In the film *Fame,* the resolution hinges round the multicultural performances and the range of abilities demonstrated by the kids (black, white and hispanic) and highlighted in the graduation show which also marks the end of the film where the performance seamlessly moves from classical to pop and then to gospel. In *Flashdance,* Alex who is poor, orphaned, and part-hispanic, is able to give up her sleazy disco dancing job when she wins a place at the prestigious ballet school. Even in the novel *Ballet Shoes* there is evidence of the classical/pop divide though here it is characterized by two of the three sisters making choices in opposite directions. While Polly goes to Hollywood where she will sing, dance, and act, Posy goes to a European ballet school.[16]

A Passion to Dance

The experience of learning to dance as a child or as a young girl, and then, later on, in adolescence the almost addictive pleasure of social dancing to an endless beat in the darkened space of the disco or nightclub, are relatively unchanging forms in the landscape of female leisure culture. They also provide a multiplicity of narrative possibilities in popular entertainment, in film, on television, and in fiction. It will be part of my argument that dance occupies a special place in feminine culture because even as a high art it has an ambiguous status—for many women and girls whose upbringing and/or education do not lend themselves to a privileging of the arts, ideas about dance made available through texts and stories serve as their introduction to the arts. The meaning of art in this context is sufficiently wide (and conventional) to allow it to signify a kind of realm of the senses, an arena which is capable of transporting the reader or viewer away from the difficulties of everyday life and which simultaneously invites the reader or viewer to imagine herself as the star, the prima ballerina. Dance therefore exists as a passion and produces a strongly emotional response on the part of young girl. The attraction of dance narratives lies in the fantasies of both passionate commitment and achievement which they afford their subjects.

In the following I will analyze the fantasies of achievement in the girls novel *Ballet Shoes,* the film and TV series *Fame,* as well as *Flashdance,* the 1983 film which attempted to build on and extend the earlier enormous success of *Fame*. Along with this focus on achievement, passion, dedication, and self-discipline, each of these works also engages with the terrain of the family romance. These two poles act as the framework for the development of the narratives. As the stories unfold, they move backwards and forwards between the desire to achieve and the constraints and expectations of the family. Work becomes an alternative romance, a dream to be pursued even if it is against the odds. Dance operates as a metaphor for an external reality which is unconstrained by the limits and expectations of gender identity and which successfully and painlessly transports its subjects from a passive to a more active psychic position. What is charted repeatedly in these stories is this transition from childhood dependency to adolescent independence which in turn is gained through achievement in dance or in the performing arts and therefore in the outside world.

All three texts are conventionally feminine texts, their readers and viewers are largely female and they are located and marketed accordingly.[17] These are unique cultural objects for the reason that they define an artistic mode as a kind of utopia and as a symbolic escape route from the more normative expectations of girls and young women found in most other forms of popular culture. It will be my contention that these narratives have proved popular precisely because they depart so strongly from the kind of narrative submissiveness associated both with girls magazine stories of the type outlined by Valerie Walkerdine in her short study of girls comics, and with teenage romantic fiction.[18] The romance of work and achievement simultaneously resolves the difficulties posed by the family romance (in psychoanalytic terms) and postpones the difficulties envisaged in the transition towards adult feminine sexuality. It does this by either disregarding sexuality altogether (*Ballet Shoes*), or by reducing real romance to a minor episode, a fleeting embrace (*Fame*), or else in the more adult world of *Flashdance* by treating it as something which can

Figure 3.2 *Fame* (1981). Leroy's "funky" black-urban dancing. Courtesy of National Film Archive, London.

be an additional, unexpected pleasure, but subordinate nonetheless to the real business of work.

In both *Fame* and *Flashdance* pop or disco dancing plays a major role in the narrative development and both films are associated either with being poor or else with being black (or both). In *Fame* jazz dancing of the type associated with Afro-American culture is given equal status with ballet and this is taken as a symbol of the school's commitment to multiculturalism and racial equality. In *Flashdance,* however, hispanic-born Alex is pleased to be able to leave her disco dancing days behind her when she eventually wins a place in the Pittsburgh Ballet School.[19] This is partly because throughout the film her go-go dancing is portrayed as overtly sexual and therefore sleazy. Unlike the "funky" dancing of Leroy in *Fame* (Figure 3.2), Alex's dancing in Mawby's bar is choreographed to sexually arouse and this is accentuated filmically by the effect she has on the men watching her perform (Figures 3.3, 3.4). However, for her audition to ballet school she returns to a more acrobatic disco style and despite the initial frosty looks from the panels she eventually manages to get them tapping their feet in enjoyment. In this penultimate moment in

Figures 3.3 and 3.4 *Flashdance* (1983). Alex as the object of the male gaze. Courtesy of National Film Archive, London.

the film we see a small gesture toward the validation of pop dancing and, by implication, pop culture, even though it remains a sign of Alex's untutored ability.

I have chosen these three narratives for a number of reasons. They address specific ages of readers and viewers (teenage and pre-teenage girls) and they have been immensely popular with them and with a wider constituency of even younger children and adults. As well as reflecting different historical moments, the texts also range from the classical to the popular in terms of taste and cultural preference. *Ballet Shoes* is a classic of girls fiction, a specifically English and middle-class portrait of fantasied childhood in inter-war Britain. *Fame* was first a film, directed by Alan Parker in 1980, after which it became a TV series achieving almost cult status two years later. Although describing the lives at the New York School of Performing Arts of a group of teenagers, the *Fame* narratives were focused towards a much younger viewer. *Fame* (the film) was also reflective of a number of media strands emerging in the early 1980s. It functioned not just as a narrativized showcase for pop music and dance performances, where the soundtrack was foregrounded and then released as an album, but it also worked visually as a high fashion text. The early 1980s saw the mass popularity of dance exercise style. *Fame* helped trigger the leggings, sweatband, and leotard look and also helped launch the success of thousands of dance classes and exercise centers (of which the Pineapple Center in London is still the best known in England). *Fame* is also interesting because of its strongly multicultural emphasis, more strongly highlighted in the film than in the TV series. Indeed the film might well be credited as one of the most racially mixed pop musicals to have been produced in recent years.

Flashdance is different in a number of respects. It is more overtly "trashy" than *Fame,* its visual overlaps with other media forms are more obvious and more derivative (critics described it as a prolonged pop video or a movie-length advertisement) and its narrative was recognized as outrageously unlikely. Ridiculous as the narrative might be, the film still holds a peculiar attraction. It has a healthy shelf-life in video shops in Britain and the U.S. (though this might be partly attributable to the films' erotic emphasis on its heroine's body), but what marks it out as different from *Fame* is not so much the sex or the romance but rather that androgy-nously named Alex is presented as more sexually knowing than her counterparts in *Fame. Flashdance* was marketed for a slighter older teen-age audience and for a less exclusively female viewer. While the narrative disavows the vulgarity of the near-pornographic dancing Alex is paid to perform in her early days as a dancer, the visuals contradict this message and at key points through the film allow the audience to dwell at length on the purely sexy gyrations of the dancers.

Let's look then in more detail at the individual texts. *Ballet Shoes,* written in 1936 by Noel Streatfield, has been reprinted almost every year since then. It is read by prepubescent girls of all social and ethnic backgrounds and the narrative is heavily overlaid by the kinds of themes which make it open to a Freudian analysis. Three foundlings are brought back to England over a period of time by the man the children come to refer to as Gum (great-uncle Matthew). They are left under the care of Nurse and Sylvia with very little money as absent-minded Gum disappears abroad to continue with his work as an explorer. The three children are called Pauline, Petrova, and Posy and they give themselves the surname of Fossil as befits their strange and unknown parentage. Orphaned and without any secure financial future the Fossils, with the encouragement of Nurse and Sylvia, set about finding ways of earning their own keep. One of the boarders living with them in genteel poverty in Kensington happens to teach in the Children's Academy of Dance and Stage Training in Bloomsbury and she manages to get them lessons in return for payment deferred until they begin to work.

As pupils at the Academy, the girls pick up an education in the arts by reading and performing in *Richard the Third, Midsummer Night's Dream,* and Maeterlinck's *Blue Bird.* Pauline shows an increasing talent as an actress, Petrova the tomboy manages to get a few parts while preferring the unfeminine world of cars and airplanes, and Posy develops the temperament of the talented ballet dancer destined for great things. The narrative spans a predictable number of auditions and disappointments and successes. It also dwells on financial difficulties and on the ways and means of overcoming them, such as pawning necklaces and making dresses from old hand-me-downs.

Through successions of wet summers, rainy winters, and endless bouts of flu, the Fossils eventually realize both the prospect of fame and the likelihood of fortune. Pauline is offered a part in a Hollywood movie, Posy is to be the most famous of the three and wins a place in a leading ballet school in Europe, and Petrova is rescued by the sudden return of Gum whose masculine interests coincide with her own.

Although the book is called *Ballet Shoes* its narrative moves well beyond the narrow confines of a ballet story. The title is instead a metaphoric summation of the curtain calls, greasepaint, and floorboards which are the real concern of the book. But what makes an old-fashioned story like this so popular with pre-teen readers? What accounts for its continuous success in a world now marked out by much more sophisticated interests? And what are the links between *Ballet Shoes* and the other narratives?

Ballet Shoes is not just a middle-class story about scrimping and saving and then succeeding. Nor is its popularity expressive of a nostalgia for a particular kind of English household management and childrearing as exemplified by Nurse's preference for brisk walks and self-reliance. *Ballet Shoes* works as a text of transition and development. It simultaneously allows its readers to fantasize a family space unencumbered by sibling rivalry and parental dictate and to contemplate a future state of being which promises reward, recognition, and happiness. The narrative also works through, in fictional form, the kind of psychic material which in itself is a product of the difficulty girls face in moving towards achieving a feminine identity. Such a non-familial space provides readers with a kind of fantasy playground where they can contemplate what it would be like to live without the symbolic constraints of the mother, father, and siblings, and where they can explore over and over again what it would be like to be an orphan, or to be without close contact with parents or relatives, to be simultaneously relieved and relinquished. More than that they can also take up and experiment with non-gender specific activities. Here the possibilities of the child's original bisexual disposition are played out as a kind of grande finale before the real world once again intrudes.

In *Ballet Shoes* the absence of both real and adoptive parents and their replacement by the more anonymous Nurse and Sylvia is transformed into an opportunity to achieve, unencumbered by the rivalries and other difficulties which, in real life, act to contain or restrict the child's desires. The reward for Pauline, Posy, and Petrova's achievement is the sudden and unexpected return of Gum. Removed from the oedipal scene for as long as is psychically reasonable, Gum is then able to take up the mantle of paternal authority without setting in motion the conflicts which his presence would have created. In short, he allows Pauline to go to Hollywood and Posy to go to a ballet school in Europe.

Central to *Ballet Shoes* is the question of feminine identity, a concern it shares not only with other classic girls novels like *Little Women* and *What Katy Did,* but also with the huge quantities of popular fiction in the forms of magazine stories consumed each week by teenage and pre-teenage girls. The narrative equivalent to *Ballet Shoes* in this respect would be the line-drawing stories found in Bunty, Mandy and Tracey, comics addressed to eight- to ten-year-olds containing between six and seven stories each week. There is no male equivalent to these forms, and although there are classic boys stories, these tend to be individual texts which do not connect up to the genres described here.

The repetitious reading described by Gill Frith,[20] the continuing popularity of a form which might otherwise have been superceded by the modern mass media, and the continual working and re-working within these texts of the question of what it is to be a girl, points to the kind of ambivalence and uncertainty which psychoanalysts, from Bruno Bettelheim to Juliet Mitchell, have seen as part of the intractable difficulty in the fixing of feminine identity and indeed in the impossibility of achieving a satisfactory resolution to the problem of femininity.[21]

In *Ballet Shoes* feminine identity is split in three and represented in the different personalities of the three girls. Pauline is good, hard-working, and responsible; Posy is gifted but spoiled, indulged, and therefore extremely selfish; and Petrova is the "boy," the narrative reminder of the child's bisexual disposition. This splitting allows the reader to see her own internal but coexisting divisions made manifest but also handled and therefore resolved through the distinct personalities of the girls. Each of these separate characteristics is validated in the end. It is not just that each girl gets what she wants, but that each of their individual quirks are recognized as necessary for them to achieve their goals. No one is punished, not even Petrova whose unfeminine interests are allowed to be pursued. In *Ballet Shoes,* an active if internally divided femininity is projected into the text and is presented to the reader as essentially enabling.

Fame, Flashdance, and Fantasies of Achievement

The success of *Fame,* first released as a feature film in 1980, led to the creation of a TV series of the same name based on several of the characters who appeared in the film and focusing each week on a number of narrative dilemmas which in the course of the episode would be satisfactorily resolved. These programs, broadcast in the U.K. during 1982 and 1983, were immediately successful with young viewers and particularly young girls. *Fame* began to develop a kind of cult status. Interest then moved back to the film which was re-released, and forward to a variety of commercial spin-offs. The "Kids From *Fame*" performed a number of live stage shows in London and in other major cities, the soundtrack reached the Top Ten, the single "Fame, I'm Gonna Live For Ever" reached number one and an additional album of *Fame* hits was released. The stars appeared on chat shows and the whole *Fame* phenomena added momentum to the exercise craze of the early 1980s.

There are a few key differences between the film and the TV series. The film version is visually a great deal more adventurous then the TV show with its style verging at points on cinéma vérité. Events unfold naturally without the foregrounding of narrative. Instead, the camera seems to drop in on rehearsals or simply record the day-to-day life of the school in an understated kind of way. The plot is skeletal. It follows the paths of a number of young hopefuls from their first auditions to graduation day three years later. Throughout the course of the film various individuals emerge. Each has a personal dilemma to work through, and most of these relate to a parental relationship. In each case the strength of the peer group friendships helps in this process. Emphasis on the family in the TV series is even more marked, sometimes dominating all of the action. In the film version, however, the viewer's attention is directed towards the performance element and the few narrative strands that emerge are more controversial. For example one boy is forced to come to grips with his homosexuality, a girl called Coco becomes involved unwittingly with a man who makes "porn" films, and Leroy's girlfriend becomes pregnant and has to have an abortion.

The film also engages more directly and in greater depth with the split between popular and high culture by drawing on a number of assumptions and stereotypes. The first of these involve crediting black music and dance with a kind of spark of authenticity missing in the colder and more austere world of the classics. These qualities of warmth, humor, and style extend, in the film, to embrace both personalities and performances. Thus Leroy is a classic "wide-boy." He knows how to manipulate the system to his own advantage. His poverty and his time spent on the street lend an even more attractive edge to his personal image. He is both sexy and stylish, admired by all and especially by his dance teacher Lydia. His talent is also a reflection of many of these natural attributes. Even without tutoring he is a born dancer and his ability impresses his white, ballet-educated peers. He is continually late for class to the annoyance of his teachers, but when he has to he shows himself to be as disciplined and committed as any of the others.

Popular culture and high culture occupy the same status in the school and are seen as equal to each other as long as they are pursued with the same degree of dedication needed to achieve in these highly competitive fields. In the world of entertainment what is important is success, not what side you come down on in the high culture/pop culture divide. Individual dedication and determination implicitly negate such unhelpful distinctions. At a personal level these are registered as choices. (Bruno upsets his father and his music teacher by preferring to play electronic progressive pop rather than the classics.) And as signs of difference, they add an exotic edge or frisson to interpersonal relationships between the pupils. In one of the most effective scenes in *Fame,* a rich white girl who looks and acts aloof and rather snobbish, is practicing alone in the long, mirrored rehearsal room. Wearing a pink leotard and dancing on blocks she performs a beautifully executed solo to a piece of classical music on tape in the background. The viewer can see that Leroy is watching, spellbound by her classical performance and attracted by her beauty. But it is unclear whether she knows that he is watching right up until the last second when the tape finishes and she completes her final pirouette. Her body language and expression convey a sense of distance, until she suddenly winks at Leroy and invites him to join her in the changing room. The asexual image of classical ballet is thus debunked and the distinction between high and pop culture is seen as surmountable.

In performance terms this moment in the film is paralleled by an earlier sequence which also acts as its reverse. Leroy and his black female dancing partner perform their audition piece to gain a place at the school. The dance teachers, all white except for Lydia, are lined up, unsmiling, severe, and, it appears, biased in favor of classical dance. Only Lydia who looks softer and is wearing make up would seem to have any time for jazz dancing. To a loud soul track Leroy and his partner take to the floor and perform an extremely sexual and gymnastic routine. At one point Leroy almost strokes his crotch as though in sexual anticipation, still in time to the beat. The camera cuts to the panel who look horrified and embarrassed except for Lydia whose expression is one of slightly shocked pleasure. She begins to move to the music as the short scene comes to an end. In doing so she is indicating that it is black culture with which she identifies, and that it does have a legitimate place in the school.

This strand is further developed and resolved in the final moments of the film, in a sequence that comprises an end of term performance for the graduating students, performed as a kind of nonstop showcase for each of the characters to display their talents. The audience is made up of parents and teachers and the camera cuts between the adults and the young performers as they get their chance to appear in the spotlight. Once again this provides an opportunity for celebrating race and cultural equality. In the closing moments of the performance where emotions have already been roused to a peak, quite suddenly and unexpectedly, the performance moves from a classical mode into a strongly black gospel mode. Black parents and children sing and clap and are joined by their white peers as gospel is also given its place in the schools' multicultural repertoire.

The New York School for the Performing Arts is therefore a perfect meritocracy and as such is a metaphor for America as it would like to see itself. Popular culture and particularly music is a unifying force. When the kids spontaneously break into dance outside the context of the rehearsal room it is always to the backdrop of black urban dance music. Even the ballet dancers "get down." Race therefore becomes just another obstacle to be overcome in a competitive world. Black students are prepared for the outside world of discrimination by one of the black male teachers who warns them they are going to have to be able to stand up for themselves by not letting prejudice get them down. But his message is not really different from that of all the other teachers, black or white. In the context of Hollywood entertainment this is an entirely appropriate way of understanding racial inequality. The more there is of it, the more reason to overcome it and get to the top. Race becomes an incentive work even harder, a self-regulating form of labor discipline (Figure 3.5).

Figure 3.5 *Fame* (1981) "Race becomes an incentive to work harder." Courtesy of National Film Archive, London.

This message is also pragmatic in a society where young black males are increasingly passed over as a result of a combination of racism and deep structural changes in technology and the labor process. There is indeed a real question of labor discipline for that section of society deemed most "dangerous." Leroy in *Fame* is a figure of white fantasy, a kind of black "head boy," a rough kid turned good, a symbol of all that young black males from a white viewpoint are not. The melting pot mentality of *Fame* is predicated on difference being sufficient to highlight how races coexist without their cultural idiosyncracies becoming real difficulties and without race raising the question of racism. This latter is avoided by stressing the rich ethnic mix of the pupils where black is only one of many identities and where each of these identities is portrayed through a range of familiar stereotypes. In the television series, ethnic is interesting where white can be neurotic. Julie, for example, white, beautiful, and unsure of herself, won't accept her parents' divorce as final and tries unsuccessfully to engineer their reconciliation. When this fails she returns to her cello for consolation, and channels all her anger and hurt into her classical music.

This raises an additional, related point. In both the film version and in the TV series art plays an emotionally cathartic and therapeutic role. It helps each of the characters to overcome the difficulties they are facing in relation to their families, but it also provides them with something in which they can lose themselves. When Coco's or Lydia's romances go wrong, when "he" doesn't turn out to be the right guy, their recognition of this fact is almost always punctuated with a solo dance alone at night in the studio. The dance movements are at once an expression of pain and a means of getting over it. A shared commitment to art is also the basis for friendship in *Fame*. Art is always an emotional space. Achievement or disappointment in the performing arts is a cause for great floods of emotion. In both the film and the series the characters each have to learn to cope with what Bettelheim has called "narcissistic disappointments."[22] These move with great regularity from family to art and back again. Only occasionally are the romances those of the kids themselves. They are kept a few steps removed from adult sexuality. Their relationships are instead still focused around the family or the peer group.

It is this which makes *Fame* such a satisfactory prepubescent text. Like *Ballet Shoes* there is also a concern with separation. In the film version one shy and timid girl is only able to discover her acting talent once she has summoned up the courage to express her anger at her anxious and over-protective mother. And the gay boy with whom she strikes up a friendship is haunted by his mother's early separation from him. Indeed it is his monologue ("We spent two whole days together and it was just like we were sweethearts") which opens the film. As in other pre-teen texts this journey of separation is made safe by the boundaries and limits set by the institution. Teachers act as surrogate parents without any of the messy emotional strings. Friendships which for the most part do not develop into sexual relationships give the kids the confidence to try new experiences and to work in an environment where there is a shared commitment to the same kind of work. This is the utopian element. In *Fame,* work is a grand passion, never just a means of earning a living.

Flashdance, in contrast, sits unevenly between the ballet story and the teen film. It is a ballet story for teenage viewers (male and female) and it suffers under the strain of the conflicting expectations of what constitutes a ballet story and what constitutes a successful teen film. Like so many of her fictive counterparts in ballet fiction, Alex is motherless. Her only adult friend is an aging emigré ballet fan named Hanna who takes her to the ballet and who encourages her to apply to ballet school even though she has never had a lesson in her life. Alex practices alone at night in her shabby warehouse apartment by copying the steps from ballet videos. Since the narrative deals with the period of time before her successful audition, there is no space for peer group culture or the institutional life of the school. Alex's only institutional support comes from the girls with whom she dances in the sleazy working-class club. And this environment is defined as cheap and nasty (Figure 3.3, 3.4). Psychologically Alex is alone until she meets the handsome son of the boss at the steel plant where she works as a welder. This introduces the sexual dimension which is a necessary part of the teenage text but which in this case has to be reconciled with Alex's great desire to get into ballet school. The narrative solution to what would otherwise be a generic difficulty lies in the introduction of a feminist slant. Alex is not typically feminine. She is doing a man's job while managing nonetheless to retain her glamorous good looks. She is not afraid to live alone and until Michael comes along she is single. This emancipated image is foregrounded throughout the film. She cycles to and from work and through the city streets at night. She has only a large dog as companion and protector and she is fiercely independent. She is also sexually liberated and actively initiates sex with Michael. She doesn't mind selling her body in Mawby's bar if it helps her earn money to pay her way. And finally she is proud of how she lives; she is neither looking for nor wants a man to rescue her though, in a sense, that is what she gets.

Alex is pretty but she has not been born with a silver spoon in her mouth. She does "go-go" dancing because that is all she has managed to learn. At her audition she performs a gymnastic dance routine where the sexuality is toned down. Her energy impresses the snobbish panel of judges who in a scene strongly reminiscent of that described earlier in relation to *Fame* reluctantly end up tapping their feet in time to the beat. It is being modern and up-to-date which works in Alex's favor. It is not that pop culture dancing is vindicated in the way it is in *Fame,* rather it

Figure 3.6   *Flashdance* (1983) Class privilege oblivious to Alex's difference. Courtesy of National Film Archive, London.

is taken as a sign of raw talent, rough at the edges but with potential for learning real (i.e. classical) dance.

Unlike *Fame*, *Flashdance* is a narrative of desired social mobility. Alex is disadvantaged by her poor background but her aspirations are to escape. She does not want to do this through a man or a romantic relationship, but she wants to get to the ballet school and that is undeniably on the other side of the tracks, in the austere and beautiful building in the city center where perfectly outfitted students practice pliés and arabesques with complete disregard for anyone outside their privileged world (Figure 3.6). Alex's achievement is that she gets there and by implication leaves behind her the steel works and the working-man's bar.

The visual subtext in the film comes into play around her body. She speaks through her body in dance; it is her only "commodity," her labor power and her artistic raw material. Cinematically, however, it is also the object of the male gaze. Michael is immediately attracted to her body as she dances in the bar. The camera lingers voyeuristically over every inch of her body as she performs (Figures 3.3 & 3.4). It is this which differentiates the cinematic style from that of *Fame*. While the dancing is sexy in *Fame*, the bodies remain the possession of their owners. The

nera at no point takes over and dwells upon them fetishistically. This
akes *Flashdance* a more adult as well as a more male-oriented film. In
arrative terms it is this sexual looking which Alex will escape when she
noves into the environment of the ballet school, but in cinematic terms
t is the sexual looking which counterpoints the feminine desire to dance
which motivates the action.

The romance of dance and the importance of work combine in these
popular narratives. There are few other places in popular culture where
girls will find such active role models and such incentives to achieve. In
almost all the examples discussed here this requires the absence or at least
the marginalization of the family and familial relationships. Because the
girl is more tightly ensconced within the family than her male peers, it is
more important for her to free herself from these ties if she is to achieve
her potential. Indeed it would be possible to attribute the success and
popularity of these fictions with pre-teen girls to the fact that they continually explore the dynamics of moving into a more independent space (which
carries with it the promise of achievement) while simultaneously holding
at bay the more adolescent dynamics of sexual success where a whole
other set of competencies come into play. In these pre-teen fictions the
body at least is speaking in a register of its own choice.

4

On the Muscle

Laurie Schulze

Working (it) Out: Feminizing Muscle

"Here She Is, Miss, Well, What?" asks the title of an article on female bodybuilders in *Sports Illustrated*. The implication is clear: the female bodybuilder is very difficult to position within any existing cultural map of the feminine. But the problem cuts through gender into sex, as the opening lines of the same article reveal: "We always knew women could never build muscles, at least not, uh, real women."[1] The female bodybuilder threatens not only current socially constructed definitions of femininity and masculinity, but the system of sexual difference itself. In a recent review of the documentary on women's bodybuilding, *Pumping Iron II: The Women* (1985), a male film critic calls the muscular female body a "kind of self-imposed freak of nature."[2] A *Newsweek Magazine* article quotes the "typical response" to Bev Francis, a world champion power lifter turned bodybuilder: "That *can't* be a woman."[3]

This body is dangerous. The deliberately muscular woman disturbs dominant notions of sex, gender, and sexuality, and any discursive field that includes her risks opening up a site of contest and conflict, anxiety and ambiguity. Some popular materials suggest that female bodybuilding is "redefining the whole idea of femininity." Some pose the question in terms of "how far" a female bodybuilder can go and still remain a "woman."[4] The most pervasive tendency, however, seems to be a recuperative strategy, an attempt to pull her back from a position outside dominant limits into a more acceptable space.

What Stuart Hall and other critics have called the "framing" function of popular forms can be traced in the ways in which popular magazines, particularly those magazines addressed to a female readership, work on

59

the image of the female bodybuilder.[5] Rather than claiming that she redefines the idea of femininity, the notion of femininity is deployed to redefine her in hegemonic terms.

If the figure of the female bodybuilder is controversial, disturbing, and transgresses established notions of what a woman is "supposed to look like," she is also capable of being positioned in a more normative regime. The fitness phenomenon of the 1980s saturates advertising and popular materials with representations of sleek, athletic female bodies. National newsmagazines like *Time* splash the leotard-covered "new ideal of beauty" across their covers.[6] "Working out," being "in shape" (and possessing the capital and leisure necessary to do so) are the new markers of feminine sexuality, desirability, and status. "Jock chic" is glamorous, high fashion, enviable.[7] With a little work, the female bodybuilder — even though she oversteps the limits of that normative map of female physicality—can be contextualized in familiar discursive and representational space. Those elements that can be assimilated to one of the accepted maps of femininity are included, and those elements that cannot be absorbed are marginalized or excluded. This redefinition takes the form of attaching certain markers of femininity to the figure of the female bodybuilder, markers that anchor her to established and accepted values. Muscle is rephrased as "flex appeal," her heterosexuality and heterosexual desirability are secured, and female bodybuilding is freighted with an ideology of control aligned with notions of competition in the workplace.

What is generally referred to as the "fitness phenomenon" indicates a shift in the definition of the "ideal body" of the 1980s (for both women and men) towards the more muscular body. Chronicling the fashions in body types over the last thirty years Alexandra Penney details the changes in the "ideal body." In the 1950s, the popular ideal for men was the "well-muscled" look, while the ideal type for women was "big bosomed and round hipped" and "well fed." In the 1960s, what Penney terms the "whippet look," the female type summed up by the model Twiggy, became fashionable for both men and women. With the 1970s, the well-maintained "healthy" body—the result of jogging and swimming—became normative for both men and women, but the "slim-line" look still controlled the overall shape this ideal body assumed. In the 1980s, however, the ideal body carries more muscle mass and is more defined, the male displaying the visible muscles of the weight-trained athlete, and now even women are using weights to "strengthen their muscles and to develop rounder contours."[8] The new female ideal of beauty," featured in a *Time* cover story, is now "taut, toned and coming on strong."[9]

The contemporary trend in fitness and current notions of health demand that women engage in the "kind of exercise that produces greater muscle definition," according to one popular magazine, which points out that "while it was very difficult to sell the defined look to women in the '70's, today a full 50 percent of the nation's 4.2 million Nautilus users are female."[10] The terms in which this is expressed articulate the commodification of the body in consumer culture. A complex net of social, economic, and ideological determinants activates the ideal body, and it is clear that fitness-related industries stand to profit if a particular female body type becomes a marketable commodity.

The normative ideal of beauty today, then, is invoked in language like "slim," "strong," "sinuous," "athletic," and "healthy." And it is against this notion of what the ideal woman's body is supposed to be that popular discourse often positions the female bodybuilder. In magazines, the professional female bodybuilder is placed either at the limits of the ideal or just beyond its boundaries. The kind of difference constructed for her in this dominant discourse of feminine beauty is posed in terms of "excess." If the female bodybuilder has transgressed the ideal, there is an attempt to ease her back into the space secured by the ideal, emphasizing certain features, suppressing others, and papering over contradictions. By examining the inscription of what Hall would refer to as the "preferred reading" of the female bodybuilder in these texts, I hope to reveal some of the specific strategies by which this domestication of a potential challenge to dominant definitions of a feminine body is accomplished.[11]

The form of address used in many articles in popular women's magazines sets a reassuring tone. Articles on bodybuilding frequently frame the issue in terms of a question for which they supply the answer. "Women's Bodybuilding: What's In It For You?" one article asks.[12] The "you" is obviously not a female bodybuilder, not one of "them," but the implication is that the regimen of the female bodybuilder could have positive effects for the "normal" woman. Typically, the articles detail those benefits in ways that connect the female bodybuilder to the feminine norm.

One strategy is to allege that weight-training for women will enhance their heterosexual desirability, and here we again find confirmation of Adrienne Rich's insight about the "compulsory" nature of heterosexuality in the way this sexuality is attached to sport.[13] Patriarchy and homophobia combine in complex ways to link female bodybuilders with lesbianism, and denying this linkage is critical to the project of framing female bodybuilding within dominant systems of meaning. The female bodybuilder must be anchored to heterosexuality; if she is not, she may slip through the cracks in the hegemonic system into an oppositional sexuality that would be irrecuperable. Female bodybuilders quoted in these magazines almost always mention "boyfriends" and their delight in the increased (sexual) attention they receive from men attracted to their physicality.[14] An interview with athlete Patrice Donnely (who played the role of Tory, a pentathlete involved in a lesbian relationship in *Personal Best* [1982]) quotes her as saying "Men have always loved my body. My boyfriend loves to show it off. He'll say to friends, 'Hey, watch Patrice flex!' "[15]

This set of meanings constructed around the female bodybuilder guarantees that weight-training makes women "more sensual." As one writer puts it, "a woman who is more aware of her physicality will . . . be more aware of her sexuality . . . sex is, after all, a form of exercise for two."[16] But of course the implication is that the exercise partner can only be male. The ultimate heterosexual, then, is an athlete, since it is now popular wisdom that weight-training increases sexual endurance.[17] That women's newly acquired sexual stamina is cut to the measurements of male desire is clearly stated.[18] For it is common sense in this discourse that *her* body work must enhance *his* sexual pleasure.[19]

Another strategy that domesticates women's bodybuilding and makes weight-training more easy to market to women is the discourse of reassurance that allays the main fear that "normal" women have about weight-training: that they will develop "excessive" muscles. A *Vogue* article elaborately protests that the "natural" differences between males and females prevent any "masculine" muscle bulk resulting from weight-training for the "average" woman. The fleshed-out argument goes like this:

> . . . for most women, the question of excessive musculature is moot, partly because they have such low levels of the basically male hormone testosterone, but mostly because only a scant minority have the genetic make-up that will allow them to develop a so-called masculine physique. Besides having to work harder for their muscles—as much as six hours a day in the gym . . . women bodybuilders must diet more strictly than men to reduce their naturally higher levels of body fat, then take diuretics to get rid of the water in their skin to achieve the veiny "ripped" effect that the judges are after. Given these facts of life, the best the average woman can hope for is a sleek, sinewy look.

The article concludes, quoting a female bodybuilder: "There is no way to change biology."[20]

Biology—this system of meaning allegedly beyond work, beyond sociality, beyond ideology—is invoked to defuse the threat female bodybuilding poses to sexual difference and gender differentiation. Those few women who do develop "masculine" muscles are biological exceptions and fanatics. If you are biologically average and use weight-training in moderation, there is no danger of acquiring the kind of physicality that will challenge the status quo. On the contrary, you will achieve the "sleek, sinewy look" that conforms to the ideal body.

And the argument goes further to reassure women that the difference between flexed and unflexed muscle is the difference between normality and excess. *Glamour* explains to its readers that competitive bodybuilders deliberately "pump up" their muscles before a contest, and that the muscle size one sees in photographs of women bodybuilders is the result. This difference is illustrated with two side-by-side photographs of a female bodybuilder labeled "Ellen with muscles flexed for competition" and "Ellen with muscles relaxed." The female bodybuilder—when not "being a bodybuilder"—looks "just like everyone else"[21] (Figure 4.1). The female bodybuilder is then invisible, except on the contest stage. This carefully brackets the threat of excessive muscularity off from the "normal" social world and confines it to the bodybuilding subculture. It also assures women who are thinking about working out with weights that they need not fear a loss of privilege or social power; despite any differences that may result from lifting weights, they will still be able to "pass." *These* muscles are a difference that won't make a difference.[22]

Channeling bodybuilding into the mainstream usually involves linking it to self-improvement, self-confidence, and self-control, and from there to the new woman who must acquire more assertiveness if she is to compete with men in the labor force. Pointing out that half of all American women are now employed full time, a recent article goes on to say that competing with men requires restructuring the female body to "fit the new *fashion* [emphasis mine: notice how social and economic equality between men and women is discursively translated into a 'fashion'] of equality."[23] According to *Glamour,* "delicate wrists [and] voluptuous curves" are no longer *au courant*. These old markers of the feminine have now become 'liabilities,' and must be replaced with the self-confident look of health and a firm body."[24] The new body is positioned as a "dress for success" fashion statement, an essential part of the image necessary to climb the corporate ladder.

Finally, the new developed body is mainstreamed as a support for the merger of work, leisure, and consumption. Mike Featherstone, in "The Body in Consumer Culture," connects "body maintenance" with "market-ability of the self." With industrialization and the development of mass production and consumption, "workers who had become used to the rhetoric of thrift, hard work and sobriety, had to be 'educated' to appreciate a new discourse centered around the hedonistic lifestyle entailing new needs and desires." This new discourse took up the ideology of continual self-improvement and self-maintenance, and one of the avenues for developing new markets was the stimulation of consumer desires connected with the body and the self, combined in contemporary currency in the notion of "lifestyle."

Advertising in the early 20th century organized a new critical attitude towards the body and imagined a "world in which individuals are made

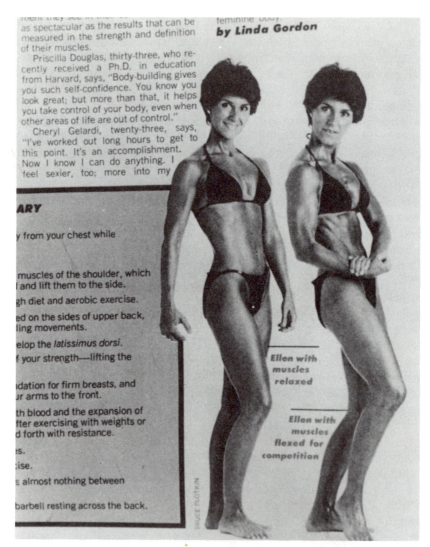

as spectacular as the results that can be measured in the strength and definition of their muscles.

Priscilla Douglas, thirty-three, who recently received a Ph.D. in education from Harvard, says, "Body-building gives you such self-confidence. You know you look great; but more than that, it helps you take control of your body, even when other areas of life are out of control."

Cheryl Gelardi, twenty-three, says, "I've worked out long hours to get to this point. It's an accomplishment. Now I know I can do anything. I feel sexier, too; more into my

feminine body.

by Linda Gordon

ARY

y from your chest while

muscles of the shoulder, which l and lift them to the side.

gh diet and aerobic exercise.

ed on the sides of upper back, ling movements.

elop the *latissimus dorsi*.

f your strength—lifting the

dation for firm breasts, and ur arms to the front.

th blood and the expansion of fter exercising with weights or d forth with resistance.

es.

ise.

almost nothing between

barbell resting across the back.

Ellen with muscles relaxed

Ellen with muscles flexed for competition

Figure 4.1 *Glamour* illustrates "pumping up". Photograph by Bruce Plotkin. Courtesy of Conde Nast Publications, NY.

to become emotionally vulnerable, constantly monitoring themselves for bodily imperfections which could no longer be regarded as natural." This body may be a carrier of "youth, beauty, energy, fitness, movement, freedom, romance, exotica, luxury, enjoyment, fun," but these benefits are not simply given. The desired and desirable qualities of the body in consumer culture are "plastic," in other words, their achievement requires work on the part of the individual. Thus it is that a certain state of anxiety is created. If an individual is not attractive, it is his or her (perhaps especially her) own fault. An improperly serviced body is the responsibility of the owner. Since the way one looks is a "reflex of the self," bodily imperfections are read as a symptom of "laziness, low self-esteem, and even moral failure." Body maintenance is a conduit to pleasure, social acceptance, and self-worth.[25]

Popular discourse harnesses female bodybuilding to this regime of hedonism and self-maintenance. It positions the bodybuilder's body as a site of heterosexual pleasure, romance, youth, fun, and beauty. Under the aegis of body maintenance, the female bodybuilder can be pulled into the hegemonic system, circulated with the ideas of hard work, self-discipline, competition, and success. Weighted down with markers of the patriarchal feminine and hailed as capitalist subject, the female bodybuilder can be transformed into a less problematic phenomenon. But only less problematic. Whether relegated to the margins of the cultural system as a freak, or recuperated as the site of "flex appeal," the female bodybuilder continues to cause considerable ideological strain.

Working It Over

In 1984, when I first begin to think about the image of professional female bodybuilding in magazines and on television, I used Stuart Hall's "preferred reading"[26] model to arrive at yet another tracing of the now "predictable mechanisms of patriarchal culture," as Jane Gaines quite aptly puts it. Rather than working from "inside" the subculture of bodybuilding (as I surely could have done, for I was and am a muscle culture fan), I took up a position "outside" female bodybuilding and instead concentrated on the strategies of preference in popular texts that attempted to make sense of these bodies by pulling them back towards a normalizing regime. I now see this choice of what to study and how to study it as limited and problematic, especially in light of recent work by scholars such as John Fiske, Janice Radway, Ellen Seiter, Ien Ang, David Morley, and others. These scholars rethink the theory and practice of cultural studies, going beyond text-centric analysis to challenge notions of the popular audience as passive and subjectified, and popular pleasures as the bait in the trap of hegemonic maintenance.[27]

There is a case to be made for the value of exposing textual structures that "prefer" dominant ideology in specific instances. If that is all that is done, however, the question of exactly what it is that makes female bodybuilding so troublesome as to attract these strategies gets left behind, and the question of what meanings and pleasures get around or go against dominant ideological control and who makes them, goes unexplored. As John Fiske argues, critical theory must now turn its attention to "the forces of resistance, evasion and opposition that constitute the tactics of the subordinate, that are the everyday means of handling the forces of domination."[28]

That I did not consider possible "forces of resistance" in my previous work (except to acknowledge alternative and oppositional readings that might be made of popular texts on female bodybuilding) is not so surprising, given the critical apparatus with which I approached the question of female bodybuilding. As Fiske has noted, one of the consequences of David Morley's use of Hall's concept of preferred readings in the "Nationwide" studies was a concentration on the text and the structures that prefer dominant readings, with the text still taking precedence over readings that might be made of it. "Preference" remains a "textual concept," and preferred readings tend to take center stage; alternative and oppositional readings are defined in relation to a predetermined preferred reading. Fiske goes on to point out a crucial shift in Morley's more recent *Family Television*. With *Family Television,* preference has given way to "relevance" which is more of a "social concept." The reader produces meanings and pleasures "that are relevant to his or her social allegiances at the moment of viewing—the criteria for relevance *preceed* the viewing moment."[29]

Morley's move from preference to relevance is emblematic of recent efforts in cultural studies to pull farther away from a text-centric criticism that privileges textual structures and the subjectivity that the text is supposed to construct, towards a retheorization of texts and readers that, as Fiske says, breaks down both the notions of the stable text and the stable audience.

> . . . the text is now no longer a stable structure of signifiers, it is not a coherent bearer of the dominant ideology nor an agent of commodification—though it may work in these ways for some viewers at some moments—and it cannot be described adequately in terms of the constant forces at work within it nor in terms of the constancy of its own structure.[30]

Just as texts cannot be considered constant, audiences can no longer be thought of as passive, unified, or fixed. The text is a "contradictory, unstable and fluid . . . concatenation of discourses," and so is the audience.[31] As Janice Radway puts it, new studies in cultural reception rethink the audience as "shifting constellations of individuals who are themselves crosscut and constituted by a multitude of social discourses, people who *act* upon the texts they encounter in multiple and different ways."[32] The focus of critical inquiry shifts from the operations of hegemony in texts to the ways in which individuals actively make meanings and take pleasures from texts in ways that may resist or evade domination, and in ways that help to make sense of aspects of their social experience. This shift asks that we begin looking for what Fiske calls the "points of purchase" that cultural forms offer to the audiences who engage with them.[33]

If we wish to investigate the making of meanings, the determinations that bear on these semio-social practices, we must ask. That is, we must "ask" the social subjects who make them. Yet how do we ask? This essentially ethnographic turn in cultural studies is crucial, but the question of how we go about researching such fluid, shifting, relatively stable practices in the everyday lives of individuals who have multiple and changing social allegiances is an open one.[34] I do not have the space here to take up this question or the larger implications of taking up these theoretical developments and research practices. I would, however, like to indicate where this shift might take further work on female bodybuilding and at least gesture towards the kind of redefinition of what to study and how to study it that might be involved.

The strategies at work in popular discourse traced in my earlier work on female bodybuilding, strategies of preference that attempt to tame female bodybuilding, occupy what Fiske identifies as the "terrain of control" in cultural production. Critical analysis of this terrain suggests that dominant ideology "works through the signifieds and the subjectivity to construct and control meanings of self and of social relations," through such forces as closure, homogeneity, sense, depth, unity, and responsibility. These strategies of domination that operate to control meaning can be opposed by the production of counter-ideologies, but Fiske proposes that "there is an alternative semiotic strategy of resistance or evasion that refuses to accept the terrain within which ideology works so well, and instead substitutes one that favors popular pleasures rather than social control." This "terrain of resistance/refusal" works through "the signifier, the body, and physical sensation," scandalizing ideology through openness, fragmentation, nonsense, surface, heterogeneity, and fun.[35] Were I to reopen an inquiry into professional female bodybuilding today, I would attempt to begin the work of mapping female muscle culture as a terrain of resistance/refusal, rather than giving ground to the terrain of control. Further, rather than limiting my analysis to the "textual structures" of cultural products that take up professional female bodybuilding—photographs, magazines, television programs, and so on—I would investigate the meanings and pleasures made by members of the bodybuilding subculture and its audiences from the experiences, performances, and texts they enjoy.

Professional female bodybuilding and its pleasures exhibit some connections with the terrain of resistance and refusal that Fiske describes. It works through the body and physicality, through sensation and through

To All My Wonderful Fans,
"I Love You"
Thanks For A Great
Four Years!

Watch For
The Revolutionary
"Rubber" Posing bikini:
Coming Soon!

Corinna Everson
4X Ms. OLYMPIA

Figure 4.2　A combination of signs which confounds common sense. Photo courtesy of Brute Enterprizes, Inc., CA.

surface. A female body displaying "extreme" muscle mass, separation and definition, yet oiled up, clad in a bikini, marked with conventionally "feminine"-styled hair and carefully applied cosmetics juxtaposes heterogeneous elements in a way that frustrates ideological unity and confounds common sense (Figure 4.2). Fiske discusses professional wrestling in terms of its "resistance to" and "refusal of" the "social identity proposed by the dominant ideology and the social control that goes with it," using Bakhtin's concept of the carnivalesque to theorize popular television and "Rock 'n' Wrestling."[36] Professional female bodybuilding seems to display some elements of Bakhtin's carnival as well, and it is tempting to extend the comparison.

Like carnival, bodybuilding is about physical excess. The popular objections to the fully developed female weight-trainer point to the excessiveness of the amount of muscle mass on her frame. Since female bodybuilders are often described as "freaks," "gross," "grotesque," and "tasteless," it would appear that they offend bourgeois taste as well as patriarchal ideology. Many people I've talked with say that female bodybuilders are "tacky," an indication of the way that bodybuilding is positioned as working class. The same accusations have historically been leveled at low carnival culture by high official culture. Bodybuilding speaks in a "low" language. Female bodybuilders "get buzzed on a pump," are "cut up" or "ripped to shreds." Female bodybuilding, like carnival, resists the laws of social control ("women aren't supposed to look like that") and inverts the conventions of the gendered body. It also interrogates patriarchy at the level of one of its essentialist foundations, patriarchy's old alibi, the "natural" physical supremacy of the male. Bodybuilding's materiality, its emphasis on the spectacular, on the sheer presence of the body and the pleasures of looking at muscle made visible (articulated as clearly as an illustration in an anatomy text), its slippage between play and display, sport and art, art and life, all seem to connect it strongly with Bakhtin's analysis of the carnivalesque. In this vein, it can be seen as a "resistance to" and "refusal of" social control.[37]

On the other hand, despite its similarities with carnival, female bodybuilding also mobilizes elements that run against the grain of carnival's characteristic liberation from social domination. Bodybuilding is highly inflected with the discourses of science: anatomy, kinesiology, exercise physiology, sports medicine, biochemistry, and nutrition. Governing bodies such as the International Federation of Bodybuilders regulate bodybuilding. Contests are judged according to an elaborate scoring system for evaluating symmetry, proportion, and overall muscularity in a series of compulsory poses and in free posing. Contestants are carefully ranked, and there are winners and losers, determined by their scores.[38]

Female bodybuilding, while it may be grotesque to some, instantiates the ideology of the perfected body beautiful, not the undisciplined, overflowing, uncontainable body of carnival. Female bodybuilders, in the discourses of the subculture, are often likened to goddesses, classical statuary, and living art. Fiske notes that the "Rock 'n' Wrestling" television bodies are the inverse of the body beautiful that sport organizes. In its articulation of ugliness, professional wrestling subverts bourgeois patriarchy with a "grotesque realism."[39] Female bodybuilding, on the other hand, takes up the classical notion that Margaret Morse refers to in her important work on television sport: kalogagathon, the Greek ideal that connects the beautiful, the good, and the political with social power.[40] Fiske argues that contemporary sport uses the ideal of kalogagathon to naturalize the links between masculinity and social and political power, and that its celebration of the beautiful male body makes this body an "active hegemonic agent for patriarchal capitalism."[41]

What, however, of the professional female bodybuilder's body? Does it, by constructing what Margaret Morse, in her analysis of aerobics terms a "body armour" that exemplifies the kalogagathon ideal, simply play patriarchy's game under patriarchy's aegis of sport?[42] Is the female bodybuilder another replay of the phallic woman Morse concludes is produced by aerobics? Morse argues insightfully that aerobics, while it may as exercise prepare a "freely-moving subjectivity which can be active in the world" and thus is able to "contradict long-prevailing notions of feminine passivity and stasis," is simultaneously "an investment in the status quo." In acquiring the body organized by aerobics, women "acquire the stamp of a particular historical ideal, reproduce a cultural cliché, buy the right to be 'feminine' . . ."[43] Is female bodybuilding netted in this system of contradictions or does female bodybuilding question patriarchy by giving the lie to its "cultural clichés"? Might a female bodybuilder, in acquiring this super body armour, create and display a social identity that refuses conformity and subordination in a much more radical way than the aerobics enthusiast?

Richard Dyer in his study of the male pin-up observes that "muscularity is the sign of power—natural, achieved, phallic."[44] Ascribing "natural" physical superiority to the male is one of patriarchy's primary supports. Although "the 'naturalness' of muscles legitimates male power and domination," says Dyer, visible muscle is not really "natural" at all, but achieved, and the male who displays it "bespeak(s) this achievement of his beauty/power." Whereas, Dyer goes on, when we look at the beauty queen, we may acknowledge that she has dieted, exercised, and used cosmetics to achieve her appearance, but all these things are "generally construed as something that has been *done to* [emphasis mine] the woman."[45] In contrast, it is impossible to read the visible muscle of the female bodybuilder as "something that has been done to the woman."[46] Muscle mass, its articulation, and the strength and power the body displays, is clearly an achievement, the product of years of intense, concentrated, deliberate work in the gym, a sign of activity, not passivity. Further, the muscles of a female bodybuilder are often displayed or represented in a flexed position, "hardened" and straining upward, one of the marks of phallic power that Dyer identifies in the male pin-up.

It is interesting, in this context, to contrast the bodybuilder's body with Dyer's analysis of the 1950s popular "psycho discourse" on female sexuality in his work on Marilyn Monroe. This 1950s discourse describes female sexual experience in a vocabulary suggesting a "vague, formless, mysterious" event, drawing on the imagery of the vagina and the ocean to invoke a "buffeting, dissolving, waterfalling ecstasy."[47] Popular criticism in that period constructed Monroe's body as a virtual "analogue" of this description, calling her walk in *Niagara* (1953) "undulating, serpentine, squiggling, wriggling," and in other cases referring to her as "soft," "moist," "quivering," "wet," and "formless."[48] I can imagine no female body less "wet" and less "formless" than a professional female bodybuilder's body. And the discourses that construct it seem antithetical to the discourse that defines woman as soft, formless, and wet.

Consider these muscle magazine descriptions of female bodybuilders in competition: "Lori Bowen was also the best she has been. Her legs, while not shredded (woe to her competitors when they are) were well-defined with clear quadricep definition." "Bev was dark, hard, and ripped. Her back and abs were second to none." "Ellen has maximum muscularity. She . . . has the unique ability to come in looking full and big, while still being cut and hard." "Cory has the structural symmetry, the right muscle sizes for her frame, the hardness, the thickness, the maturity—she has it all." And this, on Juliette Bergmann: "When she gets her diet together and learns how to control her subcutaneous water retention, her championship physique will shine through—look out."[49] "Wetness" and the "softness" produced by subcutaneous fat and water are, for the female bodybuilder, a liability. They obscure the hard edges, "fine-tuned" articulated form, and thick, full mature muscles valorized by the female bodybuilding subculture.[50]

Female bodybuilding is a direct, threatening resistance to patriarchy at its most biologist foundations. A letter to *Female Bodybuilding* from a male reader confirms this: "I read with great interest your editorial in the October issue, 'Men vs. Women.' It was good for a few laughs. Women are the weaker and physically inferior sex and always will be. Your claim . . . is ridiculous and I will prove it." The writer goes on to offer one thousand dollars to any female bodybuilder who can defeat him in a wrestling match, and ends with "I . . . am looking forward to teaching you and these various muscleheads a lesson, if any of them accept the challenge, which I doubt [sic]."[51] The possibility of a "natural" physical equality between men and women is clearly unacceptable to the writer. Against like position, however, female bodybuilding uses the same ideology of the natural, arguing that some women are endowed by nature with the potential to be men's physical equals. This position has become a tactical defense against patriarchal charges that the women who *do* are "unnatural."

Paradoxically, this defense of female bodybuilding based on the ideology of natural endowment—a subcultural tactic of resistance rallying around a female essentialism—would be understood as reactionary by feminist theorists who challenge the existence of the natural feminine body. The feminist anti-essentialist position asserts that the body is a cultural construct which does not preceed or exist naturally and unproblematically outside this construct. De Certeau speaks of the "intextuation" of the body, the body as "defined, delimited, and articulated by what writes it." He asks, "Where and when is there ever anything bodily that is not written, remade, cultured, identified by . . . a social symbolic code?"[52] In feminist theory, the anti-essentialist perspective cautions that any attempts to posit a "natural," essentially female body as the basis for a feminine identity or language (independent of patriarchy) are doomed to failure. This is because patriarchal ideology works through this same kind of naturalization of male-female difference.[53] From this point of view, the female bodybuilding subculture's tactical use of the ideology of the natural and its claim to represent its version of the essential feminine as a resistance to patriarchal subordination, would be irrevocably compromised. I think, however, that we need to look more closely at the kind of female body the discourses of the bodybuilding subculture construct before making any quick judgments about its complicity with patriarchy. For there are also strains of anti-essentialism in bodybuilding's discourse that contradict the notion of femininity as something natural and that can help us to see femininity as a cultural construct that can even be redefined by bodybuilding.

Female bodybuilders and fans are aware that more than bodies are built and articulated through pumping iron. Social subjectivity shifts with an involvement in female bodybuilding, and they shift in a way that seems to empower women. Nicole Bass, a professional bodybuilder, claims that "my self image improved all the way down to my soul. It changed my life into a 24-hour playground. I turned down dates to take care of myself. I took dance classes and changed my diet . . . I'm Russian and we were taught that women are strong and silent and don't take attention away from men. Well, I did, especially male bodybuilders, and I liked it. I found out life was fun."[54] A woman writes to the editor of *Female Bodybuilding* that "bodybuilding has earned me some respect that I might not have otherwise seen," and claims that one of her favorite competitors portrays, for her, "a strong figure without the obvious sexy poses usually associated with the exploitation of women," and stands for "pride, strength and femininity." Another fan who has been bodybuilding for just four months writes "I am committed to changing my body to what 'unknowers' [sic] may perceive as 'too muscular' or 'unfeminine.' I, obviously, don't agree with that belief (sorry, mon and dad)."[55] This letter indicates that one powerful pleasure bodybuilding offers to women is the possession of a knowledge that "unknowers" do not have. Further, it is a knowledge that involves the pleasures of being different.[56]

The bodies of female bodybuilders *are* different. Charles Gaines, in the book *Pumping Iron II,* writes that these female bodies seem "a qualitatively new thing, often disturbingly new . . . visually, existentially strange."[57] A common way of managing this "strangeness" is to push it into the familiar. People who find female muscularity aesthetically unpleasurable often claim that these bodybuilders "look just like men," or are "trying to be men." Often, too, there is the implication that female bodybuilders are lesbians. The ways in which female bodybuilders and lesbians disturb patriarchy and heterosexism, in fact, draw very similar responses from dominant culture. As Monique Wittig points out, lesbians were and are often charged with "not being 'real' women," and simultaneously "accused of wanting to be men."[58]

This certainly describes dominant culture's reaction to the professional female bodybuilder. And dominant culture often links female bodybuilding with lesbianism, further explanation for the effort spent by popular discourse to anchor female bodybuilders to heterosexuality, as I discussed earlier. As Marcia Pally points out in her article on the making of *Pumping Iron II,* ". . . women weightlifters are moving into male turf and playing with power. To folks who are comfortable with traditional arrangements, this menace hits close to home—in the body—and is tinged with lavender."[59] Pally reports that people often think that world champion Bev Francis is a lesbian, and Francis has said "The categorization annoys me more than what I'm accused of. I've been called a transsexual, a man, and a lesbian. People have to stop putting together things that don't belong together. Muscles don't make a woman a lesbian."[60] Notwithstanding, the most prevalent lesbian stereotype is arguably the "butch," the "mannish" woman whose masculine characteristics include muscularity, and the female bodybuilder can be easily "made sense of" by means of this stereotype. It is a connection that the female bodybuilding subculture is well aware of, and one that it has taken pains to fend off. As bodybuilder Carla Dunlap puts it, "Women bodybuilders have had to deal with their 'image' even more than male bodybuilders or women in other sports. We've bent over backwards to waylay accusations."[61] This is undeniably true. One clear example of how far "over backwards" the subculture will go to distance itself from lesbian sexuality can be found in *Pumping Iron II.* Christine Holmlund's analysis of the documentary reveals the narrative and representational strategies (in what is essentially a promotional film) that attempt to dissolve any association of lesbianism and female muscularity, "fetishizing women's bodies and . . . making them the object of heterosexual desire."[62]

I would certainly argue strongly against the ideological complex of patriarchy, heterosexism, and homophobia that equates muscularity and masculinity and that defines lesbianism in terms of masculinity. I am, however, provoked by the linkage of female bodybuilding with a lesbian sexual orientation across different contexts. And here there seems to be a remarkable duality at work. On the one hand, in some contexts the link seems to function as part of a patriarchal/homophobic strategy of domination in a discursive system that positions lesbianism as unnatural and "wrong" and then uses it to stigmatize bodybuilding. (The bodybuilding subculture itself seems quite complicit with this homophobia.)[63] On the other hand, friends and colleagues with whom I discussed female bodybuilders assumed, perhaps too easily, that female bodybuilding's articulation of female strength and its challenges to normative notions of gender and sexuality would make it a good candidate for reclamation by lesbian culture and that lesbians would be among female bodybuilding's biggest fans. On the face of it, the latter assumption seems persuasive, yet I question whether it does not simplify lesbian desire and presume that we could predict from one factor of a person's social identity—sexual orientation— the cultural forms she would find relevant and appealing. I decided to explore the issue empirically. And the more I talked informally with lesbians about female bodybuilding, the more I found that for many it was problematic and even offensive.

Reading the Female Bodybuilder

I do not claim any classical empirical validity for this research; there has been no attempt made to design a representative sample. Nor is this ethnographic research in any deep sense of the term. I have only talked with women I found through contacts immediately available to me, who had seen female bodybuilders in magazines and on television and film and who felt that the subculture held some relevance for them. All the women I interviewed are white, middle class or upper middle class, have graduate educations, and are in their thirties. None of the women I talked with were bodybuilding fans or bodybuilders, although all did work out with weights occasionally and participate in sports. Any hypotheses that might be formed on the basis of these interviews, then, must be very tentative. A model for ethnographic practice must be worked out and more extensive research done before I can draw any more certain conclusions.

This preliminary work suggests, (no surprisingly) that it is dangerous to make assumptions about the relevances a cultural form might offer to social subjects on the basis of an analysis of that form in isolation. It also demonstrates, as Richard Dyer and others have pointed out, that we cannot predict from a person's social position what meanings and pleasures she or he will make from a given text.[64]

"The muscles remind me of men, their power image," one woman told me. "It wasn't that I found the muscles offensive, the muscles said male and I said phooey." Another woman indicated that she dislikes the narcissism and self-absorption that she feels characterizes female bodybuilding. "There's such an emphasis on the look, they're not like other athletes who get muscular by doing what they do. I'm not saying I don't like the muscles, it's just not a sport in my mind." Perhaps, for some, the female bodybuilder's visible muscles are irrecuperably "male," even if one knows one is looking at women. That female bodybuilders are vain and narcissistic is something that the bodybuilding discourse denies. Many people outside the subculture find it narcissistic, and whether or not feminists or lesbians might object to bodybuilding on the grounds of narcissism because narcissism is an aspect of the patriarchal feminine, is something that remains to be investigated.

The same woman who was bothered by female bodybuilding's narcissism went on to say, however, that "the pumped-up, flexed body is really radical . . . it's toned and in shape, and I like all those connections. Women aren't supposed to look like that, they're not supposed to be strong or compete with men or against them and in mixed pairs they do, so they're equal." The word "radical" was meant quite positively, and stated with approval. Female bodybuilding's perceived radicalism, its difference, is one point of purchase. Its resistance to the notion that physical power is reserved for men and to the masculine colonization of sport are others. But female bodybuilding presents a very slippery sort of purchase for this woman, largely because of certain "markers" of style characteristic of professional female bodybuilders as they appear on the contest state and in most photographs in muscle magazines.

"A lot of them," she said, "would be more of a turn-on if they weren't . . . the hair, all poofed up and all that make-up. They look out of place. And it's the oil, it's too glossy. It's not like sweat, I think sweat's really sexy. The muscles look good but not the way they're displayed. If she (pointing to a photograph of a bodybuilder) were wearing shorts and a tank-top and sitting on a pier or walking on the beach, without all that other stuff, definitely." Another woman voiced similar objections: "I feel they push too hard at the real femme look." As Jane Gaines points out in the introduction to this collection, the beginning of the Second Wave of feminism was characterized by a marked hostility to "beauty culture" and glamour. Adrienne Rich, in "Compulsory Heterosexuality and Lesbian Existence," includes "feminine dress codes" and "haute couture" in her elaboration of categories describing the forms of women's subordination by patriarchy. Although, as Gaines says, feminism has begun to question its rejection of fashion (and one lesbian I talked with about feminist/lesbian "anti-fashion" exclaimed "That's so passé!"), it is clear that this stance still persists.

For some lesbians, at least, markers of conventional "feminine" glamour sit uneasily on the female bodybuilder, a heterogeneity that does not permit unproblematic identification or easy visual pleasure. For them, it compromises the difference of female bodybuilding. Perhaps these elements pull bodybuilding back towards what is perceived as the artifice of the patriarchal feminine. The look invoked by images of a female bodybuilder without make-up or elaborately styled hair, walking on the beach, dressed in shorts and a tank-top, is also certainly a construct of fashion, although it seems to counterpose an aesthetic of the natural to the constructedness of the professional female bodybuilder's look. But neither is it, however, the case that either woman rejects, out of hand, glossiness and glamour. One, for example, really likes Madonna's new look, and another's favorite movie star is Catherine Deneuve. It may be that "feminine" glamour assumes an "out of place" quality when it is juxtaposed with a radical female body that interrogates gender. Perhaps a body that is coded as athletic seems to demand a "natural" seemingly unconstructed aesthetic to achieve a pleasurable aesthetic unity. It could be, too, that despite the subculture's insistence on the femininity of the muscular female body, it is a body that most outside the subculture will see as masculine.

One woman I talked with at length said that when she first saw female bodybuilders she "really had to keep looking . . . is this a man or a woman?" She labeled the body "close to being the perfect androgynous body, because it's really hard to tell." She finds female bodybuilders appealing and sexual because of the "power," "control," and "pride" that they articulate. Especially impressive for her is the fact that this is a body that "takes up space," unlike the fashionably thin body achieved through dieting. Dieting she saw as a "form of denial, of not doing something," whereas bodybuilding in contrast, is "active." But while this woman was generally pleased that others were perfecting themselves to this degree, when the bodies display extreme muscle mass and especially extreme definition, female bodybuilding crosses over into a territory she thinks is finally terrifying.

"I find it frightening when there's no difference, when all body fat is gone, when there are no breasts, just pectoral muscles. There's . . . it's confusing, my signals get crossed. This (pointing to a photograph of Bev Francis; Figure 4.3) is a male body. There's something really scary to me that I'm not sure I'm going to be able to pinpoint." She went on to explain that, "I guess part of my sexuality is that I need a little bit of softness. There do need to be some definite female body cues . . . even an androgy-

Figure 4.3 World champions Corrina Everson and Bev Francis—Male female impersonators? Courtesy of *Female Bodybuilding* and O'Quinn Studios, NY.

nous woman has a little bit of softness." She expresses a not uncommon reaction to the professional female bodybuilder. At a certain point, the muscularity crosses over from a kind of "body-drag" or androgyneity, into something irretrievably "male." At one point in our conversation, she said that sometimes female bodybuilders look to her like "male female impersonators . . . a transvestite bodybuilder." Talking about the "clues" that mark male female impersonators ("You know, they look just like the real thing, except for a little muscle in the wrong places. It's Diana Ross, but she's got triceps"), she also said that the "theatrical" make-up often worn by female bodybuilders in contests reminded her of male transvestites. The make-up also had "working-class" connotations. "It's overdone, not like high fashion, but like make-up applied in a working-class way, a working-class attempt at glamour. It's like Tammy Wynette with muscles." The same woman compared the female bodybuilder's body to a costume that can't be removed. Female bodybuilding, she said, is "a little bit like striptease, but where a stripper takes off her costume, their costume is their body. It's a real pity they have to wear anything at all, the bikini looks silly, it breaks up the line." She spoke about wanting to touch one of those bodies, but not a body that was "really ripped." Then, however, she pointed out that if female bodybuilders weren't "so restricted to a subculture, they'd be less threatening. They wouldn't say 'male,' they'd be more familiar as 'women.'" Furthermore, she said, when she saw female bodybuilders on film or television, in motion, even the extreme muscularity wasn't so disturbing, because they "moved like women."

Female bodybuilding, then, seems to offer certain points of purchase to the women I talked with, even though they are not bodybuilding fans. If bodybuilding as a cultural form does not assume a significant place in their everyday lives and their interest in it has been intermittent, they have found certain elements appealing and meaningful. The strength in the female body, the active subjectivity that creates it, the challenge to patriarchy, the power to be different—and the courage to project a radically new body style, are all relevant to their experiences and their feminist political stance. Yet for some, female bodybuilding's juxtaposition of "feminine" elements and a radical, athletic body is problematic, and the "feminine" elements seem out of place. For others the bodies can drift out of difference, ceasing to be a radically different female body, into an unsettling sameness, a body that seems no different from a "male" body. This drift is experienced as displeasurable and disturbing.

There is much more work for us to do on the issues posed by female bodybuilding. It raises crucial questions concerning the construction of bodies, the politics of gender and sexuality, the formation of subcultures and subjectivity, and the capitalization of cultural forms. Of particular interest to me are the different pleasures and meanings bodybuilding offers to those inside as well as outside the subculture. Female bodybuilding is ideologically messy enough, open and ambiguous enough, polysemic enough to be relevant to people with very dissimilar social allegiances. For some, its pleasures slip into the dangerous, for others it is too crossed by patriarchy and capital to be radical, for still others it is a space within which the pleasures of resistance are enjoyed.[65] Female bodybuilding is currently one of those disreputable and marginalized cultural forms actively attempting to win some respectability for itself, to take over and to hold semiotic and social territory. We could learn much about the processes of cultural accommodation, resistance and refusal by attending to female bodybuilding and by listening to its fans.

5

The Female Colossus:
The Body as Facade and Threshold

Serafina K. Bathrick

Representations of Woman are everywhere and at the heart of American mass culture: from nineteenth-century monumental statues whose torches lit the way for industrial progress to the twentieth century's printed icons whose camera smiles offer present pleasure. In the age of mechanical production, the image of Woman seems basic to the legitimacy of our culture. As if to naturalize the machine-made object, women's capacity for reproduction provides the manufactured image with an artisan trace and an aura to convince us that we still experience culture "first hand." Before the age of film, when photographs were primarily accessible through studio portraiture, the female figure was reproduced for a mass audience as a lithograph or in the form of grandiose urban statuary. The first genre, an etched image often based on an original photograph, anticipated the era of halftone print when newspapers and magazines expanded their claim to bring more facts to their readers. The proliferation of female statuary recalled an era when mythic or symbolic figures, carved in stone, inspired worship or allegiance. In the nineteenth century printed images of wreathed and robed goddesses were depicted floating above newly invented technologies, machines, and manufactured goods. In one example of this, based on a popular painting by John Gast, an airily clad muse is shown hovering over a landscape filled with violent collisions between Indians, buffalo, and white men. The figure of Woman, depicted in continental scale, pays out a reel of telegraph wire as if to unify the nation through a new communication network. As columnar statue the monumental Woman appeared to represent a more earthbound nurturant guardian whose symbolic presence in the new industrial city or exposition anchored in an ancient culture. Whether as inspirational nymph or more substantial great mother, the allegorical nineteenth-century mass culture image of Woman served the ideological needs of that time.

Theodor Adorno writes that in the age of technology, "immediacy is gone for ever." While acknowledging the ways in which "modes of experience change in response to different technologies" and calling for an examination of "how these changes are reflected in works of art," he argues for the importance of an "authentic mode of experience that is able to overcome the tendency to resort to false immediacy." In this essay I will ask how Woman's image in this era has been implicated in the production of a "false immediacy," a form of culture that is assimilated to commodities while not a direct imitation of them. At the same time I will ask how actual women have been engaged in an effort to resist the impulse wherein art "becomes a mere reflex of technocracy."[1] Adorno's emphasis on the historical nature of imagery is also relevant for this examination of the concrete relations among women.

The investigation of women as historical subjects has influenced an important area of struggle in contemporary feminist film theory and history. A critique of the representation of Woman as spectacle in classical Hollywood cinema has encouraged an alternative film practice in which women produce their own historically situated narratives in order to expose and attempt to close the gap that exists between the mass media image of Woman as object of the male look and women's actual experience. There exists today a wide range of feminist films, both documentary and experimental, which have thus challenged the use of the female image as evidence of an "immediacy" which has been lost to the industrial age. This essay will explore some of the ways in which the monumental figure of Woman, an early form of mass spectacle, was often situated at the center or pinnacle of the great industrial fairs of the past century. What Adorno called "false immediacy" may thus be exemplified in the specific use of the female figure as it served to fetishize the new technical forces of production. I will also examine the related impulse within the culture industry to deny a historical consciousness in general and to implicate the image Woman in that denial.

A close examination of some historical developments related to the proliferation of such mythic female statuary is essential to this effort. For while the presence of such images serves to remind us of the deep fears of that age stemming from a new commitment to mass production, both in terms of attitudes toward natural resources and toward human labor, and in relation to the finished product, it is essential to note that, in Michèle Barrett's words, "representation is linked to historically constituted real relations."[2] In our rigidly gendered society, images of Woman are not wholly separate from specific women's concrete experiences. Such female statuary thus becomes a site of contradiction and consequently a site of feminist struggle, for while the representation of Woman is resonant with mythic and psychological meaning, making it central to the iconography of modern industrial culture, women's experience is profoundly shaped by the same culture's denial of them as active subjects. Traditionally viewed as living outside of history, women are deemed unable to change its course and thus unable to transcend the present. Simone de Beauvoir describes how women are assigned the status of man's primary other, and are thus caught "in the limbo of immanence and contingence."[3] She sums up the implications of women's status for a gendered society:

> Women have no grasp on the world of men because their experience does not teach them to use logic and technique; inversely, masculine apparatus loses its power at the frontiers of the feminine realm. There is a whole region of human experience which the male deliberately chooses to ignore because he fails to think it: this experience woman lives.[4]

De Beauvoir's notion of women's immanence is closely related to Adorno's concept of false immediacy. Both theorize the dangers implied by the ahistorical, whether in cultural forms or in human experience.

In her recent feminist psychoanalytic, *The Bonds of Love,* Jessica Benjamin notes that de Beauvoir's "analysis of gender domination as a complementarity of subject and object, each the mirror image of the other, offers a fresh perspective on the dualism that permeates Western culture."[5] This essay will explore some of the ways in which mass culture representations of Woman, namely those nineteenth-century statues associated with the manufacturing of cultural products, may catalyze or reinforce the individual "psychic structure in which one person plays subject and the other must serve as his object."[6] In order to speculate about this provocative relationship between the sexes and between mass culture and the social order, we must also explore the historically situated question of ideology and imagery. How do these mythic female figures, functioning as they do to encourage a nation's hope for the utopian promises of mass production—to facilitate a willing submission to its new and sometimes inhumane demands—provide insights into the image of Woman as key to the culture industry itself?

This essay will first investigate statuary which was constructed to commemorate the impact of technology upon manufactured goods. At this point historically, the emphasis was still on the innovative dimensions of the new machinery devised to rationalize the production of consumer goods. The monumental female statues of this era conform to the tenets of a Greco-Roman revival in the arts. They vary widely in terms of specific detail; some are adorned with wings, torchbearing hands, wreathed heads, or armored breast plates, often representing a curious collection of characteristics associated with classical goddesses and political iconography from later periods. But typically every figure is draped to her ankles in order to conceal both specific body parts and the elaborate armature that made such works into feats of modern engineering. Important academic sculptors of the period were commissioned to design and oversee the production of these figures. Some were executed as temporary monuments made of staff (a mix of plaster and fibrous material), iron, and wood—in several instances built to preside over industrial expositions, such as the World's Fairs in Philadelphia (1876), Chicago (1892), and St. Louis (1904). Some were carved of stone to endure as permanent architectural members, situated in courtyards, at entrances, and frequently on top of public buildings. Above all, these figures symbolized the Nation and its entrepreneurial spirit, their presence providing inspiration for and acceptance of what technical invention, mass production, and profits might bring. Like the mothers of twentieth-century skyscrapers, their enormous scale reflected the values of aspiring empire builders, and their public placement confirmed the birthright of those men to assume their Western European inheritance. So too their massive, solemn character suggested a distinct relationship to the Cult of True Womanhood wherein the idealized middle-class wife and mother was assigned the role of sole guardian over family and home.[7] With stern eyes and hardset angular jaws, their proliferation as larger than life objects of public admiration may be seen as a parallel to the overstated moral responsibilities assigned the American housewife, the "little woman" on the pedestal.

By looking closely at a sampling of these statues we may speculate about the meaning of such figures at a time in American history when technical development and symbolic expression could no longer co-exist. Lewis Mumford describes the end of that "happy relationship" between "pure art and pure technics," asserting that by the late nineteenth century handicraft itself could no longer mediate between "things of meaning."[8] He cites earlier cultures in which the symbolism of an object might dominate its technical meaning, elaborating on the uses of monumental female statuary during the age of Pericles. Here, "the column might be turned into the figure of a woman to form a caryatid, in order to symbolize the humiliation that had befallen the inhabitants of a certain conquered city—their women condemned to serve as the supports of the entablature."[9] Mumford's argument aims to unmask the tendency within nineteenth-century urban architecture and statuary to reproduce Grecian facades and figures in order to humanize industrial life and obscure its profit motive. Among his targets was the Beaux-Arts style that dominated the architecture at the Columbian Exposition in Chicago in 1892. For here,

the Caryatids from the Parthenon were recreated as if to hide the developments in engineering that made such scaffolding possible, while claiming
for industry the cultural aura of a Golden Age. The giant representation
of Woman so central to the industrial fair thus both embodies and obscures
the contradictions of an age where the immediacy of art as experience has
given way to the fetishization of the technical. Beyond Mumford's distaste
for the facade, it is important to consider how the monumental Woman
may also have served to compensate for feelings of loss, a sense which
substantially affected the roles of women required to resist and mediate
some of the momentous shifts in social and economic relations that took
place throughout the century. It is possible that the enormous statue of
Columbia which dominated the utopian landscape at the Chicago Exposition, unifying strangers and machines in the "White City," also served to
lament the loss of a culture that had once embodied sacred themes. The
official guidebook for the fair corroborates this possibility as it directs the
visitor's attention to new facts and information surrounding the colossal
statue of the Republic while simultaneously commending the heroic imagination and feeling that had motivated its design. Siegfried Giedion's
description of the historical context of the fair contributes to a further
understanding of how the female figure might thus contain these co-
existing impulses:

> Beginning in the nineteenth century, the power to see things in their
> totality becomes obscured. Yet the universalistic outlook did not fail
> altogether to live on. It would be a rewarding task to follow the survival
> and dying out of this tendency down to the filtering of isolation into
> the varying branches: in the state (nationalism); in the economy (monop-
> olism); in mass production; in science (specialistic approach without
> heed to universal implications); in the sphere of feeling (loneliness of
> the individual and isolation of art).[10]

It is hoped that by examining some ways in which representations of
the female body appeared at this time to address the fears of a society
where "the power to see things in their totality becomes obscured," we
can better understand both the position of American women as they have
been relegated to an ahistorical realm and the intimately related issue of
their ideological representation at the center of industrial culture. The
particular relevance of Giedion's observation for this study lies in the
fact that as the mass media published and distributed the rules of True
Womanhood, women themselves experienced the dilemma of the times
closer to home. Gerda Lerner notes that the ideology of "service and
sacrifice" that was central to their sense of self-worth has more to tell us
about a lack of order in the society than about women's actual capacities

to resolve the widening gaps between public and private life.[11] We will observe that as feminists began to question the mandate to serve and sacrifice, recognizing that a public/historical presence was essential to women, the issue of female representation became a focus of protest. For it is in conjunction with the rise of the domestic True Woman ideal as it was widely represented in women's magazines and books that the colossal female icon appeared in public spaces, representing in plaster the hopes for a nation which was losing its sense of community and its relationship to handcrafted culture. Just as women were asked to heal families divided by an industrialized economy, so too these figures soothed by providing a substitute for an artisanal age, functioning as signs of women's determination to resist the forces of history while simultaneously enabling the course of Progress. Jessica Benjamin's analysis of early mothering also becomes relevant to our discussion of these representations. We will observe that in numerous instances, the immense statue of Woman is depicted as surrounded by small construction workers or spectators, suggesting an important aspect of the mother-child relationship. It may be argued that at a psychological level these figures spoke to a generation of men whose attachment to their mothers involved them in contradictory desires: to remain connected to the idealized home where preindustrial relations might endure or to reject that community for a competitive role in the new industrial marketplace.[12]

In her detailed history of the Woman's Building at the Columbian Exposition in Chicago, Jeanne M. Weimann notes that some acknowledgment of women's public roles had occurred between the time of the Philadelphia Centennial in 1876 and the midwestern fair. She observes that at the earlier exposition many activist women had voiced their outrage at the lack of representation of women's public work on the Centennial Committees or as contributors to the exhibits themselves. Susan B. Anthony had read a "Declaration of Rights of Women" at the Philadelphia event, apparently to a receptive crowd. Weimann quotes from the suffragist's speech: " 'While the nation is buoyant with patriotism, and all the hearts are attuned to praise, it is with sorrow that we come to strike a discordant note,' she began, and went on to explain that women in 1876 had 'greater cause for discontent, rebellion, and revolution than had the men of 1776.' "[13] A brief examination of the two ways in which women were acknowledged at the Centennial reveals the basis for feminist protest.

In two distinct modes of representation, the incorporation of women into the Philadelphia fair's cultural agenda evidences the larger social and economic needs of the nation to revere and maintain past values while celebrating the machine age. First, the Women's Pavilion housed the handicrafts of middle-class wives whose needlework and painted china seemed almost to parody contemporary styles of public art. In a commemorative album produced a year after the fair, one of these wives (a True Woman to be sure), was singled out for praise. She had fashioned her contribution out of that most fragile but basic ingredient to the family kitchen: "A medallion in high relief, modelled from common butter, and representing on ideal subject, entitled 'The Dreaming Iolanthe.' "[14] Domesticity was thus officially celebrated as the source and subject of women's art.[15] While Americans turned towards the use of manufactured products for home and workplace, the good wife practiced handiwork, much of it dependent upon her abilities to use those household supplies in creative ways. Thus the housewife as artisan-consumer won public admiration for her ability to transform mass-produced goods back into handwrought bits of decoration to be enjoyed by her own family and friends. An example of how women sought to resist the takeover of mass-produced culture, we see how their efforts were neutralized by a market system that could benefit from them.

The display of leisure time made manifest in such work also served to mark the increasing difference between private and public life. Women were revered for their willingness to bridge the gap between the two worlds now separated by the advent of industrial life. In this sense the housewife was caught up in the contradictory demands of the time. Praised for her abilities to initiate "creative" modes of resistance to industrial progress, her work also functioned to help facilitate an acceptance of the new era. We see from this ideological bind how women's struggle to affirm the immediacy of experience through the production of handicraft, was in the technological age doomed to become an aspect of "false immediacy" as dictated by industrial production. The potential for women to assert themselves as historical subjects and to resist culture "as a mere reflex of technology" was thus systematically limited. It is when we look at the evidence of a second way in which Woman was represented at the Centennial that we can speculate about the conjunction between the two as they combined to legitimate the cultural significance of manufactured goods.

The Memorial Hall and Art Gallery at Philadelphia was an immense construction, intended to endure as a permanent museum for the city. Built in the modern Renaissance style, but of granite, iron, and glass, this vast hall was described in *Leslie's Historical Register* as "the best existing exemplification of the American art-idea in structure."[16] As it housed all of the "Great Artworks" that were on exhibit at the fair, it was the building that contained and incorporated literally dozens of colossal females into its architectural plan. Editor Frank Norton describes the high point of the building: "The dome is . . . built of glass and iron, and of unique design, with a colossal bell, from which the figure of 'Columbia' rises with protecting hands."[17] From lithographs and further descriptions in the *Reg-*

Figure 5.1   Placing the colossal statue of "Columbia" atop The Memorial
Hall and Art Gallery, Philadelphia Centennial Exposition, 1876.

ister, it is evident that the four cornices at the base of the dome served as
supports for four more heroic female figures, each representing a different
continent. One full-page lithograph (Figure 5.1) depicts the construction
of the dome and the placement of its statuary, and more than any written
account, conveys the complex tension that existed in the relationship
between art and manufacturing that was at the very center of this and
other nineteenth-century expositions. More than thirty tiny men are seen
climbing and balancing as they work to place the figures at the base of the
unfinished dome. Positioned in coordinated groups, the laborers lift wood
for scaffolding and tighten ropes to secure the immense figures. Conspicuous among them are three men in dress suits and homburgs who appear
to be giving instructions to the different groups of builders. As site

managers or engineers, their authoritative, somewhat static gestures are in marked contrast to the activities of the workers. As reader-spectator, one is invited to witness the construction process as a dramatic episode involving an explicit division of labor along with specific construction techniques.

Like many images in this genre, the human presence draws the viewer into a relationship with the great statues; we come closer to the feelings for a past culture that they elicit, but also to the process whereby they become the totems of an industrial age. A "behind the scenes" glimpse which privileges the spectator with a close-up view of the dome's iron ribs and the wooden beams that stay the cornice figures, the workers are presented in this illustration as artisan-members of a modern engineering effort. This work appears to grant them superhuman powers as the producers of these otherworldly figures, and indeed, one such photograph from the later Columbian Exposition is captioned "Making the Angels."[18] But at the same time that the Philadelphia laborers are posed to insure that we recognize the artisanal aura surrounding their work, by sheer size the statues reveal their dominance over the workers. Like the immense Corliss engines assembled in Machinery Hall and depicted in numerous illustrations from the same *Historical Register,* the monumental female statuary atop Memorial Hall echoes in scale the powerful industrial machine. The modern world united by new markets and manufactured goods is the other hero to this architectural narrative. In the same illustration from Philadelphia's Memorial Hall, the rendering of specific sculptural devices is used to suggest the connections between these eternal monuments to Culture and current economic growth. The central figure in the composition is the statue of a contemplative sailor seated below a colossal female figure with wings springing from its head. The presence of the male figure serves to link the allegorical—continental Woman with contemporary naval exploits—and reinforces the ideology of a world unified by modern trade and transportation.

But it is the detailed bits of drapery and the body parts of the monumental female figures which fascinate and invite us to experience this unfinished work in another light. The laborers who are posed at the feet of Columbia are all but enveloped in the folds of the statue's immense gown. The toes on one bare foot span the width of a nearby worker's torso and the giant figure's floating hand appears to hover over the entire work crew. Whether as reader or spectator at the fair, one is struck by the immensity of scale and by the necessarily fragmentary glimpses afforded when one comes close to such colossi. What are the possible psychological implications of these great mothering figures who turn the spectating masses inward, away from their awed response to the machine, to an acknowledgment of their deepest individual feelings? Jessica Benjamin describes the active state of tension that should exist between mother and infant as the latter gains her/ his sense of security and autonomy. The mother ideally accepts and communicates to the child his/her separate existence, but in order to do so, she must see herself as an individual subject. There is a paradox which the mother expresses when she looks down at her baby and says: "You belong to me, yet you are not (any longer) part of me."[19] Ideally this expression of self-assertion and recognition of the other will be the basis for a deep respect between equals. In drawing a parallel to the monumental allegorical figures positioned on the dome in Philadelphia (the mothers who symbolized the legitimate artisanal-cultural roots of the industrialized nation and celebrated the potential for a unified world of similar sister-nations), we must ask whether such imagery could possibly have confirmed the citizen-child's identity as separate subject. Or, did the imagery rather perpetuate an unequal relationship, one that insured that there would be no separation from the mother and thus little chance that women as a whole would be viewed in the society as historical subjects? Insofar as these female figures represent and reflect the ambitions and the fears of the society which designed, cast, and positioned them, we must assume that this impulse to attribute goddess-like powers to such statuary tells us a great deal about the powerlessness of men made impotent by the very world they have invented. Understandably, the ideology of "separate spheres" which radically divided and isolated men and women may have inspired a widespread longing to hold back the force of history, even to deny its dangerous course. In order for this to happen, women must be positioned outside of history. This point is corroborated by Simone de Beauvoir in the following passage which resonates with our discussion of the female colossus and the rationalized system of production whereby such images were positioned above the nineteenth century industrial exposition.

> The experience of the man is intelligible but interrupted by blanks; that of the woman is, within its own limits, mysterious and obscure but complete. This obscurity makes her weighty; in his relationships with her, the male seems light: he has the lightness of dictators, generals, bureaucrats, codes of law, and abstract principles.[20]

Let us turn now to the way in which this statuary was used to assert men's belief in the "abstract principles" of rationalized production. This same etching from the Centennial draws the viewer into an entire drama of modern construction. All stages in the labor process are included in this single image so that the privileged reader-spectator is invited to note the specific tools and techniques used to affix these Olympian figures high above the fairgrounds. The steel ribs of the dome provide the stage and the most completed figure rises beyond the top of the page, with only its stony skirt providing a backdrop for the workers who are removing the beams used to hoist it onto a pedestal. One of the continental figures stands below Columbia. Because of its placement in the foreground of the image, the workers who surround it are somewhat larger and we see more detail as they reach to untie the stays that are tied around this winged goddess's neck. At still another visual level a different stage in the construction process is represented: to the extreme left of the frame, there are men engaged in pulling a different cornice figure into place. The outline of this statue is etched loosely to imply its distant and less finished state. The assemblage of these distinct moments in the process of completing the dome above the fair suggests that this rendering was based on photographic montage. By means of this elaborate visual narrative, a primitive assembly line is emphasized by the photographic illusion of depth, and the would-be tourist is provided with factual evidence to support an appreciation for such an engineering feat.[21] The use of a modified bird's-eye view suggests another photographic genre used frequently during this time to impress the contemporary reader with the authority of the camera, its mobility and its promise of access. Invisibly located on its own scaffolding, the modern image-maker thus privileges the spectator. Thus we see how the spectacle of recorded facts co-exists with the site of the female body as a mythic repository for the cultural ideals of immediacy and community. We observe how a loss of immediacy explains the tension between a modern industrial mode of reproduction and the artisanal process and see how the abundant body of the monumental Woman must contain this conflict.

The uncertain relationship between culture and industry was an explicit focus for the *Historical Register of the Centennial Exposition*. It provided its readers a summary statement of the problem: "The great mass of the population, even including the educated, were in ignorance of the true character and importance of the relations of the arts to manufactures."[22] It is this relationship that allegorical female figures addressed. In their placement as central icons these grand-scale figures promised that the age of industry and commerce would unite and nurture a new society. Turning to the historical matter of women's experience at the Chicago fair, let us now examine the way in which actual women's handiwork was exhibited in a small "Woman's Building" and explore the debates which arose between different women's groups over the kinds of female statuary that might highlight this later industrial fair.

At the 1892 Columbian Exposition a complex relationship developed between two groups of contemporary women active in public life. The question of who might be commissioned to design the symbolic female figures essential to the fair became a central point of contention that divided these groups. In *The Fair Women*, Jeanne Weimann traces some of the tensions which existed between the two factions, each seeking to define in its own way the presence of women at the fair. While the 1876 Philadelphia Centennial Commission had effectively denied women the use of the Main Exhibit Hall and had required them to raise funds for a separate building, the groups which struggled over the same issue in Chicago now posed a more organized, albeit divided opposition to the fair's planners. One focus of the dispute between the charitable and leisured wives of the nation's businessmen and the Suffragists whose members were middle-class professional women, concerned a proposed statue of Queen Isabella. Instead of personifying the old world as a mythic female figure, the Suffragists sought to commemorate the specific historical conditions under which Christopher Columbus had gained support for his voyage. But soon after they had commissioned feminist sculptor Harriet Hosmer to design the statue, the Isabellas, as they named themselves, were opposed by the Board of Lady Managers appointed by the fair's officials to oversee the Woman's Building. It was this latter group's intent to repeat the Philadelphia strategy—to isolate artistic works by women and so limit their contribution as producers to the private sphere. So too, the Lady Managers sought refuge in the use of male-designed symbolic female statuary which clearly functioned to obscure questions about the relationship between the politics of gender and the course of history. Hosmer's plaster statue of Isabella was finally relegated to a marginal place near the Pampas Palace, a building made of California grasses that was more of an oddity than an integral part of the exposition.

In another negotiation concerning the representation of women as artists at the Chicago fair, art student Mary Lawrence was asked by her teacher, the world-famous sculptor Augustus Saint-Gaudens, to design and model a statue of Columbus, the central historical figure at this fair. Upon her arrival to oversee the placement of the statue, the invitation was revoked. The statue was then denied its place in front of the Administration Building and in the guidebooks its authorship was attributed to Saint-Gaudens.[23] That an unknown, twenty-five year old female art student should have sculpted the keynote statue for the fair was surely an anathema to the same officials who had granted authority to the Lady Managers rather than to the more political Suffragists. Mary Lawrence's Columbus was the only important sculpture by a woman to have been exhibited outside the Woman's Building, and its short history at the fair seemed to confirm the Isabellas' fear that the separation of women's art from the public arena would ultimately divide women against each other. It was the position of feminists at that time to argue against the patriarchal tradition which systematically denied women representation as historical subjects while elevating the mythic figure of Woman to a position of centrality and public awe.

Figure 5.2   *Statue of the Republic* by Daniel Chester French, the centerpiece of the Chicago Columbian Exposition, 1893. Courtesy of the Wisconsin State Historical Society.

While women's artwork was sequestered in the Woman's Building, the colossal Statue of the Republic by Daniel Chester French served to unify the Columbian Exposition (Figure 5.2). Praised widely as the centerpiece for "A Dream City" in *Harper's Monthly Magazine,* where it was said by Candace Wheeler that "certainly no one could help wishing that the great

Statue of the Republic modelled by Mr. French—a majestic woman who stands against the columned peristyle looking over the sea—could live forever, and give the future of America a national ideal of purity, simplicity, and greatness."[24] Writing as a senior member of the fair's Board of Lady Managers, Wheeler showered equal praise on president Mrs. Potter Palmer, of whom she wrote: "I have never seen the face of an adult woman who has the experience of wifehood and motherhood which retained so perfectly the flawless beauty of childhood."[25] Wheeler's description of what she saw as the eternal values symbolized by the monumental statue is drawn from the same language reserved for the True Woman whose service and sacrifice as we recall are proof of an uncorruptable and ageless "female nature." A characteristic response to the enormity of the figure is evident in Wheeler's description of Columbia as she notes that such gigantic statues humble the fair's visitors. There is the suggestion that crowds of milling strangers are both diminished by the scale and made grandiose by the modern engineering feat of the colossus: "the small human element is almost an impertinence, or, at most, something unnoticeable in the grand company of its own creation."[26] Wheeler's observation recalls the tension previously discussed in relation to the image of the unfinished dome at the Philadelphia Centennial. The masses, whether as workers or as spectators, are in danger of experiencing the loss of identity or self worth in the technological age. Compensation for this loss may be experienced in the monumental spectacle of an engineering miracle rendered as Woman.

We find the same sentiments echoed by those who observed the role of the genteel Chicago wife of 1892 who kept her home "a well-spring of repose" while the metropolis clanged and roared around it. Journalist Julian Ralph visited the city during the time of the Columbian Exposition and wrote praise for "Chicago's Gentle Side," the women "who appear not to hear the bells" of urban progress.[27] While working men and women were dehumanized by urban life and controlled by an industrial time- is-money ethic, Ralph makes it clear that the committee women married to the business elite opposed this reality by promising to live outside Chicago's political and economic parameters. Like the dominant figure of Columbia in the city within a city, these women represent the desire for a still point in a mass society where unity and community have been threatened by profiteering and harsh competition. Thus the bond between mythic female statuary and the tenets of True Womanhood functioned in an entrepreneurial context to encourage both resistance to progress and a wider participation in the new age. We see that privileged women's lives inspired and reinforced the values assigned to Woman as represented by monumental statuary and that in turn these spectacular figures provided orientation points for the crowds of strangers who toured the century's many industrial fairs. We also see exemplified what Adorno describes as the inevitable character of "art in the so-called technological age." As his words speak directly to the problem of "false immediacy" and the denial of history they help to clarify why the image of Woman became central to that tendency.

> Historical through and through, the essence of imagery would be missed
> if one were to try and replace historical imagery by an invariable one.
> To do so would be to obliterate the concrete relations among people.[28]

Adorno's emphasis is also relevant for a more psychological reading of monumental female statuary. The compelling use of the mythic Woman as unifying metaphor for the industrial exposition surely depends on some potent unconscious desires for a time in childhood when the guiding mother maintains for the child what Jessica Benjamin calls a "paradoxical balance between recognition of the other and assertion of self."[29] But as we have seen, the opportunity for women to define themselves as active historical subjects, to project themselves into an era of new technologies by voicing their own responses to that age, was severely limited. Their own subjectivity often subsumed by the cults of Motherhood and True Womanhood, there followed a breakdown of the process whereby a child learns "that sameness and difference exist simultaneously in mutual recognition."[30] Benjamin asserts that the breakdown of this "fundamental tension" provides the best point of entry to understanding the psychology of domination.[31]

In an era that demanded so much nurturing and rewarded women so publically for the reassuring roles they played in the private sphere, there developed a powerful dependency between women and the mass media. As the technological age progressed women became what Teresa de Lauretis calls "doubly bound" to the images of Woman which denied the immediacy of their own experience and implicated them in an ahistorical false immediacy. In *Alice Doesn't,* de Lauretis describes the way in which "woman is constituted as the ground of representation, the looking-glass held up to man." While her focus is on the filmic image, de Lauretis's points are useful for our examination of the pre-cinematic spectacle and recall for us that the arrival of film culture was dependent on the very technologies that were exhibited for the first time at industrial fairs. We may draw a parallel between the immense screen image of Woman and the nineteenth-century female colossus.

> . . . as historical individual, the female viewer is also positioned in the
> films of classical cinema as spectator-subject; she is thus doubly bound
> to that very representation which calls on her directly, elicits her plea-

sure, frames her identification, and makes her complicit in the production of (her) woman-ness.[32]

In his study of the Statue of Liberty, Marvin Trachtenberg observes that this monumental female functioned in two different ways during its early history: as a lofty symbol of the Enlightenment, and as a simple gesture of "welcome" to the nation's immigrant masses.[33] As both a sign communicated by men seeking to affirm the great tradition of European culture and as an historically relevant female stereotype, the Statue of Liberty is the most enduring monument to this period of rapid change in America. Likening such figures to the eternally present but elusive maternal body, Julia Kristeva provides the provocative suggestion that a figure such as Bartholdi's Liberty might operate as a "filter," a "thoroughfare, a threshold where 'nature' confronts 'culture.' "[34] In a brief discussion of this most enduring monument, let us explore Liberty as an entry point into an new age of cultural production.

The Statue of Liberty was first known to the world as a collection of parts. The hand which held the torch was on view at the Philadelphia Centennial in 1876 and the head was displayed at the Paris Exposition of 1878. Numerous published photographs and lithographs showed how the statue's huge pieces were approached by swarms of tourists, themselves transformed by its scale. Like the genre of illustration depicting workers hoisting colossal female figures onto capital domes and high cornices, these records also seemed aimed to satisfy the tourist-spectator who expected to be reassured that modern technology and industrial labor were compatible with a familiar artisan culture of the past. At the Pan-American Exposition in Buffalo in 1901, a crude staff version of Liberty's head was built as the facade and entryway to an exhibition called "Dreamland." In this instance, and in some other examples from contemporary amusement parks, the giant female face is represented with closed eyes as if to further encourage the ecstatic visitor to enter the slumbering mask to escape the surrounding chaos.[35] Within a doorway arched by a string of beads just below her neck, visitors perhaps felt safely held in the dark recesses of this colossal Woman's heart. It is significant that the potential to thus enter, to climb and play as a child in this most intimate relationship with the ideal Woman, was made possible by new engineering principles developed by men like Gustave Eiffel. Thus the moment when building innovation could be expanded from bridge and tower construction to the fabrication of an immense permanent statue was the very moment when Liberty as both facade and threshold became the unifying symbol for the nation. Representing an enduring marker of the tensions involved in our transition from artisan to industrial culture, the statue contains different manifestations of the same contradictions which coalesce in the figures of Columbia from the expositions of 1876 and 1892.

Designed by Frédèric-Auguste Bartholdi, a minor nineteenth-century French sculptor who had studied late Renaissance art and who had a "colossal vision" of a statue of his own age, Trachtenberg tells us that the sculptor's "attachment to his mother remained his deepest emotion." The sober face of Liberty is most probably drawn from his memory of her.[36] But the body of Liberty was wholly dependent upon Gustave Eiffel's engineering skills for its "hidden structural reality." Trachtenberg sums up the co-existing aspects of Bartholdi's and Eiffel's contributions and suggests the contradictory impulses contained by the statue.

> Liberty is an archetypal illustration of the esthetic tension of its time— when technology had already attained great advances and power and a hold over the mind, but when the conscious eye was still dominated by traditional imagery.[37]

But there was yet another aspect of the history of Liberty which adds to our understanding of the statue as a site of contradiction, and this involved the efforts of the American newspaper entrepreneur Joseph Pulitzer. When Liberty arrived in more than two hundred shipping crates, it sat unpacked for many months because the city lacked the money needed to assemble the statue and place it on its pedestal. It is telling that only a savvy tabloid publisher could produce the funds by harassing and coaxing the citizens of New York City into donating the money to finish the statue. The difficulty in raising the money was complicated by a class-divided response to Liberty: the rich were offended by the "populist sentiment" behind the statue, while the poor regarded the project as a "rich man's folly."[38] The female statue would personify a new kind of freedom promised by industrialization and thus contain many of the tensions produced by a new order in which culture itself was in the process of redefinition. Liberty catalyzed a little class war that was averted only by a tabloid press ploy; its whole represented an assemblage of parts which marked the end of artisanal production in the age of the engineer. Lastly, this statue provided a robed facade that would obscure its innovative construction while mobilizing the projections of a mass population whose longings for something lost had little opportunity for expression. Elizabeth Ewen's study of immigrant women in New York City gives credence to the possibility that the statue's enduring encouragement to the "huddled masses" paralleled the historical position of immigrant mothers caught up in the task of bridging the gap between old world values and new urban demands.[39] The privatized ways in which women's lives are implicated in both the preservation and the denial of cultural roots are thus related to the more public function of the monumental Woman. Again, in their immanence, both women and man-made Woman are placed outside of history, defined by the false immediacy that their roles imply. With their subjectivity defined only in relation to their roles as spectators of Woman as image, women are still deemed capable of humanizing the process whereby the past is replaced by a new industrial culture.

By the 1890s, the halftone printing process made possible the mass production and distribution of photographs. The camera thus became the image-maker for the new century. And while its claim to facticity makes it an ideal tool for an increasingly rational society, the photograph of Woman continues to function as the site of social and psychological contradictions. Surely the mass-produced icon as postcard or pin-up gains much of its contemporary acceptance and meaning from its claim to reproduce literally the female face and figure. But more important for an historical analysis of ideology and representation is the way in which the photo image also remains related to a period of conflict when the image of Woman first provided a necessary mediation between art and manufactured goods. It can be argued that while the photo image of Woman appears to be the very antithesis of the nineteenth-century's monumental figure, it is rather a new form of that image functioning in many of the same ways. It might be said that in being all that the female colossus is not—one of many, individually selected and purchased; privately positioned; small, disposal, and replaceable — the photographic picture of Woman simply reflects the values of an age where spending as opposed to saving is the mandate. It is also significant that as the increase in the production of consumer goods required the need for more women in the workforce, their increasingly visible public presence clearly shaped the new iconography. Related to this is the distinct difference between the dominant imagery of Woman as a maternal figure in the nineteenth-century and Woman as a sexual playmate in the twentieth. In order to investigate what is both new to the present period and also deeply connected to the past, let us turn briefly to two very different photographic images of Liberty, one a bit of nostalgia, another an outrageous challenge to the nineteenth-century mythic Woman launched by an early "liberated" woman. In combination these images bring us closer to understanding the age of cinematic representation.

First let us consider a World War I photograph which depicts a patriotic assemblage of 18,000 Iowa soldiers grouped on a vast frozen lake to form the gigantic body of Liberty. Reproduced as a souvenir postcard, the men at Fort Dodge in Des Moines display great care and coordination as they pose for their mass portrait. Specific men are dressed in ark or light uniforms in order to mark the folds of Liberty's drapery and delineate the lines of the figure's face and hands. Their whimsical effort makes light the rationalized life and maneuvers of a modern army, and indeed one wonders about the priorities for the Camp Dodge recruits and officers who labored to pose for this episode in which history is transformed into spectacle. Some part of its contemporaneity is surely marked by the explicit link between camera and airplane. Perhaps too the project evidences the way many early films had already begun to shape the popular image of war where minutely orchestrated armies shot from high angles filled the screen. The image is certainly related to much other World War I propaganda where Woman represents motherland. What is most interesting about this particular example is that it forms an image in which Liberty's body is entirely made up of nameless men. Like the builders and artisans who were depicted piecing together and positioning the great female statues of the previous century, we see that the photograph now records the same gesture among men whose relationship to modernity requires that they perform as soldiers. The man-made Woman is now a spectacle of military coordination. The tensions related to gender and historical change are again evident in this picture postcard: the same men who have formed the monumental figure are also diminished by the idea which she represents, even infantilized by their projection. It is only in the act of posing for a camera record of this curiously nonmilitary maneuver that they assert their relationship to an industrial age.

While the Fort Dodge soldiers construct a photographic homage to the nineteenth-century True Woman, Mae West, in a Paramount publicity shot from 1934, poses as Liberty in a direct challenge to that memory (Figure 5.3). She stands alone against a black background, her form-fitting dress composed of gleaming diagonal stripes and her crown lit up to tell us that a different representational system has produced the twentieth-century monumental Woman. More beauty queen than mother, constituted of light rather than tangible mass, Woman is now a camera creation. Where the plaster folds of the nineteenth-century goddess's gown were tucked and tied to conceal both female sensuality and engineering principles, the star's body is encased in skin-like fabric, held in place only for the duration of the camera session. In comparison with the monumental Woman, this image is virtually substanceless, but the play of light across her silvery hair, shiny breasts, and rolling hips makes this Liberty into a spectacle as grand as her namesake. An intimate fetish object for millions of fans, Mae West's "Liberty" serves a new cultural mandate. By 1934 the camera as image-maker has found its place at the center of a consumer society, and insofar as it combines a claim to represent the facts with the potential to express and respond to the desires of the age, it proposes to resolve the continuing contradictory aspects of the culture industry.

Gone is the era of the symbolic maternal Woman. Now Mae West's

Figure 5.3   Mae West, Paramount Studios publicity still, 1934. Courtesy of the Museum of Modern Art, Film Stills Archive, NY.

bawdy smile and upward gaze appear to assert the confidence needed to survive the Great Depression for Paramount Pictures as well as for the whole film industry. The darkness behind her also contributes to a parody of the patriotic as it heightens the implication that woman's body is both a source and a product of light. Given her own skyrocketing success between 1932–33 when she made her first three Hollywood films, this photo of a burlesque queen turned movie star also records a specific actress's passage from nineteenth- to twentieth-century mass culture. This woman's body has seemingly "come into the light," suggesting the more widespread acknowledgment of women's place in the public sphere. But what is the real source of this light? To what extent are we asked to celebrate the cinema rather than one woman's professional history? The contradictions are evident in every genre of promotional photography associated with motion pictures. The close-up image of woman on the screen has not brought women themselves closer to becoming agents of history as cultural producers on the scale of either the director or the architect of monuments.

Combining as it does the great inventions of the previous century, the movie industry produces a star who mocks the motionless female figure who mediated culture and industry for earlier generations. But now we must ask if the image of Woman which appears to live and move by means of light has not become a new kind of monument to a new age. To what extent are we now constructed as the fascinated voyeurs of a sexually objectified Woman rather than as the dependent children of a benevolent mother, the relationship structured by nineteenth-century statuary? Mae West's irreverent parody might suggest that we have grown into adolescence as an industrialized society. The photograph of Woman is now a temporary image: cut from a movie magazine and pinned-up on a teenager's wall it may serve briefly as a private fantasy. Featured on a calendar in a gas station, the pin-up offers a full year of visual pleasure to be found amidst the auto body parts and surrounding equipment. The men who repair the machines manufactured by machines now tack the image of Woman to their workplace walls. The photograph of a bikini-clad Woman sells new building products—power tools and step-saving compounds and adhesives—as if to assure us that craft is still alive, and that the men who manufacture and build are still artisans. In each instance, the beauty queen, the pinup, and the pornographic centerfold provide our society with an image of false immediacy, an opportunity to recall momentarily the experience feared lost to the age of industry.

6

The Carole Lombard in
Macy's Window

Charles Eckert

I

In the last quarter of the nineteenth century, American business was preoccupied with production. Most of its energy went into expanding its physical plant, increasing efficiency, and grinding the face of labor so that greater profits could be extracted and invested in production. In the last five years of the nineteenth century when, coincidentally, motion pictures were invented, American business discovered that it was up to its neck in manufactured goods for which there were no buyers. So it became sales-minded. Through the first two decades of this century, sales techniques were developed so intensely that they produced gross excesses, alienating the public and giving impetus to antibusiness and antimaterialist attitudes among intellectuals. About 1915, fixation upon sales gave way to an obsession with management, to internal restructuring and systemization. Profits were decisively improved, but the contradiction between production and consumption, between the efficient manufacture and marketing of goods and the capacity of wage-poor workers to buy them, was no closer to solution. Therefore, throughout the 1920s business became consumer-minded.

While American business was going through this process of what a Jungian would call differentiation, evolving from an oral stage in which it was given to eating its young into a rational, Apollonian stage in which it stopped thinking of workers as schmoos and began thinking of them as a sort of chicken-lickin', a synthetic substance to be fed with one hand and sliced with the other—while all of this was going forward, Hollywood

Reprinted from *Quarterly Review of Film Studies* 3, no. 1 (Winter 1978).

had evolved from a nickel and dime business to an entertainment industry funded by the likes of A.T.& T., Hayden Stone, Dillon Reid, RCA, The House of Morgan, A.P. Giannini's Bank of America, The Rockefellers' Chase National Bank, Goldman Sachs, Lohoran Brothers, Halsey Stuart—in short, all of the major banks and investment houses and several of the largest corporations in America. With the representatives of those several economic powers sitting on the directorates of the studio, and with the world of business pervaded by the new zeitgeist of consumerism, the conditions were right for Hollywood to assume a role in the phase of capitalism's life history that the emerging philosophy of consumerism was about to give birth to.

All of which brings me to a story, a sort of romance, which I shall begin, as all good storytellers used to, in Medias Res.

II

Awakened by the brakes of the train, Bette Davis pulled aside a window curtain. Beneath a winter moon the Kansas plains lay gray with late winter snow. The mail clerk glimpsed Bette's face, but was too astounded by the pullman car itself to recognize his favorite star. The pullman was totally covered with gold leaf. The rest of the train was brilliantly silvered. From one car a tall radio aerial emerged mysteriously. Lost in his wonder, the clerk barely noticed that the train was underway again. He would later tell his children about the train with the golden pullman, perhaps fashioned for some western gold baron, or for a Croesus from a foreign land. But he would never know that the interior of the train held greater wonders still.

As the cars gathered speed, other passengers shifted in their sleep, among them Laura LaPlante, Preston Foster, and numerous blond women with muscular legs (was one of them the supernal Toby Wing?). In an adjacent lounge car Claire Dodd, Lyle Talbot, and Tom Mix were still awake, attending to a reminiscing Leo Carillo. In still another car a scene as surrealistic as a Dali floated through the Kansas night. Glenda Farrell lay in her Jantzen swimsuit upon a miniature Malibu Beach beneath a manufactured California sky made up of banks of GE ultraviolet lamps. The sand on the beach was genuine sand. Everything else was unreal.

The next to the last car held no human occupants. The hum, barely discernable above the clack of the rails, emerged from the GE Monitor-top refrigerator positioned next to the GE all-electric range. When one grew accustomed to the dark, one saw that this was merely a demonstration kitchen lifted bodily, it seemed, from Macy's or Gimbels, and compressed into the oblong confines of a railway diner. In the last car was a magnificent white horse. An embroidered saddle blanket draped over a rail beside him bore the name "King." The horse was asleep.

The occasion that had gathered this congeries of actresses and appliances, cowboys and miniaturized Malibu, into one passenger train and positioned them in mid-Kansas on a night in February 1933, was the inauguration of Franklin Delano Roosevelt. If the logic of this escapes you, you simply must make the acquaintance of Charles Einfeld, sales manager for Warner Brothers.

Charles Einfeld was a dreamer. But unlike yours and mine, his dreams always came true. Charles Einfeld dreamed (and it came true) that Warner's new musical, *42nd Street,* would open in New York on the eve of Roosevelt's inauguration, that the stars of the picture (with other contract stars, if possible) would journey to New York on a train to be called the Better Times Special, and that they would then go to Washington for the inauguration itself. The film, after all, was a boost for the New Deal philosophy of pulling together to whip the Depression, and its star, Warner Baxter, played a role that was a patent allegory of F.D.R. Einfeld then sought a tie-up with a large concern that would share the expenses of the train in exchange for a quantity of egregious advertising. General Electric, already linked with Warner as a supplier of appliances for movie props, rose to the bait.

The gold and silver train was given a definitive name: The Warner-GE Better Times Special. As it crossed North America from Los Angeles to New York its radio broadcasted Dick Powell's jazzy contralto, GE ad-copy, and optimism (GE, as the parent organization of RCA and NBC, was in a position to facilitate hook-ups with local stations). When the train arrived at a major city, the stars and chorus girls motored to the largest available GE showroom and demonstrated whatever appliances they found themselves thrust up against. In the evenings, they appeared at a key theater for a mini-premiere. Their *Ultima Thule* was, of course, *42nd Street*.

On March 9 bawdy, gaudy 42nd Street looked as spiffy as a drunkard in church: American flags and red, white, and blue bunting draped the buildings; the ordinary incandescent bulbs were replaced with scintillant "golden" GE lamps; a fleet of Chrysler automobiles (a separate tie-up) and GE automotive equipment was readied for a late afternoon parade which would catch those leaving work. In the North River a cruiser stood at anchor to fire a salute—a great organ-boom to cap off a roulade of aerial bombs. As the train approached New York from New Rochelle, a pride of small airplanes accompanied it. Once it arrived, the schedule was as exacting as a coronation: a reception at Grand Central by the Forty-Second Street Property Owners and Merchants Association, the parade, a GE sales meeting at the Sam Harris Theatre, and the grand premiere at the Strand.

tunning synthesis of film, electrical, real-estate, and transportation
ation, partisan patrio-politics, and flecked-at-the-mouth star mania
. lurch fully armed from the head of Charles Einfeld, splendid
r though he was. It can only be explained in terms of the almost
uous hegemony that characterized Hollywood's relations with vast
hes of the American economy by the mid-1930s. Like most tales of
cest, this one ends badly. By 1950 Hollywood had taken to looking its
lover in the neck; the passions of the mid-1930s had become savourless
habits. But that is the end of the story. In the beginning, Hollywood was
younger than Andy Hardy and the world of industry lived just next door.

When the first movie cameraman shot the first street scene that included
a shop sign or a labeled product (Lumiere? 1895?) all of the elements of
a new advertising form were implicit: a captive audience unlikely to ignore
what was placed before it, a manufacturer, a filmmaker, and the Platonic
idea of Charles Einfeld. The short dramas and comedies of the first decade
of this century, especially those that pictured the contemporary lifestyles
of the middle and upper classes, presented innumerable opportunities for
product and brand name tie-ins. But more than this, they functioned as
living display windows for all that they contained; windows that were
occupied by marvelous mannequins and swathed in a fetish-inducing
ambiance of music and emotion.

These films merely had to be shown to Americans who lived away from
big cities, or to audiences in foreign countries, to generate a desire for the
cornucopia of material goods they proffered. Around 1912, according to
Benjamin Hampton, English and German manufacturers became alarmed
at the decline in demand for their goods and an attendant rise in American
imports. An investigation disclosed that American movies were responsible: "They began to complain to their governments that audiences saw
American sewing machines, typewriters, furniture, clothing, shoes, steam
shovels, saddles, automobiles and all shorts of things in the cinema shows,
and soon began to want these things. . . ."

From this discovery, a complex chapter of film history arose. The
periods immediately preceding and following World War I saw attempts
at the establishment of quotas for both American products and films, and
at shoring up national film industries (especially in England and Germany).
This history is tangential to our interests, but the struggle attending it
served to alert Hollywood and American industry to the full potential of
film as a merchandiser of goods. In 1926 an analyst observed:

> The peoples of many countries now consider America as the arbiter of
> manners, fashions, sports, customs and standards of living. If it were
> not for the barrier we have established, there is no doubt that the
> American movies would be bringing us a flood of immigrants. As it is,
> in a vast number of instances, the desire to come to this country is
> thwarted, and the longing to emigrate is changed into a desire to imitate.

The selling influence of this condition is proved by the demand abroad for products the use of which has been confined to this country. Word comes from several countries that swimming pools are being constructed by the wealthier classes, and that the foreign makers of bathing suits have been compelled to adapt their design to the California model. . . .

Not long ago, several large British manufacturers complained that they had been compelled to change the established styles of the shoes they made for their customers in the Far East, and they traced the change directly to the movies from America. Last year, a large demand for sewing machines in China could be credited to no other influence. (James True, *Printer's Ink,* Feb. 4, 1926)

When Joseph Kennedy brought executives of the film industry to Harvard in 1927 for a series of lectures, the topic of film and foreign trade came up again and again. Kennedy had just returned from England where diplomats had told him that American films exerted a "formidable" influence. Kent, Paramount's head of sales, ingenuously informed Harvard's undergraduates: "If you investigate the automobile situation you will find that the American automobiles are making terrific inroads on foreign makes of cars and that the greatest agency for selling American automobiles abroad is the American motion picture. Its influence is working insidiously all the time and even though all this is done without any conscious intent, the effect is that of a direct sales agency."

The demurral on conscious intent was undoubtedly directed at Kent's academic audience. Film executives spoke with another voice before government or industrial groups. William Fox told Upton Sinclair, "I tried to bring government officials to realize that American trade follows American pictures, and not the American flag. . . ." The most prominent spokesman for celluloid imperialism, however, was Will Hays. In a 1930 radio speech sponsored by *Nation's Business* he repeated a theme that he turned to many times:

Motion pictures perform a service to American business which is greater than the millions in our direct purchases, greater than our buildings. . . . The industry is a new factor in American economic life and gives us a solid basis of hope for the future by creating an increase in demand for our products. The motion picture carries to every American at home, and to millions of potential purchasers abroad, the visual, vivid perception of American manufactured products.

As if to underscore Hays's remarks, a government study published in 1929 revealed that foreign sales of bedroom and bathroom furnishings had increased 100 percent because of movies.

The mid- and late-1920s were also marked by an industrywide attempt to vitiate foreign film industries by hiring away their best stars, directors, and technicians. The logic of this development was very complex: A von Sternberg film made in Hollywood could be expected to stimulate Paramount's film rentals in Europe, to defeat foreign, chauvinist critics and quota setters, to undercut foreign competitors, and to keep the doors open for American films and products they showcased. By the early 1930s the European struggle against Americanization through films had lessened trade barriers and a worldwide Depression combined to diminish the effects of the process—for a time. From 1931 on one finds more concern among Hollywood executives with the film industry's relation to the domestic economy. Although I shall concentrate on this economy exclusively for the rest of this essay, we should bear in mind that the foreign market did not drop from Hollywood's consciousness, even though it was seldom publicly discussed. Its continued significance is illustrated in this anecdote recounted by an American fashion buyer just returned from Paris in 1935:

> Even a few years back French dressmakers were still dragging at the leash instead of bounding forward, as now, to get a preview of America's style activities. A certain gown was worn by Crawford in a picture the latter part of 1932. You will recall it, I am sure, because it is still with us and promises to become a perennial—the one with the big stiff ruffles outlining the shoulders.
>
> No sharp-eyed tipster was on the job then, for that robe swept Paris not only after it had appeared in the film but after it had been sold in New York shops. And when I took ship for America, toward the end of 1934, all the cheap little shops which have sprung up like weeds in the Champs Elysees, were still gainfully displaying it with no mention, of course, of its Pacific Coast origin.
>
> The old Paris dressmakers—those with the names which have made history for generations in the annals of French sartorial supremacy—deplore this outcropping of houses with no standards and no reverence for the French traditions. . . .
>
> Worse still, French women are crowding into the places and the streets are filled with the wearers of their output. In the old days, even the Frenchwoman of the *petite bourgeoisie* managed to achieve a certain chic; if she couldn't, she seemed to prefer to go utterly dowdy.
>
> But all that is changed. "And now," ask the exclusive dressmakers, "are Parisiennes to be caught on their own home grounds going Hollywood, and bad Hollywood at that—Hollywood that is two if not three, years behind the times? Are Joan Crawfords—but Crawfords only five feet tall and without any. . . .—to people the Bois de Boulogne on Sunday afternoon in gowns which will make Paris the laughing stock as a style center?" (*Saturday Evening Post*, May 18, 1935)

The story of Hollywood's plunge into the American marketplace involves two separate histories: that of the showcasing of fashions, furnishings, accessories, cosmetics, and other manufactured items, and that of the establishment of "tie-ups" with brand name manufacturers, corporations, and industries. The two histories are interpenetrating, but they were distinctive enough to give rise to specialists who worked independently within and without the studio.

The scope of the first history can be set forth in a sentence: At the turn of the century Hollywood possessed one clothing manufacturer (of shirts) and none of furniture; by 1937 the Associated Apparel Manufacturers of Los Angeles listed 130 members, and the Los Angeles Furniture Manufacturers Association listed 150, with an additional 330 exhibitors. Furthermore, 250 of the largest American department stores kept buyers permanently in Los Angeles.

When those intimately associated with this development reminisced about its origins, they spoke first of Cecil B. DeMille. In his autobiography DeMille maintained that the form of cinema he pioneered in the late teens and twenties was a response to pressures he received from the publicity and sales people in New York. They wanted few (preferably no) historical "costume" dramas, but much "modern stuff with plenty of clothes, rich sets, and action." DeMille brought to Paramount's studios talented architects, designers, artists, costumers, and hairdressers who both drew upon the latest styles in fashions and furnishings and created hallmarks of their own. DeMille's "modern photoplays"—films like *For Better, For Worse* and *Why Change Your Wife?*—guaranteed audiences a display of all that was chic and avant-garde. They also pioneered a cinematic style, the "DeMille style," perfectly tailored to the audience's desire to see the rich detail of furnishings and clothes.

While DeMille perfected a film display aimed at the fashion-conscious, fan magazines and studio publicity photos helped spread an indigenous Hollywood "outdoors" style made up of backless bathing suits, pedal-pushers, slacks, toppers, and skirts. By the early 1930s these styles had penetrated the smallest of American small towns and had revolutionized recreational and sport dress.

The years 1927 through 1929 saw an explosive expansion of fashion manufacture and wholesaling in Los Angeles. Some of DeMille's designers opened shops which catered to a well-heeled public. The Country Club Manufacturing Company inaugurated copyrighted styles modeled by individual stars and employing their names. It was followed by "Miss Hollywood Junior" which attached to each garment a label bearing the star's name and picture. This line was sold exclusively to one store in each major city, with the proviso that a special floor-space be set aside for display. Soon, twelve cloak and suit manufacturers banded together to form Hollywood Fashion Associates. In addition, the Associated Apparel Manufacturers began to coordinate and give national promotion to dozens of style lines. The latter association took the lead in a form of publicity that became commonplace through the 1930s: it shot thousands of photographs of stars serving as mannequins in such news-editor-pleasing locales as the Santa Anita race track, the Rose Bowl, Hollywood swimming pools, and formal film receptions. The photos were distributed free, with appropriate text, to thousands of newspapers and magazines. In a more absurd vein, the Association organized bus and airplane style shows, which ferried stars, designers and buyers to resorts and famous restaurants amid flashbulbs and a contrived sense of occasion.

If òne walked into New York's largest department stores toward the end of 1929 one could find abundant evidence of the penetration of Hollywood fashions, as well as a virulent form of moviemania. One store employed uniformed Roxy ushers as its floor managers. Another advertised for sales girls that looked like Janet Gaynor and information clerks that looked like Buddy Rogers. At Saks, Mrs. Pemberton would inform you that she was receiving five orders a day for pajamas identical with the pair that Miriam Hopkins wore in *Camel Thru a Needle's Eye*. She also had received orders for gowns and suits worn by Pauline Lord, Lynne Fontaine, Frieda Innescourt, Sylvia Fields, and Murial Kirkland.

The New York scene became organized, however, only with the advent in 1930 of Bernard Waldman and his Modern Merchandising Bureau. Waldman's concern soon played the role of fashion middleman for all the major studios except Warner Brothers (Warners, always a loner, established its own Studio Styles in 1934). By the mid-1930s Waldman's system generally operated as follows: sketches and/or photographs of styles to be worn by specific actresses in specific films were sent from the studios to the Bureau (often a year in advance of the film's release). The staff first evaluated these styles and calculated new trends. They then contracted with manufacturers to have the styles produced in time for the film's release. They next secured advertising photos and other materials which would be sent to retail shops. This ad material mentioned the film, stars, and studio as well as the theaters where the film would appear. Waldman's cut of the profits was five percent. The studios at first asked for one percent, but before 1937 provided their designs free in exchange for abundant advertising.

Waldman's concern also established the best-known chain of fashion shops, Cinema Fashions. Macy's contracted for the first of these shops in 1930 and remained a leader in the Hollywood fashion field. By 1934 there were 298 official Cinema Fashions Shops (only one permitted in each city). By 1937 there were 400, with about 1,400 other shops willing to handle some of the dozens of the Bureau's star-endorsed style lines. Cinema Fashions catered only to women capable of spending thirty dollars and more for a gown. It agreed with the studios that cheaper fashions, even though they would be eagerly received, would destroy the aura and exclusivity that surrounded a Norma Shearer or Loretta Young style. Cheaper lines might also cheapen the stars themselves, imperiling both box-office receipts and the Hollywood fashion industry.

Inevitably, competitors and cheaper lines did appear. Copyrighted styles that had had their run in the Waldman-affiliated shops were passed on to mass production (though seldom if the style was associated with a currently major star). By the later 1930s Waldman had added a line of Cinema Shops that sold informal styles at popular prices. The sale of these fashions was tremendously aided by the release of photos to newspapers (they saturated Sunday supplements), major magazines, and the dozens of fan magazines—*Hollywood, Picture Play, Photoplay, Shadowplay, Modern Movies, Screenbook, Movieland, Movie Story, Movies Stories, Modern Movies, Modern Screen, Motion Pictures,* and the rest. In monthly issues of each of these magazines, millions of readers saw Bette Davis, Joan Crawford, Claudette Colbert, and Norma Shearer in a series of roles unique to this period: as mannequins modeling clothes, furs, hats, and accessories that they would wear in forthcoming films. The intent behind these thousands of style photos is epitomized in a 1934 *Shadowplay* caption for a dress modeled by Anita Louise: "You will see the dress in action in Warner's *First Lady*." Occasionally one was informed that the fashions were "on display in leading department and ready-to-wear stores this month." The names of the leading studio designers, Adrian of MGM, Orry-Kelly of Warners, Royer of 20th Century-Fox, Edward Stevenson of RKO, Edith Head of Paramount, Walter Plunkett of Selznick, became as familiar to readers as the stars themselves.

From July 30th to August 4, 1934, Los Angeles presented the first of a twice annual series of trade fairs called, inelegantly, the Combined Market Week. More than 400 local firms displayed women's apparel, millinery, children's and men's wear, dry goods, furniture, flooring, housewares, pottery, machinery, and other lines. More than 7,000 buyers attended. By 1936 the fair attracted over 10,000 buyers and included 185 women's clothing manufacturers and 260 furniture manufacturers. In less than a decade Los Angeles had become indisputably first in the fields of sport clothes, street dress, and modern and outdoor furniture, and arguably second to New York and Paris in high fashion.

To all of this we must add Hollywood's influence upon the cosmetics industry. In a field dominated by eastern houses like Helena Rubenstein, Elizabeth Arden, and Richard Hudnut, Hollywood's Max Factor and Perc

Westmore were merely two large concerns. But Hollywood seemed to dominate the cosmetics industry because its stars appeared in the hundreds of thousands of ads that saturated the media. In the mid-1930s cosmetics ranked only second to food products in amount spent on advertising. The cycle of influence made up of films, fashion articles, "beauty hints," columns featuring stars, ads which dutifully mentioned the star's current film, and tie-in advertising in stores, made cosmetics synonymous with Hollywood. The same was true for many brands of soap, deodorants, toothpastes, hair preparations, and other toiletries. No more potent endorsements were possible than those of the women who manifestly possessed the most "radiant" and "scintillant" eyes, teeth, complexions, and hair.

Almost as significant for films as the scope of this merchandising revolution was the conception of the consumer that underpinned it. As one reads the captions beneath the style photos, the columns of beauty advice, and the articles on the coordination of wardrobes and furnishings, one senses that those who bought these things were not varied as to age, marital status, ethnicity, or any other characteristic. Out there, working as a clerk in a store and living in an apartment with a friend, was *one girl*—single, nineteen years old, Anglo-Saxon, somewhat favoring Janet Gaynor. The thousands of Hollywood-associated designers, publicity men, sales heads, beauty consultants, and merchandisers had internalized her so long ago that her psychic life had become their psychic life. They empathized with her shyness, her social awkwardness, her fear of offending. They understood her slight weight problem and her chagrin at being a trifle too tall. They could tell you what sort of man she hoped to marry and how she spent her leisure time.

They could imagine her, for instance, awakening on a Saturday, realizing that it was her day off, and excitedly preparing to do shopping. After a long soak in a bubble bath (Lux), she prepared herself to meet the critical stares of Fifth Avenue. She first applied successive coats of cleansing (Ponds), lubricating (Jergens), and foundation creams (Richard Hudnut). She then chose a coordinated group of cosmetics keyed to daylight wear and the current fashions of natural flesh tone and heavy lip color. Over a coat of light pink pancake makeup she applied a light orange rouge high and back upon the cheek-bones, accentuating the oval effect (Princess Pat). A brown eyebrow pencil, employed to extend the line back along the cheeks, and brown mascara (Lucille Young) was combined with a gray-blue eyeshadow flecked with metallic sheen, appropriate for day wear (Elizabeth Arden). A bright red-orange lipstick, richly applied (Max Factor) and a light dusting of true skin tone face powder (Lady Esther) completed her facial. From her several perfumes she chose a refreshing, outdoor type (Lentheric). She then added a "fingertip-full" of deodorant to each armpit (Mum), massaged her hands (Hinds), and applied a fresh coat of nail enamel (Revlon).

Stepping out of her dressing gown she lightly dusted herself with a body powder (Luxor), then, following a hint from Edith Head, taped her ever-so-slightly too large breasts so that they were separated as widely as possible. A Formfit bra, Undikins, a Bonnie Bright Frock (the Frances Dee model from *Of Human Bondage,* RKO, 1934), silk stockings (Humming Bird) and a pair of Nada White Buck shoes (Enna Jettick) completed her outfit. Donning her Wittnauer watch ("Watches of the Stars") and a simple necklace (the Tecla worn by Barbara Stanwyck in *Gambling Lady,* Warners, 1934), she picked up her metallic-sheen purse and left.

After several lovely hours of window-shopping she happened to pass Macy's and was thunderstruck at the sight of the original Travis Banton gown worn by Carole Lombard in her just-released film *Rumba* (also starring—in smaller print—George Raft). Rushing up to Macy's Cinema Fashions Shop she discovered a $40 copy of the gown, almost as careful in its detail as the original. Her imagination heated by this encounter, she immediately left to catch the early matinee of the film. Three dresses and a fur coat later, the gown entered. Back-lit, descending a stair, vivified by motion and music, it whispered and sighed its way into George Raft's roguish arms. Through the alchemy of his caresses it became libidinous, haunted. It slipped from Carole Lombard's shoulder and had to be lifted back again. It snaked its way across one knee, cascaded from the stairs to the floor like liquid light.

From the rear of one theater two slight moans could be heard. The first small sound, tinged with ecstasy and fulfillment, issued from the girl. The second, somewhat grosser but still redolent with satisfaction, came from Bernard Waldman.

III

Now for our second history, that of the tie-up. In mid- May 1931, a Mr. Tielhet, reporter for the *Outlook and Independent,* sat with a stopwatch in hand viewing a fifteen minute "screen-playlet" which a theater was offering as a bonus to its audiences. The next day, he published this report.

> The news reel was run off first. Then the caption, which will be called, for the purpose of this article, "Seduction— featuring Blanche la Belle," was flashed upon the screen. The scene opened in the boudoir of la Belle, and the brassy voice of the dialogue blared forth. The plot was of little importance. I was interested in counting the length in seconds that a bottle of "Seduction Fleur Parfum" was displayed before the

audience. The story with unobtrusive cunning brought out the irresistible attracting powers of a seductive perfume. It showed how a comparatively plain woman, deserted by her fiance, suddenly developed an almost overwhelming charm by the lure of this perfume. Ten times was the square bottle of "Seduction Fleur" displayed before us, for a total of seventy-eight seconds. . . . Then a seven second title was flashed, "This film is sponsored for your entertainment by the Parfum de Fleurs Company, Paris and London, Levy and Grosstein, New York, sole importers for United States and Canada."

In the lobby the two advertising men from the production company were busy interviewing as many of the audience as possible in order to determine whether the sponsored film had been successful. Next day one of the interviewers gave me his figures. He had talked with 191 men and women. So cunning was the advertising that 54 out of the 191 did not even realize that they had witnessed a sponsored film!

This was but one of a series of advertising shorts shown in early 1931, the first year of catastrophic downturn in box-office receipts. On May 13, *Variety* reported that 50 percent of the theaters were showing advertising films of some sort. Two of the hardest-pressed studios, Paramount and Warners, were seriously committed to these films. In the same month, Paramount revealed that it would produce 50 shorts in response to the favorable receptions accorded to just released *Movie Memories* (Liggett and Myers), *My Merrie Oldsmobile* and *Jolt for General Germ* (Lysol). Warners projected a dozen or more to follow its *On the Slopes of The Andes* (A & P), *Graduation Day in Bugland* (Listerine), a Chesterfield series, and others. Both studios had many signed contracts in hand. MGM was fearful of exhibitor reactions to this development and was a silent spectator. RKO was said to be "on the fence."

If a moviegoer was extremely unlucky he might encounter a Paramount advertising short on the same program with its feature film, *It Pays To Advertise,* starring Carole Lombard and Norman Foster (1931). This comedy, set in an advertising agency, aroused the anger of P. S. Harrison, editor of *Harrison's Reports,* a reviewing service directed at independent exhibitors:

The Paramount picture, "It Pays to Advertise," is nothing but a billboard of immense size. I have not been able to count all the nationally advertised articles that are spoken of by the characters, but some of them are the following: Boston Garters, Arrow Collars, Manhattan Shirts, Colgate Cream, Gillette Razors, B.V.D.'s, Hart, Schaeffner & Marx clothes, Listerine, Victor phonographs. Murad cigarettes, Florsheim shoes, Dobbs hats, Forhans toothpaste, and others. But the most subtle thing is the brand, "13 Soap, Unlucky for Dirt." A trade mark such as this does not, of course, exist; but I understand that Paramount has made the picture for the purpose of making a trade mark out of it. My information is to the effect that Colgate has offered $250,000 for it, and that Paramount is asking $500,000. I understand, in fact, that Paramount has decided to make a regular business out of creating trade marks and then selling them.

Harrison went on in this and subsequent articles to enumerate the brand names he had seen in recent feature films, including ones made by MGM, RKO, and United Artists. The response he generated from exhibitors was as angry as his own. Dozens of them supplied his articles to newspapers that were already alert to the threat to their advertising income posed by sponsored shorts.

The offers this man received were part of a reciprocal business between studio publicity people and their counterparts in business advertising agencies. The *New York Times* described the agencies' side of the operation in a 1929 editorial:

Articles to be advertised are offered as props for films in the making. Automobile manufacturers graciously offer the free use of high-priced cars to studios. Expensive furnishings for a set are willingly supplied by the makers, and even donated as permanent studio property. For kitchen scenes the manufacturers of nationally advertised food products fill cupboard shelves.

Variety reports in a Hollywood dispatch that agents eager for publicity for jewelry or wearing apparel approach movie stars directly. If they will agree to wear a certain article in their picture, it is given to them. In cases where an object is "hard to plant," the agency will even offer monetary consideration.

Given the long history behind brand name props and tie- ups, and the deepening of the Depression through 1932, it was inevitable that the restraint brought on by the excesses of 1931 would not last. By early 1933 Columbia, a studio not burned by Harrison, had moved aggressively into solicited tie-ups. Prior to the production of *Ann Carver's Profession*, a scene-by-scene breakdown was prepared and mailed to agents for manufacturers of the products that would appear in the film. Example scenes: "Scene No. 4, Bill Graham is seated at a luncheon counter, wheat cakes dominating. General Foods? Dialogue discusses flapjacks. Ann Carver is cooking, using a griddle, etc. There are a number of important utensil people who might be interested in this. Scene No. 5. Ann Carver looks at her wristwatch. Benrus? Scene No. 68. Main office of a successful law firm. Appears several times throughout the picture. Typewriters, desks— all kinds of office equipment are here prominently. Remington-Rand?" and so on through over one hundred scenes. The intent was not merely to solicit props, but to promote on-going tie-ups that would reduce studio overhead and gain advertising for films.

Through the first half of 1931 so much pressure was brought to bear upon the major studios that executives were compelled to make public statements. Carl Laemmle of Universal was unequivocally on the exhibitors' side: "I appeal to every producer not to release 'sponsored' moving pictures . . . . Believe me, if you jam advertising down their throats and pack their eyes and ears with it, you will build up a resentment that will in time damn your business." Nicholas Schenck, head of MGM, pledged his studio to the crusade. He stated that although Lowe's had been the first to be offered huge sums to produce "subsidized motion pictures," it has always refused to run commercials in its theaters.

When Harrison subsequently revealed that Paramount had threatened to run him out of business, the general reaction was one of shock. By the end of May both Paramount and Warners were compelled to apologetically disavow their practices and their future plans. Harrison announced Paramount's capitulation coldly, but commended Warners for "taking it on the chin."

This early Depression development had its antecedents in practices as old as the industry. Product display in films had become common prior to World War I. Occasionally the studios solicited props in exchange for the free advertising they could provide, or they accepted or solicited fees for foregrounding brand names or recognizable articles.

A Los Angeles advertising agent interviewed in late 1933 revealed how extensive the cooperation could become:

> Some time ago I dressed the window of 'Toler's Drug Store' on RKO's "Age of Consent" set, using conspicuous showcards and cutouts of Dr. West's products and Bromo-Seltzer (two of my accounts). Considerable action of the drama took place before these windows and that was all to the good. But when the action swung inside the 'store' there were many long shots, hence the counter racks, labels, etc., which I had planted were almost illegible when the picture was projected. On this same set, I had hung a Coca Cola electrolier well to the rear; its lettering was nearly undecipherable; yet the familiar design and trade mark got across, since it was in full view of the audience for about one-half hour of screening time. (*Sales Management,* Oct. 1, 1933)

In the next year enough brand names had returned to films to arouse critics—and the interest of manufacturer's agents. "What has particularly heated the industrialists lately," *Variety* said in June 1934, "are the great plug insertions in recent films. A particular bubble in the pot is the reference in that 'Three Little Pigs' cartoon to the Fuller Brush Man, while the three pictures centering around Greyhound buses in the past two months is another thing eating at the hearts of industrial rivals." By 1935 one could see a package of Lucky Strikes flashed in RKO's *Strangers All,* Chesterfields and Wonder Bread in a Laurel and Hardy film, and Donald Cook asking a bartender for a "Clicquot" in RKO's *Gigolette*. And if one attended RKO's *Silver Streak* one spent eighty minutes on the Burlington's streamlined "Zephyr," accompanied by Western Union, the company that timed its record run.

All this was small potatoes, however, compared to tie-up schemes fabricated at the two most powerful studios, Warners and MGM. Determined not to rekindle the controversies of 1931, these two studios evolved a form of tie-up that revolutionized sales and publicity—and permanently affected the character of films. The keystone of the method was a contractual agreement with a large established manufacturer. If the product would seem blatantly displayed if shown in a film—a bottle of Coca-Cola, for instance—the contract provided merely for a magazine and newspaper campaign that would employ pictures and endorsements of stars, and notice of recent studio releases. MGM signed a $500,000 contract with Coca-Cola in March 1933, providing that company with the vaunted "star-power" of the most star-laden studio.

There were other products, however, that could be prominently displayed in films without arousing criticism, except from the most knowledgeable. Warner's tie-up with General Electric and General Motors provided both for the use of Warner's stars in magazine ads and for the display of appliances and autos in films. Anyone familiar with the GE Monitor-top refrigerator will recognize it in a number of Warner films of this period. A tie-up with Buick (GM) provided for the display of autos in films and for a national advertising campaign that tied Buick to ten Warner films, among them *Gold Diggers of 1935, Go Into Your Dance, The Goose And The Gander, A Night At The Ritz,* and *In Caliente*.

At the end of the campaign, in May 1935, *Variety* reported, "Automobile manufacturers have gone daffy over picture names following the campaign just completed by Buick and Warners. Latter company has tied up to stars on the last 10 pictures with Buick buggies." Among the manufacturers said to be "wild on commercial tie-ups" and anxious to make deals were Auburn, Packard, Dodge, Armour Co., Jantzen Knitting Co., Walkover Shoes, Pure Oil, and Helena Rubenstein.

General Motors itself was so euphoric that it contemplated raiding the studios for stars, producing its own commercial films, and offering them free to exhibitors. It did, in fact, produce at least five of these, employing such tertiary stars as John Mack Brown, Sheila Manners, and Hedda Hopper. In April 1935, Will Hays spoke out against the return of commercial pictures, scotching General Motors' plans before they got out of hand. Only twenty exhibitors were actually offered the GM commercials.

42nd Street, discussed at the beginning of this chapter, seems to have inaugurated Warners' new order of tie-up. But major musicals which followed in 1934 and 1935 brought the technique to a refined pitch. For example, one pressbook (a large magazine-size brochure sent to exhibitors) for a typical musical, Busby Berkeley's *Dames* (1934), offered the following information. The "Exploitation" section announced "9 — Count 'em —9" prepared tie-ups. Tie-up number one: Mojud Clair-phane Silk Stockings. The manufacturers were prepared to distribute "ads, posters, die-cut window cards, counter displays, etc." Number two: Dick Powell shirts. The manufacturers placed a cardboard with a photo of Powell and a plug for the film in each shirt. They also would supply window displays, notes and copy for ads, and dealer information. Number three: *Modern Screen* magazine. "Always dependable, this fan magazine tie-up is more extensive on 'Dames' than ever before. . . ." Number four: Bendermade Breeches. "Bender Bros. are all set to work with you on this 'Dames' tie-up." They were supplying window cards, stills, and ads. Number five: Chulla Crepe, "The Fabric of the Stars!" Counter-display cards, blow-ups for windows.

In September 1934, Charles Einfeld explained the Warner's system to *Sales Management:* "Our idea is to prepare with an advertiser a scheme that works just as much to his advantage as it does to ours. Our company has prepared a special department of such tie-ups. It has pursued a definite policy of working with important nationally advertised products. We have religiously avoided the mass of small advertisers who for years have capitalized on the endorsements of movie stars with ultimate injury to both stars and the motion picture industry."

In 1934 Warners also made deals with Quaker Oats ($91,000 worth of cereal and bicycle advertising for a Joe E. Brown film, *Six Day Bike Rider*) and Farrar and Rinehart, publishers of the best-selling *Anthony Adverse.* The book was made into a major film, one that inaugurated a cycle of Warner historical films tied to highly advertised novels. To further promote *Anthony Adverse,* a $10,000 contest was announced in *Photoplay* with tie-in prizes of five Ford automobiles, a United Air Lines trip to the World's Fair, a Tecla necklace, six Orry-Kelly gowns, and Mojud stockings. *Sales Management* reported that the merchandise connected with *Anthony Adverse* was expected to develop nearly as great a dollar sales as the picture.

While Warners probably secured more major tie-ups than any other studio, MGM ran it a close race. We can illustrate its exploitational technique by examining the pressbook for *Dinner At Eight,* the studio's

Figure 6.1 Store window featuring advertising tie-ups for *Dinner at Eight* (1933). Courtesy of the Academy of Motion Picture Arts and Sciences.

most ambitiously promoted film of 1934 (Figure 6.1). A page of photos of department store displays arranged in many cities was captioned, "The merchandising value of Jean Harlow's name was never better demonstrated than by the dozens of *Dinner At Eight* fashion and show windows." The next page was headed, "Tie-ups A Million Dollars Worth of Promotion" and included this text: "250,000 Coca-Cola dealers will exploit *Dinner at Eight*. First visible evidence of the extensiveness of this national arrangement between the largest selling soft drink in America and MGM, which has individually and collectively the greatest star power names in the industry, appears in September 1933 issues of *Saturday Evening Post, Colliers, Liberty,* and the *Country Gentleman*—full color pages advertising the rare entertainment qualities of *Dinner at Eight*." In addition, Coca-Cola delivery trucks would carry side billboards advertising the film. Other tie-ups, accompanied by relevant stills from the film, included Max Factor cosmetics, Lux Soap (full page newspaper ads), Gillette Safety Razor Co., Lord and Taylor Hats, *Modern Screen,* A. S. Beck Shoes (four-column ads in New York newspapers) and Marconigrams. Dozens of opportunities for local tie-ups were provided by other products appearing in the film: furniture, dinner settings, chocolates, shaving brushes, watches, clocks, and so forth. The dress worn by Madge

Evans had been shown in Macy's window and was available in Cinema Shops.

Both studios must have monitored audience reactions carefully and half expected the epiphany of another P. S. Harrison. But the new formula worked. The audience, after all, was not assailed with brand names, merely by the products themselves. The exhibitor did not feel that his screen was obviously usurped. Perhaps most importantly, the tie-ups increased the advertising revenues of magazines and newspapers, the most effective critics of the sponsored shorts of 1931. Through the rest of the thirties, all of the major studios adopted and helped to perfect this system. In its classic—or perhaps Hellenistic—form, the head of exploitation supervised an effort that coordinated the creation of the script (tie-ups were often formative influences), the breakdown of the script into categories of products and services, and the search for sponsors. Wilma Freeman of Warners told *Nation's Business* in 1940 that she asked first to design "a product that conforms with the picture." In return Ms. Freeman offered the sponsor 12,000 theaters and an audience of 80,000,000 each week. When the product came through, a star was posed with it and the pressbook was made up. The formula, as a mathematician would say, had achieved elegance.

Because this system won wide acceptance in the late 1930s it became possible to insert some brand names into films again. They were inserted sparingly and as realistically as possible. Examples are: Kay Francis in *First Lady* (Warners, 1937) stating that "Ford always makes good cars"; Spencer Tracy in *Test Pilot* (MGM, 1938) asking for "two Coca-Colas, please"; and Barbara Stanwyck in *Always Goodbye* (20th Century-Fox, 1938), asking for a ticket "on the Normandie." The offering of props for films also became highly organized. Two of the largest agencies, the Walter E. Kline Agency and the Stanley-Murphy Service Agency, solicited properties and placed them for a small fee. Certain manufacturers sent their latest models to these agencies as a matter of course.

Before moving on to some conclusions about how all this affected films, there remains another complicity, that of the studio tie-ins with radio, to be discussed. Prior to 1932 the two major networks, CBS and NBC, did not have studio facilities in Hollywood. Warner Brothers, however, had acquired their own local station in emulation of Paramount which owned a half interest in CBS and used its nationwide facilities to advertise films and to built up stars. RKO, as we noted earlier, considered its affiliate, NBC, a major resource and used it both to advertise films and as a source of a new breed of film star, the radio personality (Amos and Andy were RKO's pride). Typical programs inaugurated prior to 1932 were the RKO HOUR, RKO THEATRE, and the PARAMOUNT PLAYHOUSE. These programs pioneered the plugging of songs from musicals and the production of abbreviated versions of the plots of soon-to-be-released films.

In 1932 NBC opened a studio in Hollywood with only one staff member, and originated a modest twelve hours of programing from it. By 1937 the staff had increased to 100 and NBC had constructed a major studio on the old Famous Players-Lasky lot. In this same year CBS began to build a new studio of its own. Over 700 hours of Hollywood programing issued from both networks in 1937. The studios had done all in their power to woo the major networks to Hollywood, offering them their rosters of stars, their copyrighted music, and advertisers eager to connect their products with star names. The following list suggests the range of programs and sponsors that came to be associated with Hollywood between 1932 and 1937: Rinso Talkie Time, Hollywood Nights (Kissproof), Hollywood Show (Sterling Drugs), Madame Sylvia (Ralston), Hollywood Hotel (Campbell Soups), Lux Radio Theatre, Mary Pickford Dramas (Royal Gelatin), Gigantic Pictures (Tastyeast), Irene Rich Dramas (Welch Juice), Sally of the Talkies (Luxor), Jimmie Fidler (Tangee), Helen Hayes Theatre (Sanka Coffee), Leslie Howard Theatre (Hinds Cream), the Fred Astaire Program (Packard Motors), and Ethel Barrymore Theatre (Bayer Aspirin).

The largest advertisers were, however, associated with the largest names. By 1937 CBS paired Al Jolson and Rinso, Eddie Cantor and Texaco, Jeanette McDonald and Vicks, Jack Oakie and Camels, and Edward G. Robinson and Kraft. NBC followed suit with Rudy Vallee and Royal Gelatin, Bing Crosby and Kraft, Amos and Andy and Pepsodent, and Jack Benny and Jello. This very potent fusion of products and performing stars aroused jealousy in the fields of recording, music publishing, and journalism. Newspapers, in particular, felt that the coalition of Hollywood and radio was drying up their advertising revenue. But the most vocal critics were theater owners. In their trade journals they protested the use of the stars they relied upon for their profits by a medium that gave its product away free. They connected declines in box-office revenue with the increased use of stars by radio, and they saw the studio sales and publicity men as madmen who had created a devouring monster in the foolish belief that they were helping the film industry. The shrewdest critics realized, however, that the tie-ups with radio advertisers gave the studios more than free advertising. Obviously lucrative contracts were involved, similar to those entered into for product tie-ups with films. By 1937 it was, in fact, common knowledge that MGM had a major contract with Maxwell House and that all requests for radio appearances and endorsements of its stars were reviewed in consultation with this company. Warners was about to sign a similar contract with Lucky Strike (without which we may never have acquired the phrase, "Don't Bogart that joint, my friend"). How many smaller contracts had been entered into over the years only the studios knew. But this oblique penetration of film into a rival medium had been carefully calculated. From about 1934 on, more and more films employed radio personalities, used radio studios as locales, and imitated the variety show format. Hollywood was not so much aiding the growth of a rival medium as it was attempting to co-opt it.

The result, at least through the mid-1930s, was a kind of symbiosis which blurred the outlines of both media. Fred Astaire became as much a radio personality who performed songs from his pictures and acted out abbreviated versions of film plots over your table model Zenith as he was a dancer and performer upon the screen. The products associated with stars in films and radio became subliminally attached to their names and their radio voices. By the late 1930s the power of film and radio as advertising mediums seemed unlimited. The Hollywood studios, with their rosters of contracted stars, had come to occupy a privileged position in the advertising industry.

We can gain considerable insight into Hollywood's role in the evolution of consumerism, and into many of the characteristics of films of the 1930s and later, by combining this history with all the elements we have so far discussed in isolation. First we have an economy suddenly aware of the importance of the consumer and of the dominant role of women in the purchasing of most consumer items. (Consumer statistics widely disseminated in the late 1920s and early 1930s show that women made 80 to 90 percent of all purchases for family use. They bought 48 percent of drugs, 96 percent of dry goods, 87 percent of raw products, 98 percent of automobiles.) Second we have a film industry committed to schemes for product display and tie- ins, schemes that brought some direct revenue to the studios but more importantly reduced prop and art department and advertising overheads. Add to all this a star system dominated by women—at MGM Shearer, Loy, Harlow, Garbo, Russell, Crawford, Goddard, Lombard, Turner, Lamarr; at Warners Davis, Francis, Stanwyck, Young, Chatterton, and so on—hundreds of women stars and starlets available to the studio publicity, sales tie-in departments as—to use the favored phrase—merchandising assets.

On one, more local, level, the combination of all these factors had some obvious and immediate effects on the kinds of films that were made. There appeared a steady output of films dominated by starlets—those hundreds of "women's films," which are of such interest to feminist critics like Molly Haskell and Marjorie Rosen. In addition, Hollywood developed a preference for "modern films," because of the opportunities they offered for product display and tie-ins. In many instances storylines were re-shaped, to provide more shooting in locales suitable for tie-ins. Movies were made in fashion salons, department stores, beauty parlors, middle- and upper-class homes with modern kitchens and bathrooms, large living rooms, and so forth.

On another level, the studio tie-ins became important far beyond the influence they exerted on the kinds of films made. It is to this more comprehensive level that I would move as I draw back from the cluttered summary I have led you through, to make some larger suggestions, not just about merchandising's contribution to Hollywood but about Hollywood's contributions to the form and character of consumerism itself. By the early 1930s, market analyses were talking about the sovereignty of the consumer, the importance of women as purchasers, and the necessity of learning more about their tastes and predilections. By the early 1940s, market research had been invented, with its studies of the hidden needs and desires of consumers and its discovery that many products were bought for their images, their associations, or the psychological gratifications they provided. Between these two movements Hollywood had cooperated in a massive effort to sell products employing a sales method that was essentially covert, associational, and linked to the deeply gratifying and habituating experiences that films provided. Furthermore, the many fine sensibilities of Hollywood's designers, artists, cameramen, lighting men, directors, and composers had lent themselves, even if coincidentally, to the establishment of powerful bonds between the emotional fantasy-generating substance of films and the material objects those films contained.

One can argue only from inference that Hollywood gave consumerism a distinctive bent, but what a massive base this inference can claim. Tens of millions of Americans provided the captive audience for the unique experiments in consumer manipulation, that the showcasing of products in films and through star endorsements constituted. And this audience reacted so predictably that every large manufacturer in America would have bought its own small MGM had this been possible. Instead they were forced to await the advent of television with its socially acceptable juxtaposition of commercials and entertainment. The form television commercials have taken, their fusion of images augmented by editing and camera techniques, with music, lyrics, and charismatic personalities, is obviously an extension of the techniques pioneered by Hollywood.

But is it equally obvious, as market researchers have claimed, that consumerism is grounded in psychological universals? What should we ascribe to the potent acculturation provided by Hollywood for several decades? Were we, as consumers, such skilled and habituated perceivers of libidinal cues, such receptive audiences for associational complexes, such romanticizers of homes, stores, and highways before Hollywood gave us *Dinner At Eight, The Big Store,* and *The Speed That Kills?* I would suggest that we were not, that Hollywood, drawing upon the resources of literature, art, and music, did as much or more than any other force in capitalist culture to smooth the operation of the production-consumption cycle by fetishizing products and putting the libido in libidinally invested advertising.

7

Fig Leaves in Hollywood:
Female Representation and
Consumer Culture

Jeanne Thomas Allen

A narrative, theorists tell us, requires a motivating enigma or problem. The de-stabilized or unresolved situation moves toward a new configuration or returns to the status quo. Making a woman's "lack" (she "hasn't a thing to wear") the propelling engine of an entire feature-length film may seem at first a *thin* plot structure and then a remarkably *transparent* ideological project. To harness "natural" female acquisitiveness to capitalist market imperatives! Containing this engine of propulsion within patriarchal prerogatives becomes the "driving force" within Howard Hawks's film of 1926, *Fig Leaves*.[1]

The film's narrative precludes the possibility of woman's economic and sexual self-reliance by casting her rebellion against her husband's control as a flight into near-prostitution (the familiar film noir dichotomy revived in *Klute* [1971] and *Fatal Attraction* [1987]). Within that narrative dynamic, women's clothing becomes the ground of a struggle, both literal and figurative, for control of women's bodies. The disclosure of a sexual double standard in the film's dramatic climax, which drops the mantle of parody and satire in an exclusively serious moment, discloses the tension which also contains the film's project—the machinery of male competitive individualism and female manipulative sexuality for economic advantage. Tensions can propel but they can also burst in the text with the possibility of alternatives. But in the case of *Fig Leaves* such a rupture depends upon the viewer and the context; the text contains the tension. This analysis of the conjuncture of text and context will explore the resources for containment and rupture in this moment of Hollywood film representation by exemplifying some of the ways in which film and social practices are related in the representation of female sexuality and identity.

Hollywood and film glamour. It is difficult to see one apart from the other. Glamour unites Hollywood production technique to consumer values, particularly around the image of woman as the ultimate product for consumption and mark of social class distinction. The conjunction of film stars with consumer products in luxurious surroundings which Charles Eckert explicates in his history of pressbook promotion reprinted here,[2] and the placement of this representation in a viewing context of similar splendor as Ben Hall and Charlotte Herzog describe in their histories of the movie palace,[3] reveal some of the ways in which consumerist social philosophy in urban America coincided with the building of a motion picture audience. Motion pictures offered the American population the image of an opulent lifestyle and the chance to rent it for a couple of hours.

Stuart Ewen has outlined consumerist social philosophy (the construction of social identity and behavior through buying) in his history of American advertising in the 1920s,[4] published only a few years before Lary May's social history of the motion picture traced the relation between movies and consumer culture, a conjuncture reminiscent of American's national birth and industrialization.[5] May describes Hollywood as a national symbol and trend-setter for the modern consumer lifestyle. A year later Richard Griffith similarly points to the films of Cecil B. DeMille as an index to a shift in social mores from Victorian thrift, hard work, and asceticism to consumerist sensuality and opulence.[6] Although Griffith cites more specific elements of mise-en-scene than May, he stops short of an explication of a single film.[7]

"The Film Viewer as Consumer," in which I consider both direct and indirect uses of film to advertise and promote consumer products, indicates a recognition of the promotional value of motion pictures in the industry's exhibition practices. In this earlier article I discuss the influence of promotion on thematic and stylistic elements in my analysis of the 1935 RKO Astaire-Rogers vehicle *Roberta*. Rather than arguing as May does that this conjuncture was a phenomenon of the 1920s, however, my study points instead to early motion picture history and an inherited legacy within the legitimate theater and other "picturing" media which bound together spectatorial entertainment, possession, and class position. Motion pictures, as I show here, would extend this alliance in the era of national chain store marketing and motion picture theater chains.[8]

Raymond Williams's discussion of "realism" in the European theater (1870–1920) acknowledges the importance of luxuriously appointed and richly detailed surroundings in establishing the material and class-inflected context of psychological realism;[9] John Berger's examination of Western European oil paintings as celebrations of the ownership of private property and its tactile qualities takes this thread of ideologically motivated representation even further back to 1500.[10] The American version of this representational tradition is seen in the last decades of the nineteenth century in the commercial trade-off which produced opulent interiors for Boston theaters: businesses donated lobby and stage ornamentation in return for credits on the program.[11]

Although May does not discuss these practices which specify the late nineteenth-century consumer/spectator's relation to props and property, he sees motion pictures as extending the spectatorial relations of the theater (incorporating the tactile aesthetic of realism described by Berger and Williams) to a mass public.[12] With the enhancement of an increasingly sophisticated set of codes which constitute Hollywood glamour, film fashions in dress became one of the codes of opulent realism that dominated the mise-en-scene. Film fashions were also inextricably tied to the bodies of women and to the representation of the female form. This was the same link that had sold theater tickets just as earlier fashion lithographs and prints had sold thousands of women's mass circulation magazines in the nineteenth century. It is this relation between representational, social, and economic practices as well as the relation between fashion and narrative that is crystallized and disclosed in the instance of *Fig Leaves*.

In *Fig Leaves,* consumerist values are cast in terms of Original Sin: forbidden, guilt-inducing, titillating, and alluring. The story alternates between a Biblical/pre-historic setting and a modern day household. In both periods, the same newly married couple argues about domestic purchases until the wife, on the sly, oversteps the bonds of matrimony to earn money for her new clothes. Original Sin is traditionally linked to a curiosity which results in a knowledge of good and evil and of sexual shame. Eve's case of the "gimmes" (Adam says, "Ever since you ate that apple, you've had the gimmes—first twin beds and now clothes"), as good a slang term for consumerism as any, indicates her knowledge of consumer products and her desire for new clothes. In this Pre-Production Code film, Adam and Eve as honeymooners display their twin beds and argue about a sale on fig leaves, blending notions of sex, sin, and consumer indulgence. After the prehistoric Adam leaves for work, Eve's friend, represented by a puppet in the form of a snake, enters her house. The subtitle tells us: "The serpent in Eden was in all likelihood a Woman who lives across the hall and sympathized with Eve." The serpent tells Eve that "men don't realize women must have pretty things" (Figure 7.1).

But by the 1920s men were not only "realizing that women must have pretty things," they were telling them that they must. A 1927 article in *Theatre Management*[13] stressed the importance of women as the primary motivators of film attendance and argued that both the appeal of the film and the allure of the theater must be geared to pleasing women's sensibilities. Art works in the lobbies and attractive interior design appealed to women's tastes for opulence and spaciousness. Music rooms and

Figure 7.1 *Fig Leaves* (1926). The serpent to Eve: "Men don't realize women must have pretty things." Courtesy of the National Film Archive, London.

comfortable lounges for reading simulated domestic intimacy. Another dimension of exhibition practice associated film viewing with shopping as early as 1910, projecting consumer products available for sale at department stores. This practice would culminate after World War II with the pre-television 16 mm Sonovision (film in a screened cabinet), and plans to make film exhibition a magnet at suburban shopping centers and recreational complexes.[14] In the 1920s the motion picture palace's aristocratic decor matched the proximity of film viewing to shopping areas as invitations to merge on-screen and off-screen surroundings.

The knowledge that trade, both domestic and international, "follows the film," was evident in the United States during the second decade of the twentieth century. A seminar at the Harvard Business School acknowledged the business community's indebtedness to film as a means of showcasing products and thereby stimulating exports.[15] The Webb-Pomerene Act of 1918 had legislated Hollywood's ability to act as a cartel, internationally advancing America's trade balance strength with an attractive product and a vehicle for the promotion of American consumer lifestyles.[16] One aspect of this was featured in *Paramount's Picture Progress,* an in-house promotional magazine which in 1916 offered articles explicitly arguing the potential of motion picture to shape consumer habits: a forecast of spring fashions designed exclusively for Paramount Pictographs and a description of the way in which fashionable women derive ideas for interior decorations by copying film sets.[17]

Initially set in a "cave man" quasi-Biblical era, *Fig Leaves* would seem an unlikely showcase for fashionable interiors. Indeed, in comparison with the exquisite clothing and lighting of the fashion show sequence, the mise-en-scene of *Fig Leaves* is low budget and drab. Although in a later interview director Howard Hawks cites the fact that only the fashion show segments appeared in color, he gives us no real explanation for this aesthetic choice. Color processes at this point were highly unusual for technical and economic reasons, but Hawks makes no reference to that element of mise-en-scene over which he had little control and which provides the *raison d'être* for color—the costumes.[18] Designed by leading Hollywood fashion designer Gilbert Adrian, the costuming is such a major "character" that Adrian competes with Hawks (perhaps as "principle source of enunciation"), a competition made more apparent by the rivalry between the Hawksian situation of comradely working men, the humor of sexual stereotypes, and the world of *haute couture*.

Given what we know from auteurist studies of Howard Hawks, his second feature seems an anomaly. But there is an affinity between the director's "screwball comedies" (*Bringing Up Baby,* 1938, and *His Girl Friday,* 1940) and this film's comedic play with gender difference. *Fig Leaves* balances the visual glamour and narrative centrality of fashion against the effete villainy and final renunciation of the couturier (if not the clothes)—a very Hawksian gesture. In *Fig Leaves,* the auteur director meets the auteur designer. Adrian was one of a handful of Hollywood fashion designers whose screen costumes had a direct influence on retail fashion marketing, although MGM never merchandized copies of his gowns as Warner Brothers marketed their designer Orry-Kelly's clothes. Adrian's entrepreneurship however, is clear in his authorial signature and in his conscious attempt to affect consumption trends.[19] While on first consideration Hawks doesn't seem to be an ideal collaborator, one might recall that his first job in the film industry was as prop man for Cecil B. DeMille, the one director whom Griffith and May both identify as the key proponent of Hollywood's consumerist lifestyle. After an apprenticeship with DeMille, Hawks scripted, directed, and financed two comic shorts at Paramount and then MGM. But his first feature as a director, *The Road To Glory* (1936), was a melodrama which failed both financially and critically. Hawks quickly recouped his losses with *Fig Leaves* which he claimed he wrote in one night. The film made back its costs at a single theater.[20]

Fig Leaves' comedy is based on gender stereotypes and the threat of role reversal. The "Adam and Eve" setting naturalizes the "battle of the sexes" into a universal, positing female greed exceeding patriarchal loyalty. Having introduced Adam and Eve in their primitive surroundings which parody and yet universalize modern lifestyles, the film reverts to a contemporary setting after Adam's departure for work on the dinosaur-drawn commuter wagon. Left to mend the very clothes which the narrative sets up as her "problem," Eve is visited by the neighborly and talkative snake. In a dissolve, the snake becomes a modern woman advising her female friend to get herself the clothes she wants by getting a job.

After Eve delivers Adam's lunch to him and charms five dollars from him for a hat, she accidentally is hit by a car carrying Joseph Andre, a famous couturier. He whisks her off to his house of fashion design to replace her damaged clothes and to woo her with charm and an offer to model his designs. Eve seeks to win Adam over to the idea but fails and decides to work for Andre without telling Adam. The neighbor who has advised Eve to get a job so that she can buy her own clothes meanwhile tries to seduce Adam, implying that she is untrustworthy and perhaps motivated in her advice by the desire to lure Eve's husband away from her. Unbeknownst to Eve, Adam has succumbed to her pleas for fancy clothes. He goes to Andre's to choose a dress for her, and instead finds his wife modeling the fanciest and skimpiest dress in the show. He denounces what he sees as her preference for clothes over her husband, although he *pays for them,* and leaves without her. Eve wins Adam back by confronting her neighbor and championing her husband who overhears her and returns. At the end, the film reverts to the "cave man" setting, and Adam suggests that they go to a party whereupon Eve complains that she hasn't "a thing to wear."

The comedy of the film rests in the incompatibility of the stereotypical man and woman whose gender is defined oppositionally and who manipulate each other's dependency rather than act on mutual self-reliance with compromise, the same incompatibility which is interpolated as tragic contradiction in melodrama. In *Fig Leaves,* gender incompatibility is explained as female acquisitiveness threatening to subvert male dominance and control, although the market imperative for acquisitiveness or the ideological imperative for patriarchal dominance is not disclosed. Instead, acquisitiveness is naturalized and mystified into a feminine essence responsible for a disturbance in the status quo, rather than the very maintenance of the status quo.

The film's solution is the comedic presentation of an endless chain of buying to reassure social class position after the struggle over ownership—the woman's possession of clothes, the man's possession of the woman. The film's denouement implies that one struggle can be resolved by another: if men continue to buy clothing to please women, they can prevent women from working and gaining economic self-sufficiency. When Adam visits the House of Andre to select a gown for his wife, suspense builds during the fashion show because of the audience's knowledge that Eve will shortly appear as a model and that she has kept the fact of her employment a secret from him. The fashion show sequences then rivet audience attention on several levels: that of the mise-en-scene because these are the only scenes in color and are lavishly lit and staged, and that of the narrative because it is constructed as building dramatic tension through suspense. In this sense, the eight minute fashion show is not a point of narrative stasis but rather a climatic crescendo. Cut-aways to and reaction shots of Adam's work partner flirting with the models as they pass the fashion show audience and another observer's question, "Which one did you like best, father? I mean the clothes," support the way the film positions the House of Andre as an expensive brothel and prepare for Adam's explosion of horror and indignation as he sees his wife modeling an especially dramatic dress, cut in a revealing manner.

The dialogue confrontation between husband and wife shortly after the modeling scene consists of this exchange:

> "What a fine wife you turned out to be."
> "But I only wanted clothes."
> "More clothes? A fig leaf would be an overcoat for you."
> "You didn't get them for me so I went out to earn them—that's every woman's right."
> "—and every man's right is to respect his wife and not have her parade around half naked. You cared more for clothes than you did for me. Keep the clothes."

This verbal exchange, marked by a lack of parody or humor, is significant for the way it intertwines positions about women's marital, sexual, and economic dependence. *Woman's right* to economic self-reliance is conflated with sexual indecency, confirming Julie Matthaei's observation that nineteenth-century Victorian patriarchal ideology constructed male potency as marked by the ability to keep a woman as a non-paid domestic servant.[21] In *Fig Leaves,* the "shop floor" is only a step away from the theatrical stage of high-class burlesque. Clothing design is featured as a male activity, evidenced by the subtitle of the fashion show program which reads: "Joseph Andre's gifts to glorious womanhood." As Jane Gaines's introduction points out, "extravagant costuming, justified as history, confirms a woman's concerns and interests by elevating them from ordinariness to the status of exquisite object. The elegant gown is an homage to woman's 'preoccupations.' " No factories staffed by woman, no female operators of textile machinery nor any sales women in clothing stores are represented. The film, however, contextualizes women's work as theatrical performance which is self-indulgent, disloyal, sexually indecent, and even adulterous. The narrative climax and resolution make it clear that for Eve, the appropriate avenue for realizing her goals is the manipulation of her husband.

Although forty to fifty percent of single women were in the labor force at any one time in the 1920s, they differed from men in that their participation was regarded as a temporary stage to be superceded after marriage by the labor of homemaking.[22] Since the whole motive in working was to serve the family, these women compromised the benefits of self-improvement. By contrast, the competitive ethic became the predominant masculine ethic, harnessing masculine competition to capital expansion. The presence of white married women in the home conferred upon their husbands the position of family provider as the essence of emerging manhood. In 1924 statistics on married women working in industrial jobs indicate that the only purpose for married women to be gainfully employed was "to provide necessities for their families or raise their standard of living."[23] Married women at work were less often pioneering new roles for women than fulfilling—in times of economic crisis—essentially domestic obligations.

Yet after World War I, Alice Kessler-Harris reports, a new generation of female wage workers emerged who hoped for more than economic survival, partly as a result of non-traditional employment opportunities during the War, the beginning of the Federal Civil Service, and the expanding need for telephone and telegraph operators as well as clerks and bookkeepers.[24] "To significant numbers of women, marriage and work no longer seemed like mutually exclusive alternatives . . . the proportion of married women (from 1920 to 1930) had jumped from 22.8 percent to 28.8 percent of the female work force—an increase of more than 25 percent."[25] Yet the earnings gap widened until at the end of the decade women's wages averaged only 57 percent of men's.[26] At the same time, advertising, seeking to locate the markets created by newly electrified and relatively prosperous households, targeted women. Eight percent of sales decisions were made by women: 82 percent of department store purchases, 81 percent of grocery stores, 75 percent of piano purchases and men's socks, 90 percent of jewelry, 80 percent of electrical supplies, 40 percent of automobiles. Women spent more on clothes than any other member of the family.[27]

Women's rights are referred to twice in the *Fig Leaves* dialogue, once in the exchange previously quoted as the right to earn money for clothes if her husband refuses to buy them and earlier when Adam commutes to work and pushes a woman from her seat so that he can sit and read. At this point the woman turns to another standing next to her and says, "Mark

my words, dearie—some day we'll get our rights." Women's rights here
are neither economic nor political independence and suffrage but the right
to Victorian paternalism. But the definition of husbands' and wives'
rights—the husband's right to contain his wife's sexuality and the wife's
right to earn money if the husband doesn't buy her what she wants, the
rights which propel the engine of capitalist patriarchy—is less apparent in
the dialogue's display of a double standard in *Fig Leaves* than in the
parallel construction of scenes organized around romantic jealousy.

Eve's seductive attempts to persuade Adam to allow her to work for
pay outside the home are unsuccessful and then interrupted by the woman
neighbor's request for assistance. Adam leaves their apartment to help
although the request is revealed as a pretense for her to flirt and ply him
with alcohol. Adam returns after a prolonged absence, disheveled and
smeared with lipstick. Berated by his wife, he mocks and laughs at her
("You're so cute when you're mad" is his familiar trivializing line). He
is neither responsible for disloyalty nor does he feel remorse for his
actions. Yet the scene in which he discovers his wife's deceitful behavior—modeling clothes behind his back— borrows the narrative conventions of a husband's discovery of adultery. The scene is free from any
marking of parody or satire, although there is no suggestion of intimacy
between the couturier and Eve analogous to the sexual "dallying" between
Adam and his neighbor. Eve has betrayed Adam with her attraction
for clothes; the film situates women's work outside the home as virtual
adultery.

The fashion show provides the vehicle of suspense building to Adam's
outraged confrontation of Eve with the evidence of her "infidelity" and
the outcome of the dramatic crisis. The spectator simultaneously experiences the greatest sensual pleasure the film offers and the anxiety of
anticipating the discovery of deceit: forbidden fruit and Original Sin. The
fact that numerous films of previous years presented extra-marital sexual
dalliance for the majority of the narrative only to satisfy conventional
morality with a swift and correct resolution helps us to understand the
fashion show as the representative stand-in for illicit sex. Further, the
show functions as a condensed version of the language of conventional
female wiles much as the gangster ballet in the musical *The Band Wagon*
(1954) condenses and formalizes the gangster genre conventions. The
pose of the fashion show model is a kind of parody of the manipulative
behavior Eve uses with her husband. Thus in the demure, coy, alternately
exhibitionistic and submissive gestures of the models we see an extrapola-
tion of the codes of wifely conduct. The seeming contradiction in Adam's
denunciation of this behavior is suppressed by the fact that the fashion
show is public, and that the models are "performing" for other men. The
striking contrast between this sequence and the rest of the film, which is

Figure 7.2   *Fig Leaves* (1926). Eve models at the House of Andre: "Be my inspiration for creative genius." Courtesy of the National Film Archive, London.

flat in lighting and design, is stylistically emphasized by cutting between the stunning depth and gloss of the models on the dias backed by draperies of silver and the reactions of the spectators. The contrast recalls the discrepancy in production costs and values between television advertisements and prime-time programs.

The sexually manipulative spectacle/object nature of fashion show modeling carries over into the models' offstage behavior in the House of Andre. They are approached consecutively by a Svengali type who offers to make them a star: "Be my inspiration for creative genius" (Figure 7.2).

One of the chief models indicates that she is not jealous of Eve because she is well provided for and reveals an expensive jeweled bracelet. The line between "true love" and economically motivated or "purchased" love in the film is a fine one, opening a web of contradiction almost endlessly imitated on American prime-time soaps. The devious woman neighbor conveys the implication that Andre bestows clothing in return for sexual favors, making ambiguous the basis of earning a wage yet holding the worker responsible. In this context, the fashion show comes to resemble the parade or "stable" for customer selection of sexual favors rather than the selection of clothes.

The rarely acknowledged parallels between the socially required behavior of wives and the socially outlawed behavior of "kept women" surface only occasionally in the American film. One recalls Julie Christie's madame in *McCabe And Mrs. Miller* (1971) instructing a prospective prostitute: "You get to keep the money—and you don't have to do any dishes." Also Eve's fashion show self-presentation—wearing a cut-away skin-tight dress with breasts thrust forward, back arched, and arms extended behind her for maximal vulnerability—is exactly the pose imitated endlessly in pornography. However, Eve's renunciation of Andre with the line, "It would take a dozen Joseph Andre's to make one Adam Smith," not only suggests a pun on the name of the early leading capitalist theorist and proponent of the division of labor, but an explicit indication that she has chosen the couturier over her husband and now regrets that choice. Working women do not gain financial independence so much as they substitute the prerogatives of a male employer for those of a husband in a situation where the employer is presumably shared among women and the women are less valued than they would be in marriage.

Woman working as fashion model has been collapsed into near-prostitution through recourse to the dramatic conventions employed in the narrative exposure of illicit, adulterous sexuality: deception, anticipation, confrontation, the sight of the transgression, and the look of horror. And in this melodramatic scenario, Andre figures as a manipulative and villainous "Don Juan." The technical and melodramatic conventions which present the fashion show and which make clothes the primary motivator of narrative action also give them the status of romance or sexual desire which are all the more alluring for their forbidden quality. Hollywood's consciousness of fans' desire to imitate the stars lends a double entendre quality to the line, "It would take a dozen Joseph Andre's to make one Adam Smith." Indeed a dozen capitalist entrepreneurs governing a female labor force might generate an economic theorist who would invent the cornerstone of mass production to generate the mass consumption which *Fig Leaves* so excellently models and showcases.

This analysis has traced the intersection of American social history (women's labor history in particular), film exhibition practices, film style and narrative structure, and the ideological contradictions surrounding women's social role in patriarchal capitalism. However, the comedic tone of the film suggests the possibility that the double standard of male and female behavior might be a subject for parody, might break out of the fissures of the narrative and its mise-en-scene. Indeed, a feminist "reading against the grain" of *Fig Leaves* might find the structural parallel between unmarried women working outside the home and married women working within it as a condition revealing signs of strain. But the melodramatic seriousness of Adam's renunciation of Eve's "wrong-doing" and her penitent return to him suggest the "rescued from a life of sin" tradition of nineteenth-century melodrama as seen in *Way Down East* (1920). I suspect that this pattern was strong enough in 1926 to override an oppositional reading. The moment of dramatic climax, when the film's ideological project synthesizes the gaze of patriarchal condemnation with the theatrical convention of adultery exposed, is unambiguously serious. Were there women in that era of strained expectations—married women entering the labor force when the gap was widening between men's and women's salaries, but advertising was increasingly pitched at women consumers—for whom the contradictions may have reached the breaking point? We have no way of knowing for certain.

The attractions of consumer culture via fashion are showcased but held out of women's reach—unless, of course, they gain them within the bounds of patriarchal respectability as wife or courtesan, the parallel which lurks here but is largely denied. The goals of subservience, dependency, and female sexual modesty are best served, *Fig Leaves* overwhelmingly maintains, within the channels of patriarchal proprietary dominance. The post-apology implication of repetition ("Let's go to a party" / "But Adam, I haven't a thing to wear") implies the continuation of the engine of capitalism—female acquisitiveness contained by male competitive individualism and patriarchal prerogative—more than the rupture of the contradictions.

8

"Powder Puff" Promotion: The Fashion Show-in-the-Film

Charlotte Herzog

According to Elizabeth Jackimowicz, fashion curator of the Chicago Historical Society, Chanel, Poiret, and Worth each claimed to have originated the first fashion show in the late teens. However, as early as the turn of the century, designers were sending models to horse shows and to other public functions to show off their creations in order to set fashion trends and promote sales.[1] The early filmed fashion show served the same purposes. Its use as a promotional tool facilitated by the tie-ins between motion pictures and women's fashions arranged in order to sell both kinds of commodities began as early as 1910.[2]

Motion picture costume historian Elizabeth Leese points out that early fashion show films, from about 1909 through 1918 were newsreel shorts or simply displays of gowns which eventually progressed to a storyline built around the display.[3] One such fashion show series was *Florence Rose Fashions,* produced in 1917. Every two weeks, one of a total of thirty-one films in this series was released with a tie-in to a dozen of the leading newspapers featuring articles about the film twelve days before it was exhibited at local theaters.[4] By reading the advance copy in these papers, a woman could find out about the design, material, cut, and detailing of each fashion item. In the theater, she could then see the same outfit modeled on a mannequin in the film. This fashion previewing facilitated an easy comparison between her body type and the screen model's. Noting how the dress would "perform" could help her to decide whether her own figure was suitable for the dress. If a woman was persuaded by the fashion preview that the dress would look good on her she could refer back to the newspaper for more information where she would presumably find department store advertisements telling her where to buy similar outfits.

The fashion parade/newsreel short with a slight storyline lasted at least until the late 1930s. For example, Fox Studio's eleven-minute *Fashion Forecast* of 1938 was widely publicized with extensive tie-ins.[5] A feature-length version of this type of film, VOGUES OF 1938, according to *Time,* had "found a formula for transforming the fashion show from a boring newsreel short to a full length revue that both men and women can sit through without squirming."[6] *Jones Magazine,* reviewing the same film, said that even though the fashions may have helped the manufacturers of the clothes by giving them free publicity, the film was still not a "commercial" picture.[7]

The fashion show as seen in newsreel shorts of the teens evolved into discrete fashion show sequences in feature-length narrative films in the twenties and thirties. Fashion promotion was thus disguised as entertainment. The commercial tie-ins and articles about stars and studio designers in fan magazines and local newspapers, along with the narrative and dialogue of these feature films provided mutually supporting channels of exploitation. Here *Roberta* (1935) is the prototype. With Irene Dunne and Ginger Rogers dressed by the notable designer Bernard Newman and cast in a musical about a French fashion house, the film had all of the ingredients for fashion tie-up promotion. According to *Fortune,* advertising agent Bernard Waldman discovered this when he produced ready-wear copies of 15 gowns from the film.[8] With the success of Bernard Waldman's Modern Merchandising Bureau, the mass production of fashions promoted through feature films became a sub-business within the ready-wear industry. Under the brand name Cinema Fashions, Waldman sold hats and dresses priced respectively from $4 and $14, and major department stores, including R. H. Macy's sometimes handled the line.[9] Through the Bureau, according to *Time,* 52 dresses, 24 hats, and various accessories featured in VOGUES OF 1938 were sold at Macy's and other stores.[10]

The existence of parasitic industries such as the Modern Merchandising Bureau suggests the ingenuity with which merchants and local exhibitors worked to get around the prohibition against mixing consumer product advertising with the regular theatrical program in the thirties. National campaigns which highlighted the ready-wear tie-ups marketed in tandem with the release of a film in which costume was a special draw, were coordinated by studio publicity departments. Pressbooks produced for each film included examples of articles on women's fashions and beauty tips suitable for reprinting on the women's page in local newspapers, encouraging a general association between the motion picture and beauty aids whether or not the studio had arranged national tie-ups with consumer product manufacturers. In addition, the pressbook contained information about how to send for lobby cards, standees, banners, window cards, and eight-by-ten glossy publicity stills of stars modeling their film costumes.

The pressbook suggestions for managers often cued them to organize fashion shows within the theater in cooperation with local stores, and if a campaign included an official fashion tie-up, as was more often the case after World War II than before, the book would include a long list of major department stores which would be carrying the official line of clothes, hats, or shoes.[11] The point here is that the films from the thirties, forties, and fifties to which I will refer were exhibited in an environment of exploitation which translated the luxuriant mise-en-scene into hats, gloves, purses, shoes, lingerie, coats, and dresses, and even directed women to the stores where affordable equivalents could be purchased.

Since the filmed fashion show sequence I will discuss is not direct advertising, the question for me becomes one of describing and defining the particular sales function of its aesthetic. Charles Eckert, in "The Carole Lombard in Macy's Window," reprinted in this collection, details the mode of operation of the fashion tie-up, but also suggests that drawing room comedies and dramas since the teens "functioned as living display windows for all that they contained." Jeanne Allen, in an earlier article, has distinguished advertising hard sell from this soft sell display to which Eckert refers.[12] In Allen's analysis of *Fig Leaves* (1926) included in this collection, she quite rightly connects the screen representation of contemporary women's fashions with traditions in Western oil painting (the richly textured and detailed oil paint surfaces of the high Renaissance canvas developing coincidentally with the new middle class; this class acquiring the very luxury goods which such a style enhanced).[13] The visual language of the fashion shows I am analyzing is neither the hard sell of direct advertising nor the soft sell display aesthetic of the contemporary drama's living rooms, boudoirs, and kitchens, but is somewhere inbetween. What I mean here by the sales function of the aesthetic is promotional suggestion which I term "powder puff" or "soft promotion." This is a subtle, illusive form of advertising where the fashion show is host to a variety of sales messages which are subsumed by the entertainment value of the show and the sum total of its attractions. Allen describes this concept of soft sell as "indirect sales messages coated with production values, glamour and humor."[14] Crucial for me will be the fact that the fashion show sequences are organized in such a way that they break down the model's costume into its saleable features, directing women viewers to look at these outfits in much the same way that they would scrutinize them in a department store fashion show.

My object of study is the feature-length narrative in which the exhibit of current styles in women's dress is the main focus of the fashion show sequence, not a pretext for something else—where the fashion show is essential, not incidental, to the storyline. For example, while I would not exclude completely such films as *Singin' In The Rain* (1952), *Easter*

Parade (1949), and *Cover Girl* (1944), each of which has a "calendar girl" song and dance number resembling a fashion show, I will argue that there is a difference between using fashion as a theme or backdrop for a song and dance, and using song and dance as an accessory to what is intended within the film to be a true exhibition of women's fashions. In my following remarks, I would like to concentrate on the entertainment value and visual style of the fashion show film and its links to the musical and the theatrical revue. I will specifically show how the fashion show exploits the way women as the primary audience see themselves in order to subtly suggest the sale of clothes to them.

Visual Style

The similarities between the fashion show film and theatrical as well as motion picture musicals, especially the revue, are striking; as both of these forms were late 19th-century contemporaries, a certain amount of cross-referencing is understandable. From the live fashion show the filmed fashion show gets its identity as a vehicle for suggestively promoting the sale of clothes, and from the live musical revue it gets its glamour and spectacle, its decor and style of presentation. The revue used clothes to enhance, that is, to "soft promote" the beauty of its models; the fashion show used the beauty of the models to enhance, that is, to "soft promote" the sale of clothes. There is a consequent difficulty in separating or seeing as separate the model and her clothes. Arlene Croce, for example, describes the Astaire-Rogers film, *Roberta,* as "the old Follies showgirl parade in couturier terms" that "had been done at least as early as 1919, in the 'Alice Blue Gown' show, 'Irene.' "[15]

Several famous couturieres designed for the Ziegfeld Follies. Lucille (Lady Duff Gordon), the supreme dictator of elegance in women's fashion during World War I, began her career with the Great Ziegfeld in 1915.[16] An entire line of her mannequins became Ziegfeld girls and some played models in silent motion pictures. Also, fashion was the theme of many of the musical numbers that featured the Ziegfeld chorus line. "Maids of Mesh," "Crinoline Days," "The Legend of Pearls," "Furs," "The Laces of the World," and "The Episode of the Chiffon" were all vehicles for spectacular costumes. According to Robert Baral, "At mere mention of the Ziegfeld Girl, one immediately gets a mental montage of silks and satins, mink and chinchilla, and Cartier—."[17] It wasn't important that none of the models could sing or dance. Ziegfeld just wanted them "to wear Lucille's gowns and walk across the stage."[18]

The decor of the Follies numbers is lavishly designed on a grand scale with "towering cascades of platforms," sweeping curvalinear ramps, shimmering backdrops, and vast folds of hanging drapery.[19] Similarly, the fashion shows in *The Dressmaker From Paris* (1925), *Mannequin* (1937), *Fashions Of 1934* (1934), *Stolen Holiday* (1937), *Roberta* (1935), *The Women* (1939), *Colleen* (1935), *Designing Woman* (1957), and *Funny Face* (1957) take place in dress salons that have stages equipped with either a ramp or a few steps. The set designs use a style of interior decor in an elite or respectable mode such as Louis XVI or Art Deco with period accoutrements—columns, vases of flowers, statuettes, chandeliers, and candelabra. The salon audience, smaller and more select than at the Follies, sits in plush chairs around tables or is lined up facing the stage. The whole atmosphere is more personal than in the Follies and has the warmth and intimacy of a living room. This intimate arrangement of space permits a greater degree of exchange between the audience and the models whose routines take them into the audience, either down a designated path or around an area resembling a dance floor, to allow for a closer inspection of the clothes. A few exceptions to this spatial arrangement are the fashion shows in *Our Blushing Brides* (1930) which uses a traditional stage and orchestra pit, *Colleen* which features a serpentine staircase and rotating dais and *Neptune's Daughter* (1949) which sets the show around an outdoor landscape and pond into which Esther Williams makes one of her sensational dives.

Lucille exploited a frosty and detached snobbishness in her models, and the famous Ziegfeld walk, fashionable in 1917, which combined, according to Baral, "Irene Castle's flare for accenting the pelvis in her stance, the lifted shoulder and a slow concentrated gait."[20] So as not to detract from the clothes, the models in filmed fashion shows display the same indifferent, aloof stance and pose with hip and shoulder tilted in an S-curve (called the "contrapposto stance"),[21] and parade in the same rhythmic, softly swaying, waltz-like manner to music that accents the comfortably slow pace.

In some of the 1930s fashion show films (*Mannequin, Fashions Of 1934, Roberta, Stolen Holiday, The Women*) the models' routines are similar. Each one enters the stage eight paces behind the model in front of her. She pauses, looks straight at the motion picture audience in a direct bodily address to the camera, and then makes a very slow continuous turn away from the camera. While her back is to the camera, she often places one arm behind her or turns her head dramatically to one side and looks over her shoulder to maintain contact with the audience. Her gestures accentuate certain features of the garments—thrusting a hand into the side of a jacket to indicate the convenience and location of a pocket, extending an arm to show a certain cut of sleeve, twirling to show the fullness of a skirt and turning climactically while removing a coat or jacket to reveal a sensational backless dress. Following a course through the audience, each model makes several more turns and gives more demonstrations highlighting the clothes before completing her "act." This cycle is repeated with each new ensemble. In *Our Blushing Brides* and *Colleen,* the fashion shows are like parades in the Follies revue style with virtually all the models on stage at one time for the duration of the show. However, in the 1950s fashion show films (*Designing Woman, Lovely To Look At* [1952], and *Funny Face*) where the slow, continuous turn is replaced with a two-part pivot (step, step, step, pivot, hold, pivot, hold, and repeat), the cadence goes at a snappier clip and the entire sequence is more like a synchronized and choreographed dance with specific steps and turns in a designated sequence.

The staging and filming of these routines emphasizes the promotional aspects of the films. In *Roberta, Stolen Holiday, Mannequin,* and *Designing Woman,* long slow horizontal pans follow each model from her entrance on stage until she stops for her turn. Providing a glimpse of the garment as a whole, the next shot is usually a static long shot at eye-level of the model and the costume centered and frontally posed in the frame as she makes a turn. This shot is followed by another static shot of the model from the waist up as she turns or pivots again, revealing the look of the garment from both the back and front but this time also disclosing details and accessories (Figures 8.1, 8.2, 8.3, 8.4). In *Roberta* the camera in long shot follows three models at one time onto the stage in an establishing shot. The editing then breaks down the establishing shot into the pattern of long shots and medium close-ups for each model individually and in succession, as I have described. The cycle is repeated again and again with a new set of three models wearing different ensembles.

There are several variants of this sequence. For example, after the initial establishing shot, all of the long shots of each individual model are shown in sequence followed by all the medium close-ups of the same models. Or, during a shot of a model turning or pivoting, the camera, maintaining the same angle, level, and distance, cuts to a completely different model and costume continuing where the other left off and completing the move (Figures 8.5, 8.6, 8.7, and 8.8). This kind of invisible editing preserves a sense of flow and continuity while the clothes actually change before the cinema spectator's eyes.

Often, the salon audience appears in these sequences. In *Roberta,* in a shot-reverse-shot, we see first the model with a portion of the audience behind her while she looks straight at the camera and the salon audience looks at the model but in the direction of the camera. Then we see a view of that same audience in front of the model still looking at her but away from the camera and back at the portion of the audience from whose point of view we saw the previous shot. Or, first we see a medium long shot of segments of the audience in both the foreground and background focusing on a model or models in the center. The camera then cuts to a closer view

Figures 8.1, 8.2, 8.3, and 8.4   *Roberta* (1935). Shot breakdown pattern in the filmed fashion show. RKO Pictures, courtesy of Film, Inc.

Figures 8.5, 8.6, 8.7, and 8.8 *Roberta* (1935). Flow and continuity between models within the show. RKO Pictures, courtesy of Films, Inc.

of the same scene, leaving out the audience in front, showing the cinema audience their point of view (Figures 8.9 and 8.10).

A similar technique is used in *Stolen Holiday* where the audience sits on only one side of the salon interior. The first and second shots from the wings backstage are of Stephan Orlaff/Claude Rains and the rest of the audience watching the show. The third is a straight-forward view of the model from the point of view of Orlaff in the audience (Figures 8.11, 8.12, and 8.13). Later in the same show we see a shot-reverse-shot alternation between Orlaff and one of the models with whom he flirts (Figures 8.14, 8.15, and 8.16). A variation on this pattern from the same film has the camera tracking into Madame Picot's dress salon on the tail of two women shoppers. It comes to a halt behind the salon audience, including them in the shot, and tracks over to the commentator all the while keeping the ongoing fashion show and the backs of members of the audience in full view. The next series of shots are of the photographers snapping pictures and are closer views of the models from the point of view of the photographers and the audience (now eliminated from the frame) (Figures 8.17, 8.18, 8.19, and 8.20). From what appears to be a front row center seat, the camera follows each model through her routine, frequently cutting to medium close-ups as she turns and looks at the audience.

As in the case of a dance number in the backstage musical, the film shifts the viewer between positions in the theater audience and the on-screen internal audience. This shift between objective views of the model as seen by the internal audience and straight-on subjective views of the model alone as in a stage performance creates the illusion for the viewer of being alternately next to and part of the internal audience.[22] This changing perspective not only suggests a very open composition and a continuity between the space of the audience in the movie theater and the space of the fashion show-in-the-film, but it also allows the real audience to identify with the depicted one, and, by proxy, to experience the performance directly and immediately. And this is the point at which classical cinema's "relay" between on-screen and off-screen spectator, first identified in Laura Mulvey's "Visual Pleasure and Narrative Cinema," is harnessed to fashion promotion.[23]

During the shift between the two audiences, entertainment becomes entertaining sales pitch. The model, when she addresses the theater audience directly, seems to project from the surface of the screen in sculptural relief. The viewer sitting in the motion picture audience has the illusion of being at an actual fashion show. The camera height, level, angle, distance, and movement and the duration and framing of each shot corresponds with the way women who attend actual fashion shows are encouraged to look at the models. Each shot is a long, lingering, scrutinizing

Figures 8.9 and 8.10 *Roberta* (1935). Merger of the on-screen and off-screen audience. RKO Pictures, courtesy of Films, Inc.

Figures 8.11, 8.12, and 8.13 *Stolen Holiday* (1937). Orlaff's controlling view of the fashion models. Warner Brothers Pictures, courtesy of Wisconsin Center for Film and Theatre Research.

Figures 8.14, 8.15, and 8.16   *Stolen Holiday* (1937). Flirtation within the shot-reverse-shot. Warner Brothers Pictures, courtesy of Wisconsin Center for Film and Theatre Research.

Figures 8.17, 8.18, 8.19, and 8.20 *Stolen Holiday* (1937). Photographers integrated into the pattern. Warner Brothers Pictures, courtesy of Wisconsin Center for Film and Theatre Research.

glance that provides valuable information about a garment and allows the audience to assess the exactness of the fit of a dress, the smoothness of its lines, the evenness of its hemline, the effectiveness of its detailing, and the appropriateness of its accessories. As in the case of Florence Rose Fashions, if a woman knows in advance that a version of the dress she is viewing is currently available in local department stores, this comparison becomes even more important from the point of view of fashion promotion.

A perfect example of the kind of camera work I've described is seen in the first fashion show in *Stolen Holiday* where we are introduced to Nicole Piccard/Kay Francis, a model who aspires to be a designer. During her routine we see a close-up of the back of her head, highlighting her hairstyle. While the shot is held, Nicole/Francis turns toward the camera so that we see her face. From this close-up, the camera cuts to two women in the audience looking at and talking about her hairstyle, then the camera cuts again to the back of her head as she has just turned to continue her modeling routine (Figures 8.21, 8.22, 8.23, and 8.24). The dialogue exchange between two female on-screen viewers suggests the kind of critical, evaluative "shopper's eye" encouraged by the cutting pattern:

"It's that new mannequin—Nicole or something."
"What a fantastic coiffeur; rather a bit shocking, so mannish."
"She'll be the rage of Paris in six months; everything is shocking to you, dear, give her her just desserts; she has ideas."

The fashion show within the film and its presentation style also taught women how to look and act like mannequins. It could be said that high fashion clothes dictate a particular behavior and comportment. The slung-out hip; the affected, delicate, limp hand; the third ballet position of the feet; and the tilted-back head, all suggest high style couture. This careful, rehearsed behavior is a way of displaying the clothes and accentuating their assets, but also it is a way of conforming to them, almost giving in to them, and here the styles themselves teach women to be mannequin-like. These classical Hollywood films, however, find ingenious ways of softening the comportment lesson as well as the sales promotion aspects of the fashion show sequence. Here is where the techniques for integration suggest a comparison with the way song and dance numbers are integrated into the narrative in the musical genre.

In some of the films I have analyzed, a backstage interlude ties the narrative to the fashion show performance. This is especially crucial in a film such as *Stolen Holiday,* a Warner Brothers' woman's film which is set primarily in a Paris fashion house. As in the backstage musical sub-genre, the narrative focus is on the success of the show business where launching the new enterprise will reverse the lower-class social circumstances of the characters. Here, Nicole/Francis is lifted out of her life as a model by Stephan Orlaff/Rains, a swindler posing as an aristocratic financier. Orlaff underwrites Nicole's couturier business. She loses the salon when his crooked deals are exposed, but the film demonstrates that the disaster is a blessing for Nicole who is released from her loyalty to Orlaff and is free to marry a better man. Because this woman's film is ostensibly about Nicole's career choice over her romantic choice, the fashion show interlude must be blended into the narrative whole. Throughout the entire fashion show in *Stolen Holiday,* the camera cuts backstage to Nicole/Francis, designer and creator of the show, helping models to dress, and reminding them to keep their shoulders back and to stay eight paces behind the model in front of them. During these shots, models we recognize from previous sequences enter the dressing room to make their change. And following these shots we see the models who are next in line appear on stage for another run-through. We see the models in contexts that define their roles as changing from mannequin/performer to non-performer and back to mannequin again.

These transitions from the fashion show to the narrative, during which we are shown the fashion show at work, are integrated into the whole. This is accomplished through shifts in the point of view of the camera which cause what Jane Feuer, in her discussion of the musical film, describes as mystification, demystification, and remystification. (An example of mystification-demystification would be a shift from the illusion of a live show, that is, from the point of view of the movie theater audience, to a subjective point of view, as from the wings of the stage as one entertainer observes another.) Because during this sequence of shots we often see the mechanics and stage paraphernalia used to put on a show, the illusion (the mystification of the first shot is demystified) temporarily becomes reality or stands for reality until there is yet another shift back to the point of view of the movie theater audience representing a new illusion/mystification or remystification.[24] With the use of this backstage musical filming style, the fashion show is sewn into the narrative in such a way that the promotional seams do not show.

In other films such as *Lovely To Look At, Our Blushing Brides, Fashions Of 1934,* and *The Women,* the fashion show is less completely integrated into the narrative and there are very few, if any, shots of the audience or the backstage mechanics during the show. In these films, the fashion show-within-the-film tends to become much more clearly a musical revue/show-window hybrid. In *Our Blushing Brides* the fashion show is like a staged musical revue shot almost entirely from the point of view of the internal audience and interspersed with Busby Berkeley-like close-ups of one or two women stepping mechanically before the camera and smiling. A similar effect is employed in *Fashions* of 1934 where the models are

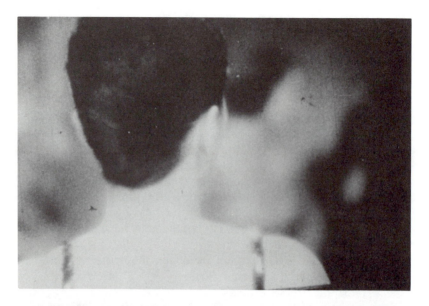

Figures 8.21, 8.22, 8.23, and 8.24 *Stolen Holiday* (1937). The camera as the female shopper's critical eye. Warner Brothers Pictures, courtesy of the Wisconsin Center for Film and Theatre Research.

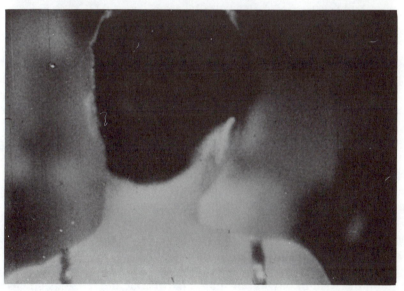

posed within the niches of a large circular stage prop and photographed one by one as the stage rotates them into place in front of the camera. When the show is over, all of the models walk single file through the audience and off-screen.

The third variation I would note is the fashion show-within-the-film which is set off as a dream sequence. For example, as the only part of the film that is in color, the fashion show in THE WOMEN is further isolated from the narrative by an animated sequence which superimposes the proscenium arch of the fashion show stage in the film over the proscenium arch of the motion picture theater in which the film is exhibited. The fashion show then fills the screen and for its duration becomes the film. With the same maneuver the on-screen audience becomes one with the real external audience. An on-screen narrator who almost immediately becomes an off-screen voice introduces the show with the following commentary:

> It gives me great pleasure to be your chaperone on our adventurous voyage into fashionland. But today, ladies, as an innovation, you will see the models go through the rhythmic movement of everyday life and you will be able to study the flow of the new line as it responds to the ever changing flow of the female form divine. Our little peek into the coming season and a glimpse of the future too.

MGM Studio News described the show as "done entirely in action with typical background for each set of costumes."[25] Each category of clothes is accompanied by complimentary sets and mood music. "Fashionland" is fantasyland and the future is represented as a dream. It is also possible to see the entire sequence as a mini-narrative of the film in fashion terms since it displays the outfits the character in the film might need to wear in the course of her day as an upper-middle society woman. In fact, later we see the Roz Russell character wearing one of the more eccentric gowns modeled in the show. If, as Feuer says, the musical sequence is an emotional catharsis or escape for the film viewer, the dream/fashion show is cathartic for the woman in the film—that is, if the relationship between the dream and reality *in* the film parallels the relationship between the dream and reality *of* the film—then the fashion show retains its promotional values because it actually becomes the film.[26] The dream/film offers to fulfill the wish of buying, owning, and wearing the fabulous gowns in the show which would be impossible for many women in real life.

Audience

The majority of filmed fashion shows are set in Parisian couturiers or exclusive dress salons. Richard Dyer elaborates on how these locales are related to wealth and culture:

It [haute couture] is worn by the elite of society; access to haute couture is denied the lower classes in three ways—original fashions are too expensive; "good taste" is not taught or acquired outside the elite, who define and enforce it; mass reproduction of the latest fashions are both significantly delayed in becoming available and inferior in cut and cloth. Wearing haute couture bespeaks luxury, wealth, refinement and, less obviously, power.[27]

Through identification with the haute couture fashion show audience in a film, the audience in the movie theater can enjoy an improved social status and an increased buying power equal to that of the cultural elite. There is also the implication that if a woman buys and wears the same dress as a movie star (who may also have worked her way up from the bottom) then she, too, can be a star. Raising one's socio-economic status and becoming famous are desirable alternatives to the discomfort of everyday life conditions created by the threat of being without and the anxiety associated with it.

While there may have been a real dress at the end of this rainbow, it was never the same as the one in the film. In an article on fashion tie-ins for *The Women,* the MGM publicity department told its exhibitors:

Of course, you will find nothing like these garments in the local shops—but that will in no way interfere with your tie- ups. Present them as the "Fashions of Tomorrow"—and they fit nicely into the displays of "Fashions of Today" the stores have to offer.[28]

Since, in practice, Hollywood designers exaggerated for the screen, their designs were much too extreme for the retail trade and most of the costumes adapted for ready-wear were complete reworkings of original conceptions.[29] Because the designs were mass produced, they were less expensive, but also less exclusive, that is, even working-class women in the mass audience could afford them. *Fashions* of 1934 includes a humorous filmic illustration of this phenomenon. In the film, William Powell plays a fashion pirate who makes it possible for a working-class woman to buy for $16.95 at Rosenblatz Basement, what appears to be the very same dress that an upper middle-class woman would pay $375 for at an exclusive dress shop after she is told the dress is straight from Paris and that there is not another like it in the world. The message is that even for $16.95 one can be part of the fashionable elite. The film (which presents each gown individually to each woman) covers up the fact of mass production: in order for one woman to buy the fantasy dress for $16.95, thousands of similar dresses had to be manufactured for thousands of other women.

With the exception of *Mannequin* and *The Woman,* the fashion show audiences within the films I've discussed so far generally consist of both men and women. We need to consider also the male in the theater audience who probably responds to the fashion show and identifies with its audience-in-the-film very differently from the way the female identifies with it. Is it possible that men in the movie theater audience identify with their counterparts in the film not because of the latters' ability to buy the clothes as much as their ability to "buy" the models who wear them, a privilege of class and a symptom of the class difference between male patrons and the women who have historically worked as models? Here we should recall the similarity between the fashion show and the live stage revue in the use of modeling as a form of seduction. But also we should consider the iconography of the fashion show sequence and its "commercial sex" connotations.

Richard Dyer relates certain types of sensual, tactile materials such as silk, satin, velvet, fur, feathers, chiffon, and taffeta to luxuriousness and commercial sex—the iconography of the brothel and the strip-tease show. "Girlie tactile fabrics are fetishistic at the level of sexuality and commodities," he says.[30] If, as I have suggested, high fashion clothes command a kind of performance, behavior, and display on the part of the wearer, then couldn't the analogy between sales and sex apply not only to fashionable clothes, but also to the posture they dictate? Guy Trebay, in an article on fashion in the 1980s says that "Selling the dress is essentially a sexual proposition . . . best exemplified by the designer who instructed her models last year to 'walk with your wombs' . . . Most runway models are small breasted and walk with their sex held forward."[31]

In an early article on images of women, Griselda Pollock equates the woman's body and sale in general.[32] But the sale of clothes is different from the sale of consumer products such as soap and garden tools. Looking at the clothes in a fashion show is inseparable from looking at the bodies of the women wearing them, which explains why the actual fashion show and the filmed fashion show borrowed so much from the live musical revue. For the female shopper since the turn of the century, an essential ritual step in the purchase of an article of clothing is trying it on in the store in front of a mirror. (My mother, who was in the dress business for thirty-five years, always repeated the saleswoman's adage that you cannot tell what a dress looks like on the hanger. If she could get a woman to try a dress on, she said, it was as good as sold. And for her male customers who were practically illiterate about women's clothes, she would model a dress or coat for them herself so that they could imagine what it might look like on their wives.) Charles Castle stresses this inseparability of the dress and the model and its impact on sales in his book on the history of modeling:

> She [the model] was as important to the dress as the cutter, the fitter, and the vendeuse in clinching a sale. The model was an integral part of the creation. If fashion were an orchestra, the designer was the conductor and the model girl the first violinist . . . The model makes the clothes "live."[33]

If modeling clothes for sale is the same as modeling the body for sale, then looking at clothes with the intention of buying (and we know that was the purpose of the fashion show) is analogous to looking at the body with the same intention. Where else but at the movies could a working-class man see a fashion show and vicariously "buy" the models for the price of admission?

Film reviews from the period allude to this form of voyeuristic sugar-daddyism. Of *Fashions* OF 1934, *Variety* would say that it was "certainly one of the most saleable pictures extant," where "the femme appeal is obvious from the billing, so that takes care of the boys also."[34] And about *The Dressmaker From Paris,* it said, "The women will want to see those clothes and the men will eat up those models."[35] In *Stolen Holiday* when Nicole finds Orlaff a chair in the front row, positioned to watch the fashion show more closely, she tells him not to "collect" all of her mannequins.

For the women in the movie audience there is also a form of identification that takes place on the level of gender that more directly links the fashion show film with the woman's film. We know from promotional material that most fashion show films were geared to appeal to female audiences. *Lovely To Look At* was supposed to give women an "eyeful of glamor" and to have an "Oriental oomph" that housewives were expected to swoon over.[36] *Lucy Gallant* (1955) provided women with an Edith Head fashion show as a topper to the story, and *The Women* was billed as "a *must* woman's show the women will flock to see" which would double and triple the matinee audience which was primarily female during the 1930s.[37]

In the late twenties, articles in trade journals began to stress the importance of booking pictures according to their appeal to female patrons. A March 1928 issue of *Exhibitors Herald and Movie Picture World* published the following:

> Woman has, in the last ten years at least, become the objective in the manager's planning, because it has become an established fact that women fans constitute the major percentage of patronage or at least cast the final vote in determining the majority patronage.[38]

Claudia Kidwell and Margaret Christman point out that the story of fashion and its promotion is overwhelmingly a story of the female side of things because the status of a woman far more than that of a man is determined by clothes.[39] If men are buying women, then women are buying clothes to get bought, or just to get a man, period. Opposite the sugar-daddy on the social climbing ladder was the gold-digger. Men wore women on their arms for status the way women wore clothes on their backs. Baral, in his book on the revue, says that between 1915 and 1922 for a man to be seen on the town with a Ziegfeld girl was a mark of distinction.[40] To quote Richard Dyer, "When wealth or status are revealed in dress, it is either shown to the exclusion of all else (the luxury escapist world of haute couture) or else is a sign of undemocratic ostentation or gold digging cupidity."[41] An analogy to this sugar-daddy/gold-digger relationship was used by one reviewer of *Lucy Gallant* who wrote that the film's fashions were not "over theatrical, but in the sound high style that any man would like to buy for his wife and daughters if he had the money," and that they would also "probably set many females busy trying to find out if he does have the money."[42] During a private showing of gowns in *Roberta,* Ginger Rogers/Countess Scharwenka, pipes up in her fake Russian accent: "That is the one I will take and the tall handsome gentleman with large bank account will be asking for my telephone number and getting it." Rogers is impersonating a Russian countess and wearing expensive gowns from Roberta's salon in order to attract a man who can match her apparent high social standing and wealth. In reality, she is Fred Astaire's girl-next-door childhood sweetheart Lizzie Gatz. Lizzie is the working-class heroine who, as Maureen Turim points out, only *appears* to be gold-digging or lusting after money, "but in fact seeks love, security, community. . ."[43]

Women are presumed to be concerned to the point of distraction about the way they look and what they wear to please and attract men. According to John Berger, a woman sees herself from the point of view of two constituent but distinct parts of her identity—the surveyed and the surveyor. As the surveyed, she is the person being looked at; as the surveyor she plays the part of a man looking at herself, judging, criticizing, and comparing herself to other women.[44] Adapting this concept of female self-surveillance, I would argue that the spectator to whom women address themselves is not just a man but also another woman. This supposition, applied to analyses of gender representation in advertisements, suggests that perhaps the models in such ads who look out at the audience coquettishly are addressing both men and women spectators and inviting women, in particular, to compare themselves to the ideal in the picture, to see how they measure up to this image.[45] If their experiences do not correspond, and if they fall short of the ideal portrayed in the advertisement, women viewers may be made to feel that they have to improve themselves. The point here is that a woman looks at herself and at other women as a man looks at her, but the male perspective is assimilated into what she thinks is her own critical eye.

Could a similar process take place in a motion picture? Might it not be that the direct address of the models in a fashion show to the audience of that show in the film, and by proxy to the audience of the film in the motion picture theater, is intended not only for the male spectator/owner but also for the woman viewer in her role as (male) surveyor, critic, judge? It is my contention that the models in the film's fashion show encourage the women in the two respective audiences—the fashion show audiences in the film and the film audience in the motion picture theater—to look to learn how to transform themselves into a "look" by comparison with another woman who is "looked at." Thus, the female spectator's perusal of the body of the model on screen is always from a point of comparison of her own body. Her looking position is then very much the "shopper's eye" to which I referred earlier. Consideration of the comparative eye of the shopper as a cinematic "look," and the critical surveillance of the other woman gives us a new vantage point on an old question. One of MGM's suggestions to exhibitors on how to promote *The Women* included a newspaper contest for women entitled "For Whom Do Women Dress?"[46] If we were to thoroughly probe the answers to this question, we might find that the arguments as to whether they dress for men, other women, or themselves would break down around lines of gender, social class, and sexual preference, for this is a case in which actual experience may be at odds with commonsense notions of heterosexual attraction.

The question "For Whom Do Women Dress?" is actually a riddle for which there is no answer but which has worked ideologically to deny the male perspective that has historically operated through women in the way they have surveyed themselves and compared themselves to other women. The interesting question we are left with is whether or not the male look then merges with the critical "shopper's eye," the eye with which women measure themselves against store mannequins and size up the cut and line of the dress into which they project their (imaginary) bodies.

9

Handmaidens of the Glamour Culture: Costumers in the Hollywood Studio System

Elizabeth Nielsen

The role call of great designers in this book should not obscure the fact that thousands of expert seamstresses, cutters and fitters, milliners and wardrobe men and women, working long hours with little reward, made the brilliant concepts reality. The giants of Hollywood stand on their shoulders and, although they are not named here, their contributions should not pass unnoticed.—David Chierichetti, *Hollywood Costume Design.*[1]

Introduction

In *Women's Oppression Today,* Michèle Barrett notes that economic discrimination against women is rooted in the structure of the family and the contrasting roles ascribed to men ("breadwinners") and women ("pin money").[2] The discriminatory division of labor in the home has historically been reinforced by the unions that controlled access to jobs.[3] The motion picture industry, for most of its history, essentially borrowed this division of labor in its determination of women's place in the work process. Women were, for the most part, restricted to a very few jobs, in fact, they held the lowest paid jobs in the industry. In addition to secretarial jobs, women's work included gluing films together in poorly ventilated film labs and sewing and handling costumes for actors. The exceptions to the rule of low pay and low status for women were those very few women who became motion picture stars, character actors, film editors, publicists, and costume designers.

In order to keep men's salaries relatively high, most Hollywood locals, like other unions throughout the country, simply refused to admit women members into their ranks until well into the 1970s when pressure from the U.S. Justice Department forced them to do so. Today, there are women in nearly all the Hollywood locals. For women who worked during the "Golden Era" (1920–1960) of the Hollywood studio system, however, horizons were very limited. In this period, the majority of women working in non-performance technical jobs were clustered in two local unions— the film lab workers and the costumers union.

The work of the costumers was indispensable to the industry as a whole since their contributions are visible to the audience, comprising as they do a key element of mise-en-scene. The following will shed some light on the work of costumers and costume manufacturing workers and on the way their work and creativity was integral to the production of Hollywood glamour culture.

It offers an internal view of the labor process—its organization and human consequences—in the Hollywood costume houses and the costume departments of the Hollywood studios.[4] Finally it is concerned with the role of costumers, especially women costumers, in the Hollywood studio system—a system that died a slow death in the 1950s and 1960s.

The Work

In the very early days of Hollywood film production, most producers depended upon the centralized collection of costumes and costume props from rental companies such as Western Costume House, or upon actors wearing their own clothes on the set. Western Costume House started around 1910 by supplying costumes for westerns. The exponential growth of film production in the 1920s, however, led the major studios to develop their own costume departments. In the large studios—Fox, Warners, Paramount, MGM, and RKO—the costume department was broken down into two sub-departments: manufacturing and finished wardrobe.

What is loosely called *manufacturing* might more aptly be called *custom creating*. Expert artisans—people with job titles such as cutter, fitter, figure maker, table lady, draper, finisher, tailor, beader, milliner, and shoemaker—transform raw sketches and bolts of every conceivable kind of material into finished garments (Figures 9.1 and 9.2). To do this, these artisans must understand the designer's ideas, use dyes expertly and have an almost instinctive command of color values. They must be able to cut, pattern, and sew the raw materials with speed and dexterity and in addition to these skills they must develop an infinite amount of patience with live fittings (Figures 9.3 and 9.4). It takes years of refinement of their skills before costumers can transform a sketch into a living garment of color, shape, personality, and authenticity on the screen. And once it is made, it is used over and over again: an alteration here, a hem lowered, an ornament added until it begins to fall apart. Then the costume is intentionally aged a bit more until it becomes an authentic-looking tattered and worn garment.[5]

Artisans working in the Hollywood studio era not only created chic or glamorous, and old or tattered clothes but also trick costumes for such films as *Alice In Wonderland* (1933), *Wizard of Oz* (1939), *Green Pastures* (1936), and *Midsummer Night's Dream* (1935). For example, the *Costumers News* reports that the costume for the Tin Man became a major studio concern during the making of *Wizard of Oz*. All of the experts—the makers of metal armor, the tin workers, the metal experts, the studio property men—were unable to make the Tin Man function properly. Finally they took the problem to the studio tailor shop where Sam Winters used metallic cloth and buckram stiffening to quickly solve the problem.[6]

Manufacturing continued to take place not only in the studio workrooms but also at Western Costume, which was founded by L. L. Burns, an Indian trader, and which, during the studio era, became the world's largest costume manufacturer. In 1949 Western's costumes were conservatively valued at ten million dollars and were produced by some two hundred skilled craft workers and artists such as Bill Emerton, a hat expert who made hats in at least two thousand different shapes and forms.[7] The Program from the Eighth Annual Costumers Ball described Western as a labyrinth of cultural artifacts:

> At first glance, as one walks through [Western's] cavernous depths, the impression is staggering. Thousands upon thousands of costumes. How many? Even Western doesn't know. Perhaps a million. And it's all there—the shoes, the hats, the accessories, the beads, bangles and baubles. If Western hasn't got it in stock, it will either make it or get it somehow. Need help on a period design? There are trained researchers constantly available to look up the most minute detail. Is it a question about the ornamentation on a Greek warrior's shield? The buttons on the waistcoat of an English dandy of the early 19th century? The frilly garters of a French can-can dancer? Name it and you'll find—as everyone does sooner or later— that the history of mankind is grist to the daily mill at Western.[8]

Much of that esoteric history can be found in Western's library which consists of thousands of rare manuscripts and books for costume researchers such as the legendary Bert Offord, an expert in police uniforms and ancient and modern weapons;[9] or Larry Purdin, who received one of the first Masters degrees in costuming and who was awarded a fellowship from the government of Haiti;[10] or Baston Duval, the Director of Research at Western in 1953 who was decorated by the Counsel General of France for his "true representation and accurate research on the national costumes of the Republic of France."[11]

But, of course, for most women and men working at Western, there were no special decorations and recognitions; there were mostly long, back-breaking working days. Agnes Henry went to work as a wardrobe "girl" for Western Costume in 1942 during her high-school summer vacation. She claims that she succeeded because she was blessed with strength and good taste: strength to work from 8 a.m. to 10 p.m. with a half hour for lunch; strength to lift heavy production dresses, which were often made out of yards and yards of velvet with huge skirts and petticoats with hoop skirts constructed out of whalebone or steel; strength to keep going when her arms and back ached from lifting these heavy dresses and carrying them to and from their racks. Agnes recalls:

> My job was to make sure the clothes fit the person. There would be racks and racks of clothes and you would have to figure out what looked best on a particular person and what would fit them best. At that time, the costumes weren't sized. You just had to look at it and guess, and then call someone in from the workroom to come in and do the actual fitting for the scene.

Someone from the studio, usually a costume supervisor, would call and tell Agnes how many people they would be working with the next day. The hours were long, the work demanding, and the pace was overwhelming:

> We came in around 8:00 a.m. and began matching up people to clothes—as many as three every fifteen minutes or five or six people per hour, depending on how complicated the clothes were. We would outfit people until 5:00 or 6:00 p.m. Then the fitter would come in and we would write up the changes that needed to be made. After that we would accessorize the costumes until ten o'clock at night.[12]

Good taste was essential since costumers had to match costumes to actors and extras. Agnes selected costumes from hundreds of racks to be certain that these clothes not only fit more properly but were appropriate to the scene. Since there were no sizes on the costumes, the job required a sense of good fit and style. It was a perfect apprenticeship for a person who would become a key costumer and the motivation to get out of the costume room was great since the strain of lifting heavy costumes twelve hours a day, six days a week was so incredible.

Gender and Ethnicity in Manufacturing

The work process in the manufacture of costumes for principal actors today has changed little from the studio era. The costume designer makes a sketch, takes it either to Western Costume or to a studio workroom, talks to the supervisor and helps to select the material. The key costumer then makes arrangements for the actor or actress to come in for extensive measurements. After the specifications and measurements, the key costumer coordinates a meeting with the actor, the designer, the head woman in the workroom, the fitter, the woman who has made the costume and her assistant(s), as well as the producer and the director. Although each of these persons may use a different standard of judgment, in fact, every

Figure 9.1   Famous-Players Lasky/Paramount Pictures, 1919. Courtesy of Marc Wanamaker Bison Archive, CA.

Figure 9.2   Paramount Pictures, 1922. Courtesy of Marc Wanamaker Bison Archive, CA.

Figure 9.3 Paramount Pictures Costume Department, 1930.
Courtesy of Marc Wanamaker Bison Archive, CA.

Figure 9.4 Metro-Goldwyn-Mayer Costume Department, 1933. Courtesy
of Marc Wanamaker Bison Archive, CA.

one of them has to pass on a costume. As Agnes Henry recalls this practice, sometimes it takes "a room full of people to get one outfit."[13]

Manufacturing involves research, design, production, cleaning, and even the aging of costumes. When Georgina Grant started work in the manufacturing department at MGM in 1935 where she would work for thirty years, the studio had seamstresses, beaders, milliners, shoemakers, and both male and female tailors who made all the suits and uniforms. With a recommendation for the job from a neighbor in Los Angeles, a Mexican-American woman who did beading work in her home for MGM, Grant was given a tryout by a designer working on *Broadway Melody* of 1936. She describes the intimidation she felt at her initial interview:

> He lined about seven or eight of us up in a row, and he handed us each an applique—white satin with braid on it—and told us to sew it to a backing. He'd pick them up and say, "You go; you stay." And when he came to me, he said, "Is that the best you can do?" I said, "No, but I thought you wanted it in a hurry." He handed me another one and said, "Do this one and give me your best work." So I did and he said, "You stay."[14]

Grant went on to perform nearly every task in the department at some point in her thirty-year career. She describes the MGM costuming process from top to bottom:

> There would be at least ten people to a cutter and fitter. In those days we had eight cutters and fitters. We had a beading department and a tailor shop. The cutters and fitters made the pattern from designs ordered by the designer. We made the pattern in cotton to show Adrian, and then he and the star would "O.K." it. Then the fitter would fit it on the person. Then you would take the cotton apart, cut the finished costume. Then a fitting again—this time with the actual costume to be used in the film. It was a long process.[15]

Although the cutters and fitters were involved in a long and often tedious process, the beaders had an even more difficult job. MGM employed at least twenty expert women beaders. They were Mexican-Americans who had carried their craft with them from Mexico. Sometimes the studio contracted the work out to a factory, and the factory hired women to work in their homes, as was the case with Georgina's neighbor. Grant recalls that the beaders had the hardest work of all in the manufacturing department:

> On a long dress like the kind Kathryn Grayson wore, the beading would go to the floor. It took a long time—months to make a single dress. It was all hand work done on a frame, with two or three women working

> on a frame—all beading, beading, beading—enormously hard work.
> Beaders worked up to twelve hours a day. Their backs hurt at the end
> of a day. At least we could move around. Men did not do this kind of
> work. They made the suits and the dress coats.[16]

Regardless of the physical strain or the tedium of the work in these years, Georgina recalled that since it was the Depression, people felt that any employment was good to have.

David Chierichetti, in his *Hollywood Costume Design,* confirms this picture of the 1930s which he has from Shelia O'Brien, a pioneer union organizer who worked in Paramount's costume department during these hard times. Costumers worked three full-time shifts—eight to four, four to midnight, and midnight to eight; the workrooms were so jammed with people that one could just barely walk through the rooms filled with enormous skirts. Paramount would get so backed up that they had to farm out the costuming on several of their pictures to Western, which was just a few blocks away. The first time the work slowed down, Chierichetti notes, was during the Second World War because all of the studios were trying so hard to conserve materials. Studios would produce less lavish pictures than they had made in the 1930s, and the films they did produce played longer and drew larger audiences so that, for instance, a film that would have run a week or two in 1939 was running for sixteen weeks in 1943.[17]

As with many other departments in the studios, the costume departments worked long hours to meet production schedules—twelve hour days were routine. If a dress was to be worn in the next day's shooting, the costumer responsible stayed into the night until it was finished. Multiple identical copies of dresses were often required to prevent production delays. An entire crew might be kept waiting if a single copy dress was damaged during filming or rehearsal. Redundancy was essential. Chierichetti explains this:

> If the costume is used in a very long sequence in a film, you need many
> copies of it. I think the record is held by Scarlett O'Hara in GONE
> WITH THE WIND, the dress she wears all through the burning of
> Atlanta up to the point that she gets back home and discovers her mother
> is dead. There were actually twenty-seven copies of that dress in various
> stages of deterioration.[18]

Many of the women and men who labored to produce so many and such elaborate costumes were immigrant laborers from such diverse countries as, in addition to Mexico, Portugal, Spain, Italy, Japan, Austria, Hungary, Czechoslovakia, Yugoslavia, and Russia. A large number of German Jews came to work as tailors and seamstresses in the costume manufacturing departments in the 1930s. The various ethnic or national groups often specialized in the manufacture of the clothing of their native lands: beaders from Mexico; crochet workers from Armenia; turban wrappers from the Middle East; embroiderers from Japan and China. In the shops, then, English was often a second language.

Although Local 705 of the Motion Picture Costumers Union always had women and many ethnic groups represented in the costume manufacturing departments, Black Americans were not among these workers. Ted Ellsworth, business agent of the costumers union in the 1940s, was determined to place Grace January, a very skilled Black seamstress, at Paramount, but the attempt was, by his account, "a disaster." He recalls that both the studio and some union members protested his placement of Grace even though she was an attractive, well-qualified person and the studio needed help. Ellsworth recalls that she quit after a week because they would either not give her any work at all or just give her dirty work to do. She then found a job with one of the affiliated companies, the non-union shops that produce specialty work such as crocheting for studios. In Ellsworth's analysis, Blacks could find employment in the specialty shops because these affiliated companies were almost one hundred percent minorities from the owners on down. Most of the extremely fine crochet workers were from Europe, and they were minorities themselves. At that time, however, Ellsworth was less concerned about the studio reaction to a Black worker than he was about the union's acceptance of her.[19]

Blacks still have a difficult time gaining admittance to the unions that control film production jobs, although some progress has been made. Local 705 was one of the few union locals that was not targeted when the Justice Department investigated minority hiring in the 1970s. Local 705 actually had Black members before the other Hollywood locals, since the first Black wardrobe men and women had been hired in the early 1960s. At the time of the Justice Department's study, Local 705 had "every race you could think of," Ellsworth recalls, in addition to Chicanos and Blacks.[20]

The Finished Wardrobe Department

Although in contrast to the manufacturing department, the finished department comprises a much smaller group, the rule still holds: for every costumer working on the set and dressing a star, there are many people behind the scenes making the clothes. Like the manufacturing department, the finished department has a sexual division of labor: women costumers work with female actors; men costumers work with male actors. In finished wardrobe, costumers analyze scripts for costume requirements and select the clothing from the manufacturing department of Western Costume or purchase clothing from a retail outlet. These costumers are responsible for insuring that the correct clothing is on the correct person at the correct time, and for maintaining accurate records as to which actor wore which costume in which scene.

For some fortunate women, working at Western Costume was a stepping stone up to working on the set as a key costumer—as we have seen was the case with Agnes Henry who moved from Western to the RKO stock room where she classified garments and returned them to the rack. Shortly thereafter she began working on what the finished costumers call "the firing line," or daily work on the set. In the 1940s, the "set girl," as Henry was called, and costumer supervisor, were often one and the same person. In fact, in these years the distinction between designers and costumers was often blurred, although later contract agreements prohibited crossing over from one job classification to another without the appropriate union card. The fluidity of job categories at the time Henry began working at RKO meant that she could more easily rise to the position of key costumer—the primary supervisor for all costume work on the set.

Agnes Henry describes the work by key costumer as overseeing the others who actually handle the costumes on the set, but it also involves reading the script, making a chronological wardrobe plot breakdown (actresses only), and noting the names of the characters and the scenes in which they appear. She then meets with twenty or thirty department heads to coordinate hair dressers, make-up artists, and cinematographers.[21] Chierichetti contends that the technological complexity of the old feature films made such extensive pre-production meetings necessary. These consultations no longer take place in regular television series or smaller budget features.[22] Key costumers, however, do consult with the costume designers and make suggestions that are often incorporated into a scene. For example, Henry told the designer of the costumes for the Enterprise crew in the STAR TREK films that George Takei's uniform should not be yellow, since it would not offer enough contrast with his skin color. The designer agreed and made the change.[23]

The main assistant to the women's key costumer is the "set girl," a position more important than it sounds since on big productions the set girl has assistants under her. As a means of making sure the right costumes are in the right scenes she keeps books with polaroid snapshots and descriptions of the jewelry worn and the color of the costume matched to the correct scene. Finally, the set girl checks the call sheet before she leaves at night in preparation for any unexpected changes in the next day's shooting schedule.[24] This is crucial since at the end of every day it is the costumer's job to see that every costume to be worn in the next day of shooting is cleaned, pressed, the dress shields changed, and the costume even repaired if necessary. Frequently costumers are called upon to do emergency cleaning jobs on costumes, especially if make-up has to be removed from collars and sleeves. Such maintenance work is usually done by costumers in the manufacturing department, except when the film is being shot on location at some distance from Los Angeles.

Shooting on location, a more common practice today than in the studio era, places special demands on costumers because of the need to use every hour of daylight. If the motion picture or television program is shot on location in the Los Angeles area, for example, costumers leave home before the sun comes up, driving first to the studio to pick up costumes and then traveling from forty-five minutes to an hour to the location where they must see that the actors have their costumes in order and are ready to perform when the first light comes through. The crew shoots until it is dark. After checking the call sheet for possible changes for the next day, the costumers then return the costumes to the studio for cleaning and pressing. Only then can they drive home and get their short night's sleep—usually six hours or less.

Creativity

What costumers call "creativity" is synonymous with resourcefulness. It is a kind of spontaneous adaptability found in individuals who because of necessity have to do something with very limited resources. And among costumers some of the challenges to this resourcefulness are legendary. For example, the program from the Eighth Annual Costumers Ball tells the story of a Cecil B. DeMille costuming unit arriving in Egypt for the filming of *The Ten Commandments* (1956) and discovering that instead of the costumes for three thousand extras which they had brought with them from the studio, director DeMille wanted them to both find and make clothes for fifteen thousand extras.[25]

Contracts with actors and extras today specify that they receive bonuses for wearing their own clothing and accessories which are appropriate to the scene. This encourages on-camera performers to maintain their own wardrobes, which means a savings for the producers, but a limitation which taxes the resourcefulness of the costumer. Chierichetti describes the way he had to transform extras into bathing beauties to save time and money on a film.

> I was working on a film that took place on a ship. There were all these extras who had been told to show up in formal evening clothes, which they did. We did the scene in the ballroom and then, on the spot, they rewrote the script to include a daytime scene. So suddenly we were doing a scene out on the deck and the extras were sitting around on the

deck playing cards and so forth. The director said there should be some of them sunbathing. Well, this was the middle of winter, and it was fairly cold out. Very few of the extras had brought their bathing suits along. The director asked me if I thought I could get more bathing suits, and I said, "I doubt it. It's the middle of January." He told me to do the best I could do in two hours. We were in the middle of Long Beach, and they got me a limousine. I went into downtown Long Beach, but there were no bathing suits in any of the department stores. I went into a sporting goods store, and there were tennis suits on sale. I bought as many as I could get and took them back to the set. If I couldn't get a good fit, I pinned them up in the back. One extra was wearing a pink bra under her blouse—that became a swimsuit top. You just have to think very fast on the job.[26]

Resourcefulness, or what one costumer calls "creativity," then, translates into substantial savings for the producer. Agnes Henry confirms this correlation between the tightness of the budget and the resourcefulness of the costumer in her description of the transition between work on feature films and telefilms:

I was in TV in the very beginning. I worked at Four-Star Television in the 1950s. I had more responsibility because I was on my own. I talked with the producer, did the script breakdown for costumes, rented or bought clothing at retail stores, brought the clothes back to the set and arranged fittings for the actors. There was no big head of the department, and the atmosphere was much friendlier. The pace of the work was incredibly fast. TV shows were made in a week, whereas you had months to do feature film. Because of the low budgets, TV was harder but also required you to be more creative.[27]

Of course this is not the flamboyant sense of creativity that is flaunted at the Academy Awards ceremony. It is rather the *spontaneous* productive sense of creativity—the ability to find cheap and fast solutions to production problems, such as knowing how to "cheat" a bit on period costumes by altering contemporary clothes bought in retail stores to look like period costumers as Chierichetti describes:

With men's suits, for instance, if you're doing a 1930s or 1940s show, you can find in the stores today a pin-stripe suit that looks just right except that the lapels are a little off. You can have the changes made and that is a lot cheaper than having something made from scratch.[28]

In the manufacturing departments, costumers also develop this spontaneous ability to make do in a hurry with very few resources. Georgina Grant recalls that in manufacturing the costumers had to make everything themselves and sometimes the entire project depended on their own use of imagination and ingenuity. She recollects that one time she created long stoles out of nothing more than string. She was more surprised than anyone when they were used on the women in the chorus line. For Georgina Grant, and others like her, the work in the manufacturing department was tiresome and demanding, but it also had its special rewards. Grant still has souvenirs of photos and swatches of cloth that she worked with at MGM. She recalls:

> I did mostly hand work. If there was anything rather fussy to be done, I got it. On the big screen, every stitch could be seen. The clothes were so beautiful in these days. You would work weeks and weeks and weeks on a period dress. You would have rows and rows of petticoats underneath before you ever got to the top. You had to make everything yourself.[29]

Costumers prided themselves on creating fabulous costumes seen on the "most beautiful women in the world" on giant screens. The studios could then count on the loyalty of these workers because of the degree of personal satisfaction they found in their jobs which became the "intrinsic reward" for thirty-five years of low pay, low status, and backbreaking work.

Transitional Period: The Changing Image of Women

For the costumers working in the transitional period between the studio and television eras, patterns of employment changed drastically. The most significant change was that the studios no longer kept production staff on the payroll full-time. People who had worked at the same studios for more than thirty years found themselves adrift as freelance workers. The exceptions to this rule were those people who were fortunate enough to secure a job on a long-running television series, or those who worked at specialized facilities, such as the film labs or the costume houses.[30]

Film producers are free to hire any member of Local 705 as a costumer as long as they are of the proper classification—finished wardrobe or manufacturing. When producers run short of help, they can either call costumers directly or call the union hall to contact additional help. Such calls to Local 705 are filled by the members of the local who have been out of work the longest. The union calls the people starting at the top of the unemployed list until all the available jobs have been filled. Unemployed costumers thus stay close to their phones in the afternoon to get possible calls from the union or from key costumers who may have already been hired by the assistant director or producer. Getting a call from a key costumer is largely a matter of personal contacts in the industry. Although there is a base line of skill that all finished costumers must have in order to secure employment, finding work on a regular basis requires contacts in the industry, or ideally star actors will request specific people to handle their wardrobe. In other instances, costumers or key costumers are hired on the basis of their specialized knowledge; Bert Offord, for example, always found work because his knowledge of historical military uniforms was encyclopedic.[31]

Agnes Henry was part of the "new breed of women" who were hired in the finished departments during World War II. As Ted Ellsworth explains, before the war the wardrobe women's duties corresponded to what people in the theater call "dressers." Everything was prepared for them, and they just took the clothes from the racks to the set and helped dress the women actors when necessary. None had university degrees. Few had high school educations. People had no respect for them and they functioned more or less like servants. These women costumers often came from the theatrical industry themselves or were married to men who worked in the theater. At that time the motion picture industry was operating in the same way that the theater operated: that is, if they needed wardrobe women, stagehands brought in their wives to do the work. Ellsworth describes the situation before and during the war:

> All wardrobe department heads were men. With one exception, men ran both the men's and women's wardrobe. Any decisions affecting the mix of employees were made by a man, and usually it was men who received the benefits. Universal was the exception. Vera West, a costumer and designer, ran both the men's and the women's department. Technically there was a man in charge of the men's wardrobe, but for twenty years Vera called all the shots. She was the first woman who didn't take orders from anyone but production people. She never had the title of department head, but she had all the responsibility.[32]

Although Vera West may have "called all the shots" and had all the responsibility, she never officially headed the department. The head still had to be a man. During the Second World War, however, such sex discrimination practices began to change. The union began hiring articulate, educated, career- oriented women who ultimately changed the status of women working on the set. This change coincided with the rebound of the industry during the war. The studios were turning record box office receipts back into the studios to avoid paying excess profit taxes levied during the war, and the wardrobe departments could hire new people. When Ellsworth became business agent for the costumers' local union in 1942, he was in a good position to push for improved status for both men and women costumers working in the studios and in the shops.

Today the new women on the set, as Ellsworth describes them, are bright, creative, and innovative. Many have taken courses in film in colleges and art schools from which they now have degrees. Women are now in supervisory positions and have the same status as men, that is, if they are young or "well-preserved" in their maturity. Ellsworth notes, however, that there is still residual discrimination in the industry's preference for younger women:

> They don't like old women around. They want younger girls. The average in the union now is ten years younger than in the 1930s. The average is thirty-five or forty, but that average is brought up by some women in their fifties or sixties. If women work themselves up as one of the people producers and directors have confidence in, there is no problem. In new people, they want younger women; but they have some very experienced women in their late fifties who are in demand all the time because they are good. . . .[33]

In order to break into the industry today, a woman must not only be knowledgeable but she must be young and attractive. Unfortunately there are very different expectations for women and men in this job, as it doesn't seem to matter to anyone how the male costumers dress for work.

The Union

Although Clara Kimball Young, a dramatic and glamorous silent-film star, established the importance of costumes for a leading lady as early as 1914, studio executives were generally indifferent to the clothing worn by actors. "So isolated and unorganized was the very concept of costume that it was not until approximately the mid-1920s that Famous Players-Lasky, forerunner of today's Paramount, felt impelled to establish its own costuming department."[34] But still, costuming was not respected and costumers were only called on the set now and then when an emergency arose.

In the union today, there are more than 60 classifications and more than forty-five rates of pay.[35] For over half a century, costumers have created garments that have exerted enormous influence throughout the world. In order to understand how the costumers' position in the Hollywood industry has changed over the past fifty years, we must look at the motivation of the first unionized costumers, the role the union has played in the development of the art of costuming, and the costumer's sense of professionalism.

Nineteen finished wardrobe women and men formed the first motion picture costumers union in 1929, organized as a federally chartered union of the American Federation of Labor. Until the late 1930s, the manufacturing and finished departments of the studios and costume houses continued to operate as open shops, that is, an individual could work in the studios without belonging to a union. In the early days of the Hollywood studio system, the costume department was a favorite place for studio bosses to place "girlfriends" and inept relatives for whom they could find no other job in the studios. This practice undermined serious union organization and also contributed to the generally low regard in which the costumers were held by their co-workers in other departments. Conditions and wages for the costumers were among the worst in the motion picture industry. As was the case with most unions in Hollywood before the New Deal legislation supporting union organization and collective bargaining, members of the costumers union caught soliciting other workers for union membership were often fired from their jobs. The early members of the motion picture unions had to be particularly dedicated and militant in their efforts to secure bargaining rights for better wages and working conditions.[36]

Georgina Grant, the daughter of a Scottish union organizer, was one of those early militant workers in the manufacturing branch of the industry. She has vivid memories of those aspects of her own job that led her to become a union member and organizer:

> Before unionization, I would go in at 7:00 a.m., get no break, and not get lunch at one o'clock. We worked Saturday and Sunday for the same wages we got during the week—18 dollars a week for six days a week for as many hours as they told you to stay. There was no vacation pay, holiday pay, or overtime—only straight salary. Sometimes, they would work you four hours and send you home and dock your weekly pay. You would get a day off during the week if they weren't busy. When I first went there, they could call me to work at four in the afternoon, just when you were sitting down to eat, and they would tell you, "Come in right now. And work these hours and find your way home any way you like." Women were afraid to walk home at night. There was always the pressure, and you didn't want to lose your job, so you kept your mouth shut lots of times. In 1935, any work was good work.[37]

This was during a period in which there was no social security, no unemployment compensation, and no pension plan. The union wanted to obtain several rights for its members, including protection from harassment for union activities, higher salaries, a guaranteed eight-hour work day, time and one half for any hours more than eight worked in a single day, specified lunch and break periods, and eight hours turnaround time between shifts worked by individual employees.

The studio manufacturing department employees were organized in the mid-1930s and joined Local 705 in 1941. Grant, who was instrumental in organizing the women in the MGM shop, recalls that she helped organize the union which she joined before 1937 at a great personal risk. The cutters and the fitters she worked with at that time were interested in the union so they had meetings in their homes. The "table ladies" (shop supervisors in women's manufacturing), didn't like union organizing because at that time they were in command, and such union activity threatened their power. Grant recalls:

> As in most places, the head of the workroom was quite powerful. They domineered us and this hurt us—hurt our feelings. I organized the whole work room, and all the girls joined. When the union finally began to get involved, the table ladies had to kowtow a bit and observe the rules.[38]

The costume house employees were the last to be organized and finally joined the union in 1944.[39]

Women costumers in both the manufacturing and finished departments were especially interested in getting equal pay for comparable work. In 1945, the costumers in manufacturing became the first group of craft workers in the studios to successfully negotiate a contract with the producers that afforded equal pay for male and female costumers in equivalent classifications. Although the tailors strenuously objected, the union equalized wages for seamstresses and tailors, largely because the women, according to Ted Ellsworth, "raised so much hell."[40]

Male costumers, doing the same work as female costumers on the set, were paid more on the basis of their "head of household" status, but this reasoning was galling to many of the women. Agnes Henry describes how her vote for the union was inspired by a different reasoning—that women's wardrobe is at least equal to and perhaps more important than men's because of the very nature of the industry:

> Personally, I felt that ladies' wardrobe was just as important as men's. With ladies, there is more required in putting everything together than there is with men—especially when you consider how Hollywood focuses on women and their role in being beautiful. When I could vote for equal pay, I put my hand up.[41]

Regardless of the focus of the industry and the complexity of their jobs, however, women in the finished department did not receive equal wages for comparable work until the 1970s.

Local 705 has had close to an equal number of men and women members for many years. Yet, unlike other Hollywood talent and craft unions with significant female membership, the members of Local 705 have never elected women as business agent or president. Ted Ellsworth, who served as business agent of Local 705 from the early 1940s to the early 1950s, felt that it was not a question of discrimination: "Women never wanted those positions; I've never considered why. Women have played important roles on committees, thought."[42] Agnes Henry, who did serve on committees and ran unsuccessfully for local vice-president in 1984, suggested that the union has never had a woman business agent because the small minority of members who actively participate in the union's internal affairs are afraid that a woman would not be as strong as a man at the bargaining table or in handling grievances. Henry notes a trend among younger women who tend to be less active in union affairs:

> I think the young people in the union might make changes, but they don't seem to have the time to come to meetings. I talk to young girls on the set and try to get them involved. A lot of them get complacent once they get into the union and feel that someone else should do the work.[43]

Henry's description of the younger women's attitudes might confirm Judith Stacey's analysis of the phenomenon of post-feminism—younger women who disassociate themselves from feminism as well as unionism and who take their current status for granted.[44] Nevertheless, Henry tries to get the younger, newer union members to understand that they need to actively participate in the union and that it was the struggles of women and men in recent history that made their current working conditions possible.

One long-time member of Local 705 stands out as a prime mover in the women's struggle for equity in the film industry and exemplifies the changes in the last forty years. Sheila O'Brien started in the Paramount manufacturing work room, moved into finished wardrobe, onto the set at MGM, and eventually became a costumer designer. Ted Ellsworth feels that the equalization of salaries for seamstresses and tailors in 1945 was due entirely to the efforts of Sheila and outspoken others who "simply wouldn't stand for lower pay for women."[45] O'Brien had been part of the Local 705 negotiating committee since the 1930s, and by the mid-1940s she had the respect of the producers' negotiating them. Thus, although O'Brien never was elected to the key positions in Local 705, she actually was a powerful behind-the-scenes force in Hollywood labor circles and served for many years on the executive board of Local 705.

In the late 1940s, O'Brien became a costume designer for Joan Crawford and for a period of time she worked both as a costumer and a designer. The costume designers had a guild in the 1950s, but this organization did not participate in collective bargaining with the producers. As the studio system broke down, long-term contracts with designers were dissolved. It was Sheila O'Brien who once again rose to the task, turning the informal guild into Costume Designer Guild IATSE Local 892. She became its first business agent and negotiated the first collective bargaining agreement between the designers and the producers.[46]

During the studio era, Local 705 was concerned with more than wages, benefits, grievances, and hiring practices. One special function that the union has undertaken since 1948 has been to sponsor the "Costumers' Ball," an annual event that serves the dual purpose of raising funds for the costumers' welfare fund and of recognizing the best costume work in the industry over the past year. The statuettes given out at the awards banquet, attended each year by the costumers as well as the stars they help to create, are appropriately called the "Adam and Eve" awards.

Conclusion

The union played a large part in developing a sense of professionalism among the costumers. It gave them better wages, conditions, and a sense of self-respect which costumers never had enjoyed in the pre-union days. It gave the costumers themselves, not the studio bosses, the chance to judge whether or not an individual was fit to be a co-worker.

On the one hand, to study the costumers' Local 705 is to study a microcosm of unions in general and sexism in the society at large. Women in Local 705 have never held the top positions of president or business agent, although they have typically agitated behind the scenes to alter the course of the union history. In the finished department, women have to be young, attractive, and knowledgeable to get the job, and personable, "well-kept," and proven excellent in the field in order to continue to be in demand.

On the other hand, the costumers have historically stood in a different relation to other unions and to U.S. society as a whole. In many respects, the costumers do *not* reflect the attitudes toward women of society at large in that they are one of the few unions in the U.S. that have had women members as founders and a nearly half-female membership. As early as 1945, the union successfully dealt with the issues of comparable worth in manufacturing, but it wasn't until the 1970s that the union resolved the comparable worth issues in the finished department.

During the studio era, skilled artisans were drawn to Hollywood to create clothing that was not only meant for actors to wear but for people to see. Since the wages of manufacturing employees were so low in the 1930s, one must assume that there was a special attraction in creating clothing that would become "bigger than life" on motion picture theater screens. For the manufacturing group, although the quality and manner of work has changed very little through the years—they must still be the very best seamstresses and tailors available—there are far fewer opportunities for employment today than there were in the studio era. For the finished group, the work for women has changed from that of maids and dressers to that of genuine creative collaborators in motion picture production. The choices that key costumers exercise in selecting costumes affect the way in which audiences "read" characters in films and the nitpicking attention of the set costumers helps to avoid breaks in continuity, thus aiding in the all-important suspension of disbelief requisite to our enjoyment of the entertainment.

10

Costume and Narrative: How Dress Tells the Woman's Story

Jane Gaines

In *The Costume Designer,* a 1949 educational short on Hollywood studio production, Edith Head, in voiceover, describes the thought processes of the designer as film clips illustrating her method of costuming character appear on the screen. Head describes the character as a twenty-year-old woman from a wealthy family. The young woman is dressing for an evening social engagement with an old friend, but she is unhappy because she has just quarreled with the man she loves. "Should the costumer put her in something white, gay, and frothy, or in a more sophisticated and clinging jersey?" asks Head. "But wait a minute! She *cries* just before she leaves for her date. That's a big emotional moment and deserves all the emphasis it can get," the designer explains. As the costume of the actress on the screen dissolves from a slinky, sequined evening dress to white flowing chiffon, Head describes this softer effect as her solution to the narrative problem.

Edith Head's decision is based on the motion picture costumer's code which weighs design against dramatic content. Of all of the designers from the classical period, Head most fully articulated this costume-narrative tension and she continually returned to this theme in numerous interviews and magazine articles as well as in her autobiographies.[1] As Maureen Turim emphasizes elsewhere in this collection, Head was often credited with producing 'storytelling wardrobes." Her examples, then, demonstrate more clearly for us what Hollywood creative personnel meant by letting the costume "tell the woman's story," a phrase which appears frequently in screen designers' descriptions of their craft. A closer examination of the work of key designers, however, shows that costume was severely restricted in what it was allowed to "tell," with some exceptions which I will discuss. This restriction has to do with the primary function of costuming in classical realist cinema where every element in the mise-en-scene—from painted backdrop to prop to lighting cue—serves the higher purpose of the narrative.

In this essay, then, I will consider the constraint on screen design in terms of the antithetical relation between costume and narrative. Clothes, as lower elements in a hierarchy of screen discourses, primarily work to reinforce narrative ideas. On occasion, an accessory planted as a prop may come to narrative fruition. A telltale glove or shoe (or Head's own example, the scarf with which the heroine is strangled), may start out as part of an ensemble and later serve to advance the narrative.[2] But primarily costumes are fitted to characters as a second skin, working in this capacity for the cause of narrative by relaying informationto the viewer about a "person." Thus, I will also be concerned here with the nineteenth-century notion of "personality" as it applies to the clothing of the self.

Since the following is the briefest introduction to an area that has thus far been literally untouched by film scholars, I am limiting my examples as much as possible to black and white contemporary dress drama. In the first two parts, I sketch out some of the history of motion picture costume design, taking account of the transition from silent to sound technology. A third part describes the classical star-designer relationship. The special problems posed by color processes and period dress, and the exceptions represented by such genres as the western and the musical are beyond the scope of this basic inquiry.[3] However, in the fourth and last section I will make some remarks about melodramatic form as well as the woman's picture as genre since historically it is the *woman's* story that is told in dress. Although all characters, regardless of gender, are conceived as "costumed" in motion pictures, a woman's dress and demeanor, much more than a man's, indexes psychology; if costume represents interiority, it is she who is turned inside out on screen.

Costume in Silent Film

From the mid-teens, I find such a close link made between dressing the part and playing the part that it is almost as though "acting" for the female silent film player consisted of nothing more than stepping into and out of different costumes. This conception may have to do with the way motion pictures were costumed before the advent of the studio designers. Originally, the aspiring actress was expected to purchase her own contemporary screen wardrobe which had to include at least one evening dress and an outfit for every possible daytime occasion.[4] "Dressing for the Movies," one of the earliest articles on the subject, appearing in *Photoplay* in 1915, describes the job of the actress as entailing designing as well as sewing the costumes required by the part.[5] Interpreting the role for the silent actress also meant translating character into costume by means of the "dress plot," a kind of scenario indicating all of her wardrobe changes. In later years, under the studio system, the designer rather than the actress translated the script into a costume plot; after designers were phased out, this "plot" was treated as the kind of continuity record which Elizabeth Nielsen describes in her history of the costumers union included this collection. Before Before Erté, Chanel, and Schiaparelli were hired to bring French couture to the screen, actresses were literally their own designers, although as they became stars they no longer did their own sewing.[6] Instead, the stars' original designs were rendered by a personal tailor or modiste.[7] Significant here is the evolution of the distinction between street wear and motion picture costume, a change which paralleled the development of stardom. The issue of ordinary clothing versus costume was first expressed in the predicament of the struggling picture actresses who, to make ends meet, had to appear in different roles wearing the same gowns, or, had to make their screen clothes double as everyday dress.[8] Behind this doubling-up function is the assumption that costume for contemporary motion picture drama was not different from ordinary dress, and for a brief period in the early teens, these practices were defended on the basis of verisimilitude. Very quickly, however, the development of a costume aesthetic specifically fitted to the screen began to pose a challenge to the realist position which favored everyday wear over special costuming.[9] Eventually, discourse about costume would become locked into this contradiction which came to a head in the mixed message of costumers' advice to female viewers circulated by publicity departments: *Do* copy what the stars wear on the screen, but *don't* wear screen styles because they are too exaggerated.

One unusual article from the teens, "How I Teach My Gowns to Act," exemplifies again this idea of the costume as actually taking a role or part, but goes on to attempt a definition of a cinematic costume aesthetic. Actress Marguerite Courtot is quoted on the importance of line, contrast, and tone value. The need to "render" color in black and white, she says, points up the advantage of a specifically cinematic dress as opposed to an ordinary dress which might not make a strong enough screen statement.[10] In the process of formulating the new rules of screen costume, these early articles espouse two antithetical values at once: costume must *register* on the screen at the same time it must *recede*. However, during these years, costume had more opportunity to register than it would in later years. Silent film costuming was marked by a gratuitous flourishing which was "toned down" after sound. In the earlier period, one finds examples of camera concentration on a costume detail; aesthetic coordination of costume and sets (Natasha Rambova's art nouveau costume designs for *Camille* [1921] and *Salome* [1923]); and camera movement organized

Figure 10.1 *The Kiss* (1929). Adrian's costumes for Garbo coordinated with the art deco interior. MGM, courtesy of BFI Stills Archive.

around the display of an entire costume. An especially interesting example of all of these possibilities can be found in Jacques Feyder's *The Kiss* (1929), in which costume is coordinated with the art deco decor (Figure 10.1), but also, as in the opening sequence where Greta Garbo meets her lover in an art museum, camerawork and editing seek out all of the details of her Adrian-designed fox fur-trimmed coat, afternoon dress, and cloche hat. A clue to the attitude that costume can be a dangerous signifier is the containment of unbridled visual display within dream sequences (*Forbidden Fruit*, 1921 and *Male and Female*, 1919), and fashion sequences (*Fig Leaves*, 1926) (discussed elsewhere in this collection by Jeanne Allen and Charlotte Herzog). Outside these conventional boundaries, in the dining room or parlor, the elaborate costume, like poor etiquette at a dinner party, could claim undue attention for its wearer. Thus Courtot, in describing a cerise velvet gown featuring black chiffon sleeves with matching fox fur trim and silver lace at the hem, explains that "one must see to it that these daring bits of fur must never over-act," for "any subtle acting of the wearer would be lost along side of the gown screaming its presence."[11]

And yet the opposite of the detail which "overacted," the dress with no distinctive styling or detail whatever, could not "act" at all according to Courtot who thus describes the problem:

> For instance, the other day I was shown a draped chiffon gown of exquisite orchid shades. Not only were the variations of tone insufficient to register any contrast on the screen, but the ineffectual, caught-here-and-there draperies were meaningless. These hanging lengths of lovely color could neither festoon with joy nor droop for dejection . . .[12]

What this suggests, however, is that not only did the screen costume need to exhibit a sufficient contrast of light and dark and a strong line in order to make an interesting photographic composition, but that it had to have the kind of style and fabric combination which served the narrative by restating the emotions which the actress conveyed through gesture and movement. Stepping into a costume, *was* like stepping into a role. Costumes, furthermore, were expected to express the *same* feelings ("joy" or "dejection") called for in the part. And here I emphasize "same" to call attention to a pair of assumptions underlying these early discussions of character and costume. One assumption is that a role can and should only be costumed *with* rather than against the personality of the character. (For Courtot, the design qualities which contradict her conception of her role do not signify disguise or discrepancy, a counter-meaning, but "meaninglessness.")

In other words, there is a notion of personhood in operation here which assumes a continuity between inner and outer rather than two discrepant parts. But the other related assumption (only too familiar to us at the end of the twentieth century), is that dress is a key to the personality of the wearer. In fact, in this discourse, dress becomes somewhat more than a key or an indicator since "personality" and "dress" are so often confused that it would seem that they have become the same thing. We are, after all, talking about two distinct orders of things—human beings and material goods. Why ascribe the same attributes to clothing as one would ascribe to a person?

The idea of dress as the key to the self is not confined to discussions of acting and costuming, but also informs the practice of silent film screenwriting. Frederick Palmer, in the chapter on "Visualization" in his 1922 manual, tells aspiring screenwriters to study character by observing gloves, shoes, and jewelry, because "So much of character is told in one's manner of wearing clothes."[13] Clothes and mannerisms in these early manuals are not vehicles for conveying the sense of a "real" person nor are they elements utilized in the craft of character construction, they are "truths" told about persons. Character writing here depends on an idea that real selves (rather than types) can be studied by reading appearance signs which are communicated in public. Another manual contains this advice:

> Not one of us but is shouting his or her personal characteristics every minute of every day by the clothes we wear and the way we wear them,and the creative writer can be on the lookout for these tiny indications.[14]

For the observer as well as the aspiring actress, choosing clothes is conflated into the manner of wearing them. They are simply a matter of the expression of the self. This kind of observation was then a much simpler matter before Erving Goffman called our attention to the difference between the expressions which a person "gives" as opposed to those he "gives off," as well as to the problem of the impression which is received by others.[15]

This notion of clothes as self-expression is a product of a combination of the late nineteenth-century sense of public self-in-urban-space developing in Western industrial culture and a Platonic understanding of the matter/spirit dichotomy. Carlyle expresses this in his admission that, although clothes are "despicable" they are unquestionably significant because they are vehicles for the soul. Clothes should thus be seen as the matter necessary to "body forth an idea."[16] The problem of the public self which made immediate impressions and the true self which was within, was dealt with in the possibility of personality management and improvement which historians of modern society find emerging at the turn of the century. Not surprisingly, the evolution of the contemporary sense of "how to" make a personal impression on others coincides with the appearance of the vanguard institutions of the consumer culture—the department store and the nickelodeon.[17]

In the century before, as Richard Sennett tells us, the social vogue had been marked by a sense of the discontinuity between the person and the dress, or the belief that the true self was quite safe from public eyes which might see connections between one's body and one's soul.[18] At the root of this earlier version of selfhood was the Enlightenment conviction that natural character, which connected all humans, was fixed at birth.[19] The exterior, divorced from the interior, could be used ironically in any imaginable way—hence the eighteenth-century moment in costume history in which the body was most literally nothing more than a mannequin on which to hang clothes.[20] As Sennett describes the historical abandonment of the permanently fixed natural character and the adoption of the modern personality, the new notion no longer depended upon an idea of separate parts, but on the inextricable connection between the inner and the outer. While it would seem that this understanding of the personality as a constructed or cultivated self would give individuals a sense of social confidence in facing a world of strangers, the Victorians, as Sennett describes them, assumed a sophisticated anonymity in their dress and demeanor out of concern that their exterior appearance (and details of sexuality and class in particular) would betray them.[21]

One has to ask if this idea of the involuntary expression is not fundamentally at odds with a new conviction that personality could be acquired and perfected. (But this, as we know, is still an enigma to us in the later part of the twentieth century!) In "Expression of the Emotions," a series of articles by Eugene Brewster appearing in the early years of *Photoplay,* the author explains silent film acting in terms of the exteriorized social personality which he understands as a combination of contrivance and involuntary expression. He bases a case for the ease with which which audiences followed silent acting techniques on this theory of the personality:

> We learn to drive a sharp bargain, to put our best foot forward, to conceal our weaknesses, to exaggerate our good points, and in various ways to create a good impression, all of which necessitate acquiring control of our emotions and of our modes of expressing them. And in so doing we learn to express false emotions.[22]

We want to ask how the motion picture theatergoer could be assured that he or she could correctly read silent film gesture, posture, or dress by pointing out the incidence of dissemblance in human self-presentation. Although the same notion of personality as a socially decipherable self whose inner and outer layers were in tune informed both social costuming and theatrical stage dress, a dual set of rules was involved. Where the former was thought to involve some subterfuge, the latter was expected to reveal a character (confirming how people of different gender, age, nationality, and social class were thought to be in "real life"), for the convenient comprehension of an audience.[23]

In some ways, silent film costuming developed along with the same psychological realism seen in the evolution of theatrical as well as motion picture acting styles in the teens.[24] A new code of naturalism stressed individuated characters over types and emphasized the face, eyes, and lips as conveyors of "interiority."[25] It is in the discussion of acting (which costuming discourse has historically echoed) that one finds the articulation of the idea that the interior can be registered visibly on the theory that there is a direct line of communication between interior and exterior. Although this early literature does not suggest that an actor or actress drew on previous experience in the portrayal of character emotion (as it later would), acting did involve drawing from an existing reserve within; costuming evidenced this evocation at the same time it facilitated it. Clara Kimball Young, in an early *Photoplay* article describes the way the color in the costume she wore brought out "latent elements" in herself:

> To some women red is like a fire, bringing out the glow. To others red is deadening, as if it killed their paler fires. Unless a woman feels that red is essentially related to something within herself, she should avoid wearing it as she would the plague. On the other hand, if she can wear red, she should wear it at such times as she desires to express these qualities that its warmth and richness bring out by its contact with herself.[26]

The notion that costuming "brought forth" traits would continue into the sound era and appear repeatedly as one of the justifications for the lavishness of star costuming in the studio era. In the production of black and white films, the special care taken with the use of color was generally attributed to the boon it afforded the actors who could not be expected to project realistic emotions if they were costumed only in shades of grey. A legendary mystique even seems to have arisen around the invisible detail which secretly helped certain actresses to perform, a variation on the actor's practice of putting on a costume as a means of learning about a character. The painstaking work of the costumer—embroidering the star's initial on the inside of a glove, lining a jacket with silk crepe, or adding extra rows of lace to the bottom of a petticoat—was elevated because it aided an actress in the realization of the character.[27]

Thus in the discourse on costume, dress, like an expression of emotion, seemed to grow out of the mysteries of the body. This close association with the body helped to construct costume as behavior, an indicator which in popular usage could subsume the social, moral, and psychological:

> The dowd dresses dowdily, the woman of spirit and originality dresses that way, the business woman dresses in simple tailor-made things, and the adventuress dresses to lure.[28]

But note here that dress is charged with expressing only one trait or reinforcing one quality. While the body was used in acting to express emotional complexities and to enunciate subtle gradations of feeling, costume was expected to simplify. Costume detail was "fixed" in the Panofskian sense in that it stood, again and again, for the same thing, and could be counted on to provide the most basic information about a character for the spectator, that is, it typified.[29] And because of this typifying function, I would contend, film theory has historically lumped costume along with furniture under the category of iconography.

Not only did costume, like decor, provide iconographic cues related to typage and narrative conventions; in the absence of sound it was seen as a substitute for speech. "Dressing for the Movies" goes on to describe how "The elimination of voice from the picture dramas calls the greater attention to movement and raiment."[30] Since these elements were conceived as standing in for the missing dialogue, for audiences, attending to costume and gesture was somewhat like listening. Mary Ann Doane describes the displacement of speech in silent cinema, "The absent voice re-emerges in gestures and the contortions of the face—it is spread over the body of the actor."[31] If the voice is spread over the body, however, it is spread unevenly, with expressivity concentrated on the upper parts. Yes, vocal enunciation is dispersed over the body, but the uneven distribution of "speech," favoring the fingers, eyes, and lips, suggests the hierarchy of vehicles of expression alluded to earlier. Dress, even in coordination with the movement of the torso and arms, is not conceived as having the eloquence of eyes or lips. If it "speaks," it is treated rather like the flat character who is never given more than one line to deliver. In silent cinema, this line was usually either: "I am the vamp" or "I am the straight girl."[32]

Costume in the Sound Era

The rules of costume and typage—that the dress should place a character quickly and efficiently, identifying her in one symbolic sweep—were held over into the sound era where they coexisted with ideas about a new realism in dress which meant both subtlety and contemporary fashion-consciousness. Edith Head, who began work at Paramount after the silent era, has insisted that costume should carry enough information about characters so that the audience could tell something about them if the sound went off in the theater.[33] Since in the sound era narrative came to depend more and more on dialogue to establish identity and reveal interiority, this might have meant that costume could be relieved of its old responsibility. But the discourse on costume still remained centered on character coherence. The use of bold design, enlarged detail, and exaggerated shapes was consistently defended not as aesthetic interest in and of itself but as the need to make a character statement.

The legacy of the silent era was really a tendency toward metaphorical literalization in costume design. Take, for example, costuming for the type of the dangerous woman in both silent and sound periods. In 1914, vampiress Theda Bara, in *A Fool There Was,* is literally embalmed to the neck in the sack-like full-length coats and dresses she wore in scenes where she attached herself to the throats of her victims. As a man-trap in *I'm No Angel* (1933), Mae West is costumed by Travis Banton in a black

Figure 10.2 *I'm No Angel* (1934). Travis Banton's rhinestone spiderweb pattern on Mae West. Paramount Pictures, courtesy of the Museum of Modern Art Stills Archives.

chiffon with diaphonous sleeves decorated with rhinestones in the design of a spiderweb (Figure 10.2). In *The Little Foxes* (1941), Bette Davis, the predatory Regina, wears a huge hat decorated with a literal bird of prey (Figure 10.3). All of Davis's dresses in this period film (designed by Orry-Kelly) feature long tight sleeves, some of which extend beyond the hand like claws.

As Edith Head's commentary on characterization reveals, a designer is

Figure 10.3 *The Little Foxes* (1941). Orry-Kelly transforms Bette Davis into a bird of prey. Warner Brothers, courtesy of the Museum of Modern Art Stills Archives.

desinger is using

using metaphors in this way every time he or she translates a character trait—such as that of "female" wickedness or destructiveness—into an item of apparel. Asked in an interview how she would costume various types, Head does not hesitate, saying that to her, a self-centered woman translated into a "covered-up look," a generous woman into "clothes that look easy and give a little," and a shy or rigid woman into clothing with a collar standing up around her face, cuffs that extend over her hands, and ruffles.[34] What is interesting here is that while this stated theory of costuming was committed to the humanist notion of a unified self, unstated costume practice, when not reined in by producers, could and did suggest characters as complexly divided selves.

The stated theory of character costuming, then, holds that the costumer's creative process works through equivalences and is like other processes of adaptation in which different artistic systems are consciously compared. Dudley Andrew's work on transposing novels into film is relevant here, particularly as he discusses adaptation as a common aesthetic practice which often goes unnoticed. Essentially, adaptation is nothing more than a kind of borrowing in which one aesthetic domain is raided to enrich another, he says. The search for equivalence, more specifically, has to do with lining up two domains and "matching" the terms in each. Citing the work of art historians E.H. Gombrich and Nelson Goodman, whose analyses of adaptation as systematic exchange predate semiotic theory, Andrew describes adaptation as "searching two systems of communication for elements of equivalent position in the systems capable of eliciting a signified at a given level of pertinence. . ."[35] By pairing signifieds, colors are translated into musical tones, vegetables are understood as animals, and fabrics are transposed into character traits. In the fabric system, for instance, wool tweed corresponds with "serious," black satin with "wicked" or "decadent," and tulle is "lighthearted." Such an equivalence between fabric and mood informs Carole Lombard's warning, "Don't discuss politics in tulle!"[36]

In costume discourse, what is semiotically nothing more than a mis-matching of two systems, whether mood, occasion, or personality system, often takes on connotations of moral prohibition and becomes an "inappropriate" choice. "Appropriate" costuming for character is rather like the value of fidelity in literary-film adaptation. It depends on creating the impression of "rightness" by striving for exact connotative equivalence for items drawn from relatively unlike systems. Frequent use of such combinations or coupling of items establishes the rule or code, and eventually this coding becomes "naturalized."

The highly ideological process of naturalization, as Stuart Hall describes it, depends on customary use. Or, as he says, the existence of naturalized codes is the result of the "degree of habituation produced when there is fundamental alignment and reciprocity . . . between the encoding and decoding sides of an exchange of meanings."[37] The perfect connotative match between systems also makes an easy argument for an existential connection between two terms, and, in the case of costume, this naturalization helps to reassert again that the personality finds its direct manifestation in manner of dress. The naturalization of the costume/character relation is such that the more perfect the fit between the two systems, the less the

Figure 10.4 *No More Ladies* (1935). Crawford's starched pique collar—Adrian's costume excess unmotivated by character. MGM, courtesy of the Museum of Modern Art Stills Archives.

costume will be seen as costume; at some point, we will see a character as merely wearing clothes.

Film scholars have theorized classical realist cinema as a finely tuned naturalization machine which presents to the viewer a perfectly contained world that is an apparent continuation of the one in which he or she lives. The smooth running of the narrative is produced by erasing any signs that it is different from the actual world and by tightly coordinating its various parts. In this economy of classical cinema, costume signs are rationed for the sake of the unity of the work. As much as is possible, the presence of costume must be justified or motivated by characterization.

To give an example of what can happen when a stylistic flourish is not adequately motivated by character, one could compare two different collars designed by Adrian for Joan Crawford. The starched pique collar seen on the Marcia character in *No More Ladies* (1935), a farce about infidelity, went so far beyond the function of characterization that fan magazine writers singled it out for humorous commentary, referring to it as a nun's habit turned upside down (Figure 10.4). In contrast, on the stenographer Flaemmchen in *Grand Hotel* (1932), Adrian's asymmetrical collar is justified, as it helps to create the characterization of a loose-moraled woman whose clothes are always slightly askew (Figures 10.5 & 10.6). Or, designer Walter Plunkett could attach a life-size bird resting on a branch to the bodice of Jennifer Jones's gown in *Madame Bovary* (1949), since it signifies Emma's misinterpretation of aristocratic tastes (Figure 10.7).

In the service of narrative ideas costume is assigned one main function: characterization. In this capacity, costume also works to blend straggling physiological signifiers so that they contribute to character. Here, Stephen Heath, describing the circularity of the actor, person, and character relation, has referred to costume as well as make-up as "absorbing face and body into character significance."[38] (As I point out in the introduction to this volume, however, the actual process is less benign, since actresses' bodies are often painfully restructured by designers.) Costume assimilates bodily signifiers into character, but body as a whole engulfs the dress. Hence the paradox of costume transparency. Costume historian Anne Hollander explains the invisibility of theatrical dress:

> Costumes are so thoroughly identified with bodies that the messages they send are received without acknowledgement, even though an extraordinary emotional power can be generated by the use of very specific, noticeable things—the right use of a black cape, a white scarf, or a pair of bare feet.[39]

Thus it is that costume is eclipsed by both character and body at the expense of developing its own aesthetic discourse. Bound to character and body, it is socialized, conventionalized, tamed. Like make-up on the face, costume is invisible as it is present,[40] and the irony of the concern over costume superfluity is that the real but unforeseen danger is not in too much costume, but in the total absence of it—the body naked.

With the coming of sound, and eventually color, those additional details which seemed to promise the approximation of the real also became a threat to the establishment of the realist aesthetic itself. Here I want to call particular attention to the importance of narrative continuity as it constructs the illusion of the real. Costume, like sound and color, has the potential to distract the viewer from the narrative, which could result in breaking the illusion and the spell of realism. An early Society of Motion Picture and Television Engineers manual on color technology uses costume as a comparison with color to illustrate the rules of continuity cinema. Color, like costume detail, could become "clutter" on the screen unless restricted and held to its character identification function.[41] But costume was to be given little more to do than insure that the character was clearly *seen*. If costume did not "punctuate" the actor against the backdrop the

Figure 10.5 Adrian's asymmetrical collar on Crawford's loose-moraled stenographer—design motivated by character. MGM, courtesy of Academy of Motion Pictures Arts and Sciences Stills Archives.

viewer might not be able to "follow the story."[42] Here, costume helps to tell the story merely by insuring that the viewer can distinguish the narrative agent from other elements in the mise-en-scene. In the ecosystem of classical cinema, telling the story requires subordinating an especially evocative aesthetic to narrative designs.

Figure 10.6   Adrian's asymmetrical collar on Crawford's loose-moraled stenographer—design motivated by character. MGM, courtesy of Academy of Motion Pictures Arts and Sciences Stills Archives.

Hollywood directors in the sound era, when asked about costuming, have consistently insisted that the costume's contribution to telling the story called for subservience to it. George Cukor, who can be associated with some of the most interesting designing for black and white sound film, such as Adrian's work on *Camille* (1936) and *The Women* (1939), is quoted in an interview as saying that he did not have a favorite costume because the ideal costume was the one that most perfectly "suited the scene." If the costume "knocked your eye out," he goes on, it was not good for the scene or for the entire film.[43] The rule is that costumes should be modulated, much like orchestral underscoring for Hollywood melodrama which was so carefully matched with emotional connotations that it was heard but not noticed. The costumer's formula, as Alice Evans Field defines it, requires that clothes be "*harmonized*" to the mood, be it

Figure 10.7 *Madame Bovary* (1949). The awkward and ridiculous bird perched on the bodice of Emma's ball gown—Walter Plunkett's design for Jennifer Jones. MGM, courtesy of Academy of Motion Pictures Arts and Sciences Stills Archives.

comedy, tragedy or romance; they must add subtly to the *grace* of the wearer; and they must enhance the rhythmic flow of the story. Never must they call undue attention to themselves, unless for sharp definition of character, and they must have originality of detail within the certain bounds of good taste."[44] Narrative realism dictates that costume be curtailed by conventional dress codes; continuity requires that it be monitored for the telltale continuity error; economy requires that it reinforce causality.

The directorial practices informed by this notion of costume as servant of narrative ideas, then, were at odds with any vision of costume as spectacular design that might have no other purpose than to feed a visual appetite. Directors might plan compositions that would lop off exquisitely detailed handiwork around a hem, or block a scene with indifference to the back interest focal point of a gown, as is the case with Adrian's bias-cut satin gown with cut-out sleeves, scarcely seen on Jean Harlow in *China Seas* (1935) (Figure 10.8). The practice of cutting films for narrative coherence and visual continuity meant that close-ups which featured design interest around the collar disappeared in the final print and even that many costumes created for the production would be edited out of the film

Figure 10.8   *China Seas* (1935). Back interest in Adrian's bias-cut dress for Jean Harlow. MGM, courtesy of Academy of Motion Pictures Arts and Sciences Stills Archives.

but would show up in studio publicity stills.[44] As a guide to costume in motion pictures in the studio era, old fan magazines, star biographies, and glossy cocktail table books are often misleading since they reconstruct the golden age from production stills which are pre-release records of the publicity image of a new production. In comparison with these production stills, the costumes as filmed in final scenes are often a disappointment.

The fashion coverage in popular magazines from the period, as well as the nostalgia books read in retrospect, portray the contemporary trend-setting on the screen as unproblematic, as though all Hollywood creative personnel had as much enthusiasm for fashion developments as the women in the audiences. Directors, however, disassociated themselves from this trend-setting, and generally held the belief that motion pictures should not "cater" to fashion.[46] In addition, the designers themselves often denied that they were trying to "set styles." Costume extravagance came to be associated with consumerism, which meant that it was a double threat— to narrative coherence as we have seen—and to a notion of art that stands apart from the vicissitudes of commerce.

Certainly there is a contradiction here since Hollywood productions have historically been unabashedly commercial. The motion picture industry in this period, however, represented its product as uplifting entertainment which stood outside time and was never "dated." The industry avoided tying in so closely with the woman's fashion trade that it would be required to refer to the seasonal shifts which stimulated the retail clothing business. The 1930s phenomenon described in Charles Eckert's article reprinted here was an exception. In part, the retail tie-in was cooperative advertising, an effort to counteract the economic effects of the Depression. However, it is best to see the collaboration between Hollywood and Seventh Avenue as a publicist's vision, a reality at the distribution, not the production, end. Because of the tensions created within the film itself by competing discourses—the rhetoric of costume and contemporary style consciousness as against narrative coherence and economy—the interest in style and the work of the studio designers had to be deflected elsewhere. And here the institution of stardom worked to divert the superfluity which could not be contained in the ninety-minute feature.

Star Designing

The institution of stardom directed the superfluity of costume (and the crasser extremes of commerce) away from the film itself and then redirected interest back to it. As I see stardom in relation to costume in the 1920s through the 1950s, the institution establishes a marketable entity which could carry the extra charge of glamour and the overload of emotion. Building on the work of Richard Dyer (who originally theorized the star actor and the sum of his or her star vehicles as a continuous text), I am suggesting that there was an easy carry over of the costume excesses from film to star.[47] The "clothes horse" stars, Joan Crawford and Kay Francis, were thus produced as style-setting tangents to their star vehicles. A fan could even follow these stars or the lesser fashion plate figures—Claudette Colbert, Loretta Young, and Delores Del Rio—without ever seeing them in their motion picture roles, for they were each constructed as much by publicity releases and women's page fashion features as by their performances. Looking at the phenomenon of high visibility celebrity, semiotic theory sees the constant deferral of meaning in which the multiplicity of determinations keeps the star semiotically active. Stephen Heath's theorization of the "shifting circulation" between narrative agent, character, person, and image, in which no term "settles" or exclusively determines the contents of stardom, explains why commonsense knowledge finds it so difficult to reduce the star to a final key to the meaning of contemporary society.[48] But an understanding of stardom as circulating also explains why different interests have been able to exploit the star from so many angles while still maintaining the fiction of a person and the requisite single point of coherence.

The companion institution and ideology of the star designer—the artist genius who invented the actress much as the Svengali-likedirector—was instrumental; he helped to formulate a point of coherence and to channel the costume excess into the star as a marketable entity. I say "he" because the Svengali model developed in the classic cases (Travis Banton-Marlene Dietrich, Orry-Kelly-Bette Davis, Gilbert Adrian-Joan Crawford and Greta Garbo) remained the dominant one. Edith Head, in contrast, is not seen as having created Dorothy Lamour, Barbara Stanwyck, or Elizabeth Taylor in the same way, and although Mae West would design her own image, it still was executed in costume terms by Travis Banton and Edith Head.

What I would argue is that the star designer had a particular role in the maintenance of two mutually supportive monopolies—the studio's exclusive control of the star property and the star's exclusive right to the construction which he or she claimed as a "self." While the fact that the studio exercised complete control over the action during this period has been well established, the idea of the star's control of the self as a "personal monopoly" comes from Barry King's recent work on the star actor. As King analyzes the economics of the star system, the "personal monopoly" is a response to an oversupply of actors and significant here is the development of an inextricable link between the person and the screen image. This unity, King says, depends on the creation of an off-screen life or public "conduct" predicated on the existential connection between person and image.[49] King replaces Richard Dyer's concept of "star image" in his theory with the notion of persona (the person and image united), which has the advantage of positing this synthetic amalgam as yet another character.[50]

The persona is the marketable character which takes material form in the star designer's costuming; the work of the designer was especially important here, for he created the overriding persona through the medium of the star's personal wardrobe, one which was a continuation of the costumes the designer made for the star's characters. The earliest view of costuming, the silent film dictum that motion picture costumes for "true-to-life" characters should be no different from street clothes was then reversed. The off-screen wardrobe now had to be similar to the on-screen costume in its exaggerated qualities and had to carry over a definitive style, testifying that the woman who wore the off- as well as the on-screen clothes by the star designer was, in fact, the same individual. In the service of the star's personal monopoly, personality (as expressed through dress) takes on a new importance as the guarantee of the real person in the role— the insurance that the off-screen and on-screen characters are the same.

In the era of the studio designer, costuming no longer "brings out" traits in the actress of its own accord (as Clara Kimball Young described the actress-costume relation in silent film). Star designing effects the synthesis between character and actress, intermingling traits in such a way that the two become indistinguishable. By way of example, let me quote a representative description of the star designing process as explained to the fan magazine reader:

> First: Take stock, not of your body, but of your mind! That is what Adrian does to each star with whom he works. Even before attempting sketches he talks with her, gets her slant on life. Not, if you please, the life she totes out for the benefit of her public, but her private one which is the key to her personality. He tries to feel what is really going on inside that beautiful head of hers. Then, if he designs her clothes for private life, they are the expression of that, and that alone. For picture purposes, of course, Adrian must also determine how the character she is to portray thinks, and then blend the two—for that is how she will appear on thescreen.[51]

To illustrate this, Adrian explains his conception of the character in *Queen Christina* (1933) as a "blend" of Garbo's "originality" and the real queen's "cleverness."[52]

But why the insistence that the "truth" of the self is a product of the mind rather than the body? For one thing, this insistence affirms the need for the designer, the expert who will interpret the person and whose costume diagnosis will "bring out" hidden traits. This emphasis on personality over body also stresses uniqueness and individuation which serves to divert our attention from the way the star always functions as a type, one of the most important assertions of Richard Dyer's work on star acting.[53] Furthermore, to add to Dyer, the notion of a real personality as opposed to a body type masks the way in which star image/persona is often a kind of caricature or emblem derived from the actress's underlying skeletal structure. The characterization of Garbo as having the "quality of old world repose," for instance, is an articulation of the famous slouch, and Norma Shearer, who was physically short and compact, became known for her "tailored personality," which combined her fashion diagnosis based on body type with an idea of a real self.[54] The irony of the use of costuming to demark personalities is that at the same time the artist designer individuated actresses, he created for an ideal impossible body. Adrian's sketch of a gown for Norma Shearer in *Escape* (1940) is the long-limbed, slim-hipped, broad-shouldered shape which fashion myth holds he derived from Joan Crawford's body (Figure 10.9). Actually, Adrian sketched this same 1940s silhouette for every model for nearly thirty years.

Star designing as it supports star acting, then, creates a personal monopoly as it articulates a quickly comprehensible character, the entity which includes person and image and guarantees that an individual with a distinct personality stands behind this public character. Since star acting as a mode of performance often appears to be self-evident because of its prevalence, let me suggest how it compares with another model of performance, and, finally, how star designing as opposed to other costume traditions and practices serves particular economic interests. Pertinent here is the principle Richard Dyer has called the star-character "fit," a principle which has undergone some refinement in Barry King's analysis of star acting.[55] King makes a distinction between the theatrical ideal of impersonation (in which the actor's performance so successfully foregrounds the role that the actor "disappears" into the character) and star acting (which is effectively personification). Schools of acting (and audiences who subscribe to the notion of believability) value impersonation, the performance in which the actor is effaced. These naturalistic schools hold that physiognomy as well as technique must evaporate on stage. Personification, held in less esteem because it is popularly understood as an actor "playing himself or herself," is based on the coincidence of character and person and thought to require no "acting" in the traditional histrionic sense.[56]

Although star designing is thoroughly committed to foregrounding the star, the value of impersonation over personificationhas still held. The ideal in this way becomes the transformation of the star that plays on a fascination with masquerade while remaining a transformation that stops short of complete disguise. Edith Head expresses this contradictory ideal in her comment that what the designer strives for is to "shock" the viewer into saying, "I don't believe that's Grace Kelly after all."[57] The job of the star designer, then, is to be sure that the actress does not completely disappear into the character, for the eclipse of the star in the film is akin to marketing a consumer good without prominent placement of the manufacturer's trademark. Something of the way the star design functioned historically to secure the monopoly the studio held on the star

Figure 10.9   *Escape* (1940). Adrian's idealized sketch for Norma Shearer. MGM, courtesy of Academy of Motion Pictures Arts and Sciences Stills Archives.

product is suggested in Jack Warner's worry that Paul Muni was so convincing in his role in *Juarez* (1939), that audiences would not recognize the expensive Warner Brothers property.[58] Costume as total disguise, as a misleading indicator of identity, as remnant of an older theatrical tradition, of carnival and ritual, is also incompatible with the narrative rule of coherence. As tangent to the film, then, the star carries off the artifice and the extravagance where it can be relished and reclaimed by female fans, costume collectors, and her gay camp following, thus recycling the excess which returns these enthusiasts to the films for years later.[59]

Costume and Melos

Finally I want to suggest what happens in some genres during particular periods in cinema history when costume has not been reined in, and where the relative sartorial effulgence suggests a larger connotative investment in this layer of mise- en-scene. This is the case with the melodramas produced by the major studios in the 1920s through the 1950s, and I would argue that the work of the designers on these films can be read as the most fully developed rhetoric of motion picture costume. The costumes in many of the films which have come to constitute the canon for melodrama studies are the work of the legendary design talent who, with the studio resources behind them, saw their wildest visions and most outrageous whims made into clothes.

To give only a few examples, *Now Voyager* (1942) and *Dark Victory* (1939), as well as the majority of the Bette Davis star vehicles at Warner Brothers, were designed by Orry-Kelly. Travis Banton, Paramount's star designer, discussed by Gaylyn Studlar within this collection in relation to his costumes for Marlene Dietrich, also designed *Imitation Of Life* (1934) and *Letter From An Unknown Woman* (1948). Howard Greer and Walter Plunkett (best remembered for his work on *Gone With The Wind* 1939), both designed costumes for *Christopher Strong* (1934), and Jean Louis (recalled for Rita Hayworth's *Gilda* dress) was responsible for Lana Turner's wardrobe in *Imitation Of Life* (1958). At MGM, Gilbert Adrian designed *Camille* (1936) and *Anna Karenina* (1935), and later, after he had left to start his own couture business, Warner Brothers hired him to create some of Joan Crawford's costumes for *Humoresque* (1946) and *Possessed* (1947).

Although feminist critics have often remarked about the costuming in these women's pictures, the work on costume and melos still lags behind the work on musical scoring in the genre. The comparison with music is an important one, and not only because music has also been seen as a subordinate system in the classical narrative scheme. Like the musical code, the vestural code has a basic typifying function as well as an elaborative function, the later accessing the realm of emotion and compensating for the expressive deficiencies of the dialogue.[60] At the basic level, musical motif and costume motif alike borrow popular conceptions to locate types. For instance, the wide apron identifies the mammy, the feather boa the floozie, and the turban with bananas, the Latin American rhumba dancer—visual shorthand which depends, like musical typage, on ideological premises lodged in this iconography.[61] It is this "type" costuming which best exemplifies the ideological dimension of naturalization as I have referred to it, that is, costuming which tends to disappear as it confirms commonsense notions. And corollary to this, costuming which exceeds the typifying function can constitute a threat to the narrative—like the virtuoso composition which suddenly calls attention to itself in a scene and is *heard* as music.

For the most part, in Hollywood films of this period, generic convention keeps costume as spectacle in check by motivating it as show business in the musical, or as visual pun, parody, or humorous incongruity in comedy (as in Bernard Newman's designs for *Theodora Goes Wild* [1936], Travis Banton's for *My Man Godfrey* [1936], and Adrian's for *Bombshell* [1935] and *The Women* [1939]). But classic Hollywood domestic melodrama offers a somewhat different case in point. On the one hand, plotwise and stylistically, it depends on the extraordinary; on the other, it consistently keeps one foot in everyday life (as signified by its verisimilitudinous mise-en-scene). The costuming extremes that I am interested in here escape from the strict realism of contemporary dress. Often they eschew historical realism in the representation of period clothes. Sometimes they even exceed the realism of social class, that is, they exhibit a wealth beyond the means of the character. These, then, are the residues that represent the "much too much" sensibility which characterizes the genre as a whole.

Melodrama, as Peter Brooks has theorized it, is characterized by a "rhetorical excess," a hyperbole which exceeds verbal language.[62] Like the nineteenth-century novel, melodrama tries to convey its meanings through the conventions at hand. But the realist aesthetic is never sufficient to melodrama's project, a project which requires vehicles that can express the grandiose and the profuse. In film melodrama, as Thomas Elsaesser discusses it, the vehicles of melodramatic rhetoric are those aspects of mise-en-scene which verge on the non-representational—gesture, lighting, camera movement, decor, and costume. Likening the excesses of visual style in silent film and Hollywood 1950s melodramas to the musical counterpoint of the original organ grinder who played a "commentary" on theatrical action, Elsaesser maps out the register of the melodramatic for film theory, suggesting that what is inexpressible in the narrative overflows into the more absorbant, purely aesthetic vehicles where it assumes an antithetical relation to the action. As Elsaesser describes the 1950s Technicolor melodramas, emotion is exteriorized in the lush mise-en-scene, almost as though the characters are turned inside out and their interiority displayed (in coded form) in the decor. Here, his analogy between the text and the psychoanalytic patient emphasizes the involuntary, unauthorized, and disjunctive aspect of melodramatic rhetoric: It is always a symptom of something elsewhere. Elsaesser's discussion of the mise-en-scene of *Written On The Wind* (1956) provides one starting point for seeing costume as melodramatic rhetoric, particularly in the women's film which, in the period I am concerned with here, tends toward an aesthetic luxuriance which sometimes matches the emotional opulence. Like the passions in these films, the costuming is unrestrained and relatively indulgent. Elsaesser singles out the black satin bow the wind detatches from the funereal wreath at the end of *Written On The Wind,* which, it seems to him, carries emotional qualities.[63] What is significant about this moment is that the bow, in its detachment from the wreath, is relieved of its representational obligations, and in this form it seems to carry the strongest charge. It is this kind of emotional charge which may be carried by the lavish costuming in the women's film.

However, designers as well as directors in this period also adhered to a code which stipulated an inverse relationship between costume design and emotionality; in other words, the actress should be dressed down for the high emotional scenes and dressed up for the less significant moments. And yet,in the women's film, the costume for the "big" scene, in terms used by designers, had to be "important," especially if the occasion called for formality. In my analysis, we need to make a distinction here between textural extravagance (and, later, color) and design extravagance, often referred to as "style." As we shall see, each of these aesthetics could be troublesome in its own way, but of the two, textural density could be seen as working somewhat like music in its function as affective supplement to a scene. For on the bodies of the female heroines, such fabrics as lamé, silk velvet, duchesse satin and chiffon, simulate skin and thus seem to render tangible an emotional hypersensitivity.

My distinction, however, is still imperfect since texture and style also work together in the more lavish melodramas to stimulate the viewer's visual appetite for a crescendo of opulence as well as emotion. Part of the the pleasure of watching these films is in the prolongation of this excitation in the surprise aspect of the designing which carries over the fascination into transitional scenes. In these superfluous scenes the heroine may do nothing more than answer the telephone or pen a note, but she carries out this mundane task in the most visually stunning and complex costume featured in the entire film. And here lies the danger. The costume plot organizes an idiolect with its own motifs, variations, surprises, anticipations, and resolutions which unfold in a temporality which does not correspond with narrative developments, whose climaxes occur in alternation with key dramatic scenes, in the undramatic moments.

Here, also, is where the comparison with music must end. Much more, of course, needs to be done with the contrast between costume idiolects and musical structures as carriers of affect, and between the eye and the ear as receivers, perhaps following E.H. Gombrich's suggestion that while the "eardrum vibrates sympathetically" with instrumental music, "light energies [impinge] on the rods and cones" of the eye.[64] Our clue to the hyperactivity of the eye is the costumer's postulate that design extravagance (style) is in competition with emotional content since such artistry encourages a kind of visual intellection at odds with delicate nuances of feeling. The basic principles of dress design adhered to in motion picture costuming during this period relate style to the roving eye which could be rerouted on the body. The eye may be directed inward, for instance, so that it is "entrapped," or upward so that it "travels" beyond the figure.[65] In the heyday of the studio designer, from about 1929 to 1940, one can see numerous examples of activity for the eye which was routed around the bodies of actresses in unpredictable directions. The mark of "style" for the virtuoso designers literalizes Barthes's understanding of the "aberrant message which '*surprises*' the code," and as exemplified by Adrian's work during this period, it is both startling and deviant.[66] By stylistic deviance I mean oversized buttons, misplaced pockets, asymmetrical collars, and unconventional use of fabrics. Adrian himself described his characteristic exaggeration as "tabloid fashioning," the design which involved "keeping to the point, yet embroidering the facts."[67] This, then, is the kind of "eye-catching" surprise which George Cukor and Alfred Hitchcock saw as endangering subtle moments in a scene.[68]

Whereas stylistic eccentricity is thought to be the potential ruin of a scene, texture and color may be more easily shaped to fit narrative priorities. Design which maps out the proairetic in visual terms as, for instance, Orry-Kelly's costuming for Bette Davis in *Juarez* (1939) (in which the gradation from white to black parallels the mental disintegration of the Empress Carlotta), achieves the kind of harmony with narrative goals for which directors strive. Costuming, however, cannot anticipate narrative developments so closely that it gives away the plot. The heroine cannot wear all-black *before* the tragedy.

The questions of narrative suspense and affectivity merge in the problem of how to costume the heroine for the scene in which she kills her lover. Some of the costuming solutions to this problem that I have considered suggest that the intensity of the scene requires the banishment of style but the presence of some other strong costuming statement that would reiterate the intensity of the passion and echo the fear. One solution is to strip the heroine down to dark shades with no accessories or detailing (as seen in the simple dress Joan Crawford wears when she shoots her ex-lover [Van Heflin] in *Possessed* [1947]). In *Mandalay* (1934), Orry-Kelly has Kay Francis wear a thin pale-colored shimmering satin robe to watch her ex-lover drink from the glass she has filled with poison. Orry-Kelly solves a more difficult problem in *The Letter* (1940) in which Bette Davis/Leslie Crosbie shoots her lover a few seconds after the opening credits. Here,

Leslie's guilt or innocence hinges upon the question of her relationship to the dead man. If the viewer is watching closely she may note that Davis kills the man who has betrayed her in a full-length black-checked chiffon with diaphonous sleeves and a strapless black underdress (a cross between an evening gown and a lounging robe), and that she quickly changes into a white blouse and tailored skirt before her husband and the investigators arrive. Considered retrospectively, the first costume confirms the character's guilt, establishes the murder motive as jealous passion, and even hints (in the wide white collar) at the prudishness Leslie hides behind (Figure 10.10).

What is similar in these costumes is that, in comparison with the other costumes the heroines wear in the same films, they have relatively simple lines and virtually no decoration, but do feature what we might call empathetic textures. But then, there are significant exceptions to the conventions of costuming the scene of passion, ones which suggest that melodrama encourages rule-breaking. Banished as style, the overblown comes back as texture. Here I am thinking of the scene in *Letty Lynton* (1932) where Adrian puts Joan Crawford in a two-piece silver lamé suit dress to poison the Nils Ascher character (Figure 10.11). The costume works to divert our expectations, since the enigma posed is whether Letty will drink the poison herself or whether she will leave it for him. The costume accommodates both the daring stubbornness of the sophisticated "society girl" determined to have her own way with the villain and the stunning ruthlessness of the murderess into which she must be transformed without the aid of a costume change. Relative to the other costumes Crawford wears in this film, the lamé suit is not the most spectacular design—indeed, it does not compete with the puffy-sleeved white *mouse-lline de soi* which the film made famous.[69] But the textural rigidity (heartlessness) of the silver lamé fabric, overwhelming even the design features (the asymmetrical cut of the cape-like collar as well as the peplum) is a visual "knockout" in its own way. While some directors might see such visual brilliance as undercutting the scene, to me it is one of a few cases in which the connotative charge in the one system is at least equal to that of the other.

The problem of costuming scenes of passion recalls Edith Head's commentary in *The Costume Designer* quoted at the beginning of this article. As the sign of emotion most eloquent and subtle at the same time, tears are easily overwhelmed by sequins, dismissed by chintz, or upstaged by white fox, hence Head's decision to soften her character's outfit. In the woman's films I am concerned with here, however, this principle works somewhat differently, since such melodrama stars as Bette Davis and Joan Crawford are not known for displaying tears at all, hence the institution of the "surrogate sufferer," the friend or relative who assumes the burden

Figure 10.10 *The Letter* (1940). Bette Davis shoots her lover in Orry-Kelly's black-checked chiffon. Warner Brothers, courtesy of BFI Stills Archives.

of feeling.[70] The empathetic costuming of the woman's film heroine in the depths of despondency works somewhat like the surrogate sufferer device. Richness of feeling deserves enriched texture, and velvet, wool jersey, chiffon, satin, bugle-beading, or sable are often used on the bodies of these heroines. These fabrics seem to capture and hold the pathos before our eyes.

But the crucial point here is that in order to capture and hold, the camera has to linger. And yet, as I have said, it *will not* be waylaid by costume

Figure 10.11   *Letty Lynton* (1932). Joan Crawford poisons her lover wearing Adrian's silver lamé suit. MGM, courtesy of the Museum of Modern Art Stills Archives.

detail. The moments when the costuming eludes meaning, when affect becomes ascendant, then, are those moments in which the camera is held on the heroine for some other dramatic reason. The costume detail is trapped in the frame! Two examples come to mind,both of them cases of costuming which is connotatively rich enough to match the volume of suffering. One recalls Orry-Kelly's fox hat and matching bolero-length jacket worn by Bette Davis as Judith Traherne in *Dark Victory* (1939)

Figure 10.12 *Dark Victory* (1939). Bette Davis's suffering exteriorized in Orry-Kelley's fox hat and matching jacket. Warner Brothers, courtesy of Wisconsin State Historical Society Stills Archives.

(Figure 10.12). This is the outfit she is wearing for the close-ups in three crucial scenes, the first of which is the scene in which she reads her fate in the words "Prognosis Negative," highlighted on the pages of Dr. Steele's medical file. But what is it about the fur fringe creeping into Bette Davis's eyes? And the incongruous mass of it on her shoulders? How can an image be horrible and beautiful at once, unless what we are looking at is the image of her glorious suffering intermingled with the disease itself?[71] One also thinks of the cherries on Greta Garbo's Empress Eugenie-style black velvet hat, cocked over one eye as seen in the last frames of *Anna Karenina*. The artificial cherries, magnified in the close-up over Garbo's lowered eyes (stunned by the train wheels in her contemplation of suicide), are empathetic in their drooping shape, and disconcertingly sensual. The presence of these cherries is strange and inexplicable, the more strange and inexplicable the *longer one thinks about it*. Is this what Barthes means by "inexpressibility" and "obtuseness" in his essay "The Third Meaning" (which has clearly informed my analysis of these scenes)?[72]

Yes and no. One needs to recall that Barthes derives his theory of the third meaning from scrutinizing frame enlargements from Eisenstein's *Ivan The Terrible,* not from watching women's pictures. The notion of cinematic excess derived from the Barthes essay and the notion of melodramatic excess have yet to meet and establish some ground rules. While the costume idiolect does threaten to cohere into a different temporality and a different film, this other (more wonderful) film is not completely "indifferent" to story (as is Barthes's third meaning), although it may appear at an obtuse angle to the narrative.[73] My preliminary findings suggest that in terms of costume surplus, film melodrama can absorb and motivate beyond the capacity of other genres.[74] This may call into question the use of the concept of narrative unity without reference to genre in relation to a notion of cinematic excess. Here, then, is the question: Does the woman's film narrative so thoroughly motivate costume that all apparent excesses (even style extravagance) are not excessive *within* the film, but only in relation to films in other genres? Is this why, as we watch these films, we are so often left unsatisfied in our craving for costuming which crescendos to meet the heights of the passions the films strive to dramatize?

11

Designing Women:
The Emergence of the
New Sweetheart Line

Maureen Turim

A tight bare bodice, a nipped-in, accentuated waist, a full, billowing skirt—such are the lines of a gown that came to dominate the image of women in America from 1947 through the mid-fifties. The story of this gown is one that cuts across the film and fashion industries. It helps us understand the specific role of the studio fashion designer in the dissemination of style, how the designer manipulates dress design in relationship to characterization and spectacle in the large budget films of this period. And it is a story that tells us much about the historical motivation and ideological meaning of fashion.

As background it is important to consider the effects of World War II on both the fashion industry and the costume design departments of the Hollywood studios. The British and American austerity programs emphasized practicality in clothing. Tailored dress and suit design utilizing a minimal amount of material were suggested by war production board guidelines in both countries. This tailored look harmonized with the uniforms women were wearing in newly acquired wartime industrial jobs and in the military, and was in keeping with a program of rationing and economy aimed at the consumer on the homefront.

As for studio costume design, it was restricted by the U.S. Government's war order L85, to limited budgets.[1] Certain textiles such as silk and rubber were prohibited, and many other luxury fabrics were simply unavailable during the war. Adrian's broad-shouldered geometric suits are well-known examples of design from the war period. These were only sporadically seen on the screen after Adrian resigned as head of costume design at MGM in 1941, in part because of the budget restrictions, to

Reprinted from *Wide Angle* 6, no. 2 (1984).

open his own boutique.[2] The sculptured lines of Adrian's suits—the sure, severe, yet graceful angles—connote power. And while the silhouette is broad-shouldered and slim-hipped, this masculine line is tempered by the use of the shapes and lines of modernist abstraction. Less abstractly, design detailing accentuated the bust and waist, and these suits were worn in the 1940s with obligatory hats and high heels, thus augmenting the power connotations through a very sophisticated manipulation of fetishism. Few women could afford the elegance and opulence of these Adrian designs. After all, geometric piecing and shaping are not so much economy measures as they are extravagant use of fabric and labor. But compared to the rather plain "utility suit" the British wore, American women dressed "smartly" in less expensive versions of this amalgam of power and glamour. In January of 1942 even *Vogue* magazine displayed what it called "Unflinching Flannels" and "Busy Black Woolens" under the heading "The Tailored Suit, . . . Your 1942 Uniform."[3]

The dominant style through 1946 was a broad-shouldered, straight cut jacket or blouse worn over a straight skirt with a hemline just below the knees (Figure 11.1). It was worn in countless wartime films. By 1945, in *Mildred Pierce,* however, the style garnered the connotation of a too-masculine ruthlessness. *Spellbound* (1945), the following year, elaborated the masculine connotation by using psychoanalyst Constance Peterson's tailored suits as an emblem of her neurotic avoidance of men. In *Spellbound* Constance (Ingrid Bergman) voices a desire to change, to transform herself through feminine attire as a result of her new-found love: "I always loved very feminine clothes, but never quite dared to wear them. But I am going to after this. I'm going to wear whatever pleases me, . . . and you." These lines of dialogue speak to more than just Constance's character within screenwriter Ben Hecht and director Alfred Hitchcock's fiction. Towards the end of the war, the fashion industry and perhaps even some women themselves were looking forward to a new "refeminization" of style. Ads for girdles appeared once the promise of a supply of rubber and the need for a peacetime market became imminent; the ads clearly tied the cinching of the waist to welcoming home the warrior, and even made the connection between the "true-womenhood" of the corseted 1890s and a newly envisioned program of "feminine mystique."[4] *Mademoiselle* magazine instructed WACS and WAVES how to convert their uniforms to civilian style, but told them that new ball gowns of flowing proportions would nonetheless have to be purchased.[5] The fashion industry's self-conscious conversion from wartime to peacetime provides an instance to be considered in the long-standing debate in theories of fashion as to whether changes in fashion obey arbitrary, but structured internal patterns or are socially determined. In recent history it has been the industry itself, in its advertising and magazine copy that prepares for a new cycle by

Figure 11.1   Adrian's high fashion version of the 1940's silhouette. Courtesy of John Engstead.

tapping the mood of the moment. Evidently the American fashion industry was ready to introduce a new style to celebrate the return of unrestricted and unashamed consumerism. It actively instructed women to adopt a new style so that they could embody the "spirit" of the armistice.

The New Look—High Fashion Leads

The lead, however, was to come from Paris, from the Paris whose world-dominating fashion industry had been in an ambiguous state of Occupation, partially dormant or passively resisting, partially collaborating. Lucien Lelong remained as president of the Chambre Syndicale de la Couture Parisienne from 1937–1946, but he sent Elsa Schiaparelli to America as a public relations agent for the industry. Her article in a September 1940 *Vogue* chronicles the months before the capitulation, but stops short of questioning how the industry would be kept "alive" as she promised it would be once the only buyers were Nazis and Petainists.[6]

Thus, the historical motivation for the New Look from the French point of view was to overcome the damages of war and to reinstate the French fashion industry in America's good graces and desires. Christian Dior, assistant designer-turned-soldier, returned to Paris from Southern France to accomplish this coup with his first independent collection. Funded by a major French financier and textile manufacturer, Michel Boussac, Dior presented the New Look of 1947. It was given enormous play in fashion journals anxious to leave behind their wartime sobriety and return to covering the charity balls of the very wealthy. The New Look was characterized by a soft shoulder, a "wasp waist," and a full skirt. It was simple and tailored for daytime wear, with the fullness supplied by draping, and extravagantly full for evening.

The New Look was not actually that new. The lines that characterized it had been introduced in the Paris collections of 1939, the last collection that American buyers attended.[7] At that time the Lane sisters, Hollywood celebrities, appeared in a newsreel to protest this reimposition of the wasp waist, a look that Dior had previously characterized the corseted silhouette of late nineteenth-century fashion.

Hollywood fashion design had also anticipated this look in period costume dramas produced in the late 1930s. From Adrian's *Marie-Antoinette* (1936) to Walter Plunkett's *Gone With The Wind* (1939), the period picture displayed elegance as a variation of the corseted bodice and hoop skirt, referring as they did to the two periods whose silhouette matched the New Look; the eighteenth century (the courts of Louis XV, Louis XVI) and the later half of the nineteenth century (Figure 11.2). The film that serves as a real liaison between this costume drama tradition of the late 1930s and Hollywood's version of the New Look is *Meet Me In St. Louis* (1944), designed by Irene and Irene Sharaff in 1944. While still a period costume film, this collaboration of Hollywood's two Irenes on a large budget color musical towards the end of the war, marked the true initiation of a dress whose form and function would be central to so many similar productions of the post-war period.

Hollywood, the Sweetheart Line, and Mass Consumption

High fashion began to vary the "New Look" just two years after its introduction. By 1949 Dior's collection was dominated by very tight

Figure 11.2 *Gone With the Wind* (1939) Walter Plunkett's period costumes for the film anticipate the New Look.

straight skirts embellished by trains of material that maintained a modified bell shape in the skirt line.[8] By the 1950s high fashion showed a straight and full skirt simultaneously (something rare in the history of fashion). Then, in 1953, high fashion attempted to reintroduce the straight chemise line and a dropped waist reminiscent of the 1920s, a look which did not gain more general popularity until 1957.

Resisting the lead of high fashion, popular culture and the mass of consumers retained the silhouette of the belted waist and the full skirt through the mid-1950s. The shape that I am calling the "sweetheart line" produced for the Hollywood screen and reproduced by the garment industry, was created from a mixture of period nostalgia and the high fashion lead of the New Look. The sweetheart line depended on bras that were molded to a point and often strapless, corsets or girdles, and crinolines—layered, ruffled slips made of stiffened organza and net that supported the bell-shaped skirts to their great width at the hemline. It was a style of dress that dominated the evening gown, in tulle, lace, satin, or organza, and was also common in daytime dresses, particularly spring and summer cottons. The "princess," the "true-women," the "debutante," and the "bride" were all connotations born by this dress as it enveloped America's would-be sweethearts (Figure 11.3). These connotations were sewn into the style not only by the history of fashion but by the way Hollywood costume design seized upon it, prolonged its life, and positioned it as a reinforcement of narrative ideas.

Hollywood fashion design had a resurgence after the war. Design departments regained their prestige and large budgets at the major studios. Academy awards for costume design were established in 1949 in two categories: Black and White and Color. The Hollywood Designers Guild was formed in 1953 at which time it began giving out its own Figleaf award, an Adam and Eve statuette. Chart A (at the end of the article) shows the design heads or most prominent designers at the major studios during the 1950s. Note that in each case new supervising designers came to prominence during or just after the war, replacing such famous designers as Adrian, Travis Banton, Herschel, and Howard Greer. This group includes some key women: Edith Head, the first woman to head a design department, who retained that post and won more academy awards and nominations that any other artist in Hollywood history; Irene Lentz Gibbons, known as "Irene;" Irene Sharaff, whose career included much Broadway designing; and Helen Rose. In addition to these women, many others were active as designers during this period (see Chart B). Many of these women seemed to bring with them a personal investment in the sweetheart line, although photos of the designers rarely depict them wearing this style of dress (with the exception of the academy awards when the designers wore a version of their own designs). Their attachment to the sweetheart line as a style, however, is evidenced not only in their design but in statements they made in interviews. Edith Head's often quoted statement is an example: "My dress for Taylor was taken up by a manufacturer of debutante party dresses. Someone at Paramount once counted at a party, 37 Elizabeth Taylors dancing!"[9] And Helen Rose has said: "I loved that period. Grace was beautiful and in love with the prince

Figure 11.3   Grace Kelly wears the Princess neckline version of the 1950's "Sweetheart Line".

and life was divine. I have always been extremely proud that Grace chose me to design her wedding gown as practically every designer in the world vied for this honor."[10]

Edith Head's designs for Bette Davis in *June Bride* (1948) have been called Davis's first New Look wardrobe, and we can see how directly Head borrowed from the previous year's French designer collection (Figure 11.4). Davis plays an established newspaperwoman doing a story on a midwestern June bride, only to become one herself by the end of the

Figure 11.4 *June Bride* (1948) Edith Head designs Bette Davis's first New Look wardrobe.

film. The New Look was again put to use in *All About Eve* (1950), when Davis convinced Head that her suit should have skirts full enough to indicate Margo's femininity in scenes where she might otherwise seem completely tyrannical. In both films Davis plays women no longer "young" who rediscover their "femininity" and consecrate that discovery with marriage. This is a transitional post-war narrative with a message for a group of women who had worked and worried and waited out the war, and the New Look served it well.

Figure 11.5 *Father of the Bride* (1950) "Sweetheart line" as transition from bobby soxer to woman.

But the real work for the sweetheart line was to grace the young, to establish the transition to womanhood and marriage for women coming of age in the 1950s. An example of this function can be seen in *Father Of The Bride* (1950), in which Elizabeth Taylor is transformed from bobby soxer in blue jeans to a glorious rendition of nuptial splendor while her father, Spencer Tracy, provides a satirical commentary on the costly ritual (Figure 11.5). During this period the sweetheart line came to signify "bride" and "bridal gowns," held to this traditional style long after it vanished from other fashion. Upper class, middle class, even Hollywood in its real life, everyone, that is, everyone except the very poor, engaged in this extravagant costuming to celebrate the most important social ritual of the post-war years: the wedding. Thus a film like *Father Of The Bride* not only simultaneously mocked and rectified this ritual, it proscribed the style that meant "proper wedding." This same style of wedding dress is used at the close of *Gentlemen Prefer Blondes* (1953) to signify through costume the legitimacy granted the showgirls in their transformation to wives.

The power of the sweetheart line to affect ideological transformation is shown in quite a different way in the case of George Stevens's *A Place*

Figure 11.6 *A Place in the Sun* (1951) Edith Head's famous strapless bouffant dress for Elizabeth Taylor.

In The Sun. Adapted from Theodore Dreiser's *An American Tragedy,* the 1951 film displaces the novel's emphasis on social tragedy. Instead of focusing on the loss of human values as a tragic consequence of striving to enter the capitalist class, the film focuses on the way an unfortunate past destroys a man's entrance into a fairy tale romance with the proper sweetheart. The sweetheart, Angela Vickers, is played by Elizabeth Taylor, and her gowns, designed by Edith Head, are a major factor in creating that ideological shift. The four gowns, three white and one black, do not simply signify Angela Vickers's wealth; rather, the appearance is almost magical, ethereal (Figure 11.6). Embroidered flowers or lace perfectly outline and adorn Taylor's breasts, representing both her sexuality and her maiden innocence. The cloth of the dress and the lines of the body seem to respond to each other so rhythmically that social context almost seems to disappear. And this seductive charm of the garments destroys sympathy for the non-sweetheart, the "dowdy working girl" as she is called by *Life*.[11]

Edith Head won an academy award for designing the gowns in *A Place In The Sun,* and the film received tremendous publicity for displaying them. In interviews and articles, Head is often credited with the manner in which her designs established character and served narrative functions, and as such might be called "storytelling wardrobes." The dresses, then, became significant auxiliary signs within the semic coding. By this I mean that they are signifiers that establish the character, Angela Vickers, in a most fundamental way. But in the case of *A Place In The Sun,* they exceed this function and help to eradicate any potential critique of Angela Vickers's shallowness and privilege. These gowns recall the *Father Of The Bride* dress and even Helen Rose's gowns for Taylor in *A Date With Judy* (1947), thus linking Angela Vickers with more innocent and desirable sweethearts (Figure 11.7).

Surely *A Place In The Sun* played an important role in the dissemination of such gowns to middle-class America. The *Variety* review mentioned the gowns as a selling point of the film, saying, "most commendable are the gowns designed by Edith Head and worn so fetchingly by Miss Taylor."[12] The film received *Life Magazine*'s "Picture of the Week" and *Seventeen* magazine's "Picture of the Month" awards. Articles announcing the awards in both magazines were illustrated by photos that displayed the dresses. True debutantes would have already been familiar with these gowns through their reading of *Vogue* and *Harper's Bazaar,* magazines which had featured such designs since 1947. The film helped to bring the style to mass audiences and mass manufacture for such middle-class social events as high school proms and sorority balls (Figure 11.8).

Two advertisements that appeared in *Life* in 1951 show how the sweetheart dress style could be used decoratively to sell other commodities. Such ads were certain signs of the dispersion of this style and its myth to a mass public. In one, a woman wearing a flowing sweetheart gown leans against her male companion, her bare arms and shoulders surrounded by text inserts describing the benefits of wearing Fresh deodorant. In another, a woman seated in a sweetheart dress has a glass of ale poured for her by the male companion.[13] The featured products, it is important to note, are not champagne, wine, or expensive cologne, but deodorant and ale. The market is middle and working class, but the myth is sweetheart elegance and romance. During this period, sweetheart line dresses were also used to sell kitchen and laundry appliances and accoutrements using the theme "waltzing through washday." Rather than merely claiming to make housework easier, advertisers disguised work as decorative romance, not unlike the daily life of Angela Vickers, by borrowing her dresses. This was the

Figure 11.7 *A Date With Judy* (1947) Helen Rose designs for Taylor as the ideal sweetheart.

sweetheart line's contribution to another social myth elaborated in the 1950s: the myth that housework was not real labor.

Another connotation of the sweetheart line was that of ballerina, important in this period when classical ballet and modern dance were beginning to capture America's attention. Alicia Markova was adopted as a national sweetheart.[14] In film this ballerina infatuation was translated into costume design for choreographed musicals. The sweetheart line was used in many

Figure 11.8 Homecoming, 1959—Thornton Township High School, Harvey, Illinois. Charlotte Kopac and date. Courtesy of Charlotte Herzog.

of the MGM musicals far into the 1950s. Edith Head was later to reveal that Elizabeth Taylor had been so tightly bound in corsets in order to wear her Head-designed sweetheart dresses, that she could barely breathe, but Leslie Caron and Cyd Charisse performed freely in versions adapted to dance movements, whirling the full skirts to great advantage. Helen Rose designed sweetheart line dresses for all the women in *Brigadoon* (1954), adding rustic detailing to the extras' costumes only. The pale yellow dress

Charisse wears is midcalf length with a scoop neckline, tightly cinched waist, and crinoline underskirts of deep orange. "Bonnie Jean" wears a blue sweetheart dress for her wedding, while Charisse wears bright red. The colors and contemporary lines of the lead's costumes can be explained only by the studio's desire to exploit Technicolor and the audience's fashion expectations. By the mid-1950s, this dance variation of the sweetheart dress was brought into the mass market. As the dress got progressively shorter, it reached a style known as the ballerina length.

The sweetheart line was often used in opposition to the slinkier tight skirt. In *Gentlemen Prefer Blondes,* tight skirts represent women as sexual warriors and golddiggers and the sweetheart bridal gowns establish their legitimation as wives. In *How To Marry A Millionaire* (1953), Marilyn Monroe, Lauren Bacall, and Betty Grable supposedly refused to wear the full skirts of the sweetheart line, possibly fearful of the effect Cinemascope might have in distorting the already wide proportions of such skirts. As David Cherichetti tells it in his book, *Hollywood Costume Design,* "Each wanted the slimest possible skirts." Charles LeMaire did not want Fox designers to appear ignorant of current fashion, so he called a meeting. Grable finally agreed to wear a cancan petticoat under a very full blue taffeta dress in the first scenes; Bacall wore a full-skirted printed shirtwaist in the fashion show, and several of her other costumes had flared skirts; but Monroe was completely intransigent and insisted on tight skirts.[15] Whatever the truth of this anecdote, films in the mid-1950s began to display a very different prototype for audiences to follow. The slim skirt, either as tight and sexy, or looser and chic, began to replace the full skirt.

However, some films from late in the decade provide a humorous critical comment on the style. In *Les Girls* (1957), designer Orry-Kelly uses the dance numbers to comment on the sweetheart style. First, he has one of the dancers audition in a costume that turns Head's *A Place In The Sun* inside-out. This costume features a wire armature on the exterior as a support for the decoration—the flowers—which were held inside. Then, in another dance number, he costumes the *Les Girls* trio in Marie Antoinette ball gowns in which he satirizes the elegance of this style by rendering it with a pornographic posterior. This gives us the historical antecedent of the 1950s' sweetheart dress collapsed upon its decline into pornographic display. This blending had been seriously presented, as in Marilyn Monroe's costume for *River Of No Return* (1954), where the sweetheart line is slit at intervals in the full skirt to expose a complete view of Monroe's fishnet-covered legs. The flashback structure of *Les Girls* also allows Orry-Kelly to cleverly contrast earlier 1950s sweetheart gowns with the more dramatic, severe black dresses of the later 1950s worn by the women in the courtroom frame-story set in the present. The gowns the women wear to their farewell party three years before their lawsuit reunion exemplify the sweetheart line, but develop its relationship to the pornographic eighteenth-century costumes seen earlier through visual matching. These costumes also emphasize how ribbons placed on the sweetheart style can render its wearers as gift-wrapped presents offered up to the male.

Another commentary on the fashion design of the past decade is offered by Jean-Luc Godard's *A Bout De Souffle* (1959), when Michel Poiccard interrupts his urban perambulations to run up behind a woman crossing a boulevard and lift up her full skirt from behind. Later, when Patricia (Jean Seberg) buys a dress for her first professional interview, she selects a black-and-white striped sweetheart-styled Christian Dior. The dress is black-and-white striped not only for graphic pleasure, but also to recall the headlines, the text, the newspaper appearance throughout the film, and Patricia's desire to become a serious professional writer. But the sweetheart line dress will forever bind her to being a decorative woman; her interviewee, a male writer, tells her that he knows the place for a woman with a very pretty dress like hers. We are left, of course, to assume that this place is *not* posing questions about the role of women in contemporary society, as Patricia had tried to do in the interview.

Symbolic and Ideological Investments

These late 1950s metacommentaries on fashion bring us to the question of the social and psychological meanings of the sweetheart line. We have seen that the dress has been used to signify "femininity" and have traced part of the explanation for this to its reference to historical periods where the feminine was an exaggerated "other" within upper-class and bourgeois society. But the question is still why this shape should carry those connotations and, therefore, why it is able to annex the connotations of princess, debutante, or bride that became attached to this exaggerated feminine. The answer can be found in part by examining the outline of the dress.

Not coincidentally, the sweetheart line has become the image used for the symbol of a woman's toilet, as contrasted with the male outline that is represented by broad shoulders and trousered legs. The outline can also be seen as a combination to heart shapes; one with the curves at the breasts to a point at the waist, another inverted from a point at the waist to a scalloped hem. The dress shape follows the curves of an idealized average of a woman's body shape and proportion, but spreads out discreetly from the wider hips to conceal the real sign of sexual difference, the pubic area. It inverts the triangle of pubic veil to provide this cover. Then it further metaphorizes its function as cover to the woman's sexual organs by layers of ruffles and folds, in laces, tulles, organzas, satins, chiffons—materials that are soft, translucent, transparent, or shiny. The flowers that often adorn the dress are again metaphorically referred to by one's imaginary view of this full-skirted style from underneath. Freud's young male discovering sexual difference through his fictional crawl underneath his mother's skirt would here only be exposed to the terrain of metaphor.

The ideology that surrounds this metaphor is one that functions through opposition, restriction, and limitation. Just as these decorative dresses were often very uncomfortable and impractical to wear, so the decorative and passive function assigned to women by their metaphorical inscription in such clothing was the ugly underside of the charming appearance. In fact, the sweetheart line can also be seen as a form of guilded bondage. For clothing goes beyond a temporary usage, a specific ritual function, a temporary fantasy. It establishes identities. This style, by enforcing symbolic femininity, allowed for a great restriction of the female role to be attached to the very notion of the feminine.

CHART A
Major Studios—Postwar Costume Design Supervisors

MGM
1942–1949   Irene
1949–1967   Helen Rose
1947–1966   Walter Plunket, with Irene Sharaff for Musicals

Columbia
1944–1958   Jean-Louise

Paramount
1938–1967   Edith Head

Fox
1943–1949   Charles Lemaire, with Bonnie Cashin (1944–1949)
1950–1953   Edward Stevenson

Universal
1957–1950   Orry-Kelly
1950–1960   Rosemary Odell, Bill Thomas, Jay Morley, Jr.

Warners
1951–1960
Moss Mabrey

RKO
1949–1954
Michael Wolfe

Republic
1938–1957   Adele Palmer, with Orry-Kelly freelancing for Fox, Universal, RKO, & MGM after leaving Warners in 1943

CHART B
Post-war Women Designers with Supervisory Control

Edith Head—Paramount 1938–1967
Irene—MGM 1942–1949
Helen Rose—MGM 1942–1967
Irene Sharaff—MGM 1943–1961
Adele Palmer—Republic 1938–1957; Fox 1954–1959

Other Post-war Women Designers

Bonnie Cashin—Fox 1943–1950
Dorothy Jeakins—Fox 1948–1958
Elois Jenssen—Stromberg 1947–1950; Fox 1951–1953
Ann Hill Johnstone—Kazan 1950s
Mary Ann Nyporg—MGM 1952–1953; then Fox and U.A.—Freelance
Kay Nelson—Fox 1943–1955
Elizabeth Haffenden—MGM 1950s
Sheila O'Brien—Warners 1950s
Mary Wills—Fox 1948–1962
Adele Balkan—RKO 1947–1952; Fox 1955–1960
Yvonne Wood—Fox 1941–1945; Universal 1945–1951
Leah Rhodes—Warners 1941–1952
Rosemary Odell—Universal 1950–1960
Marjorie Best—Warners 1949–1959

12

Masochism, Masquerade, and the Erotic Metamorphoses of Marlene Dietrich

Gaylyn Studlar

"Venus in Furs!" I cried, pointing at the picture.
"That is how I saw her in my dream."
"I, too," said Severin, "but I was dreaming with my eyes open."
—Leopold von Sacher-Masoch, *Venus in Furs*

In feminist film theory's attempt to explain how sexual difference is represented in the cinema, costuming has been a surprisingly neglected factor. Part of the explanation of this neglect lies in the appropriation of psychoanalysis in feminism's approach to classical Hollywood cinema. The Freudian and Lacanian accounts of spectatorship that have dominated this theory tend to assume that fascination with classical realist cinema depends upon the solicitation and satisfaction of deeper unconscious pleasures for a spectatorship usually defined as male by film's patriarchal system. In such a system, women are constructed as images for the pleasure of male looking. Female costuming, as part of that construct, is designed to attract the attention of the male gaze to the sexual spectacle of woman's body while the interest of women viewers in watching such a spectacle of female exhibitionism is explained as a narcissistic identification with the star. Envy and emulation of the actress's attire reflects the viewer's culturally inculcated wish to attract male attention through an enhancement of her own attractiveness. This process helps fulfill the patriarchy's desire to channel women's desires into a "happily-ever-after" heterosexual union privileging male power.

Although this outline of feminist-psychoanalytic theory's view of the function of costuming in dominant cinema obviously simplifies complex theoretical paradigms, it is undeniable that the role of costuming in forming the pleasures of viewing remain undertheorized within current psychoanalytic discourse on film. Therefore, the purpose of this article is to show how costuming can be incorporated within a psychoanalytic theory of visual pleasure that accounts for some subversive spectatorial possibilities available through Hollywood texts. These pleasures are subversive in that they result in forms of identification and desire that question rather than reaffirm male domination, that disrupt traditional male/female gender roles, and that may even subvert the heterosexual presumption.

To accomplish this task, I am calling upon Gilles Deleuze's revisionary theory of masochism.[1] While it may seem curious that a theory of masochism can be used to theorize the subversive possibilities of pleasure offered through classical Hollywood cinema, I will demonstrate how Deleuze's analysis of masochism as a mother-centered, pre-Oedipal phenomenon may be used to challenge Oedipally centered Freudian and Lacanian interpretations of female representation. Simultaneously, it can be used to reveal how costuming can be an extremely important element in producing pleasures for male and female spectators that are neither ideologically regressive nor immediately recuperable into the sexual agendas of patriarchal domination.

Any discussion of issues of sexual difference, looking, and narrative cinema necessitates a return to Laura Mulvey's seminal "Visual Pleasure and Narrative Cinema," the single most influential feminist-psychoanalytic analysis of women's representation in the Hollywood cinema and of male spectatorial response.[2] In it, she claims that dominant cinema speaks neither *for* women nor *of* women, but rather speaks a discourse of male Oedipal desire, a possessive, sadistic desire haunted by the fear of sexual difference defined as the mother's castration by the Father. Relying on Freud's essay on fetishism, Mulvey suggests that the erotic spectacle of woman unconsciously reactivates the moment in which the male child discovers his mother's lack of a penis. His discovery of sexual difference, at first denied, is then interpreted as a difference brought about by the mother's castration by the father. Freud believed all males experience absolute horror at this discovery. Those who resolutely attempt to deny the mother's castration become fetishists who resort to a *disavowal* based on a formula of denial, of "I know but nevertheless." Disavowal leads to taking a fetish—an object such as a shoe or a body part—as the symbolic replacement of the mother's missing penis; otherwise women's disgusting difference would make them unacceptable as sexual objects.[3]

From a literal reading of Freud's theory of fetishism, Mulvey, and many psychoanalytic-feminist theorists in her wake, assert that film represents women through a fetishistic visual process that simultaneously denies and asserts their sexual difference, a difference defined by men as a castration threat. Woman is objectified by the male's controlling gaze, constituted in film as a relay between the camera, the spectators (assumed to be male), and the male hero who often aggressively seeks to investigate the woman's mysterious sexuality.[4]

In this theoretical explanation, women's costuming becomes an inevitable reflection of a fetishistic process that disguises the woman's "castration" and attempts to render her difference harmless. The woman has only to be represented to be "fetishized" through available cinematic technique: lighting, costuming, camera placement, and editing. She is typically fetishized into a part object with visual emphasis added through perspective, angle, or lighting to the legs (Marlene Dietrich), buttocks and breasts (Marilyn Monroe), hair (Rita Hayworth), or face (Greta Garbo). But cinematic fetishism, as defined by common usage, also offers the woman as a comforting phallicized totality with her body encased in a "phallic dress" of the type worn by Mae West.[5] If, as Mulvey has claimed, women are phallic substitutes whose erotic spectacle is constructed to cover their lack, then the superficial details of costuming ultimately must be dismissed as unimportant in determining the deeper unconscious pleasures which film provides for its male spectator: Mae West's phallicized representation providing essentially the same fetishistic psychological pleasures as Jayne Mansfield's décolleté or Dietrich's "gams."

During the last decade, this interpretation of woman as phallic substitute has been adopted as a key premise in feminist film criticism's discussion of film costuming as an oppressive mechanism that fashions the female into the passive spectacle for the male look. Such an approach is illustrated by E. Ann Kaplan's Mulveyian/Lacanian analysis of Josef von Sternberg's *Blonde Venus* (1933). Citing Mulvey, Kaplan says that the melodrama is "clearly constructed for the male spectator" and uses fetishization "as its method of dominating women . . ."[6] She also follows Mulvey's suggestion that films directed by von Sternberg demonstrate, in Mulvey's words, "a pure fetishistic scopophilia" in which Dietrich becomes "the ultimate fetish" whose eroticized presence as a "perfect product" transforms her into a "reassuring rather than dangerous" object, an assuagement rather than an instigator of male castration fear.[7] Kaplan characterizes all of Dietrich's costuming as fetishistic, from the star's carefully controlled suggestion of nudity in the film's opening scene, to the man's white tuxedo that makes Dietrich "most spectularly fetishized" in her Paris nightclub act, to the final costume, a black coatdress bordered in fur and glittering beads that paradoxically marks Dietrich/Helen Faraday's return to the life of a struggling hausfrau and devoted mother (Figure 12.1). Kaplan argues that although the woman spectator may read "against the grain" of the film to see a subversive woman-to-woman bonding in Dietrich's assumption of male attire, the male spectator, too heavily invested in the pleasure of watching the woman as an erotic fetish constructed for him, would, like the film's director, fail to see the contradictions created between "woman as erotic object (or narcissistic phallic replacement) and woman as Mother."[8]

Kaplan's reading shows the manner in which feminist film theory has often subsumed a specific textual analysis of costuming under the rubric of a broader psychoanalytic approach that aligns male visual pleasure with

Figure 12.1   *Blonde Venus* (1933) A glittering coatdress marks Helen's return to motherhood. Paramount Pictures, courtesy of Cinema Collectors, CA.

fetishism as an indicator of castration fear and Oedipal conflict. Her reading also faithfully adheres to Mulvey's explanation that male looking takes two related forms, a sadistic voyeurism often expressed through a narrative pattern that proves the woman's guilt so that she may be punished or saved by the hero, and a *fetishistic scopophilia* that "builds up the physical beauty of the object, transforming it into something satisfying in itself." The latter stifles narrative progress in favor of a woman-centered spectacle that focuses "the erotic instinct on the look alone."[9] The result, which Mulvey observes in *Blonde Venus* (1932), is that such films are missing the powerful, controlling look of the male protagonist who usually anchors spectatorial identification. Instead, the spectator is in "direct erotic rapport" with the woman who becomes "the direct recipient of the spectators' look . . ."[10] I will later demonstrate how the notion of direct, unmediated "erotic rapport" can be used to re-theorize the subversive relationship of the female spectator to Dietrich in these films although Mulvey herself is mute on the subject of the woman spectator within this particular essay.[11] In spite of the narrowly drawn boundaries of her theoretical premise, Mulvey's account of male spectatorial looking has proven to be crucial to the last decade of feminist theory's analysis of the cinema and spectatorial pleasure. However, her theory has also been implicated in some troubling theoretical impasses that suggest the need to further analyze the power dynamics and pleasures of gender-differentiated looking.

In his reconsideration of Mulvey's thesis, D. N. Rodowick notes that there is a disturbing blind spot in her theory. She readily pairs voyeurism with sadism, but avoids the logical pairing of fetishistic scopophilia with *masochism*. For Mulvey to admit that pleasurable male looking might encompass masochism or a submission to the object, says Rodowick, would endanger the political focus of her argument: that the male gaze always asserts its control over the passive figure of woman as the "bearer of the bleeding wound."[12]

It is ironically because of Mulvey's failure to include masochism in her theory that we can formulate an alternative meaning to the dynamics of looking—to fetishism, and to costuming in *Blonde Venus,* to all the von Sternberg/Dietrich films, and to Hollywood cinematic practice in general. Even though masochism or "sadomasochism" has often been attributed by critics to the sexual dynamics created between von Sternberg's characters,[13] never has masochism defined as a distinct set of signs served as the tool of describing and explaining the interaction of all the elements—including costuming—that make the von Sternbergian universe. As I have argued elsewhere,[14] the von Sternberg/Dietrich films, including *Blonde Venus,* are not "sadomasochistic," neither are they centered around unconscious Oedipal conflicts and pleasures; they offer instead a totally predictable aesthetic system based on the formal, narrative, and psychological requirements of masochism as a pre-Oedipal, mother-centered fixation as described by Gilles Deleuze in his analysis of the novels of Leopold von Sacher-Masoch.

The use of Deleuze rather than Freud or Lacan is a key difference that marks my analysis of visual pleasure and costuming as a radical alternative to theories of feminine representation that emphasize Oedipal fantasy, castration fear, and feminine lack. In complete contrast to Freud, Deleuze regards masochism as an oral stage phenomenon in which the subject's sexuality is fixated at an infantile (i.e. pregenital and therefore "perverse") level.[15] Deleuze argues that the conflation of masochism and sadism into "sadomasochism" confuses their psychodynamic structures, their fantasies, *and* their representation of the female. The sadist lives by the mechanisms of an Oedipal negation, and in particular, a negation of the female so that the father may be exalted. The masochist does not desire to despoil or destroy the woman, but to idealize her, to submit to her, and to be punished by her so that the father (in himself) may be symbolically punished and denied. The unconscious fantasy underlying this masochistic disavowal of the father is the wish for a re-symbiosis with and fantastical rebirth from the powerful pre-Oedipal mother that will result in the "new sexless man" who owes nothing to the father and phallic sexuality. Rebirth is equated with castration, which is not an obstacle but rather a "precondition of its success with the mother." As a result, Deleuze turns Freud's Oedipal theory of masochism upside down; it is not the child who is guilty, but the father who, remarks Deleuze, "is deprived of all symbolic function."[16]

Reading from Deleuze's pre-Oedipal theory of masochism, the end of *Blonde Venus* might be interpreted as a very open expression of a fundamental masochistic fantasy in which the mother, Helen Faraday (Marlene Dietrich) is bound into a erotically charged relationship with her child, Johnny (Dickie Moore), whose sexualized bond with her undermines the patriarchal family and proves the father (Herbert Marshall) to be sexually and economically superfluous. In the final reel, Helen returns to the dismal, dirty New York flat of her husband, Ned, who has blamed Helen for the family's disintegration. He is characterized by Helen as weak, and the film confirms his weakness. Ned has tried to make Johnny forget Helen, but his revenge has failed. Johnny has not forgotten his mother's face, he still cannot read or write "Father," and continues to sleep in a crib. Helen's return is motivated by her love for Johnny, not Ned. Although it may be argued that the reunion scene reinstates Helen into the repressive patriarchal institution of marriage, Ned's Oedipal revenge has failed, and it is the perverse bond of mother and infantilized child that is reaffirmed. There is high irony (and typically understated Sternbergian humor) in the fact that in the last scene, Dietrich does not reveal her body. But, behind the doors of Johnny's bedroom, she removes her coatdress beneath which she is wearing an evening gown which remarkably is cut low in both the front and the back and bares her shoulders at the same time. As Kaplan claims, Dietrich's "fetishization" may be aimed toward the male spectator, but the implications of that fetishistic process seem much more textually and psychologically complex than Kaplan allows, especially within the context of a film that, as Robin Wood has so convincingly shown, seems to very knowingly (rather than unconsciously as Kaplan says) undermine patriarchal norms.[17]

A revisionary theory of masochism built on Deleuze and pre-Oedipal object relations theory, allows us to posit a fetishism in which the child does not disavow the mother's supposed castration, but separation from her body and his difference from her as the representative of a "femininity posited as lacking nothing."[18] From such a revised perspective, fetishism's link to masochism explains a specific kind of pleasure in looking, reflecting the desire to reconstruct the powerful pre-Oedipal mothering imago and to submit to her power in inseparable plenitude. Many researchers claim fetishism should be understood as having pre-Oedipal determinants that express the need to preserve primary identification with the authoritative pre-Oedipal mother; this research also affirms Deleuze's suggestion that fetishism and masochism have a particular affinity.[19] In masochism, the fetishistic treatment of the woman reflects an idealization of the mother, the disavowal of her separateness, and the wish for reunion with her (resymbiosis). However, ambivalence marks this wish: it registers fear of being overwhelmed by the mother as well as the hope of a resymbiosis, not to be achieved in reality, but a plenitude recaptured only in the fantasy reunion of Death.

Thus, if fetishism is understood as a phenomenon in which the desire to overcome distance is immobilized by a fear of the wished-for re-bonding of mother and child, then the interplay between the tactile implications of costuming as fetish (the texture of fur, satin, etc.) and its visual aspects (the pleasure of looking at a distance) begins to make sense, as does *fetishistic scopophilia* as a form of looking that is not Oedipal, but pre-Oedipal, not sadistic and destructive in intent, but disavowing and masochistic.

In the masochistic fantasy of the male subject, patriarchal norms of gender-defined dominance (male) and submission (female) are reversed. Consequently, while a Deleuzean theory of masochism frees us to challenge the notion of the female as a fetish signifying only castration/lack, it also challenges the notion that Hollywood film always constructs a controlling, masterful pleasure for male spectators that negates any possibility that men might identify with the represented female as an active, authoritative figure.

"Especially When She is Behaving Cruelly"

Josef von Sternberg's films with Marlene Dietrich, *The Blue Angel* (1930), *Morocco* (1930), *Dishonored* (1931), *Shanghai Express* (1932), *The Scarlet Empress* (1934), *The Devil Is A Woman* (1935), and *Blonde Venus* (1932) are the filmic equivalents to Sacher-Masoch's novels. The masochistic subject is most often inscribed in these films through the presence of male actors who resemble von Sternberg, while Dietrich's powerfully sexual, androgynous presence is asserted in a series of characters who have most frequently been labeled as *femme fatales*. Yet it would be a mistake to give the impression that Dietrich is an unvarying *femme fatale*, nor do her actions belong to the domain of sadism, as critics frequently suggest.[20] Deleuze explains that in masochism the punishing woman is not sadistic, but exhibits the pseudo-sadism (punishing functions) required within the purely masochistic narrative.[21]

Unlike sadism which demands a true victim, masochism is a contractual alliance. The willing victim (in this case, the male) provocatively inspires and goes so far as to formally arrange these punishments at the hands of a beautiful woman. He may even seek to guarantee the often reluctant dominatrix's costuming through a contract, as in Sacher-Masoch's agreement with Fanny von Pistor in which she agrees to "to wear furs as often as possible, especially when she is behaving cruelly."[22]

Not surprisingly, the contract appears as a major motif in von Sternberg's *Blonde Venus* and *The Devil Is A Woman,* and Dietrich's appearance in furs is a foregone conclusion in all of the films except those set in warm climates. (*Morocco,* however, contains a reference to the sables Amy Jolly once owned.) The Sternbergian heroine's *femme fatale* status usually depends, not on a written contract, but upon the implied projection of the male's desire for submission to her. For example, in *The Devil Is A Woman,* Don Pasquale, the masochistic male, masquerades behind a mask of passivity as he attempts to displace responsibility for his fate onto Concha Perez. She is an actively elusive figure, first glimpsed by the film audience as a fleeting, masked figure in a pre-Lenten carnival parade. Don Pasquale admits that he chose to pursue Concha in defiance of his better judgment: "I had two options," he laments, "to leave her or to kill her." He admits: "I chose a third." This echoes a statement made by Severin, the protagonist of Sacher-Masoch's most famous novel, *Venus in Furs:* "The comic side of my situation . . . is that I could escape, but do not want to."[23] In an interview in the 1960s, von Sternberg discusses the male's complicity in a sexual alliance of self-punishment. Commenting on the relationship between Lola Lola, perhaps the most famous Dietrich *femme fatale* and her "victim," Professor Rath in *The Blue Angel,* von Sternberg says: "She did not destroy him—he destroyed himself. It was his mistake—he should have never taken up with her. That's what the story is."[24] Here, then, in the von Sternberg/Dietrich films' relationship between the *femme fatale* and the willing victim we find the crystallization of the contradictions in Mulvey's elision of masochism in her theory. How can the fetishized *femme fatale* assuage castration fear? And if the figure of the woman is not a phallic substitute in the masochistic dynamic, then how does costuming, given its emphasis within the von Sternberg/Dietrich films, relate to the deeper unconscious pleasures of spectatorship?

Mothers in Metamorphoses

Iris Barry once despairingly referred to Dietrich as a "mere clotheshorse" in what she dismissed as von Sternberg's "succession of deplorable films, each one more lavish and stupider than the others."[25] Dietrich must be a clotheshorse in the sense that costumes and masks are the masochistic props par excellence. The feathers, furs, the whips, headdresses, helmets, and masks everpresent in Sacher-Masoch's novels and in von Sternberg's films conform to the need to fetishistically idealize the woman as they are used to play out the masochistic rituals of punishment and disguise. Unlike the Sadean heterocosm with its prototype in the novels of the Marquis de Sade, von Sternberg's masochistic heterocosm, like Sacher-Masoch's, is neither obscene nor pornographic; instead it plays upon the "striptease," or as Barthes says, the "staging of an appearance-as-disappearance"[26] within a strategy of continuous masquerade, of erotic metamorphoses in the service of desire. Sacher-Masoch's novels abound in almost mystical descriptions of the exquisite torturess who is rarely if ever naked, but always adorned in sable, silk, or satin. Severin describes the object of his desire in *Venus in Furs:* "At the sight of her lying on the red velvet cushions, her precious body peeping out between the folds of sable, I realized how powerfully sensuality and lust are aroused by flesh that is only partly revealed."[27] The suggestive power of the partially concealed body manifests the play of anticipation and suspense that structures masochistic temporality. Masochism obsessively recreates the suspended movement between concealment and revelation, disappearance and appearance, seduction and rejection, in emulation of the ambivalent response to the mother who the child fears may either abandon or overwhelm him. The control of desire through theatrical ritualization of fantasy in masochistic masquerade delays the genital consummation of desire, a sexual act that would restore the symbolic presence of the Oedipal father, the phallic intrusion into the symbiotic merger of mother and child.[28]

Consequently, the male masochist wants to be led in a round robin of pretense, misunderstanding, and sexual disguise in order to prolong the pleasure of desire unfulfilled. Through costuming, the woman creates a game of appearance and disappearance propelling the male masochist's pursuit in which pleasure is experienced in fetishistic "foreplay" rather than in sexual union. The female's transformations deflect and confuse the male gaze in order to keep the masochistic charade alive. Wanda, the heroine of *Venus in Furs,* appears first as an aloof goddess in gleaming white satin who suddenly comes to life under the moonlight, then as a cruel mistress in ermine-trimmed jacket and toque "such as Catherine the Great liked to wear," and finally as a diffident traveler, leading her male slave in a *fort/da* game of desire, costumed in "a kind of Amazon's travelling dress in black linen . . . bordered with dark fur."[29]

Dietrich's transformations through costume bear uncanny resemblance to Masoch's descriptions of his heroines. They also work in tandem with her fabled air of insolence to create the coldly erotic atmosphere necessary for masochism to work "to suppress pagan sexuality and keep sadistic sensuality at bay."[30] Silvia Bovenschen has remarked that Dietrich is a myth "in spite of her disdain for men."[31] Perhaps she is also a myth *because of* her disdain since Dietrich's indifference to male desire and her elusive costuming exemplify the cold feminine ideal of masochistic fantasy. Psychoanalyst Victor Smirnoff has suggested that this ideal reflects the ambivalence of the desiring child who sees the mother as simultaneously loving and rejecting. As projections of the child's ambivalence, the bad and good mothering imagos, imposed on a single person, cannot be expressed through a "physical core" but must be represented through clothing: "The dual structure of the love object is clearly stated, since clothes more than the physical core, determine the status of the love object; and this dual structure must remain throughout the whole story . . ."[32]

Smirnoff's view is compatible with that of Deleuze who believes that the mother figure in the masochistic fantasy absorbs the functions of three mothering imagos from the child's psychosexual development. The two "bad" figures merge in the ideal figure of the good oral mother who represents the oral period of perfect nurturing and symbiotic merger. Costuming functions here as a primary means of distinguishing these mythically evocative mothering imagos: the hetaeric primitive uterine mother (Sacher-Masoch's "Grecian woman") associated with prostitution, paganism, and confusion of gender roles; the Oedipal mother who administers punishment or is punished by the father; and the good oral mother, loving, coolly distant, and holding the promise of a fantasmical reunion of unimaginable bliss. These three figures also play a part in the subject's disavowal and redistribution of the father's phallic power onto the authoritative, active pre-Oedipal mother. The good oral mother takes on all of these maternal functions as she transforms and idealizes them so that "the father is excluded and completely nullified."[33]

In guaranteeing the pleasurable pain of desiring, the von Sternberg/Dietrich films evidence the masochistic projection of these multiple mothering imagos onto Dietrich. In *Shanghai Express* Shanghai Lily (Dietrich) appears as Sacher-Masoch's Grecian woman. She lives for momentary pleasure, defends the independence of women, and fulfills Severin's remarks in *Venus in Furs:* "If I cannot find a noble and spirited woman . . . then give me no half-measures, no lukewarm compromises. I prefer to be at the mercy of a woman without virtue, fidelity or pity, for she is also my ideal . . ."[34] Lily's costume of enveloping black feathers, veils, and lace chemises advertise her sexual availability (Figure 12.2). They also seem to adhere to the model of "excess femininity" that Mary Ann Doane says men "necessarily regard as evil incarnate."[35] However, Lily, like the most of the other Dietrich/von Sternberg *femme fatales,* is not "evil incarnate" although she is initially vilified by other characters as a woman who, like some sexual typhoon, has "wrecked men up and down the Chinese coast." Lily was once Madeleine, the faithful fiancée of Donald "Doc" Harvey, a British army surgeon who wrongfully accused her of being unfaithful. When he finds her years later, Doc's fascination with her is unabated although Lily announces to the world through costume

Figure 12.2 *Shanghai Express* (1932) Lily's costume "advertises her sexual availability". Paramount Pictures, courtesy of Cinema Collectors, CA.

that she has become the metamorphic extreme of the type of woman he believed her to be. This costume is a disguise: Shanghai Lily proves her moral superiority as the ideal cold oral mother in a scenario that, like Sacher-Masoch's, uses the thinnest of plot pretexts to sustain the male's humiliating pursuit of the woman.

Chinese revolutionaries stop the train on which Doc and Lily ride. Doc is threatened with blindness; Lily offers to give herself to the revolutionaries' general to save him. By the end of the film, the cynical Lily has prayed to save her man's life, but she does not conform (or reform) to the de-eroticized model that Mulvey posits as the model of classical Hollywood norms. No costuming signs mark her as Doc Harvey's possession, indicating that she will, in Mulvey's words, become "his property, losing her outward glamourous characteristics, her generalized sexuality, her show-girl connotations," thus allowing the male spectator, by way of identification with the hero, to "indirectly possess her too."[36] On the contrary, the happily-ever-after of *Shanghai Express* like that of *Blonde Venus,* is a reversal of traditional male-female power relations. Lily remains in her prostitute's costume of swaying black feathers. Doc follows her. Finally, they embrace. She takes his riding crop in her gloved hand, confirming the power relations already evident between them, relations that are more than slightly reminiscent of *Venus in Furs* in which Severin describes Wanda: "The supple furs greedily caressed her cold marble body. Her left arm . . . lay like a sleeping swan amid the dark sable, while her right hand toyed with the whip."[37]

In *The Devil Is A Woman,* Concha Perez also appears as the capricious hetaeric mothering imago. She is first glimpsed by Don Pasquale as she sits on a snowbound train amidst the bustle of an overcrowded third-class compartment. Her circumspect, nunlike costuming consists of a wimple-like headcover, shawl, and a cross hanging from a necklace (Figure 12.3). Yet Dietrich's famed arched and plucked eyebrows, exaggerated to an even greater degree here, hint that her clothing is a masquerade, that it is not based on a cause/effect relationship between signifier (her attire) and signified (her personality). Concha is neither a nun, nor a simple peasant girl, in spite of the goose she holds in a basket. She petulantly trips a woman, twiddles her thumbs and rolls her eyes in feigned innocence, then proceeds to trip her again. A fight ensues. Concha must be restrained by the captain of the guard, Don Pasquale, who will play Severin to her Wanda. Don Pasquale is smitten by Concha, but she smilingly rejects him saying, "What do you take me for? . . . Mother says, a closed mouth never catches flies." Pasquale later "accidently" encounters Concha when he tours a cigarette factory. He pretends to be on official business but admits he was "looking for a pretty girl." He finds Concha. She looks and acts like a completely different person as she casually accepts his advances and his gold coins. Her lovers become numerous, but to Don Pasquale's dismay, her nunnish unavailability, suggested in their first meeting, still holds true for him. Later, she appears as a vision of cascading icy white-ness, in dripping mantilla and fringed white gown, to become the visual correlative to Don Pasquale's declaration: "that one has ice where her heart ought to be" (Figure 12.4). In this instance, Concha's costuming also displays the metaphorical ability of costuming to communicate the quality of coldness necessary to keep sensuality at bay in the play of

Figure 12.3 *The Devil is a Woman* (1935) Concha's nun's habit as masquerade. Paramount Pictures, courtesy of Cinema Collectors, CA.

masochistic desire. Only in the film's ambiguous hallucinatory ending does she, like Shanghai Lily, "redeem" herself: she abandons her young lover to return to Don Pasquale, who lies dying in a hospital after he has willingly permitted himself to be shot in a duel to spare her lover, Antonio. Swathed in yards of black satin, lace gloves, and a broad-brimmed hat dripping with black veiling, Concha becomes the physical correlative for death, the site of Don Pasquale's final masochistic triumph (Figure 12.5).

The protean transformations of the woman without such a dynamic of cold sensuality serve more than a purely unconscious purpose. Although they reflect the changing maternal imagos and the projected ambivalence of the desiring subject, these visual transformations through costuming ensure the female's survival as she attempts to cope with her position as economic and sexual commodity in patriarchy. This function is most obvious in *The Scarlet Empress* and *Blonde Venus*. In the latter, Helen Faraday's changes of costume and social identity are initially part of her attempt to obtain money to save her husband's life. She assumes a succession of masquerades as part of her investment in herself as a sexual commodity, as the fabulous "Blonde Venus." It is only by capitalizing on her value as a sexual spectacle (on stage) and a sexual commodity (in a politician's bed) that she saves her husband from a lingering disease

Figure 12.4   *The Devil is a Woman* (1935) Concha as a "vision of icy white-
ness". Paramount Pictures, courtesy of Cinema Collectors.

brought on by his own chemical experiments. When her husband discovers
that his cure has been bought at the price of her adultery, he condemns
her for her actions and threatens to take her son from her. His attitude
would seem to support Kaplan's assertion that sexuality and mothering
are incompatible under patriarchy, but this is not to say that *Blonde Venus*
encourages the spectator to side with the father. Helen takes her son and
flees. Reduced to poverty and prostitution, her ability to camouflage
herself then becomes a survival technique in a society that judges and
exploits her according to her image. Even the detective sent to find her
does not recognize that Helen Faraday hides beneath the battered straw

Figure 12.5   *The Devil is a Woman* (1935) Concha as Black-veiled
death. Paramount Pictures, courtesy of Cinema Collectors, CA.

brim and smear of heavy lipstick of a Galveston prostitute. "You don't
look anything like these other women," he cheerfully tells his new friend.
"Just give me time," she cynically replies.

By creating herself through masquerade and performance, Helen Faraday and Marlene Dietrich are part of a process in which the woman obtains
power through her knowledge of how others see her. As many critics have
noted, Dietrich possesses an aloofness that suggests a distanciation from
her constructed image, a refusal to emotionally invest in her "femininity"
and its assumed aim of attracting men. This cannot be interpreted as a
liberation by any means, but it does locate a certain resistance to patriarchal
norms even as von Sternberg's films seem to constantly remind the masochistic male character and the spectator that the gaze determines but
cannot control the object of desire. This is explicitly demonstrated in the
cabaret scene in *Morocco* in which Amy Jolly defies the attempt of a man
in the audience to hold her by her costume and is echoed in Concha's

disdainful remark to Don Pasquale: "How can you lose what you never possessed?"

Is This a Man, A Woman, or Both?

Within feminist theory, the issue of distanciation from the image has been addressed in terms of the masquerade. Defined from a Lacanian perspective by Michèle Montrelay, masquerade emerges as a process in which, "a woman uses her own body to disguise herself"; femininity is created with a masquerade of "dotty objects, feathers, hats, strange baroque constructions," the purpose of which is "to say nothing."[38] Montrelay adheres to Lacan's assertion that the masquerade (like fetishism) is used to disavow feminine lack. Joan Riviere, however, offers a very different interpretation of the woman's assumption of excessive feminine accoutrements. She links this masquerade to a defensive attempt "to hide the possession of masculinity and to avert the reprisals expected if she was found to possess it."[39] Doane suggests that such a masquerade may construct a distance between the woman and her public assumption of femininity even as it "carries a threat of disarticulating male systems of viewing."[40] The masquerade confuses male looking even as it provides the woman with a way to achieve a certain distance between herself and the sexual identity demanded of her by the patriarchy.

Masquerade as a disguise of femininity may indeed destabilize a specific form of the male gaze: the sadistic and Oedipal variety, but it sustains *fetishistic scopophilia*'s dialectic of distance and intimacy within a dynamic of masochistic male looking. A masquerade of "excess femininity" is perfectly at home in masochism in which masquerade—in many forms including but not limited to excess femininity—functions as a mechanism to help maintain the dialectical play of distance and closeness necessitated by the subject's ambivalence towards the symbiotic union of mother and subject/child.

Dietrich's distanciation from all her assumed costumes—whether the ambiguously masculine or the excessively feminine—is typical of masochistic masquerade, in which the participants operate on the belief that sexual and social identity is as easily assumed and rejected as a piece of clothing. In Sacher-Masoch's *Venus in Furs*, "The Greek" sometimes dresses like a woman and is courted by other men. His rival for Wanda, Severin, assumes the varied costumes of a servant. Wanda tells him at one point: "You are whatever I want you to be, a man, a thing, an animal."[41] To prove her point, female servants then tie Severin to a plough and push him into the field. Within the acting out of masochistic fantasy, characters also recognize that roles of dominance and submission are not natural, but constructs to be assumed and played at. In *Venus in Furs*, the theatrical excess of masochism is apparent in an exchange between Severin and Wanda: " 'Tread on me!' I cry, throwing myself before her. 'I dislike play-acting,' says Wanda impatiently. 'Then hurt me in earnest.' "[42]

Falling outside either Montrelay's or Doane's definitions of masquerade, cross-dressing appears as a particularly important type of masquerade in the masochistic dynamic. It is also a trademark of Dietrich, who assumes male attire in *Blonde Venus, Morocco, Dishonored,* and *The Scarlet Empress* and limited variations on it in *Shanghai Express* and *The Blue Angel.* The significance of this motif in Sacher-Masoch's "Grecian woman" (hetaeric mother) relates to masochism's underlying refusal to accept the "reality" of the Oedipal regime in which the father's genital sexuality dominates within rigidly defined gender and sex role boundaries. Instead, the polymorphous possibilities of bisexuality are symbolically maintained through cross-dressing and other masquerades that break down the patriarchal polarity of sexual difference and provide the visual vehicle for expressing the masochist's belief that it is possible to become both sexes.

In von Sternberg's masochistic heterocosm, carnival celebrations frequently provide the excuse for masquerades which confuse gender identity and permit a mobility of desire through visual transformation. In *Dishonored,* Magda (Dietrich) attends a dance ball dressed in a glittering lamé and black chain mail cape, plumed headgear and a half-mask. Looking like a cross between a black bird of prey and a medieval knight, she seems to have shifted her shape in the manner of a Greek god rather than assumed a costume. Her masquerade gives her the appearance of a prenatural creature of ambiguous gender: her legs are female, but her swagger is masculine. She appears to be of an entirely different gender than the other women who are attired in conventional ball gowns. At the same time, Magda's masculinized manner combines with her costume to visually contradict her mission of heterosexual seduction in the service of the Austrian government, a mission which would seem to depend on clearly defined sexual difference within established "natural" boundaries of sexual role playing.

Similarly, in *Morocco,* Dietrich appears on stage in a rowdy Moroccan nightclub clad in a man's black tuxedo, white tie, and top hat. In the first backstage scene, her gestures do not soften her masculine attire to safely recuperate "femininity"; on the contrary, she appears unequivocally butch (Figure 12.6). She silently takes the stage and gazes down on an effeminized Gary Cooper, who later wears a flower behind his ear and carries a fan. After her song, she accepts the accolades of the audience and stops to give a woman in the audience a kiss on the mouth. Similarly, in *Blonde Venus,* Dietrich dons an all-white tuxedo ensemble and flirts with a chorus of dancers dressed as harem girls (Figure 12.7). Her performance in drag

Figure 12.6 *Morocco* (1930) Amy Jolly is "unequivocally butch" in tuxedo and tails. Paramount Pictures, courtesy of Cinema Collectors, CA.

Figure 12.7 *Blonde Venus* (1932) The "fluidity of sexual identity". Paramount Pictures, courtesy of Cinema Collectors, CA.

serves to demonstrate the fluidity of sexual identity even as it parodies male narcissism. Clothes "make the man": with only the exterior trappings of "masculinity" she assumes the male's prerogative of sexual assertiveness. Her tuxedo and same-sex flirtations confuse the norms of sexual difference and the expectations of heterosexual desire. That desire, like her clothes, appears as a consciously chosen momentary pleasure rather than a biologically determined compulsion.

In donning male attire, Dietrich transforms the spectacle of female representation into a ritualized acting out of bisexual identification. Clothes provide a way of carrying out magical body change and the wish to become both sexes without requiring the complete rejection of the original gender identity.[43] Through the changing spectacle of masquerade, the limits of a single gender identity and one body-ego are pleasurably transcended.

The Woman All Women Love to See

There is no question that Dietrich is an eroticized image in these films. She is coded as a sexual, "fetishized" object, but for whom and to what purpose? Is she constructed for the sole pleasure of the male spectator as Kaplan claims? In much of current theoretical discourse, the female spectator's reaction to the representation of women is said to be channeled by Hollywood film into two narrow avenues for pleasure: either a masochistic (or narcissistic) overidentification with the passively exhibitionist female or an identification with the privileged male position/gaze for whom the spectacle of woman is constructed. Doane, among others, asserts that in this process, the woman spectator shifts between the "masculinized" or "transvestite" identification with the camera whose look is mediated by the film's central active male character, and a masochistic overidentification with the woman character defined as the object of the camera's "masculine" look.[44] Yet writers as varied as Molly Haskell, Kathryn Weibel, and Julia Lesage have remarked on the complex appeal of Dietrich to women, an appeal that appears to extend beyond either of the two spectatorial alternatives described by Doane.[45]

Dietrich's appeal to women is neither a new nor an easily explained phenomenon. In its time, *Morocco* advertised its star as "the woman all women love to see," and von Sternberg commented in his autobiography that he was unsure whether women like glamorous female stars because they wish to emulate them or they are "confused" and find them sexually desirable.[46] Julia Lesage has remarked that Dietrich is a powerful subculture icon who " . . . fascinates women as a lesbian figure with whom they identify."[47] This view of Dietrich is supported by the films' suggestions of lesbianism, their incorporation of cross-dressing, and perhaps also by rumors concerning the star's private life.[48] But others have suggested that Dietrich's fascination, even for lesbian audiences, is not one of identification, but as an erotic object of woman-to-woman desire.[49] Dietrich's appeal to both straight and lesbian women spectators points to a dynamic of pleasurable looking that is more complex than either the normative model of narcissistic, heterosexual identification or the alternative model of a similarly motivated lesbian identification. To probe the source of this fascination we need to return to the von Sternberg/Dietrich films as a masochistic formal system.

In the von Sternberg films, Dietrich's representation of a sensual androgyny is subversively paired with a change in the construction of the relay of the gaze. Not only is the male gaze altered in its aim of submission rather than control, but a change is also evident in the formal construction of the trajectory of looking (spectators/camera/characters). As I discussed earlier, Mulvey notes the absence of a strong male protagonist who could mediate between spectatorial looking and Dietrich as the object of the gaze of von Sternberg's camera. Without a strong controlling male gaze situated within the diegetic space, the image of Dietrich is brought into a fetishistic "direct erotic rapport with the spectator."[50]

What Mulvey does not consider in her analysis of *fetishistic scopophilia*, however, is the effect of that "direct erotic rapport" on women spectators. Mulvey's notion of unmediated pleasurable looking, combined with a revisionary concept of a pre-Oedipal fetishism, creates the theoretical means for reconsidering the source of Dietrich's fascination for female audiences. Unmediated by a male gaze, I would argue, this "direct erotic rapport" encourages a potentially subversive female to female looking that also evokes pre-Oedipal pleasures and ambivalences. Although Dietrich may be constructed according to a masochistic male fantasy and for the primary pleasure of a masochistic male gaze, the absence of male mediation of the look, as well as the sexual ambiguity of Dietrich's erotic image, encourage a female looking that defies heterosexual norms and the accepted dominance/submission agenda of patriarchal sexual politics. The mechanisms of masochism disturb the power of the "phallic" gaze to create space for an erotically charged female gaze fixed on the woman star. The result is a system of looking that elicits both female spectatorial identification with and *desire for* the powerful *femme fatale*.

The von Sternberg/Dietrich films demonstrate a psychodynamic and formal system with complex signifying implications. Through a theory of masochism, as I have shown, the relationship between costuming, fantasy, and visual pleasure can be analyzed with attention to the function of specific modes of costuming and visualization. Undeniably, the von Sternberg/Dietrich films reflect the projection of male fantasy onto the female. Nevertheless, the protean metamorphoses of the woman, the scandalous change of sexual identity through cross-dressing, and the suggestive power of Dietrich as the maternal object of masochistic fetishism suggest the existence of forms of Hollywood narrative film and forms of spectatorship that may subvert patriarchal power relations and heterosexual norms. Even as these pleasures resist explanation through a single monolithic Oedipal/castration model of Hollywood film, they also, in spite of analysis and re-analysis, remain—like a Dietrich masquerade—as fascinatingly elusive as they are powerfully enticing.

Notes

1. Fabricating the Female Body

1. Annette Kuhn, *The Power of the Image: Essays in Representation and Sexuality* (London: Routledge & Kegan Paul, 1985), 13.

2. Judith Williamson, "Images of 'Woman,' " *Screen* 24, No. 6 (November-December 1983): 102; rpt. in Judith Williamson, *Consuming Passions: The Dynamics of Popular Culture* (London: Marion Boyars, 1986).

3. Anne Hollander, *Seeing Through Clothes* (New York: Viking Press, 1975), xiii.

4. Edward Maeder, "The Celluloid Image: Historical Dress in Film," *Hollywood and History: Costume Design in Film,* ed. Edward Maeder (New York: Thames and Hudson, 1987), 13.

5. Roland Barthes, *Erté, (Romain de Tirtoff),* trans. William Weaver (Parma: Franco Maria Ricci, 1972), 26; trans. Richard Howard, as "Erté or À la lettre," in Roland Barthes, *The Responsibility of Forms* (New York: Hill and Wang, 1985).

6. Sandra Lee Bartky, "Narcissism, Femininity and Alienation," *Social Theory and Practice* 8, (Summer 1982): 137–38.

7. Simone de Beauvoir, *The Second Sex,* trans. H.M. Parshley (New York: Knopf, 1953), 529.

8. John Berger, *Ways of Seeing* (London: Penguin, 1972).

9. Adrienne Rich, "Compulsory Heterosexuality and Lesbian Existence," *Powers of Desire: The Politics of Sexuality,* ed. Ann Snitow, Christine Stansell, and Sharon Thompson (New York: Monthly Review Press, 1983), 184.

10. Rayna Rapp and Ellen Ross, "The Twenties' Backlash: Compulsory Heterosexuality, the Consumer Family, and the Waning of Feminism," *Class, Race, and Sex: The Dynamics of Control,* ed. Amy Swerdlow and Hanna Lessinger (Boston: G.K. Hall, 1983), 103; Historian Lois Banner, takes a similar position as she analyzes the first Miss America pageant in 1921 as marking the "triumph of the fashion culture over feminism." See *American Beauty* (New York: Knopf, 1983), 16.

11. The basic texts associated with the "images of woman" approach are Molly Haskell,

From Reverence to Rape: The Treatment of Women in the Movies (New York: Holt, Rinehart and Winston, 1973); Marjorie Rosen, *Popcorn Venus: Women, Movies and the American Dream* (New York: Avon Books, 1973); and Joan Mellen, *Women and Their Sexuality in the New Film* (New York: Horizon Press, 1974). A critique of this position can be found in Griselda Pollock, "What's Wrong with Images of Women?" *Screen Education* 24 (Summer 1977): 25–33; Claire Johnston, "Feminist Politics and Film History," *Screen* 16, no. 3 (Autumn 1975): 115–24; Diane Waldman, "What's Wrong with Positive Images?," *Jump Cut* no. 18 (August 1978): 31–32; rpt., *Jump Cut: Hollywood, Politics and Counter-Cinema*, ed. Peter Steven (New York: Praeger, 1985).

12. Sheila Rowbotham, *Woman's Consciousness, Man's World* (Harmondsworth: Pelican, 1973), 109.

13. See Judith Walkowitz, *Prostitution and Victorian Society: Women, Class and the State* (Cambridge [Cambridgeshire], N.Y.: Cambridge University Press, 1980); Elizabeth Ewen, *Immigrant Women in the Land of Dollars: Life and Culture on the Lower East Side 1890–1925* (New York: Monthly Review Press, 1985); Gwen Robinson, *Crowning Glory: A Historical Analysis of the Afro-American Beauty Industry and Tradition* (Urbana: University of Illinois Press, forthcoming).

14. The Barnard Papers were published in *Pleasure and Danger: Exploring Female Sexuality*, ed. Carole S. Vance (Boston: Routledge & Kegan Paul, 1984). A more recent formulation of some of the issues raised around feminism and pleasure can be found in *Caught Looking: Feminism, Pornography and Censorship*, ed. Kate Ellis et. al. (New York: Caught Looking, 1987).

15. See Mary Ann Doane, Patricia Mellencamp, and Linda Williams, eds. *Revision: Essays in Feminist Film Criticism* (Frederick, Md.: University Publications of America, 1984), 9; E. Ann Kaplan, "Feminist Film Criticism: Current Issues and Problems," *Studies in Literary Imagination* 19 (1986): 7–20; E. Ann Kaplan, "The Hidden Agenda: *Re-Vision: Essays in Feminist Literary Criticism*," *Camera Obscura* 13–14 (1985): 235–249.

16. See Bret Harvey, "No More Nice Girls," *Pleasure and Danger*, ed. Vance, 204–209.

17. Roland Barthes, trans. Richard Miller, *The Pleasure of the Text* (New York: Hill and Wang, 1975); Jane Gallop gives us the history of the fate of *plaisir* and *jouissance* in their translation into English. See *Thinking Through the Body* (New York: Columbia University Press, 1988), 120–23.

18. Kuhn, *The Power of the Image*, 8.

19. "Lesbians for Lipstick" is a group of lesbians in Durham, North Carolina who have circulated a newsletter as a spoof on lesbian anti-fashion style and commercial beauty culture.

20. Cindy Patton, "Brave New Lesbians," *Village Voice*, 2 July, 1985, 24; Joan Nestle, "The Fem Question," *Pleasure and Danger*, ed. Vance, 236.

21. Carol Ascher, "Narcissism and Women's Clothing," *Socialist Review* 11, no. 3 (May-June 1981): 77, 81; For a discussion of the "rhetoric of the natural" in contemporary lesbian culture, see Richard Dyer, "Seen to be Believed: Some Problems in the Representation of Gay People as Typical," *Studies in Visual Communication* 9, (1983): 15.

22. Elizabeth Wilson, *Adorned in Dreams: Fashion and Modernity* (London: Virago, 1985), 13.

23. Monique Wittig, "The Category of Sex," *Feminist Issues* (1976).

24. Mary Ann Doane, "Woman's Stake: Filming the Female Body," *October* no. 17 (1981): 25; rpt. *Feminism and Film Theory,* ed. Constance Penley (New York: Routledge, 1988).

25. For a thorough introduction to this approach, see Stuart Hall, "Cultural Studies at the Centre: Some Problematics and Problems," *Culture, Media, Language,* ed. Stuart Hall, Dorothy Hobson, Andrew Lowe, and Paul Willis (London: Hutchinson, 1980), 25–47.

26. V. N. Volosinov, *Marxism and the Philosophy of Language,* trans. Ladislav Matejk and I. R. Titunik (New York: Seminar Press, 1973), 11.

27. Stuart Hall, "Signification, Representation, Ideology: Althusser and the Post-Structuralist Debates," *Critical Studies in Mass Communication* 2 (1985): 99.

28. Dick Hebdige, *Subculture: The Meaning of Style* (New York and London: Methuen, 1979); Stuart Hall and Tony Jefferson, eds. *Resistance Through Rituals: Youth Subculture in Post-War Britain* (London: Hutchinson, 1976).

29. Angela McRobbie, "Settling Accounts with Subcultures," *Screen Education* no. 34 (1980): 37–49; rpt., *Culture, Ideology, and Social Process: A Reader,* ed. Tony Bennett et al. (London: The Open University, 1981), 43.

30. Angela McRobbie, "Working Class Girls and the Culture of Femininity," *Women Take Issue,* ed. Women's Study Group (London: Hutchinson, 1978), 104.

31. Noelle Caskey, "Interpreting Anorexia Nervosa," *The Female Body in Western Culture: Contemporary Perspectives,* ed. Susan Rubin Suleiman (Cambridge, Mass.: Harvard University Press, 1986), 184, 179.

32. Caskey, "Anorexia Nervosa," 184.

33. Susan Willis, "Work (ing) Out," *Cultural Studies* (forthcoming).

34. Margaret Morse, "Artemis Aging: Exercise and the Female Body on Video," *Discourse* 10 (1987–1988): 25.

35. Williamson, *Consuming Passions,* 230.

36. See David Frisby, "George Simmel: First Sociologist of Modernity," *Theory, Culture and Society* 2 (1985): 49–67.

37. Georg Simmel, *On Individuality and Social Forms,* ed. Donald N. Levine (Chicago: University of Chicago Press, 1971), 296.

38. Thorstein Veblen, *The Theory of the Leisure Class: An Economic Study of Institutions* (1899; rpt., New York: Macmillan, 1912).

39. Theodor W. Adorno and Max Horkheimer, *Dialectic of Enlightenment,* trans. John Cumming (1944; rpt., New York: Continuum, 1987); Georg Lukács, *History and Class Consciousness,* trans. Rodney Livingstone (1922; rpt., Cambridge, Mass.: MIT Press, 1971), 86–91.

40. Guy Debord, *Society of the Spectacle* (1967; rpt., Detroit: Black and Red, 1983), 67.

41. Henri Lefebvre, *Everyday Life in the Modern World,* trans. Sacha Rabinovitch (1967; reprint, London: Penguin, 1971).

42. Stuart Ewen, *Captains of Consciousness: Advertising and the Social Roots of the Consumer Culture* (New York: McGraw-Hill, 1976).

43. Fredric Jameson, "Reification and Utopia in Mass Culture," *Social Text* 1 (1979): 144.

44. Siegfried Kracauer, *Theory of Film: The Redemption of Physical Reality* (New York: Oxford University Press, 1960).

45. Siegfried Kracauer, "The Little Shop Girls Go to the Movies," trans. Thomas Y. Levin, *The Mass Ornament* (Cambridge, Mass.: Harvard University, forthcoming); For further discussion of Kracauer's earlier journalistic work see Sabine Hake, "Girls and Crisis: The Other Side of Diversion," *New German Critique* 40 (1987): 147–66; Heide Schlüpmann, "Phenomenology of Film: On Siegfried Kracauer's Writings of the 1920s," *New German Critique* 40 (1987): 97–114.

46. Siegfried Kracauer, "Cult of Distraction: On Berlin's Picture Palaces," trans. Thomas Y. Levin, *New German Critique* 40 (1987): 91–96.

47. Adorno and Horkheimer, *Dialectic of Enlightenment*, 145.

48. Theodor W. Adorno, *Prisms*, trans. Samuel and Sheirry Weber (1967; rpt., Cambridge, Mass.: MIT Press, 1982), 87.

49. For an example of the way Benjamin has been claimed for cultural studies, see Simon Frith, *Sound Effects: Youth, Leisure, and the Politics of Rock 'n' Roll* (New York: Pantheon, 1981), 47.

50. Walter Benjamin, "Art in the Age of Mechanical Reproduction," trans. Harry Zohn, *Illuminations* (Glasgow: Fontana/Collins, 1973); For a report on the progress of the English translation of *Passagen-Werk* as well as a discussion of its promise see Irving Wohlgarth, "Re-fusing Theology: Some First Responses to Walter Benjamin's Arcades Project," *New German Critique* 39 (Fall 1986): 3–24.

51. Susan Buck-Morss, "Benjamin's *Passagen-Werk:* Redeeming Mass Culture for the Revolution," *New German Critique* 29 (1983): 220.

52. Buck-Morss, "Benjamin's *Passagen-Werk*," 233.

53. Michel de Certeau, *The Practice of Everyday Life*, trans. Steven Rendall (Berkeley: University of California Press, 1984), 31.

54. John Fiske, "Popular Forces and the Culture of Everyday Life," *Southern Review* 21, no. 3 (November 1989).

55. Susan Porter Bensen, *Counter Culture: Saleswomen, Managers, and Customers in American Department Stores, 1890–1940* (Urbana: University of Illinois Press, 1986).

56. John Fiske, in conversation with the author.

57. Michael Miller, *The Bon Marché: Bourgeois Culture and the Department Store, 1869–1920* (London: Allen and Unwin, 1981), 197.

58. For an overview of the literature on this see David Chaney, "The Department Store as a Cultural Form," *Theory, Culture and Society* 1 (1983): 22–31. Also see Rachel Bowlby, *Just Looking: Consumer Culture in Dreiser, Gissing, and Zola* (New York and London: Methuen, 1985).

59. Miller, *The Bon Marché*, 201.

60. Jeanne Thomas Allen, "The Film Viewer as Consumer," *Quarterly Review of Film Studies* 5, no. 4 (Fall 1980): 481–99.

61. Mary Ann Doane, *The Desire to Desire: The Woman's Film of the 1940s* (Bloomington: Indiana University Press, 1987), 177.

62. Raymond Williams, *Problems in Materialism and Culture* (London: Verso, 1980), 187.

63. Jean Baudrillard, *For a Critique of the Political Economy of the Sign,* trans. Charles Levin (St. Louis: Telos Press, 1981), 115.

64. An important cross-cultural perspective and some distance on this problem of how to talk about commodities outside the context of advanced capitalism is offered by Igor Kopytoff, "The Cultural Biography of Things: Commoditization as Process," *The Social Life of Things: Commodities in Cultural Perspective,* ed. Arjun Appadurai (Cambridge: Cambridge University Press, 1986).

65. Diane Waldman, "From Midnight Shows to Marriage Vows: Woman, Exploitation, and Exhibition," *Wide Angle* 6, no. 2 (1984): 40–48.

66. Charles Eckert, "Shirley Temple and the House of Rockefeller," *Jump Cut* no. 2 (1974): 1, 17–20; rpt., *Jump Cut: Hollywood, Politics and Counter-Cinema,* ed. Steven; "The Anatomy of a Proletarian Film: Warner's MARKED WOMAN," *Film Quarterly* 17, no. 2 (Winter 1973–74): 10–24; rpt., *Movies and Methods II,* ed. Bill Nichols (Berkeley: University of California press, 1985).

67. See my "Film and Television Costume and Everyday Dress" (unpublished paper).

68. Herbert Blumer, *Movies and Conduct* (New York: Macmillan, 1933), 198, 132.

69. Angela McRobbie, "Postmodernism and Popular Culture," *Postmodernism: ICA Documents 4,* ed. Lisa Appignanesi (London: Institute of Contemporary Arts, 1986), 55, 57; rpt. *Journal of Communication Inquiry* 10 (1986): 108–16.

70. Edgar Morin, *The Stars,* trans. Richard Howard (New York: Grove Press, 1961), 165, 166–67.

71. James Laver, *Clothes* (New York: Horizon press, 1953), 122–52.

72. See Sally Mitchell's introduction to Ellen Price Wood, *East Lynne* (1861; rpt. New Brunswick: Rutgers University Press, 1984), xi.

73. Janice Radway, *Reading the Romance: Women, Patriarchy, and Popular Literature* (Chapel Hill and London: University of North Carolina Press, 1984), 193.

74. For a discussion of the coexistence of the ordinary and the extraordinary in melodrama see Steve Neale, "Melodrama and Tears," *Screen* 27, no. 6 (1986): 7.

75. For an analysis of historical costume and sexuality, see Sue Harper, "Gainsborough: What's in a Costume," *Monthly Film Bulletin* 52 (1985): 324–27; rev. and rpt., *Home is Where the Heart Is: Studies in Melodrama and the Woman's Film,* ed. Christine Gledhill (London: British Film Institute, 1987).

76. David Chierichetti, *Hollywood Costume Design* (New York: Crown, 1976), 18.

77. Edith Head and Paddy Calistro, *Edith Head's Hollywood* (New York: E.P. Dutton, 1983), 42–45.

78. Chierichetti, *Hollywood Costume Design,* 125, quotes Bill Travilla who used this metaphor to describe designing for Marilyn Monroe.

79. My discussion is in "Women and Representation: Can We Enjoy Alternative Pleasure?," *American Media and Mass Culture: Left Perspectives,* ed. Donald Lazere (Berkely and London: University of California Press, 1987); "Visual Pleasure and Narrative Cinema" was first published in *Screen* 16, no. 3 (Autumn 1975): 6–18, and has most recently been reprinted for at least the sixth time in *Feminism and Film Theory,* ed. Constance Penley (Routledge 1988). For an overview of the critical response to this seminal article see Mandy Merck, "Introduction– Difference

and its Discontents," *Screen* 28 (1987): 2 – 9; "Morocco," *Cahiers du Cinéma* no. 225 (1970), rpt. *Sternberg,* trans. Diana Matias, ed. Peter Baxter (London: British Film Institute, 1980).

80. John Fletcher, "Versions of Masquerade," *Screen* 29 (1988): 48–50; Claire Johnston, "Femininity and the Masquerade: Anne Of The Indies," *Jacques Tourneur,* ed. Claire Johnston and Paul Willeman (Edinburgh: Edinburgh Film Festival, 1975).

81. Fletcher, "Versions of Masquerade," 50. I would argue that some of the images which contributed to Mulvey's vision of the phallic woman can be found in Alan Jones's misogynist fetishes. See Laura Mulvey, "You Don't Know What is Happening, Do You, Mr. Jones?," *Spare Rib* 8 (February 1973); rpt., *Spare Rib Reader,* ed. Marsha Rowe (London: Penguin, 1982).

82. Mulvey, "Visual Pleasure and Narrative Cinema," 17.

83. Mulvey, "Visual Pleasure and Narrative Cinema."

84. Dale McConathy and Diana Vreeland, *Hollywood Costume: Glamour! Glitter! Romance!* (New York: H.N. Abrams, 1976), 40; Erté, *Things I Remember: An Autobiography* (New York: Quadrangle, 1975).

85. Roland Barthes, *Erté,* 38; Barthes, however, is speaking as much about his own fascination with linguistics-based systems of meaning which produced his study of fashion imagery as language. See *The Fashion System,* trans. Matthew Ward and Richard Howard (New York: Hill and Wang, 1983).

86. See Lucy Fischer, "The Image of Woman as Image: The Optical Politics of *Dames,*" *Genre: The Musical* ed. Rick Altman (London: Routledge & Kegan Paul, 1981), 74, for the reference to the way Busby Berkeley matched his chorus girls like pearls.

87. Maureen Turim, "Gentlemen Consume Blondes," *Wide Angle* 1 (1979): 52–59; rpt., *Movies and Methods II,* ed. Nichols, 374, 378.

88. *Cahiers du Cinéma* collective text, 92.

89. See John Ellis, *Visible Fictions: Cinema, Television, Video* (London: Routledge & Kegan Paul, 1982), 45, 47.

90. Anne Friedberg, "Identification and the Star: A Refusal of Difference," *Star Signs,* ed. Christine Gledhill et al. (London: British Film Institute, 1982), 50.

91. Ellis, *Visible Fictions,* 47.

92. Baudrillard, *For a Critique of the Political Economy of the Sign,* 88–97.

93. Helene Roberts, "The Exquisite Slave: The Role of Clothes in the Making of the Victorian Woman." *Signs* (1977): 554–79; Joanna Russ, "Comment on Helene E. Robert's 'The Exquisite Slave: The Role of Clothes in the Making of the Victorian Woman' and David Kunzle's 'Dress Reform as Antifeminism,' " *Signs* 2, no. 3 (1977): 521; David Kunzle, *Fashion and Fetishism: A Social History of the Corset, Tight-Lacing and other Forms of Body-Sculpture in the West* (Totowa, N.J.: Rowan and Littlefield, 1982).

94. Wilson, *Adorned in Dreams,* 100, suggests, citing Beatrice Faust, *Women, Sex, and Pornography* (Harmondsworth: Penguin, 1981) that girdles could be auto-erotic.

95. Fletcher, "Versions of Masquerade," 48–49; Janet Bergstrom, "Rereading the Work of Claire Johnston," *Camera Obscura* nos. 3–4 (Summer 1979): 21–31, very

early noted Johnston's indebtedness to *Cahiers du Cinéma's* theorization of the progressive text.

96. Claire Johnston, "Women's Cinema as Counter-Cinema," *Notes on Women's Cinema,* ed. Claire Johnston (London: Society for Education in Film and Television, 1973), 26; rpt. *Movies and Methods,* ed. Bill Nichols (Berkeley and London: University of California Press, 1976).

97. Tania Modleski, *Loving with a Vengeance: Mass-Produced Fantasies for Women* (New York: Methuen, 1982).

98. Mary Ann Doane, "Film and the Masquerade—Theorising the Female Spectator," *Screen* 23 (1982): 85; For Mulvey's earlier formulation see "Afterthoughts on 'Visual Pleasure and Narrative Cinema' inspired by *Duel In The Sun,*" *Framework* 6, nos. 15–17 (1981): 12, rpt. *Feminism and Film Theory,* ed. Penley.

99. Doane *The Desire to Desire,* 181–82.

100. See Claire Whitaker, "Hollywood Transformed: Interviews with Lesbian Viewers," and Edith Becker, Michelle Citron, Julia Lesage and B. Ruby Rich, "Lesbians and Film," *Jump Cut: Hollywood, Politics and Counter-Cinema,* ed. Steven; Caroline Sheldon, "Lesbians and Film: Some Thoughts," *Gays and Film,* ed. Richard Dyer, rev. ed. (New York: Zoetrope, 1984).

101. Miriam Hansen, "Pleasure, Ambivalence, Identification: Valentino and Female Spectatorship," *Cinema Journal* 25, no. 4 (Summer 1986): 8.

102. For an extremely lucid discussion of these formulations and the significance to feminist film theory see Tania Modleski, *The Women Who Knew Too Much: Hitchcock and Feminist Theory* (New York and London: Methuen, 1988), 10–13.

103. E. Ann Kaplan, *Women and Film: Both Sides of the Camera* (New York and London: Methuen, 1983), 53–56.

104. Chris Straayer, "Redressing 'the Natural.' " Paper delivered at Athens Film Conference, March, 1984; See also Arny Christine Straayer, "Sexual Subjects: Signification, Viewership, and Pleasure in Film and Video." Unpublished Ph.D. dissertation, Northwestern University, Evanston, Illinois (June 1989), chaps. 6 and 7.

105. Cynthia Cris, "Pretty in Pink," *Afterimage* 16, no. 1 (Summer 1988): 13, reviewing Mariette Pathy Allen's *The Woman Who Lives Inside: Portraits of Men as Women* (New York: E.P. Dutton, 1989), considers transvestitism in a way that poses an alternative to the cross-dresser as phallic woman:

But the phallic woman is one that exists in denial of castration, and I would question if the denial of castration is the primary function of cross-dressing. When the transvestite "becomes" a woman by means of feminine clothing, cosmetics, and behavior, he denies his masculinity. His cross-dressing veils the penis. It places a disclaimer on the physical and behavioral sign of phallic power. Rather than deny castration, the transvestite defers to it and takes on the signs of femininity to prove it.

106. Gayatri Chakravorty Spivak, "Displacement and the Discourse of Woman," *Displacement: Derrida and After,* ed. Mark Krupnick (Bloomington: Indiana University Press, 1983), 186.

107. Spivak, "Displacement and the Discourse of Woman."

108. Kuhn, *The Power of the Image,* 48–54.

2. All the Rage

1. Quentin Bell, *On Human Finery* (London: The Hogarth Press, 1947).

2. See Stella Mary Newton, *Health, Art and Reason: Dress Reformers of the Nineteenth Century* (London: John Murray, 1974).

3. See David Kunzle, *Fashion and Fetishism* (Totowa, N.J.: Rowan and Littlefield, 1982).

4. James Laver, the British costume historian, for example, has popularized this view in a number of very influential books and articles.

5. Thorstein Veblen, *The Theory of the Leisure Class: An Economic Study of Institutions* (1899; rpt. New York: Macmillan, 1912).

6. See Kunzle, *Fashion and Fetishism* and also Valerie Steele, *Fashion and Eroticism* (New York: Oxford University Press, 1985) who takes issue with feminists such as Helene Roberts, "The Exquisite Slave: The Role of Clothes in the Making of the Victorian Woman," *Signs* 2, no. 3 (Spring 1977), who too readily position women as submissive victims.

7. Stuart Ewen and Elizabeth Ewen, *Channels of Desire: Mass Images and the Shaping of American Consciousnesss* (New York: McGraw-Hill, 1982), 237.

8. Bernice Martin, *A Sociology of Contemporary Cultural Change* (Oxford: Basil Blackwell, 1981), 51.

9. Theodor W. Adorno and Max Horkheimer, *Dialectic of Enlightenment,* trans. John Cumming (1944; rpt. New York: Continuum, 1987).

10. Dick Hebdige, *Subculture: The Meaning of Style* (London: Methuen, 1979).

11. For example, Alison Lurie, *The Language of Clothes* (London: Heinemann, 1981).

12. Sheila Rowbotham, Lynne Segal, and Hilary Wainwright, *Beyond the Fragments* (London: Merlin Press, 1979). Following the publication of this book, which argued for feminism's greater influence on non-aligned socialism, there were a number of conferences to discuss its ideas and an attempt to found an organization to put them into practice.

3. *Fame, Flashdance,* and the Fantasy of Social Integration

1. Gladys Malvern, *Dancing Star* (London: Collins, 1965).

2. Suzanne Langer, *Feeling and Form: A Theory of Art* (New York: Scribner, 1953).

3. Helen Thomas, "Movement, Modernism and Contemporary Culture: Issues for a Critical Sociology of Dance" (Ph.D. diss., University of London, 1986).

4. Romola Nijinsky, *Nijinsky* (London: Penguin, 1960).

5. Peter Wollen, "Fashion/Orientalism/The Body," *New Formations* 1 (Spring 1987): 5–34.

6. See also Eric Cahm, "Revolt, Conservatism, and Reaction to Paris 1905–1925," *Modernism: 1890–1930,* ed. Malcolm Bradbury and James Macfarlane (London: Penguin, 1976) for an interesting discussion following the same lines as Wollen, concentrating on the dramatic effect Diaghilev's *Rite of Spring* with music by Stravinsky had on Paris audiences: "Fighting broke out and the hubbub practically drowned the music; the refined innovations of Debussy were one thing, but these private rites of Russian tribalism another."

7. Wollen, "Fashion/Orientalism/The Body," 28.

8. Ian Chambers, *Urban Rhythms: Pop Music and Popular Culture* (London: Macmillan, 1985).

9. Chambers, *Urban Ryhthms*.

10. Elizabeth Ewen, *Immigrant Women in the Land of Dollars* (New York: Monthly Review Press, 1985) and Kathy Peiss, *Cheap Amusements: Working Women and Leisure in New York City, 1880 to 1920* (Philadelphia: Temple University Press, 1986).

11. Jean McCrindle and Sheila Rowbotham, *Dutiful Daughters* (London: Penguin, 1977).

12. Robert Roberts, *The Classic Slum* (London: Penguin, 1971).

13. Phil Cohen, "Subculture Conflict and Working Class Community," *Culture, Media, Language,* ed. Stuart Hall et al (London: Hutchinson, 1980).

14. Dick Hebdige, *Subculture: The Meaning of Style* (London: Methuen, 1979).

15. Paul Gilroy, *There Ain't No Black in the Union Jack: The Cultural Politics of Race and Nation* (London: Hutchinson, 1987).

16. Noel Streatfield, *Ballet Shoes* (1936; London: Puffin, 1984).

17. *Flashdance* was marketed as a teen dance film. The publicity still and the TV advertisements for the film drew attention to the erotic dimension, focusing particularly on one moment in the film when Alex appears to be dancing under a shower. It might be suggested that the narrative was designed to attract a female interest and the visual subtext to appeal to men.

18. Valerie Walkerdine, "Some Day My Prince Will Come," *Gender and Generation,* ed. Angela McRobbie and Mica Nava (London: Macmillan, 1984).

19. See Kathryn Kalinak, "*Flashdance*: The Dead-End Kid," *Jump Cut* no. 29 (1984): 3–5, for more on racial typage in this film.

20. Gill Frith, " 'The Time of Your Life': The Meaning of the School Story," *Gender Under Scrutiny,* ed. G. Weiner and M. Arnot (London: Hutchinson, 1987).

21. Angela McRobbie, "Interview with Juliet Mitchell," *New Left Review,* no. 170 (August 1988).

22. Bruno Bettelheim, *The Uses of Enchantment* (London: Thames and Hudson, 1976).

4. On The Muscle

1. David Levin, "Here She Is, Miss, Well, What?," *Sports Illustrated,* 17 March 1980, 66.

2. Richard Corliss, "Real People in a Reel Peephole," *Time,* 6 May 1985, 86.

3. Charles Leerhsen and Pamela Abramson, "The New Flex Appeal," *Newsweek,* 6 May 1985, 82.

4. Charles Gaines and George Butler, "Iron Sisters," *Psychology Today* (November 1983): 67.

5. See Stuart Hall, "Culture, the Media and the 'Ideological Effect,' " *Mass Communication and Society,* ed. James Curran, Michael Gurevitch, and Janet Woollacott (Beverly Hills: Sage Publications, 1979), 315–48; Stuart Hall, "Encoding/Decod-

ing," *Culture, Media, Language,* ed. Stuart Hall, Dorothy Hobson, Andrew Lowe, and Paul Willis (London: Hutchinson, 1980), 128–39.

6. Richard Corliss, "The New Ideal of Beauty," *Time,* 30 August 1982, cover.

7. Alexandra Penney, "Showing Some New Muscle," *New York Times Magazine,* 15 June 1980, 58.

8. Penney, "Showing Some New Muscle."

9. Corliss, "The New Ideal of Beauty," 72.

10. Leerhsen and Abramson, "The New Flex Appeal," 83.

11. Hall, "Encoding/Decoding."

12. Linda Gordon, "Women's Bodybuilding: What's In It For You?," *Glamour* (October 1981): 116.

13. Adrienne Rich, "Compulsory Heterosexuality and Lesbian Existence," *Signs* 5, no. 4 (Summer 1980): 631–60.

14. Jim Calio, "Shades of Charles Atlas," *People,* 26 May 1980, 87.

15. Corliss, "The New Ideal of Beauty," 76.

16. Corliss, "The New Ideal of Beauty".

17. Calio, "Shades," 87. Bodybuilder Lisa Lyon states that "your sexual endurance is better" as a result of weight-training.

18. Corliss, "The New Ideal of Beauty," 76, quotes the editor of *Cosmopolitan,* Helen Gurley Brown, who observes that "women are becoming real sexual athletes now. Health gives women stamina that allows them to give full range to their sex drive."

19. Corliss, "The New Ideal of Beauty." Corliss writes: "the new body is here and men may decide it is sexy for one basic reason: it can enhance sex," 76.

20. "Strength . . . The Good Reason Women are Weight Training," *Vogue* (September 1983): 316; Leerhsen and Abramson, 83.

21. Gordon, "Women's Bodybuilding," 116.

22. Calio, "Shades," 87.

23. Corliss, "The New Ideal of Beauty," 72–77.

24. Janice Kaplan, "The New Ideal Female Body: Standards of Feminine Appeal are Definitely Changing," *Glamour* (July 1981): 58.

25. Mike Featherstone, "The Body in Consumer Culture," *Theory, Culture and Society* 1 (Autumn 1982): 18–26.

26. Hall, "Encoding/Decoding."

27. See, for instance, John Fiske, "British Cultural Studies and Television," *Channels of Discourse,* ed. Robert C. Allen (Chapel Hill: University of North Carolina Press, 1987); Janice A. Radway, *Reading the Romance: Women, Patriarchy, and Popular Literature* (Chapel Hill: University of North Carolina Press, 1984); Ien Ang, *Watching Dallas: Soap Opera and the Melodramatic Imagination* (London: Methuen, 1985); David Morley, *Family Television: Cultural Power and Domestic Leisure* (London: Comedia, 1986). See also papers presented at the February 1987 symposium in Blaubeuren, West Germany, "Rethinking the Audience: New Tendencies in Television Research," which introduce important and provocative work on reconceptualizing the audience and research methods: Ellen Seiter, Gabriele Kreutzner, Eva-Maria Warth, and Hans Borchers, "Don't Treat Us Like We're So Stupid and Naive: Towards an Ethnography of Soap Opera Viewers";

Ien Ang, "Wanted: Audiences: On the Politics of Empirical Audience Studies"; John Fiske, "Moments of Television: Neither the Text nor the Audience"; Martin Allor, "Relocating the Site of the Audience: Reconstructive Theory and the Social Subject." Reprinted in Ellen Seiter, Hans Borchers, Gabriele Kreutzner, Eva-Maria Warth, eds. *Remote Control: Television, Audience and Cultural Power* (London and New York: Routledge, 1989).

28. John Fiske, "Critical Response: Meaningful Moments," *Critical Studies in Mass Communication* 5 (September 1988): 249.

29. Fiske, "Critical Response," 247.

30. Fiske, "Critical Response."

31. Fiske, "Critical Response."

32. Janice A. Radway, "Where is 'the Field?': Ethnography, Audiences, and the Redesign of Research Practice" (unpublished paper), 5.

33. Fiske, "Critical Response," 247.

34. For a very insightful discussion of the complex issues clustered around the projects that attempt to rethink the audience, see Radway's "Where is 'the Field?' "

35. John Fiske, *Television Culture* (New York: Methuen, 1987), 240.

36. Fiske, *Television Culture*, 241–43.

37. Fiske, *Television Culture*, 245.

38. Fiske, *Television Culture*, 247. Fiske states that bodybuilding contests are not the "free for all" of professional wrestling where rules exist to be broken and the referees are more often than not ignored or pulled into the fray.

39. Fiske, *Television Culture*, 248.

40. Margaret Morse, "Sport on Television: Replay and Display," *Regarding Television: Critical Approaches—An Anthology*, ed. E. Ann Kaplan (Frederick, Md.: University Publications of America, 1983), 58.

41. Fiske, *Television Culture*, 248.

42. Margaret Morse, "Artemis Aging: Exercise and the Female Body on Video," *Discourse* 10 (Fall-Winter 1987–88): 25.

43. Morse, "Artemis Aging," 24, 42. The terms "mature," "full," and "thick" are significant here in distinguishing the female bodybuilder's look from the cultural norm, which Morse describes as "thin and muscular, hard and curvaceous," suggesting "power and yet a slender boyishness." Boyishness and thinness do not compete with the mature, full muscle of the adult male. They connote the powerlessness of adolescence. The female bodybuilder thus challenges patriarchy on this ground as well.

44. Richard Dyer, "Don't Look Now," *Screen* 23 (September-October 1982): 68.

45. Dyer, "Don't Look Now," 71.

46. Steroids are a very sticky issue for bodybuilding. Bodybuilding magazines like *Muscle & Fitness, Flex,* and *Female Bodybuilding* feature numerous articles warning their readers of the dangers of steroids and urging bodybuilders not to use them. On the other hand, while few male or female bodybuilders will personally go on record acknowledging that they use steroids, the general consensus seems to be that many bodybuilders have used them and continue to use them. Some bodybuilding contests, however, are now testing for steroids and disqualifying competitors if

they test positive. In any case, steroids can certainly be defined as something that has been "done to" a female bodybuilder, and not a few people I talked with about female bodybuilding said that the muscles weren't real because they were the product of drugs.

47. Richard Dyer, *Heavenly Bodies: Film Stars and Society* (New York: St. Martin's Press, 1986), 55.

48. Dyer, *Heavenly Bodies,* 57–59.

49. "Ms. Olympia 1987," *Female Bodybuilding* (May 1988): 31–33; Bill Dobins, "Shoot-out in Toronto," *Muscle & Fitness* (October 1984): 41.

50. Morse, "Artemis Aging," 25.

51. "Letters to the Editor," *Female Bodybuilding* (May 1988): 6.

52. Michel de Certeau, *The Practice of Everyday Life,* trans. Steven Rendall (Berkeley: University of California Press, 1984), 139–40, 147.

53. For a useful discussion of the anti-essentialist and essentialist positions in feminist work on the body, see Mary Ann Doane, "Woman's Stake: Filming the Female Body," *October* 17 (Summer 1981): 23–36.

54. J. M. Manion, "One on One," *Flex* (June 1988): 92–93.

55. "Letters to the Editor," *Female Bodybuilding* (May 1988): 6–7.

56. Fiske, *Television Culture,* 234.

57. Charles Gaines and George Butler, *Pumping Iron II: The Unprecedented Woman* (New York: Simon & Schuster, 1984), 132.

58. Monique Wittig, "One is not Born a Woman," *Feminist Issues* (Winter 1981): 49.

59. Marcia Pally, "Women of 'Iron,' " *Film Comment* 21 (July–August 1985): 62.

60. Pally, "Women of 'Iron.' "

61. Pally, "Women of 'Iron.' ".

62. Christine Holmlund, "Visible Difference and Flex Appeal: The Body, Sex, Sexuality and Race in the *Pumping Iron* Films" *Cinema Journal* 28, no. 4 (Summer 1989).

63. Gaines and Butler, *Pumping Iron II,* 64. In Charles Gaines's apologetic for female bodybuilders, "dikey" is included in the list of things the normal female bodybuilder is *not,* along with feminist, revolutionary, blue-collar, and urban.

64. Richard Dyer, "Victim: Hermeneutic Project," *Film Form* 1 (Autumn 1977), quoted in David Morley, *Family Television,* 43.

65. One crucial issue that needs to be explored empirically is the kind(s) of erotic appeal the female bodybuilder does have for some heterosexual men. The promoters of bodybuilding certainly attempt to position the female bodybuilder as the object of heterosexual masculine desire. I think, though, that empirical work with female bodybuilding's male fans must be done to investigate the range of erotic meanings and pleasures produced, and by whom. We might find, for instance, that for some male fans, the pleasures of female bodybuilding as erotic spectacle may not necessarily be entirely complicit with patriarchal and heterosexist ideologies.

5. The Female Colossus: The Body as Facade and Threshold

1. Theodor Adorno, *Aesthetic Theory,* trans. C. Lenhardt (London and New York: Routledge & Kegan Paul, 1984), 311.

2. Michèle Barrett, "Ideology and the Cultural Production of Gender," *Feminist Criticism and Social Change: Sex, Class and Race in Literature and Culture,* ed. Judith Newton and Deborah Rosenfelt (New York: Methuen, 1985), 70.

3. Simone de Beauvoir, *The Second Sex,* trans. H. M. Parshley (New York: Knopf, 1952), 575.

4. De Beauvoir, *The Second Sex,* 575–76.

5. Jessica Benjamin, *The Bonds of Love: Psychoanalysis, Feminism, and the Problem of Domination* (New York: Random House, 1988), 7.

6. Benjamin, *The Bonds of Love.*

7. Barbara Welter, "The Cult of True Womanhood, 1820–1860," *American Quarterly* 18 (Summer 1966). See also Mary Ryan, *The Empire of the Mother: American Writing About Domesticity, 1830 to 1860* (New York: The Institute for Research in History and the Haworth Press, 1982).

8. Lewis Mumford, *Art and Technics* (New York: Columbia University Press, 1952), 6.

9. Mumford, *Art and Technics,* 61.

10. Siegfried Giedion, *Mechanization Takes Command, A Contribution to Anonymous History* (New York: Norton, 1969), 30.

11. Gerda Lerner, "Placing Women in History: Definitions and Challenges," *Feminist Studies* 3 (Fall 1975): 7.

12. Nancy Chodorow, *The Reproduction of Mothering: Psychoanalysis and the Sociology of Gender* (Berkeley: University of California Press, 1978). This formative work has encouraged feminist cultural critique to explore the relationship between historical developments and human psychology.

13. Jeanne Madeline Weimann, *The Fair Women* (Chicago: Academy Chicago, 1981), 4.

14. *Frank Leslie's Historical Register of the United States Centennial Exposition 1876,* ed. Frank H. Norton (New York: Frank Leslie, 1877), 156.

15. Weimann, *The Fair Women,* 3. Here the author notes that the "Butter Woman" became "the butt of many jokes and some bitterness," suggesting the frustration felt by those who opposed the isolation of women's art in the Women's Pavilion.

16. *Frank Leslie's Historical Register,* 174.

17. *Frank Leslie's Historical Register,* 20.

18. *The Dream City: A Portfolio of Photographic Views of the World's Columbian Exposition,* ed. Halsey C. Ives (St. Louis: N. D. Publishing Co., 1893), n.p. See two juxtaposed photographs of men working on scaffolds to complete the female figures who represent "Art" and "Industry." It is interesting to note that "Art" is an angel with bared breasts while the winged figure of "Industry" is robed and carries a shield.

19. Benjamin, *The Bonds of Love,* 15.

20. De Beauvoir, *The Second Sex,* 577.

21. *Frank Leslie's Historical Register,* 42–49. Note here a collection of lithographs which shows viewers watching workers as they assemble a number of different gigantic statues and put the decorating touches on them. The basic principles of assembly line work are shown to be most fascinating as the tiny spectators and

22. Matthaei, *Economic History of Women,* 155–56.

23. Leslie Woodcock Tentler, *Wage-Earning Women* (New York: Oxford University Press, 1979), 142.

24. Alice Kessler-Harris, *Out to Work: A History of Wage-Earning Women in the United States* (New York: Oxford University Press, 1982), 226.

25. Kessler-Harris, *Out To Work,* 229.

26. Kessler-Harris, *Out To Work.*

27. Alice Kessler-Harris, *Women Have Always Worked: A Historical Overview* (Old Westbury, N.Y.: The Feminist Press, 1982), 133.

8. "Powder Puff" Promotion: The Fashion Show-in-the-Film

1. Elizabeth Jackimowicz, interview with the author, 17 April 1983.

2. Elizabeth Leese, *Costume Design in the Movies* (New York: Frederick Ungar Publishing Co., 1976), 9.

3. Leese, *Costume Design,* 8–12.

4. Leese, *Costume Design,* 11.

5. Leese, *Costume Design,* 12.

6. "Vogues of 1938," *Time,* 30 August 1937, 23.

7. "Vogues of 1938," *Jones Magazine* 1, no. 4 (November 1937): 3.

8. "Cinema Fashions," *Fortune* 15, no. 1 (January 1937): 44.

9. "Cinema Fashions," *Fortune* 15, no. 1 (January 1937): 44.

10. "Vogues of 1938," *Time,* 30 August 1937, 23.

11. Jane Gaines, "Film and Television Costume and Everyday Dress" (unpublished paper).

12. Jeanne Allen, "The Film Viewer as Consumer," *Quarterly Review of Film Studies* 5, no. 4 (Fall 1980): 490.

13. Also see John Berger, *Ways of Seeing* (New York: Penguin Books, 1972), 83–112.

14. Allen, "The Film Viewer as Consumer," 490.

15. Arlene Croce, *The Fred Astaire and Ginger Rogers Book* (New York: Outerbridge & Lazard, Inc., 1972), 46.

16. Robert Baral, *Revue: A Nostalgic Reprise of the Great Broadway Period* (New York: Fleet Publishing Corporation, 1962), 55.

17. Baral, *Revue,* 33.

18. Baral, *Revue,* 61.

19. Richard Dyer, "Social Values of Entertainment and Show Business" (Ph.D. Dissertation, Center for Contemporary Cultural Studies, Birmingham University, Birmingham, England, 1972), 339.

20. Baral, *Revue,* 61.

21. The contrapposto stance is an art historical term used to describe a particular pose developed by the Greeks for their statues of male nude athletes to make them look more naturalistic. These statues are shown with the weight of the entire body on one leg and the other leg bent and its heel off the ground as if walking or about to take a step (the pose is also called the "walking pose"). This makes the hips and

shoulders uneven and the head tilted slightly sideways. From the front the body looks like the letter "S" thus the term "S-curve" also used to describe the pose.

22. Jane Feuer, *The Hollywood Musical* (London: Macmillan, 1982), 26–30.

23. Laura Mulvey, "Visual Pleasure and Narrative Cinema," *Screen* 16, no. 3 (Autumn 1975): 6–18; Stephen Heath, "Film Performance," *Ciné-Tracts* 2 (Summer 1977): 11.

24. Feuer, *The Hollywood Musical,* 42–44.

25. *MGM Studio News,* 2 September 1939, 3–11.

26. Feuer, *The Hollywood Musical,* 26–30.

27. Dyer, "Social Values of Entertainment," 341, 343.

28. *MGM Studio News,* 2 September 1939, 3–11.

29. Charlotte Cornelia Herzog and Jane Marie Gaines, " 'Puffed Sleeves Before Tea-time': Joan Crawford, Adrian and Women Audiences," *Wide Angle* 6, no. 4 (1985): 25.

30. Dyer, "Social Values of Entertainment," 341.

31. Guy Trebay, "Selling the Dress," *Village Voice,* 3 May 1983, 67.

32. Griselda Pollock, "What's Wrong with Images of Women?," *Screen Education* 24 (Autumn 1977): 27–28.

33. Charles Castle and David Castle, *Model Girls* (London: Chartwell Books, 1977), 137.

34. FASHIONS OF 1934 file, news item from *Variety,* 23 January 1934, n.p., Academy of Motion Picture Arts and Science, hereafter AMPAS.

35. *The Dressmaker From Paris* file, news item from *Variety,* 18 March 1925, n.p., AMPAS.

36. *Look,* 22 April 1952, 121.

37. *Lucy Gallant* file, news item dated 29 September 1955, n.p., AMPAS; *MGM Studio News,* 2 September 1939, 3–11.

38. As quoted in Jeanne Allen, "The Film Viewer as Consumer," 486.

39. Claudia B. Kidwell and Margaret C. Christman, *Suiting Everyone: The Democratization of Clothing in America* (Washington, D.C.: The Smithsonian Institution Press, 1974), 177.

40. Baral, *Revue,* 54.

41. Dyer, "Social Values of Entertainment," 347.

42. *Lucy Gallant* file, news item dated 29 September 1955, n.p., AMPAS.

43. Maureen Turim, "Gentlemen Consume Blondes," *Wide Angle* 1, no. 1 (1979); rpt., *Movies and Methods II,* ed. Bill Nichols (Berkeley: University of California Press, 1985), 377.

44. Berger, *Ways of Seeing,* 46–47.

45. Peter Steven, "Body Politics: Some Notes on the Stealing and Selling of Non-Verbal Communication," *Film Reader* 5 (1982): 205.

46. *MGM Studio News,* 2 September 1939, 3–11.

9. Handmaidens of the Glamour Culture:
Costumers in the Hollywood Studio System

1. David Chierichetti, *Hollywood Costume Design* (New York: Harmony Books, 1976), 10.

2. Michèle Barrett, *Women's Oppression Today* (London: Verso, 1980).

3. Ruth Milkman, "Organizing the Sexual Division of Labor: Historical Perspectives on 'Women's Work' and the American Labor Movement," *Socialist Review* 10, no. 1 (Jan-Feb 1980): 95–150.

4. The primary sources for this article are interviews conducted in Los Angeles in the summer of 1985 with Georgina Grant (costumer manufacturing), Agnes Henry (key costumer), David Chierichetti (costumer), and Ted Ellsworth (union business agent) of the International Alliance of Theatrical and State Employees (IATSE) Motion Picture Costumers Local 705. Also, officials of Local 705 generously shared their union records dating back to 1942. These records are the source of all the following references to Motion Picture Costumers Records, hereafter MPCR.

5. MPCR, program from the Eighth Annual Costumers Ball, 29 September 1956.

6. MPCR, *Costumers News* (August 1954).

7. MPCR, program from the Eighth Annual Costumers Ball, 29 September 1956.

8. MPCR, program from the Eighth Annual Costumers Ball, 29 September 1956.

9. MPCR, *Costumers News* (March 1949) and (May 1950).

10. MPCR, *Costumers News* (November 1951).

11. MPCR, *Costumers News* (June 1953).

12. Agnes Henry, interview with author, Los Angeles, California, 11 June 1985.

13. Henry, interview, 11 June 1985.

14. Georgina Grant, interview with author, Los Angeles, California, 12 June 1985.

15. Grant, interview, 12 June 1985.

16. Grant, interview, 12 June 1985.

17. David Chierichetti, interview with author, Los Angeles, California, 14 June 1985.

18. Chierichetti, interview, 14 June 1985.

19. Ted Ellsworth, interview with author, Los Angeles, California, 13 June 1985.

20. Ellsworth, interview, 13 June 1985.

21. Henry, interview, 11 June 1985.

22. Chierichetti, interview, 14 June 1985.

23. Henry, interview, 11 June 1985.

24. Henry, interview, 11 June 1985.

25. MPCR, program from the Eighth Annual Costumers Ball, 29 September 1956.

26. Chierichetti, interview, 14 June 1985.

27. Henry, interview, 11 June 1985.

28. Chierichetti, interview, 14 June 1985.

29. Grant, interview, 12 June 1985.

30. Ellsworth, interview, 13 June 1985.

31. MPCR, program from the Eighth Annual Costumers Ball, 29 September 1956; also, Bert Offord wrote a regular column in the *Costumers News* in the 1940s.

32. Ellsworth, interview, 13 June 1985.

33. Ellsworth, interview, 13 June 1985.

34. MPCR, program from the Eighth Annual Costumers Ball, 29 September 1956.

35. MPCR, Contracts between Costumers Local 705, and Western Costume House.

36. MPCR, *Costumers News* (June 1950) and (August 1954).

37. Grant, interview, 12 June 1985.

38. Grant, interview, 12 June 1985.

39. Hugh Lovell and Tasile Carter, *Collective Bargaining in the Motion Picture Industry: A Struggle for Stability* (Berkeley: Institute of Industrial Relations, University of California, 1955), 30–32.

40. Ellsworth, interview, 13 June 1985.

41. Henry, interview, 11 June 1985.

42. Ellsworth, interview, 13 June 1985.

43. Henry, interview, 11 June 1985.

44. Judith Stacey, "Sexism by a Subtler Name? Post Industrial Conditions and Post Feminism in the Silicon Valley," *Socialist Review* 96 (November/December 1987): 7–28.

45. Ellsworth, interview, 13 June 1985.

46. Ellsworth, interview, 13 June 1985; Chierichetti, interview, 14 June 1985.

10. Costume and Narrative: How Dress Tells the Woman's Story

1. For example, Beryl Williams, *Fashion is Our Business* (Philadelphia: J. B. Lippincott, 1945), chap. 9; Edith Head and Jane Kesner Ardmore, *The Dress Doctor* (Boston: Little, Brown and Co., 1959); Edith Head and Paddy Calistro, *Edith Head's Hollywood* (New York: E.P. Dutton, 1983).

2. Transcript of American Film Institute seminar with Edith Head, 23 November 1977, 17. (Edith Head Collection, Folder 57, Academy of Motion Picture Arts and Sciences)

3. See my entry, "Costume in the Western," *Companion to the Western,* ed. Ed Buscombe (London: British Film Institute/Andre Deutsch, 1987).

4. John Emerson and Anita Loos, *Breaking into Movies* (New York: McCann, 1921), 23. The authors also note that an actress was often awarded a role based on her "ability to wear" costumes; Dorothy Hobson says that British soap opera actresses often wear their own clothes in order to situate a character as realistic. See her *"Crossroads": The Drama of a Soap Opera* (London: Methuen, 1982), 82.

5. Clara Kimball Young, "Dressing for the Movies," *Photoplay* 7, no. 2 (January 1915): 117.

6. For background see Gorham Kindem, "Hollywood's Movie Star System: A Historical Overview," *The American Movie Industry: the Business of Motion Pictures,* ed. Gorham Kindem (Carbondale: So. Illinois University Press, 1982), 79–93.

7. *Photoplay* 8, no. 6 (November 1915): 26–32.

8. Margaret I. MacDonald, "Alice Brady Talks About Dress and Make-up," *Moving*

Picture World, 21 July 1917, 426. Brady is also quoted as saying, "I try to buy clothes that fit the part I am playing; consequently very often I go around looking like the character because I don't want to throw the clothes away."

9. MacDonald, "Alice Brady," 426. Alice Brady expresses this early idea that screen costume was not necessarily different from everyday dress: "Ordinarily anything that is becoming on the street is becoming in a picture, unless, of course, the gown happens to be one that is largely dependent on color for its beauty."

10. Louise Howard, " 'How I Teach My Gowns to Act'," *Photoplay* 9, no. 3 (February 1916): 92.

11. Howard, " 'How I Teach,' " 93.

12. Howard, " 'How I Teach,' " 92.

13. Frederick Palmer, *Photoplay Plot Encyclopedia,* 2nd. ed. (Los Angeles: Palmer Photoplay Corp., 1922), 28.

14. Murray Sheehan, *Hints on Scenario Writing* (Girard, Kansas: Haldeman-Julius Co., 1923), 12.

15. Erving Goffman, *The Presentation of Self in Everyday Life* (New York: Anchor Books, 1959), 2.

16. Thomas Carlyle, *Sartor Resartus, English Prose of the Victorian Era,* ed. Charles F. Harrold and William D. Templeman (Oxford: Oxford University Press, 1938), 94.

17. See Warren I. Susman, *Culture as History: The Transformation of American Society in the Twentieth Century* (New York: Pantheon, 1984), chap. 9; Mike Featherstone, "The Body in Consumer Culture," *Theory, Culture and Society* 1 (1982): 18–26.

18. Richard Sennett, *The Fall of Public Man* (New York: Random House, 1974), 68.

19. Sennett, *Fall of Public Man,* 152.

20. Sennett, *Fall of Public Man,* 69.

21. Sennett, *Fall of Public Man,* 163.

22. Eugene Brewster, "Expression of the Emotions," *Motion Picture Magazine* 8, no. 7 (August 1914): 102.

23. Sennett, *Fall of Public Man,* 174.

24. See James Naremore, *Acting in the Cinema* (Berkeley: University of California Press, 1988), 51–56, for an overview of this change in acting styles as it pertains to the silent film.

25. Janet Staiger, "The Eyes are Really the Focus: Photoplay Acting and Film Form and Style," *Wide Angle* 6, no. 4 (1985): 20.

26. Young, "Dressing for the Movies," 118.

27. Naremore, *Acting in the Cinema,* 83.

28. Ruth Roland, "Personality in Dress," *Photoplay* 8, no. 1 (June 1915): 134.

29. Erwin Panofsky, "Style and Medium in the Motion Pictures," *Film Theory and Criticism,* ed. Gerald Mast and Marshall Cohen, 3rd ed. (New York: Oxford University Press, 1985), 224.

30. Young, "Dressing for the Movies," 118.

31. Mary Ann Doane, "The Voice in the Cinema: The Articulation of Body and Space,"

Yale French Studies no. 60 (1980): 33; rpt. *Film Sound: Theory and Practice,* ed. Elisabeth Weis and John Belton (New York: Columbia University Press, 1985).

32. See Panofsky, "Style and Medium," 224.

33. "Dialogue on Film: Edith Head," *American Film* 3, no. 7 (May 1978): 36.

34. "Dialogue on Film: Edith Head."

35. Dudley Andrew, *Concepts in Film Theory* (New York and London: Oxford University Press, 1984), 102.

36. Virginia Lane, "How Lombard's Clothes Match Moods," *Movie Classic* (September 1935): 45.

37. Stuart Hall, "Encoding/Decoding," *Culture, Media, Language,* ed. Stuart Hall, Dorothy Hobson, Andrew Lowe, and Paul Willis (London: Hutchinson, 1980), 132.

38. Stephen Heath, "Film and System: Terms of Analysis, Pt. II," *Screen* 16, no. 2 (1975): 104.

39. Anne Hollander, "Costume and Convention," *American Scholar* 42 (1972–73): 674.

40. Trevor Pateman, "The Painted Face of Capitalism: The Technique of Film and Television Make-up for Color and Black and White," *Women and Film* 1, nos. 5–6 (1974): 98.

41. *Elements of Color in Professional Motion Pictures* (New York: Society of Motion Picture and Television Engineers, 1957), 41; Steve Neale also discusses the fear that Technicolor posed a "threat" to the narrative. See *Cinema and Technology: Image, Sound, Color* (Bloomington: Indiana University Press, 1985), 145–51.

42. *Elements of Color in Professional Motion Pictures,* 43.

43. "Dialogue on Film: George Cukor," *American Film* 3, no. 4 (1978): 43.

44. Alice Evans Field, "Costume Design," *Hollywood, U.S.A.: From Script to Screen* (New York: Vantage, 1952), 115.

45. See Edith Head, "A Costume Problem: From Shop to Stage to Screen," *Hollywood Quarterly* 2, no. 1 (1946): 40–44, on designing for close-ups; Gerald Mast describes the way the studio system systematically eradicated the personal style of all creative personnel, an irony considering the case made for understanding the feature film as the work of an auteur. See *A Short History of the Movies* (Indianapolis: Bobbs-Merrill, 1976), 268.

46. Margaret Bailey, *Those Glorious Glamour Years* (Secaucus: The Citadel Press, 1982), 8, quotes George Cukor as saying:

    Hollywood wardrobes are created *all to serve the picture—not to make fashion.* They must fulfill two requirements: 1) they must serve the dramatic purpose of the script by helping to make the character believable and not distract from the scene, and 2) they must be photogenically best for the actress.

47. Richard Dyer, *Stars* (London: British Film Institute, 1979).

48. Heath, "Film and System," 105–6.

49. Barry King, "Articulating Stardom," *Screen* 26, no. 5 (September–October 1985): 46.

50. King, "Articulating Stardom," 47. The advantage of Dyer's notion of the star image

is that it retains the reference to representation and some of the sense that stardom is industrially produced.

51. Helen Harrison, "Adrian's Fashion Secrets," *Hollywood* 23, no. 9 (September 1934): 42.

52. Harrison, "Adrian's Fashion Secrets," 43.

53. Richard Dyer,"Stereotyping,"*Gays and Film,* ed. Richard Dyer (New York: Zoetrope, 1984), 27–39.

54. Harrison, "Adrian's Fashion Secrets," 43; Mayme Ober Peak, "Study the Stars and Dress Your Line," *Ladies Home Journal* 49, no. 6 (June 1932): 9.

55. Dyer, *Stars,* 146–49.

56. King, "Articulating Stardom," 30; See Naremore, *Acting in the Cinema,* 44, on how naturalistic styles are designed to conceal the very devices an actor uses.

57. "Dialogue on Film: Edith Head," 36.

58. As quoted in King, "Articulating Stardom," 41.

59. For a thorough account of the gay male camp appropriation of Judy Garland, see Richard Dyer, *Heavenly Bodies: Film Stars and Society* (London: British Film Institute, 1987), chap. 3.

60. Claudia Gorbman, *Unheard Melodies: Narrative Film Music* (Bloomington: Indiana University Press, 1987), 67.

61. See Gorbman, *Unheard Melodies,* 83, for examples of the way musical motifs construct types.

62. Peter Brooks, *The Melodramatic Imagination: Balzac, Henry James, Melodrama, and the Mode of Excess* (New York: Columbia University Press, 1985), 36.

63. Thomas Elsaesser, "Tales of Sound and Fury: Observations on the Family Melodrama," *Movies and Methods II,* ed. Bill Nichols (Berkeley and London: University of California Press, 1985), 165–89.

64. E. H.Gombrich, *The Sense of Order: A Study in the Psychology of Decorative Art* (Ithaca: Cornell University Press, 1984), 286. This observation is from the Epilogue in which Gombrich draws analogies between ornamental design and musical structures.

65. These principles of design are discussed in Margaret Story, *How to Dress Well* (New York: Funk and Wagnalls, 1924) and Laurene Hempstead, *Color and Line in Dress* (New York: Prentice-Hall, 1947).

66. Roland Barthes, "Style and Its Image," in Roland Barthes, *The Rustle of Language,* trans. Richard Howard (New York: Hill and Wang, 1986), 94.

67. Helen Harrison, "Headline Fashions!," *Screenland* 30, no. 4 (February 1935): 82.

68. Edith Head recalls that Alfred Hitchcock had a phobia about "eye-catchers" which he feared would divert attention from significant scenes. See Transcript of American Film Institute seminar with Edith Head, 20.

69. See Charlotte C. Herzog and Jane M. Gaines, " 'Puffed Sleeves Before Teatime': Joan Crawford, Adrian, and Woman Audiences," *Wide Angle* 6, no. 4 (1985): 24–33, for further discussion of the Letty Lynton dress. LETTY LYNTON has not been exhibited since the early 1930s because of the outcome of a lawsuit (*Sheldon v. Metro-Goldwyn Pictures Corp.,* 1936). Although few have seen this film since 1933, the notoriety of the Letty Lynton dress is kept alive by the production stills

and the George Hurrell photographs reproduced so often, as well as by the myth that Macy's sold 500,000 copies of the dress.

70. See Bernard F. Dick, "Introduction: The Fine Art of Dying," *Dark Victory*, ed. Bernard F. Dick (Madison: University of Wisconsin Press, 1981), 24, for a discussion of Ann King along these lines. Thanks to Joanne Yeck for calling my attention to this concept.

71. See Mary Ann Doane, *The Desire to Desire: The Woman's Film of the 1940s* (Bloomington: Indiana University Press, 1987), 178. From a psychoanalytic vantage point, Doane discusses DARK VICTORY in terms of the symptomatic registration of the disease on the body of the heroine, so that the disease becomes the "body fully in sympathy with the psyche."

72. Roland Barthes, "The Third Meaning," *Image/Music/Text*, trans. Stephen Heath (New York: Hill and Wang, 1977), 52–68.

73. Barthes, "The Third Meaning," 61.

74. Kristin Thompson has undertaken the most thorough history and analysis of the concept of "excess" as it has come to be used in film theory, and it is her reworking which locates the "excessive" as that which cannot be motivated by the narrative or organized by the structuring devices. See "The Concept of Cinematic Excess," *Narrative/Apparatus/Ideology*, ed. Philip Rosen (New York; Columbia University Press, 1986), 130–42; More recently, Rick Altman takes issue with this definition of excess and suggests that we are no longer talking about the same thing Barthes was trying to identify. See "Dickens, Griffith, and Film Theory Today," *South Atlantic Quarterly* 88, no. 2 (Spring 1989): 321–359; Christine Gledhill asks yet another crucial question about the relationship between excess and genre, that is, "if melodramatic rhetoric informs westerns, gangster and horror films, psychological thrillers and family melodramas alike, how tenable is it to constitute melodrama in a critical, disruptive relation to the classic realist/narrative text?" See "The Melodramatic Field: An Investigation," in *Home is Where the Heart Is: Studies in Melodrama and the Woman's Film,* ed. Christine Gledhill (London: British Film Institute, 1987), 13.

11. Designing Women: The Emergence of the New Sweetheart Line

1. War Production Board Government War Order L85 was announced in the *Report of Production Management Office Relating to Allocations and Priorities of War Materials,* December 1942. Edith Head's reaction to L85 was quite different from many of her colleagues. In a 1944 interview, Head is quoted as saying: "L85 was the greatest boom that ever came to fashion design in Hollywood. . . . It banished super luxury and brought us all down to earth. . . . Today we create sensible designs for women, the kind they can actually wear" (Clippings file, Academy of Motion Picture Arts and Sciences). As we shall see, luxury does return in the 1950s, however, though Head's concern with wearable designs is interesting in terms of the mass marketing of even the most extravagant evening dresses she produced for films after the war (see note 9).

2. Sarah Tomerlin Lee, ed., *American Fashion: The Life and Lines of Adrian, Mainbocher, McCardell, Norell, Trigère* (New York: Quadrangle/New York Times Book Co., 1975), 47–55.

3. "The Tailored Suit . . . 1942 Uniform," *Vogue* 15 (January 1942): 36–37. The fashion section of this issue is called "Double-Duty Lives—War Work Home

Work," and includes short essays on women's contributions to the war effort. This theme continues in *Vogue* throughout the war.

4. *Mademoiselle* (August 1945): 7; (September 1945): 7; and (November 1945): 7, 210.

5. Shirley White (ex-yeoman, USNR), "WAVE to Civilian," and Sergeant Sylvia Margulies, "WAC to Civilian," *Mademoiselle* (November 1945): 160–63.

6. Elsa Shiaparelli, "Needles and Guns," *Vogue* 1 (September 1940): 57.

7. Christian Dior, *Talking About Fashion,* trans. Eugenia Shepard (New York: Putnam, 1954).

8. Dior, *Talking About Fashion.*

9. A different version of the same story appears in other sources such as the documentary film on Edith Head produced in 1980 by Blackhawk Films, where she changes the number of dresses at the party. A similar story is credited to a "fashion commentator" writing in 1951 by David Chierichetti in *Hollywood Costume Design* (New York: Harmony Books, 1976), 69: "Go to any party this summer and you'll see at least ten [copies of Head's designs for *A Place In the Sun*]." In Edith Head and Paddy Calistro, *Edith Head's Hollywood* (New York: E. P. Dutton, 1983), 97–98, the authors say that Head had been quoted as saying that anywhere from seven to thirty-seven girls wore this dress to the same party.

10. Helen Rose, *Just Make Them Beautiful: The Many Worlds of a Designing Woman* (Santa Monica: Dennis-Landman Publishers, 1976).

11. *Life,* 28 May 1951, 47–48+.

12. *Variety* 8 (July 1951): 6.

13. *Life,* 28 May 1951.

14. Bryan Holme, comp., *The Journal of the Century* (New York: Viking, 1976), 250.

15. Chierichetti, *Hollywood Costume Design,* 128.

12. Masochism, Masquerade, and the Erotic Metamorphoses of Marlene Dietrich

1. Gilles Deleuze, *Masochism: An Interpretation of Coldness and Cruelty* (New York: George Braziller, 1971).

2. Laura Mulvey, "Visual Pleasure and Narrative Cinema," *Screen* 16, no. 3 (Autumn 1975): 6–18.

3. Mulvey, "Visual Pleasure," 6–7; 13–14. See also Sigmund Freud, "Fetishism" (1927) *The Standard Edition of the Complete Psychological Works* 3d ed., trans. and ed. James Strachey, 23 vols. (London: Hogarth Press, 1953–1966), 21: 151–163 (hereafter cited as *SE*).

4. Mulvey, "Visual Pleasure," 11–12.

5. On Mae West see Claire Johnston, "Woman's Cinema as Counter- Cinema," *Notes on Women's Cinema,* ed. Claire Johnston (London: Society for Education in Film and Television, 1973), 26.

6. E. Ann Kaplan, *Women and Film: Both Sides of the Camera* (New York: Methuen, 1983), 50.

7. Mulvey, "Visual Pleasure," 14; Kaplan, *Women and Film,* 50–53.

8. Kaplan, *Women and Film,* 50–58.

9. Mulvey, "Visual Pleasure," 14.

10. Mulvey, "Visual Pleasure."

11. Mulvey addresses the question of the female spectator in "Afterthoughts on 'Visual Pleasure and Narrative Cinema' inspired by DUEL IN THE SUN," *Framework,* nos. 15/16/17 (Summer 1981): 12–15. Miriam Hansen, "Visual Pleasure, Fetishism and the Problem of Female Discourse: Ulrike Ottinger's *Ticket of No Return*," *New German Critique,* no. 31 (Winter 1984): 102, suggests in passing that Mulvey's point contains the potential for considering the subversive aspect of the unmediated gaze.

12. D. N. Rodowick, "The Difficulty of Difference," *Wide Angle* 5 (1982): 7. The quoted phrase is Mulvey's, "Visual Pleasure," 7.

13. "Morocco," *Cahiers du Cinéma* (a collective text), no. 225 (November/December 1970): 5–13, rpt. *Sternberg,* trans. Diana Matiae, ed. Peter Baxter (London: British Film Institute, 1980): 81–94; Robin Wood, "Venus de Marlene," *Film Comment* 14 (March/April 1978): 62, writes that the film's male characters confirm "one's sense of Sternberg's personal involvement" in their humiliation.

14. See my *In the Realm of Pleasure: Von Sternberg, Dietrich, and the Masochistic Aesthetic* (Urbana and Chicago: University of Illinois Press, 1988), 9–28. See Deleuze, *Masochism,* 18, on the impossibility of "sadomasochism."

15. Deleuze, *Masochism,* 49. Freud in "Three Essays on the Theory of Sexuality" (1905), *SE* 7: 231, regarded polymorphous perversity as the normal mode of childhood sexuality. It became pathological in adult life only when it replaced genital sexuality instead of coexisting with it.

16. Deleuze, *Masochism,* 56.

17. Wood, "Venus de Marlene," 58–63.

18. Deleuze, *Masochism,* 59.

19. Deleuze, *Masochism,* 29–30, 63–64. Deleuze notes: "Fetishism, as defined by the process of disavowal and suspension of belief belongs essentially to masochism . . . fetishism only occurs in sadism in a secondary and distorted sense." Joseph C. Solomon, "Transitional Phenomena and Obsessive-Compulsive States," *Between Reality and Fantasy: Transitional Objects and Phenomena,* ed. Simon A. Grolnick, Leonard Barkin, and Werner Muensterberger (New York: Jason Aronson, 1978), 250, writes: "Fetishism . . . may have its pregenital origin in the threatened loss of the mother. Here both survival and erotic powers are transferred to the object."

20. See Raymond Durgnat, "Six Films of Josef von Sternberg," *Movie* 13 (Summer 1965): 29–30.

21. Deleuze, *Masochism,* 36–38.

22. "Two Contracts of Masoch," Appendix II, in Deleuze, *Masochism,* 234. Born in 1835 in Lemberg, Galicia (part of the Austro-Hungarian Empire), Sacher-Masoch's early career was as a professor of history at Graz. He became a much acclaimed author, enjoying popular and critical success in Europe and abroad with his numerous plays and novels, including *Venus in Pelz,* first published in 1870. *Venus* is based on Sacher-Masoch's relationship with Fanny von Pistor, who wrote him a fan letter praising his novels and asking him to evaluate her own literary efforts. Sacher-Masoch's first wife, Wanda (who called herself Wanda von Dunajew, after the heroine of *Venus*) wrote a flog-and-tell autobiography, *Meine Lebensbeichte,*

published in 1906, (republished in French as *Confessions de ma vie*, [Paris: Tchou, 1967]). She and Sacher-Masoch signed many contracts, including one in which he promised to stop using the fictional character of the cruel woman if Wanda would assume that role in their own marriage. This agreement was inspired by Wanda's having called his attention to the critical disfavor that this predictable character was bringing to his novels.

23. Leopold von Sacher-Masoch, *Venus in Furs*, trans. Jean McNeil, reprinted in Deleuze, *Masochism*, 169. When his name became associated with "masochism," the term first used by sexologist Richard von Krafft-Ebing in *Psychopathia Sexualis* (1886), Sacher-Masoch was devastated. With his death in 1895, he left incomplete an immense cycle of historical novels called *The Heritage of Cain*, begun some twenty- five years before. Sacher-Masoch had finished over a dozen novels for this cycle, which illustrated the theme of humanity's inherited burden of suffering. By the time that Krafft-Ebing linked Sacher-Masoch's name to sexual pathology, his work was already beginning to fall into neglect. That neglect continues today. In print, English-language editions are rare. His *Jewish Tales* is available (New York: Gordon Press, n.d.), as is *Venus in Furs* (together with *The Black Czarina*) in a British edition translated from the German by H. J. Stenning (London: Luxor Press, 1970). An out of print, English language edition of Sacher-Masoch can occasionally be located, most frequently *Venus and Adonis* (New York: Windsor Pub. Co., 1933) and the woefully inadequate Sylvan Press translation of *Venus in Furs* (New York: Priv. print. for the Sylvan Press, 1947).

24. Von Sternberg quoted in Peter Bogdanovich, "Encounters with Josef von Sternberg," *Movie* 13 (Summer 1965): 25.

25. Iris Barry, quoted in Josef von Sternberg, *Fun in a Chinese Laundry* (New York: Collier, 1965), 260.

26. Roland Barthes, *The Pleasure of the Text*, trans. Richard Miller (New York: Hill & Wang, 1975), 10.

27. Sacher-Masoch, *Venus in Furs*, 201.

28. Deleuze, *Masochism*, 57–60.

29. Sacher-Masoch, *Venus in Furs*, 128–30, 172–73.

30. Deleuze, *Masochism*, 46.

31. Silvia Bovenschen, "Is There a Feminine Aesthetic?," *New German Critique*, no. 10 (Winter 1977): 128–29.

32. Victor Smirnoff, "The Masochistic Contract," *International Journal of Psycho-Analysis* 50 (1969): 669.

33. Deleuze, *Masochism*, 54–55, 8–60; Deleuze, *Masochism*, 110, maintains that the mother is phallicized through fetishism, and that this phallus "does not have a sexual character" but is "the ideal organ of a neutral energy" that works to cancel out the father and his law from the symbolic order. Some theorists of fetishism regard the phallic fetish, the imagined fantasy penis of the mother, as the boy's way of expressing his own wish to be both sexes, to overcome sexual difference and emulate the mother's procreative power. Deleuze, *Masochism*, 59–60, says that the masochist believes that it is possible to become both sexes. See Charles Socarides, "The Development of a Fetishistic Perversion: The Contribution of PreOedipal Phase Conflict," *Journal of the American Psychoanalytic Association* 8 (April 1960): 306–7 and also Eva Feder Kittay, "Womb Envy: An Explanatory Concept," *Mothering: Essays in Feminist Theory*, ed. Joyce Trebilcot (Totowa,

N.J.: Rowan & Allanheld, 1984), 125. For another view on bisexuality and fetish-ism, see Robert Bak, "Distortions in the Concept of Fetishism," *The Psychoanalytic Study of the Child* 29 (1974): 205.

34. Sacher-Masoch, *Venus in Furs,* 143.

35. Mary Ann Doane, "Film and the Masquerade: Theorising the Female Spectator," *Screen* 23 (1982): 82.

36. Mulvey, "Visual Pleasure," 13. On the subject of possession, Deleuze, *Masochism,* 20, writes "Possession is the sadist's particular form of madness just as the pact is the masochist's."

37. Sacher-Masoch, *Venus in Furs,* 201–2.

38. Michèle Montrelay, "Recherches sur la fémininité," *Critique,* no. 278 (July 1970): 654–74 quoted in *Cahiers du Cinéma,* no. 225 (November-December, 1970): 93.

39. Joan Riviere, "Womanliness as a Masquerade," *Psychoanalysis and Female Sexual-ity,* eds. Hendrik M. Ruitenbeek (New Haven: College and University Press Ser-vices, 1966), 213. John Fletcher, "Versions of Masquerade," *Screen* 29 (Summer 1988): 50, 57, compares the various definitions of masquerade that have been applied in film theory to the female subject. He identifies filmic examples of "the distinctive scenario of the masquerade" as theorized by Riviere to show how this scenario "generates images and stories of a double female subject . . . [and] tells the story of the fetish from the other side of the screen." Fletcher points out that neither the definition offered by Riviere nor Lacan's (as taken up by Claire Johnston as well as by *Cahiers du Cinéma* in their analysis of MOROCCO) adequately explain the *masculine* masquerade assumed by Dietrich in the von Sternberg films. He also shows that in her recent analysis of female-centered films, Mary Ann Doane, *The Desire to Desire: The Woman's Film of the 1940s* (Bloomington: Indiana University Press, 1987) ignores the possibilities of her own theorization of the masquerade. See also Claire Johnston, "Femininity and the Masquerade: *Anne of the Indies," Jacques Tourneur,* ed. Claire Johnston and Paul Willemen (Edinburgh: Edinburgh Film Festival, 1975).

40. Doane, "Film and the Masquerade," 82.

41. Sacher-Masoch, *Venus in Furs,* 155.

42. Sacher-Masoch, *Venus in Furs,* 194.

43. On costume as a magical body change see Lawrence Kubie, "The Drive to Become Both Sexes," *Symbols and Neurosis: Selected Papers of L. S. Kubie,* ed. Herbert J. Schlesinger (New York: International Universities Press, 1978), 195–202. This imaginative investment in "body change" is a positive, playful pleasure rather than the purely defensive or neurotic mechanism that Riviere's theory of masquerade emphasizes.

44. Doane, "Film and the Masquerade," 80, states: "Given the structures of cinematic narrative, the woman who identifies with a female character must adopt a passive or masochistic position, while identification with the active hero necessarily entails an acceptance of . . . a certain 'masculinisation' of spectatorship." On the oscilla-tion of women's spectatorial identifications, see also Mulvey, "Afterthoughts," 12–15. Of course, a positive, female-to-female identification would also seem possible for women's spectatorship, but theorizing such a response from a psychoanalytic perspective has proven to be difficult.

45. Molly Haskell, *From Reverence to Rape: The Treatment of Women in the Movies* (New York: Holt, Rinehart & Winston, 1973), 101, 112; Kathryn Weibel, *Mirror*

Mirror: Images of Women Reflected in Popular Culture (New York: Doubleday, 1977), 105, 178–80; Julia Lesage quoted in Silvia Bovenschen, "Women and Film," *New German Critique,* no. 13 (Winter 1978): 89–90.

46. For von Sternberg on female spectators' identification with women stars see his *Fun in a Chinese Laundry,* 68–69.

47. Lesage quoted in Bovenschen, "Women and Film," 89–90.

48. Alex de Jonge, *The Weimar Chronicles: Prelude to Hitler* (London and New York: Paddington Press, 1978), 152, relates how Friedrich Holländer, composer of the songs for THE BLUE ANGEL, searched for Dietrich to tell her she had won the role of Lola Lola. Holländer finally located her in "Silhouette," one of the most popular of Berlin's many lesbian bars.

49. In "Hollywood Transformed," *Jump Cut: Hollywood, Politics and Counter-Cinema,* ed. Peter Steven (New York: Praeger, 1985), 115, Claire Whitaker interviews nine lesbian women about their film-viewing to produce some interesting remarks concerning Dietrich. One woman mentions being "enthralled with Dietrich" but she didn't think that she identified with the star, rather it was "Lust, childhood lust, I'm sure."

50. Mulvey, "Visual Pleasure," 14. Doane, *The Desire to Desire,* 169, argues (as she does in "Film and the Masquerade"), that women cannot properly distance themselves from the cinema's imaging of women. They cannot maintain the balancing act of a fetishistic gaze at the screen since they are "deprived of castration anxiety." While I believe it is counterproductive to trade Freudianisms in the search for female subjectivity, it should be noted that even Freud, "Female Sexuality," (1931) *SE* 21: 233, suggested that little girls learn to disavow through their reaction of "penis envy."

Bibliography

Hollywood Costumes

Adrian. "Setting Styles Through the Stars." *Ladies Home Journal* 50 (February 1933): 10–11,40.

———. "Costumes for the Screen." In *Movie Merry-Go-Round,* edited by John Paddy Carstairs. London: Newnes, 1937.

———. "Clothes." In *Behind the Screen: How Films Are Made,* edited by Stephen Watts. London: Barker, 1938.

Bailey, Margaret. *Those Glorious Glamour Years.* Seacus, N.J.: Citadel, 1982.

Beaton, Cecil. "Hollywood Goes Refined." *Vogue* 77 (June 1931): 34–35, 98.

Chierichetti, David. "Sheila O'Brien." *Film Fan Monthly* 148 (October 1973): 19–24.

———. *Hollywood Costume Design.* New York: Crown, 1976.

———. "Star Style: Hollywood's Legendary Fashion Firsts." *Los Angeles Times.* 27 October, 1978: 6.

Cooke, Alistair. *Garbo and the Night Watchmen.* New York: McGraw-Hill, 1971.

Costume Institute. *Romantic and Glamourous Hollywood Design.* New York: Metropolitan Museum of Art, 1974.

Cukor, George. "Dialogue on Film: George Cukor." *American Film* 3 (February 1978): 33–48.

Duff Gordon, Lady Lucille. *Discretions & Indiscretions.* New York: Stokes, 1932.

Erté. *Things I Remember: An Autobiography.* New York: Quardrangle/New York Times, 1975.

Fernandez, Rick. "Designing for the Stars: Interview with Walter Plunkett." *The Velvet Light Trap* 18 (1978): 27–29.

Field, Alice Evans. "Costume Design." In *Hollywood U.S.A.: From Script to Screen,* ed. Alice Evans Field. New York: Vantage, 1952.

Glyn, Elinor. *Romantic Adventure: Being the Autobiography of Elinor Glyn.* New York: E.P. Dutton, 1937.

Greer, Howard. *Designing Male.* New York: Putnam's, 1949.

Gustafson, Robert. "The Power of the Screen: The Influence of Edith Head's Film Designs on the Retail Fashion Market." *The Velvet Light Trap* 19 (1982): 8–15.

Harris, Julie. "Costume Designing." *Films and Filming* 4 (November 1957): 17.

Harrison, Helen. "Adrian's Fashion Secrets." *Hollywood* 23 (September 1934): 42–43, 55.

————. "Headline Fashions!" *Screenland* 30 (February 1935): 82–24.

Hawes, Elizabeth. *Fashion is Spinach*. New York: Random House, 1938.

————. "Hollywood Fashion Is Spinach." *Screenland* 37 (October 1938): 24–27.

Head, Edith, as told to Gladys Hall. "Dress Your Type." *Screenland* 68 (September 1944): 33–37, 78, 80.

————. "A Costume Problem: From Shop to Stage to Screen." *Hollywood Quarterly* 2 (October 1946): 44–44.

————. "Dialogue on Film: Edith Head." *American Film* 3 (May 1978): 33–48.

————. "Hold that Line." In *Hollywood in the 1940's,* edited by Ivy Crane Wilson. New York: Frederick Ungar Publishing Co., 1980.

Head, Edith and Jane Kesner Ardmore. *The Dress Doctor*. Boston: Little, Brown and Co., 1959.

Head, Edith and Joe Hymans. *How to Dress for Success*. New York: Random House, 1967.

Head, Edith and Paddy Calistro. *Edith Head's Hollywood*. New York: E.P. Dutton, 1983.

LaValley, Satch. "Hollywood and Seventh Avenue: The Impact of Period Films on Fashion." In *Hollywood and History: Costume Design in Film,* edited by Edward Maeder. New York: Thames and Hudson, 1987.

Laver, James. "Dates and Dresses." *Sight and Sound* 8 (1939): 50–51.

LaVine, W. Robert. *In Glamorous Fashion*. New York: Charles Scribner & Sons, 1980.

Leese, Elizabeth. *Costume Design in the Movies*. Isle of Wight, England: BCW Publishing, 1976.

Le Roy, Mervin. *It Takes More Than Talent*. New York: Knopf, 1952.

McConathy, Dale and Diana Vreeland. *Hollywood Costume: Glamour! Glitter! Romance!* New York: H.N. Abrams, 1976.

Maeder, Edward. "The Celluloid Image: Historical Dress in Film." In *Hollywood and History: Costume Design in Film,* edited by Edward Maeder. New York: Thames and Hudson, 1987.

Peak, Mayme Ober. "Study the Stars and Dress Your Line." *Ladies Home Journal* 49 (June 1932): 8–9, 105.

Picken, Mary Brook, *The Secrets of Distinctive Dress*. Scranton, Pa.: The Woman's Institute of Domestic Arts and Sciences, 1918.

Pratt, Polly. "Dressing Up: Costume Design." *American Film* 2 (February 1977): 75–76.

Prichard Perez, Susan. *Film Costume: An Annotated Bibliography*. Metuchen, N.J. and London: Scarecrow Press, 1981.

Rickey, Carrie. "The Couture Theory: A Fashionable Guide to Clotheshorse Films on Cassette." *American Film* 7 (December 1982): 57–61.

Riley, Robert. "Adrian." In *American Fashion,* edited by Sarah Tomerlin Lee. New York: Quadrangle, 1975.

Rose, Helen. *Just Make Them Beautiful: The Many Worlds of a Designing Woman*. Santa Monica: Dennis-Landman, 1976.

Rosen, Marjorie. "Movie Costumes." *Film Comment* 40 (1975): 34–35.

Schiaparelli, Elsa. *Shocking Life*. New York: Dutton, 1954.

Sharaff, Irene. *Broadway and Hollywood: Costume Design by Irene Sharaff*. New York: Von Nostrand Rinehold, 1976.

Simms, Joseph. "Adrian—American Artist and Designer." *Costume* 8 (1974): n.p.

Spencer, Charles. *Erté*. New York: Potter, 1970.

Webb, Michael, ed. *Hollywood: Legend and Reality*. Boston: Little, Brown and Co., 1986.

Fashion/Body/Consumer Culture

Ackroyd, Peter. *Dressing Up: Transvestism and Drag: The History of an Obsession*. London: Thames and Hudson, 1979.

Banner, Lois W. *American Beauty*. New York: Knopf, 1983.

Barber, Bernard and Lyle S. Lobel. " 'Fashion' in Women's Clothes and the American Social System." *Social Forces* 32 (1952): 124–131.

Bell, Quentin. *On Human Finery*. 2nd ed. New York: Schocken Books, 1976.

Benedict, Ruth. "Dress." In *Encyclopedia of Social Sciences,* vol 5. New York: MacMillan Co., 1931.

Berch, Bettina. *Radical by Design: The Life and Style of Elizabeth Hawes, Fashion Designer, Union Organizer, Best-Selling Author*. New York: Dutton, 1989.

Bergler, Edmund. *Fashion and the Unconscious*. New York: Robert Frunner, 1953.

Blum, Stella, ed. *Everyday Fashion of the Twenties as Pictured in Sears and Other Catalogues*. New York: Dover, 1981.

Blumer, Herbert. *Movies and Conduct*. New York: Macmillan, 1933.

———. "Fashion: From Class Differentiation to Collective Selection." *The Sociological Quarterly* 10 (1969): 275–291.

Boorstin, Daniel J. *The Americans: The Democratic Experience*. New York: Random House, 1973.

Braudel, Fernand. Translated by Miriam Kochan. *Capitalism and Material Life: 1400–1800*. New York: Harper and Row, 1982.

———. *The Structure of Everyday Life: The Limits of the Possible*. New York: Harper and Row, 1982.

Brenninkmeyer, Ingrid. *The Sociology of Fashion*. Paris: Libraire du Recueil Sirey, 1963.

Brockman, Helen L. *The Theory of Fashion Design*. New York: Wiley, 1965.

Brownmiller, Susan. *Femininity*. New York: Simon & Schuster, 1984.

Castle, Charles and David Castle. *Model Girls*. London: Chartwell Books, 1977.

Chambers, Bernice. *Color and Design in Apparel*. New York: Prentice-Hall, 1942.

———. *Fashion Fundamentals*. New York: Prentice-Hall, 1947.

Chase, Edna Woolman and Ilka Chase. *Always in Vogue*. Garden City: Doubleday and Co., 1954.

Crawford, M.D. *The Ways of Fashion*. New York: Fairchild Publishing Co., 1948.

Daves, Jessica. *Ready-made Miracle: The American Story of Fashion for the Millions*. New York: G.P. Putnam's Sons, 1967.

Dior, Christian. *Talking About Fashion.* Translated by Eugenia Shepard. New York: Putnam, 1954.

Dooley, William H. *Economics of Clothing and Textiles.* Boston: D.C. Heath, 1933.

Ewing, Elizabeth. *History of 20th Century Fashion.* New York: Scribner, 1974.

Gernsheim, Alison. *Victorian and Edwardian Fashion: A Photographic Survey.* New York: Dover, 1981.

Glynn, Prudence. *In Fashion: Dress in the Twentieth Century.* New York: Oxford University Press, 1978.

Goffman, Erving. *The Presentation of the Self in Everyday Life.* Garden City: Doubleday, 1959.

Grace, Evelyn. *Introduction to Fashion.* New York: Prentice-Hall, 1978.

Hall-Duncan, Nancy. *The History of Fashion Photography.* New York: Alpine Book Co., 1979.

Hanna, Judith Lynne. *Dance, Sex and Gender: Signs of Identity, Defiance and Desire.* Berkeley: University of California Press, 1988.

Hardy, Kay. *Costume Design.* New York: McGraw-Hill, 1948.

Hempstead, Laurene. *Color and Line in Dress.* New York: Prentice-Hall, 1947.

Hendrickson, Robert. *The Grand Emporiums.* New York: Stein and Day, 1979.

Hollander, Anne. *Seeing Through Clothes.* New York: Viking Press, 1975.

———. "Costumes and Convention." *American Scholar* 42 (1972–73): 671–675.

Hopkins, Marguerite. *Dress Design and Selection.* New York: Macmillan, 1935.

Howell, Georgiana. *In Vogue.* London: Allen Lane, 1975.

Kasson, John F. *Amusing the Millions: Coney Island at the Turn of the Century.* New York: McGraw Hill, 1978.

Kemper, Rachel A. *A History of Costume.* New York: Alfred A. Knopf, 1963.

Kettunen, Marietta. *Fundamentals of Dress.* New York: McGraw-Hill, 1941.

Kidwell, Claudia B. and Margaret C. Christman. *Suiting Everyone: The Democratization of Clothing in America.* Washington, D.C.: The Smithsonian Institution Press, 1974.

Kimball, Gayle, ed. *Women's Culture: The Woman's Renaissance of the 1970's.* Metuchen, N.J. and London: Scarecrow Press, 1981.

König, René. *The Restless Image: A Sociology of Fashion.* Translated by F. Bradley. London: George Allen and Unwin Ltd., 1973.

Kopytoff, Igor. "The Cultural Biography of Things: Commoditization as Process." In *The Social Life of Things: Commodities in Cultural Perspective,* edited by Arjun Appadurai. Cambridge: Cambridge University Press, 1986.

Kunzle, David. *Fashion and Fetishism: A Social History of the Corset, Tight-Lacing and Other Forms of Body Sculpture in the West.* Totowa, N.J.: Rowan and Littlefield, 1982.

Lakoff, Robin Tolmach and Raquel L. Scherr. *Face Value: The Politics of Beauty.* Boston and London: Routledge & Kegan Paul, 1984.

Lang, Kurt and Gladys Long. "Fashion: Identification and Differentiation in the Mass Society." In *Dress, Adornment, and the Social Order,* edited by Mary Ellen Roach and Joanne Bubolz Eicher. New York: Wyley, 1965.

Laver, James. *Taste and Fashion: From the French Revolution Until Today.* London: George G. Harrap, 1937.

———. *Clothes.* New York: Horizon Press, 1953.

———. *Women's Dress in the Jazz Age.* London: Hamish Hamilton, 1964.

———. *Costume and Fashion: A Concise History*. New York: Oxford University Press, 1983.

Lee, Sarah Tomerlin, ed. *American Fashion: The Life and Lines of Adrian, Mainbocher, McCardell, Norell, and Trigère*. New York: Quadrangle/New York Times Book Co., 1975.

Ley, Sandra. *Fashion for Everyone: The Story of Ready-to-Wear (1870s–1970s)*. New York: Charles Scribner's, 1975.

Lowe, John W.G. and Elizabeth D. Lowe. "Cultural Pattern and Process: A Study of Stylistic Change in Women's Dress." *American Anthropologist* 84 (1982): 521–544.

Lurie, Alison. *The Language of Clothes*. New York: Random House, 1981.

Lynam, Ruth. *Couture: An Illustrated History of the Great Paris Designers and Their Creations*. New York: Doubleday and Co., 1972.

McKendrick, Neil. "The Commercialization of Fashion." In *The Birth of a Consumer Society: The Commercialization of Eighteenth Century England,* edited by Neil McKendrick, John Brewer and J.H. Plumb. Bloomington: Indiana University Press, 1982.

Marcus, Leonard. *The American Store Window*. New York: Whitney Library, 1978.

May, Lary. *Screening Out the Past: The Birth of Mass Culture and the Motion Picture Industry*. Chicago: University of Chicago Press, 1980.

Miller, Michael B. *The Bon Marché: Bourgeois Culture and the Department Store, 1869–1920*. Princeton: Princton University Press, 1981.

Nystrom, Paul. *Economic Principles of Consumption*. New York: Ronald Press Co., 1929.

———. *The Economics of Fashion*. New York: Ronald Press Co., 1928.

———. *Fashion Merchandising*. New York: Ronald Press Co., 1932.

Poiret, Paul. *My First Fifty Years*. London: Victor Gollancz, 1931.

Polhemus, Ted, ed. *The Body Reader: Social Aspects of the Human Body*. New York: Pantheon, 1978.

Polhemus, Ted and Lynn Procter. *Fashion and Anti-Fashion: Anthropology of Clothing and Adornment*. London: Thames & Hudson, 1978.

Richards, Florence S. *The Ready-To-Wear Industry 1900–1950*. New York: Fairchild Publications, Inc., 1951.

Richardson, Jane and A.L. Kroeber. "Three Centuries of Women's Dress Fashions: A Qualitative Analysis." *Anthropological Records,* vol.5, no.6. Berkeley and Los Angeles: University of California Press, 1940.

Riley, Robert and Walter Vecchio. *The Fashion Makers*. New York: Crown, 1967.

Rittenhouse, Anne. *The Well-Dressed Woman*. New York: Harpers, 1924.

Robinson, D.E. "The Importance of Fashions in Taste to Business History." *Business History Review* 37 (1963): 5–38.

Robinson, Gwen. *Crowning Glory: A Historical Analysis of the Afro-American Beauty Industry and Tradition*. Urbana: University of Illinois Press, forthcoming.

Rosencranz, Mary Lou. *Clothing Concepts*. New York: Macmillan Co., 1972.

Saisselin, Rémy. *The Bourgeois and the Bibelot*. New Brunswick: Rutgers University Press, 1984.

Sapir, Edward. "Fashion." In *Encyclopedia of the Social Sciences,* vol.6. New York: Macmillan Co., 1931.

Sennett, Richard. *The Fall of Public Man: On the Social Psychology of Capitalism*. New York: Knopf, 1977.

Shorter, Edward. *A History of Women's Bodies*. New York: Basic Books, 1982.

Silverman, Debora. *Selling Culture: Bloomingdale's Diana Vreeland, and the New Aristocracy of Taste in Reagan's America*. New York: Pantheon, 1986.

Sombart, Werner. *Luxury and Capitalism*. 1913. Reprint. Ann Arbor: University of Michigan Press, 1967.

Sproles. George B. "Analyzing Fashion Life Cycles: Principles and Perspectives." *Journal of Marketing* 45 (Fall 1981): 116–124.

Steele, Valerie. *Fashion and Eroticism: Ideals of Feminine Beauty from the Victorian through the Jazz Age*. New York: Oxford University Press, 1985.

Story, Margaret. *How to Dress Well*. New York: Funk & Wagnalls, 1924.

Swinney, John B. *Merchandizing of Fashions*. New York: Ronald Press Co., 1942.

Tate, Sharon Lee. *Inside Fashion*. 2nd ed. New York: Harper and Row, 1984.

Turner, Bryan S. *The Body and Society: Explorations in Social Theory*. Oxford: Basil Blackwell, 1984.

Veblen, Thorstein. *The Theory of the Leisure Class: An Economic Study of Institutions*. 1899. Reprint. New York: Macmillan, 1912.

Waugh, Norah. *The Cut of Women's Clothes 1600–1930*. London: Faber & Faber, 1968.

Wilcox, R. Turner. *The Mode in Costume*. New York: Charles Scribner's Sons, 1942.

———. *The Mode in Hats and Headdress*. New York: Charles Scribner's Sons, 1948.

Willett, C. and Phillis Cunningham. *The History of Underclothes*. 1951. Reprint. London & Boston: Faber & Faber, 1981.

Williams, Beryl. *Fashion is Our Business*. Philadelphia: Lippincott, 1945.

Young, Agnes B. *Recurring Cycles of Fashion*. New York: Harper's, 1937.

Feminism and Cultural Studies

Adorno, Theodor. *Aesthetic Theory*. Translated by C. Lenhardt. 1970. Reprint. London and New York: Routledge & Kegan Paul, 1984.

———. *Prisms*. Translated by Samuel Weber and Shierry Weber. 1967. Reprint. Cambridge, Mass.: MIT Press, 1982.

Adorno, Theodor and Max Horkheimer. *Dialectic of Enlightenment*. Translated by John Cumming. 1944. Reprint. New York: Continuum, 1987.

Affron, Charles. *Star Acting: Gish, Garbo, Davis*. New York: E.P. Dutton, 1977.

Allen, Jeanne Thomas. "The Film Viewer as Consumer." *Quarterly Review of Film Studies* 5, no. 4 (1980): 481–499.

Alloway, Lawrence. "Lawrence Alloway on Iconography in the Movies." In *Movie Reader*, edited by Ian Cameron. New York: Praeger, 1972.

Anderson, Rae. "The Dance of the Scarecrow Bride." In *Body Invaders: Sexuality and the Postmodern Condition*, edited by Arthur Kroker and Marilouise Kroker. London: Macmillan, 1988.

Ang, Ien. *Watching Dallas: Soap Opera and the Melodramatic Imagination*. London: Methuen, 1985.

Ascher, Carol. "Narcissism and Women's Clothing." *Socialist Review* 11, no. 3 (May-June 1981): 75–86.

Banks, Jane and Patricia R. Zimmerman. "The Mary Kay Way: The Feminization of a Corporate Discourse." *Journal of Communication Inquiry* 11 (1987): 85–97.

Barrett, Michèle. *Women's Oppression Today*. London: Verso, 1980.

————. "Ideology and the Cultural Production of Gender." In *Feminist Criticism and Social Change,* edited by Judith Newton and Deborah Rosenfelt. New York: Methuen, 1985.

Barry, Judith. "Casual Imagination." *Discourse* 4 (1981–82): 336–359.

Barthes, Roland. "Le Bleu est à la Mode cette année." *Revue Française de Sociologie* 1 no. 2 (April-June 1960): 147–162.

————. *Erté (Romain de Tirtoff)*. Translated by William Weaver. Parma: Franco Maria Ricci, 1972.

————. *Mythologies*. Translated by Annette Lavers. New York: Hill and Wang, 1972.

————. *The Pleasure of the Text*. Translated by Richard Miller. New York: Hill and Wang, 1975.

————. *The Fashion System*. Translated by Matthew Ward and Richard Howard. New York: Hill and Wang, 1983.

————. *The Responsibility of Forms*. Translated by Richard Howard. New York: Hill and Wang, 1985.

————. "Erté, or À la lettre." Translated by Richard Howard. In *The Responsibility of Forms*. New York: Hill and Wang, 1985.

Baudrillard, Jean. *For a Critique of the Political Economy of the Sign*. Translated by Charles Levin. St. Louis: Telos Press, 1981.

————. *Simulations*. Translated by Paul Foss. New York: Semiotext(e), 1983.

Beauvoir, Simone de. *The Second Sex*. Translated by H.M. Parshley. New York: Knopf, 1953.

Becker, Edith, Julia Lesage, Michelle Citron, and B. Ruby Rich. "Lesbians and Film: Introduction to Special Section." *Jump Cut* 24–25 (March 1981): 17–21. Reprinted in *Jump Cut: Hollywood, Politics and Counter-Cinema,* edited by Peter Steven. New York: Praeger, 1985.

Bell-Metereau, Rebecca. *Hollywood Androgyny*. New York: Columbia University Press, 1985.

Bellour, Raymond. "Interview with Roland Barthes." *Discourse* 2 (1980): 3–17.

Benjamin, Walter. "Art in the Age of Mechanical Reproduction." Translated by Harry Zohn. In *Illuminations,* edited by Hannah Arendt. Glasgow: Fontana/Collins, 1973.

————. "N. [Theoretics of Knowledge; Theory of Progress]." Translated by Mark Ritter. *The Philosophical Forum* 15, nos. 1–2 (Fall-Winter 1983–1984): 1–51.

Benson, Susan Porter. *Counter Cultures: Saleswomen, Managers, and Customers in American Department Stores, 1890–1940*. Urbana: University of Illinois Press, 1986.

Berger, John. *Ways of Seeing*. New York: Viking Press, 1972.

Bergstrom, Janet. "Androids and Androgyny." *Camera Obscura* 15 (1986): 37–64.

————. "Rereading the Work of Claire Johnston." *Camera Obscura* nos. 3–4 (Summer 1979): 21–31. Reprinted in *Feminism and Film,* edited by Constance Penley. New York: Routledge, 1988.

Betterton, Rosemary, ed. *Looking On: Images of Femininity in the Visual Arts and Media*. London and New York: Pandora, 1987.

Bogatyrev, Petr. "Costume as Sign." In *Semiotics of Art,* edited by Ladislav Matejka and Irwin R. Titunik. Cambridge, Mass.: MIT Press, 1976.

Bolton, Richard. "In the American East: Avedon Incorporated." *Afterimage* 5 (1987): 12–17.

Boone, Sylvia Ardyn. *Radiance from the Waters: Ideals of Feminine Beauty in Mende Art.* New Haven, Ct.: Yale University Press, 1986.

Borinsky, Alicia. "Jean Rhys: Poses of a Woman as Guest." In *The Body in Western Culture: Contemporary Perspectives,* edited by Susan Suleiman Rubin. Cambridge, Mass.: Harvard University Press, 1986.

Bowlby, Rachel. *Just Looking: Consumer Culture in Dreiser, Gissing, and Zola.* New York and London: Methuen, 1985.

Branigan, Ed. "The Articulation of Color in a Filmic System: *Two Or Three Things I Know About Her.*" *Wide Angle* 1 (1976): 20–31.

Britton, Andrew. *Katherine Hepburn: The Thirties and After.* Newcastle upon Tyne: Tyneside Cinema, 1984.

Brown, Beverly and Parveen Adams. "The Feminist Body and Feminist Politics." *m/f* no.3 (1979): 35–50.

Brumberg, Joan Jacobs. *Fasting Girls: The Emergence of Anorexia Nervosa as a Modern Disease.* Cambridge Mass.: Harvard University Press, 1988.

Brunsdon, Charlotte, ed. *Films for Women.* London: British Film Institute, 1986.

Buck-Morss, Susan. "Benjamin's *Passagen-Werk:* Redeeming Mass Culture for the Revolution." *New German Critique* 29 (1983): 212–240.

——. "The Flaneur, the Sandwichman and the Whore: The Politics of Loitering." *New German Critique* 39 (Fall 1986): 99–140.

Cahiers du Cinéma (collective text) no. 225 "MOROCCO." 1970. Translated by Diana Matias. Reprinted in *Sternberg,* edited by Peter Baxter. London: British Film Institute, 1980.

Carter, Angela. *Nothing Sacred: Selected Writings.* London: Virago, 1982.

Carter, Erica. "Alice in the Consumer Wonderland." In *Gender and Generation,* edited by Angela McRobbie and Mica Nava. London: Macmillan, 1984.

Caskey, Noelle, "Interpreting Anorexia Nervosa." In *The Female Body in Western Culture: Contemporary Perspectives,* edited by Susan Rubin Suleiman. Cambridge, Mass.: Harvard University Press, 1986.

Chaney, David. "The Department Store as a Cultural Form." *Theory, Culture and Society* 1, no.3 (1983): 22–31.

Chapkis, Wendy. *Beauty Secrets: Women and the Politics of Appearance.* Boston: South End Press, 1986.

Chernin, Kim. *The Obsession: Reflections on the Tyranny of Slenderness.* New York: Harper, 1981.

Chodorow, Nancy. *The Reproduction of Mothering: Psychoanalysis and the Sociology of Gender.* Berkeley: University of California Press, 1978.

Chris, Cynthia. "Pretty in Pink." *Afterimage* 16 (1988): 12–13.

Coward, Rosalind. *Female Desires: How They are Sought, Bought, and Packaged.* New York: Grove Press, 1985.

Cowie, Elizabeth. "Fantasia." *m/f* 9 (1984): 71–105.

Debord, Guy. *Society of the Spectacle.* 1967. Reprint. Detroit: Black and Red, 1983.

De Certeau, Michel. *The Practice of Everyday Life.* Translated by Steven F. Rendall. Berkeley: University of California Press, 1984.

De Cordova, Richard. "The Emergence of the Star System in America." *Wide Angle* 6, no.4 (1985): 4–13.

———. "The Emergence of the Star System in America: An Examination of the Institutional and Ideological Function of the Star." Ph.D. diss., University of California at Los Angeles, 1986.

De Lauretis, Teresa. *Alice Doesn't: Feminism, Semiotics, Cinema.* Bloomington: Indiana University Press, 1984.

———. *Technologies of Gender: Essays on Theory, Film, and Fiction.* Bloomington: Indiana University Press, 1987.

———. "Sexual Indifference and Lesbian Representation." *Theatre Journal* 40 (1988): 155–177.

Deutelbaum, Marshall. "Costuming and the Color System of LEAVE HER TO HEAVEN." *Film Criticism* 11, no.3 (1987): 11–20.

Diamond, Nicky. "Thin is the Feminist Issue." *Feminist Review* 19 (March 1985): 45–64.

Doane, Mary Ann. "Film and the Masquerade—Theorising the Female Spectator." *Screen* 23 (1982): 74–87.

———. *The Desire to Desire: The Woman's Film of the 1940s.* Bloomington: Indiana University Press, 1987.

———. "Woman's Stake: Filming the Female Body." *October* no. 17 (1981): 23–36. Reprinted in *Feminism and Film Theory,* edited by Constance Penley. New York: Routledge, 1988.

Doane, Mary Ann, Patricia Mellencamp, and Linda Williams, eds. *Re-Vision: Essays in Feminist Film Criticism.* Frederick, Md.: University Publications of America, 1984.

Dyer, Richard. "Social Values of Entertainment and Show Business." Ph.D. diss., Birmingham University, 1972.

———. "Entertainment and Utopia." *Movie* no. 24 (1977): 2–13.

———. "Resistance Through Charisma: Rita Hayworth and *Gilda.*" In *Women in Film Noir,* edited by E. Ann Kaplan. London: British Film Institute, 1978.

———. *Stars.* London: British Film Institute, 1979.

———. "Seen to be Believed: Some Problems in the Representation of Gay People as Typical." *Studies in Visual Communication* 9, no.2 (Spring 1983): 2–18.

———. *Heavenly Bodies: Film Stars and Society.* London: Macmillan, 1987.

Eckert, Charles. "The Anatomy of a Proletarian Film: Warner's MARKED WOMAN." *Film Quarterly* 17, no.2 (Winter 1973–74): 10–24. Reprinted in *Movies and Methods II,* edited by Bill Nichols. Berkeley: University of California Press, 1985.

———. "Shirley Temple and the House of Rockefeller." *Jump Cut* no. 2 (1974): 1, 17–20. Reprinted in *Jump Cut: Hollywood, Politics and Counter-Cinema,* edited by Peter Steven. New York: Praeger, 1985 and *American Media and Mass Culture: Left Perspectives,* edited by Donald Lazere. Berkeley: University of California Press, 1987.

Ellis, John. *Visible Fictions: Cinema, Television, Video.* London: Routledge & Kegan Paul, 1982.

Ellis, Kate et al., eds. *Caught Looking: Feminism, Pornography and Censorship.* New York: Caught Looking, Inc., 1987.

Ellsworth, Elizabeth. "Illicit Pleasures: Feminist Spectators and PERSONAL BEST." *Wide Angle* 8, no.2 (1986): 46–56.

Ellwanger, Karen and Eva-Maria Warth. *"Die Frau Meiner Träume (Woman Of My*

Dreams): Weiblichkeit und Maskerade: eine Untersuchung zu Form und Funktion von Kleidung als Zeichensystem im Film." *Frauen und Film* 38 (1985): 58–71.

Erens, Patricia, ed. *Sexual Stratagems: The World of Women in Film.* New York: Horizon Press, 1979.

Ewen, Elizabeth. *Immigrant Women in the Land of Dollars: Life and Culture on the Lower East Side, 1890–1925.* New York: Monthly Review Press, 1985.

Ewen, Elizabeth and Stuart Ewen. "Americanization and Consumption." *Telos* 37 (1978): 42–51.

Ewen, Stuart and Elizabeth Ewen. *Channels of Desire: Mass Images and the Shaping of American Consciousness.* New York: McGraw-Hill, 1982.

Ewen, Stuart. *Captains of Consciousness: Advertising and the Social Roots of the Consumer Culture.* New York: McGraw-Hill, 1976.

Ewen, Stuart. *All Consuming Images: The Politics of Style in Contemporary Culture.* New York: Basic Books, 1988.

Faurschou, Gail. "Fashion and the Cultural Logic of Postmodernity." In *Body Invaders: Sexuality and the Postmodern Condition,* edited by Arthur Kroker and Marilouise Kroker. London: Macmillan, 1988.

Featherstone, Mike. "The Body in Consumer Culture." *Theory, Culture and Society* 1 (1982): 18–26.

———. "Consumer Culture: An Introduction." *Theory, Culture and Society.* 1 (1982): 4–9.

Feuer, Jane. *The Hollywood Musical.* London: Macmillan, 1982.

———. "Reading DYNASTY: Television and Reception Theory." *South Atlantic Quarterly* 88, no.2 (1989).

Finch, Mark. "Sex and Address in 'Dynasty.' " *Screen* 27 (1986): 24–42.

Fischer, Lucy. "The Image of Woman as Image: The Optical Politics of DAMES." In *Sexual Strategems: The World of Women in Film,* edited by Patricia Erens. New York: Horizon Press, 1979.

Fiske, John. "British Cultural Studies and Television." In *Channels of Discourse,* edited by Robert C. Allen. Chapel Hill: University of North Carolina Press, 1987.

———. *Television Culture.* New York: Methuen, 1987.

———. "Critical Response: Meaningful Moments." *Critical Studies in Mass Communication* 5 (September 1988): 246–251.

Fletcher, John. "Versions of Masquerade." *Screen* 29 (1988): 43–70.

Fox-Genovese, Elizabeth. "Yves Saint-Laurent's Peasant Revolution." *Marxist Perspectives* no. 2 (1978): 216–240.

Friedberg, Anne. "Identification and the Star: A Refusal of Difference." In *Star Signs,* edited by Christine Gledhill et al. London: British Film Institute, 1982.

Frisby, David. "Georg Simmel: First Sociologist of Modernity." *Theory, Culture and Society* 2, no. 3 (1985): 49–67.

Frith, Simon. *Sound Effects: Youth, Leisure and the Politics of Rock 'n' Roll.* New York: Pantheon, 1981.

Gaines, Jane M. "Women and Representation: Can We Enjoy Alternative Pleasure?" In *American Media and Mass Culture: Left Perspectives,* edited by Donald Lazere. Berkeley: University of California Press, 1987.

———. "The *Queen Christina* Tie-ups: Convergence of Show Window and Screen." *Quarterly Review of Film and Video* 11, no. 1 (1989).

Gaines, Jane M. and Charlotte C. Herzog. "Hildy Johnson and the 'Man-Tailored Suit': The Comedy of Inequality." *Film Reader* 5 (Winter 1982): 232–246.

Gallagher, Catherine and Thomas Laqueur, eds. *The Making of the Modern Body: Sexuality and Society in the Nineteenth Century*. Berkeley: University of California Press, 1987.

Galler, Roberta. "The Myth of the Perfect Body." In *Pleasure and Danger*, edited by Carole S. Vance. Boston: Routledge & Kegan Paul, 1984.

Gallop, Jane. *Thinking Through the Body*. New York: Columbia University Press, 1988.

Gamman, Lorraine and Margaret Marshment, eds. *The Female Gaze: Women as Viewers of Popular Culture*. London: The Women's Press, 1988.

Gledhill, Christine, ed. *Home is Where the Heart Is: Studies in Melodrama and the Woman's Film*. London: British Film Institute, 1987.

Gilbert, Sandra M. "Costumes of the Mind: Transvestism as Metaphor in Modern Literature." In *Writing and Sexual Difference*, edited by Elizabeth Abel. Chicago: Universtity of Chicago Press, 1982.

Goldberg, Marianne. "Ballerinas and Ball Passing." *Women and Performance: A Journal of Feminist Theory* 3, no.2 (1987–1988): 7–31.

———. "The Body, Discourse, and *The Man Who Envied Women*." *Women and Performance: A Journal of Feminist Theory* 3, no. 2 (1987–1988): 97–102.

Gornich, Vivian. "Introduction." In Erving Goffman. *Gender Advertisements*. New York: Harper's, 1979.

Grossberg, Larry. " 'I'd Rather Feel Bad Than Not Feel Anything at All': Rock and Roll, Pleasure and Power." *Enclitic* 8, nos. 1–2 (1984): 94–111.

Hake, Sabine. "Girls and Crisis: The Other Side of Diversion." *New German Critique* 40 (Winter 1987): 147–166.

Hall, Stuart and Tony Jefferson, eds. *Resistance through Rituals: Youth Subcultures in Post-War Britain*. London: Hutchinson, 1976.

Hall, Stuart. "Culture, the Media and the 'Ideological Effect.' " In *Mass Communication and Society*, edited by James Curran, Michael Gurevitch, and Janet Woolacott. Beverly Hills: Sage Publications, 1979.

———. "Cultural Studies at the Center: Some Problematics and Problems." In *Culture, Media, Language*, edited by Stuart Hall, Dorothy Hobson, Andrew Lowe, and Paul Willis. London: Hutchinson, 1980.

———. "Encoding/Decoding." In *Culture, Media, Language*, edited by Stuart Hall, Dorothy Hobson, Andrew Lowe, and Paul Willis. London: Hutchinson, 1980.

Hansen, Joseph and Evelyn Reed. *Cosmetics, Fashions, and the Exploitation of Women*. New York: Pathfinder, 1986.

Hansen, Miriam. "Pleasure, Ambivalence, Identification: Valentino and Female Spectatorship." *Cinema Journal* 25, no.4 (Summer 1986): 6–32.

———. "Benjamin, Cinema and Experience: 'The Blue Flower in the Land of Technology.' " *New German Critique* 40 (Winter 1987): 179–224.

Harper, Sue. "Art Direction and Costume Design." In *Gainsborough Melodrama*, edited by Sue Aspinall and Robert Murphy. London: British Film Institute, 1983.

———. "Historical Pleasures: Gainsborough Costume Melodrama." In *Home is Where the Heart Is*, edited by Christine Gledhill. London: British Film Institute, 1987.

Haskell, Molly. *From Reverence to Rape: The Treatment of Women in the Movies*. New York: Holt, Rinehart & Winston, 1973.

Haug, W.F. *Critique of Commodity Aesthetics: Appearance, Sexuality and Advertising in*

Capitalist Society. Translated by Wolfgang Fritz Haug. Minneapolis: University of Minnesota Press, 1986.

Heath, Stephen. "Film Performance." *Ciné-tracts*. 2 (1977): 7–17.

Hebdige, Dick. *Subculture: The Meaning of Style*. (London: Methuen, 1979).

Herzog, Charlotte C. and Jane M. Gaines. " 'Puffed Sleeves Before Teatime': Joan Crawford, Adrian and Women Audiences." *Wide Angle* 6, no. 4. (1985): 24–33.

Hoggart, Richard. *The Uses of Literacy*. 1957. Reprint. New York: Oxford University Press, 1970.

Hollander, Anne. "Moving Pictures." *Raritan* 5 (Winter 1986): 82–102.

Huyssen, Andreas. "Introduction to Adorno." *New German Critique* 6 (Fall 1975): 3–19

Jameson, Fredric. "Reification and Utopia in Mass Culture." *Social Text* 1 (Winter 1979): 129–148.

Jardine, Alice. "Alice in Wonderland: Looking for the Body." In *Utopia Post Utopia: Configurations of Nature and Culture in Recent Sculpture and Photography* catalogue of exhibition, Institute of Contemporary Art, Boston, Jan. 29-March 27, 1988, Cambridge, Mass.: MIT Press, 1988.

Johnston, Claire. "Woman's Cinema as Counter-Cinema." In *Notes on Women's Cinema,* edited by Claire Johnston. London: Society for Education in Film and Television, 1973. Reprinted in *Movies and Methods,* edited by Bill Nichols. Berkeley: University of California Press, 1976.

———. "Femininity and the Masquerade: ANNE OF THE INDIES." In *Jacques Tourneur,* edited by Claire Johnston and Paul Willeman. Edinburgh: Edinburgh Film Festival, 1975.

Kaite, Berkeley. "The Pornographic Body Double: Transgression is the Law." In *Body Invaders: Sexuality and the Postmodern Condition,* edited by Arthur Kroker and Marilouise Kroker. London: Macmillan, 1988.

Kalinak, Kathryn. "FLASHDANCE: The Dead-End Kid." *Jump Cut* no. 29 (February 1984): 3–5.

Kaplan, E. Ann, ed. *Women in Film Noir*. London: British Film Institute, 1978.

Kaplan, E. Ann. *Women and Film: Both Sides of the Camera*. New York: Methuen, 1983.

Kay, Karyn and Gerald Peary. *Women and the Cinema: A Critical Anthology*. New York: E.P. Dutton, 1977.

Kellner, Douglas. "Critical Theory, Commodities and the Consumer Society." *Theory, Culture and Society* 1 (1983): 66–81.

Kimball, Barbara. "Women and Fashion." In *Women's Culture,* edited by Gayle Kimball. Metuchen, N.J.: Scarecrow Press, 1981.

King, Barry. "The Hollywood Star System." Ph.D. diss., University of London, 1984.

———. "The Star and the Commodity: Notes Towards a Performance Theory of Stardom." *Cultural Studies* 1, no.2 (May 1987): 145–161.

Kirby, Lynn. "Fassbinder's Debt to Poussin." *Camera Obscura* 13/14 (1985): 5–23.

Kleinhans, Chuck. "Fashioning the Fetish: The Social Semiotics of High Heel Shoe Images." Unpublished paper.

———. "SHAMPOO: Oedipal Symmetries and Heterosexual Satire." *Jump Cut* no. 26 (December 1981): 12–18.

Kracauer, Siegfried. "Cult of Distraction: On Berlin's Picture Palaces." Translated by Thomas Y. Levin. *New German Critique* 40 (1987): 91–96.

————. *The Mass Ornament*. Translated by Thomas Y. Levin. Cambridge, Mass.: Harvard University Press, forthcoming.

Kristeva, Julia. *Desire in Language: A Semiotic Approach to Literature and Art*. New York: Columbia University Press, 1980.

Kroker, Arthur and Marilouise Kroker, eds. *Body Invaders: Sexuality and the Postmodern Condition*. London: Macmillan, 1988.

————. *The Power of the Image: Essays in Representation and Sexuality*. London: Routledge & Kegan Paul, 1985.

Kuhn, Annette. *Women's Pictures: Feminism and Cinema*. London: Routledge & Kegan Paul, 1982.

LaPlace Maria. "Producing and Consuming the Woman's Film: Discursive Struggle in *Now, Voyager*." In *Home is Where the Heart Is,* edited by Christine Gledhill. London: British Film Institute, 1987.

Lefebvre, Henri. *Everyday Life in the Modern World*. Translated by Sacha Rabinovitch. 1967. Reprint. London: Penguin, 1971.

Lesage, Julia. "*Celine and Julie Go Boating:* Subversive Fantasy." *Jump Cut* nos. 24–25 (March 1981): 36–43.

Lewis, Lisa A. "Female Address in Music Video." *Journal of Communcation Inquiry* 11 (1987): 73–84.

————. "Female Address in Music Video: The Emergence of a Contradictory Cultural Discourse." Ph.D. diss., University of Texas-Austin, 1987.

Lippard, Lucy R. *Get the Message? A Decade of Art for Social Change*. New York: E.P. Dutton, 1984.

Lovell, Terry. *Consuming Fiction*. London: Verso, 1987.

McRobbie, Angela. "Working Class Girls and the Culture of Femininity." In *Women Take Issue,* edited by Women's Study Group. London: Hutchinson, 1978.

————. "Settling Accounts with Subcultures." In *Culture, Ideology, and Social Process: A Reader,* edited by Tony Bennett et al. London: The Open University, 1981.

————. "*Jackie:* The Ideology of Adolescent Femininity." In *Popular Culture: Past and Present,* edited by Bernard Waites, Tony Bennett, and Graham Martin. London: Croom Helm, 1982.

————. "Dance and Social Fantasy." In *Gender and Generation,* edited by Angela McRobbie and Mica Nava. London: Macmillan, 1984.

————. "Fashion and Sexuality." *Women's Review* 13 (1986): 13–14.

————. "Postmodernism and Popular Culture." In *Postmodernism: ICA Documents* 4, edited by Lisa Appignanesi. London: Institute of Contemporary Arts, 1986. Reprinted in *Journal of Communication Inquiry* 10, no.2 (Summer 1986): 108–116.

McRobbie, Angela and Mica Nava, eds. *Gender and Generation*. London: Macmillan, 1984.

Marchetti, Gina. "Readings on Women and Pornography." *Jump Cut* no. 26 (December 1981): 46–47.

Matthews, Peter. "Garbo and Phallic Motherhood—A 'Homosexual' Visual Economy." *Screen* 29 (1988): 43–80.

Mayne, Judith. "Immigrants and Spectators." *Wide Angle* 5 (1982): 32–40.

Mellencamp, Patricia. "Spectacle and Spectator: Looking Through the American Musical Comedy." *Ciné-tracts* 1 (1977): 27–35.

Merck, Mandy. "Introduction—Difference and Its Discontents." *Screen* 28 (1987): 2–9.

Modleski, Tania. *Loving with a Vengeance: Mass-Produced Fantasies for Women*. New York: Methuen, 1982.

―――, ed. *Studies in Entertainment: Critical Approaches to Mass Culture*. Bloomington: Indiana University Press, 1986.

―――. *The Women Who Knew Too Much: Hitchcock and Feminist Theory*. New York and London: Methuen, 1988.

Morin, Edgar. *The Stars*. Translated by Richard Howard. London and New York: Grove Press, 1961.

Morse, Margaret. "Sport on Television: Replay and Display." In *Regarding Television: Critical Approaches—An Anthology*, edited by E. Ann Kaplan. Frederick, Md.: University Publications of America, 1983.

―――. "Artemis Aging: Exercise and the Female Body on Video." *Discourse* 10 (1987–88): 20–53.

Mulvey, Laura. "Visual Pleasure and Narrative Cinema." *Screen* 16 (1975): 6–18. Reprinted in *Feminism and Film Theory*, edited by Constance Penley. New York: Routledge, 1988.

―――. "Afterthoughts on 'Visual Pleasure and Narrative Cinema' inspired by *Duel In The Sun*." *Framework* 6, nos. 15–17 (Summer 1981): 12–15. Reprinted in *Feminism and Film Theory*, edited by Constance Penley. New York: Routledge, 1988.

―――. "You Don't Know What's Happening Do You, Mr. Jones?" In *Spare Rib Reader*, edited by Marsha Rowe. London: Penguin, 1982.

―――. "Changes." *Discourse* 7 (Fall 1985): 11–30.

―――. "Melodrama In and Out of the Home." In *High Theory/Low Culture*, edited by Colin MacCabe. New York: St. Martin's Press, 1986.

―――. *Visual and Other Pleasures*. Bloomington: Indiana University Press, 1989.

Mulvey, Laura and Peter Wollen. "The Discourse of the Body." In *Looking On: Images of Femininity in the Visual Arts and Media*, edited by Rosemary Betterton. London and New York: Pandora, 1987.

Murray, Timothy. "Subliminal Libraries: Showing Lady Liberty and Documenting Death." *Discourse* 9 (1987): 107–124.

Myers, Kathy. "Fashion 'n' Passion." *Screen* 3–4 (1982): 89–97. Reprinted in *Looking On: Images of Femininity in the Visual Arts and Media*, edited by Rosemary Betterton. London and New York: Pandora, 1987.

―――. "Towards a Feminist Erotica." In *Looking On: Images of Femininity in the Visual Arts and Media*, edited by Rosemary Betterton. London and New York: Pandora, 1987.

Nava, Mica. "Consumerism and its Contradictions." *Cultural Studies* 1, no.2 (May 1987): 204–210.

Neale, Steve. "Melodrama and Tears." *Screen* 27 (1986): 6–22.

Nichols, Bill, ed. *Movies and Methods*. Berkeley: University of California Press, 1976.

―――. *Movies and Methods II*. Berkeley: University of California Press, 1985.

Owens, Craig. "The Discourse of Others: Feminism and Postmodernism." In *The Anti-Aesthetic*, edited by Hal Foster. Port Townsend, Wa.: Bay Press, 1983.

―――. "Posing." In *Difference: On Representation and Sexuality*, edited by Kate Linker and Jane Weinstock. New York: The New Museum of Contemporary Art, 1985.

Pacteau, Francette. "The Impossible Referent: Representation of the Androgyne." In *Formations of Fantasy*, edited by Victor Burgin, James Donald, and Cora Kaplan. New York: Methuen, 1986.

Parker, Rozsika. *The Subversive Stitch: Embroidery and the Making of the Feminine.* London: The Women's Press, 1984.

Patton, Cindy. "Brave New Lesbians." *Village Voice,* 2 July 1985, 24–25.

Peiss, Kathy. *Cheap Amusements: Working Women and Leisure in New York City, 1880 to 1920.* Philadelphia: Temple University Press, 1986.

Penley, Constance, ed. *Feminism and Film Theory.* New York: Routledge, 1988.

Polan, Dana. " 'Above All Else to Make You See': Cinema and the Ideology of Spectacle." *Boundary* 2 (1982–83): 129–144.

Pollock, Griselda. "What's Wrong with Images of Women?" *Screen Education* 24 (1977): 25–33. Reprinted in *Looking On: Images of Femininity in the Visual Arts and Media,* edited by Rosemary Betterton. London and New York: Pandora, 1987.

Prisco, Dorothy D. "Women and Social Change as Reflected in a Major Fashion Magazine." *Journalism Quarterly* 59 (1982): 131–134.

Probyn, Elspeth. "The Anorexic Body." In *Body Invaders: Sexuality and the Postmodern Condition,* edited by Arthur Kroker and Marilouise Kroker. London: Macmillan, 1988.

Pumphery, Martin. "The Flapper, the Housewife and the Making of Modernity." *Cultural Studies* 1, no.2 (May 1987): 179–194.

Radway, Janice A. *Reading the Romance: Women, Patriarchy, and Popular Literature.* Chapel Hill: University of North Carolina Press, 1984.

Rapp, Rayna and Ellen Ross. "The Twenties' Backlash: Compulsory Heterosexuality, the Consumer Family, and the Waning of Feminism." In *Class, Race and Sex: The Dynamics of Control,* edited by Amy Swerdlow and Hanna Lessinger. Boston: G.K. Hall, 1983.

Roach, Jacqui and Peter Felix. "Black Looks." In *The Female Gaze: Women as Viewers of Popular Culture,* edited by Lorraine Gamman and Margaret Marchment. London: The Women's Press, 1988.

Roberts, Helene E. "The Exquisite Slave: The Role of Clothes in the Making of the Victorian Woman." *Signs* 2, no.3 (1977): 554–579.

———. "Submission, Masochism and Narcissism: Three Aspects of Women's Role as Reflected in Dress." In *Women's Lives: Perspectives on Progress and Change,* edited by Virginia Lee Lussier and Joyce Jennings Walstedt. Newark, Del.: University of Delaware, 1977.

Russ, Joanna. *Magic Mommas, Trembling Sisters, Puritans and Perverts: Feminist Essays.* Trumansburg, N.Y.: Crossing Press, 1985.

Scarry, Elaine. *The Body in Pain: The Making and Remaking of the World.* London and New York: Oxford University Press, 1985.

Schiebinger, Londa. "Skeletons in the Closet: The First Illustrations of the Female Skeleton in Nineteenth-Century Anatomy." *Representations* 14 (Spring 1986): 42–82.

Schlüpmann, Heidi. "Politik als Schuld. Zur Funktion des historischen Kostüms in Weiblichkeitsbildern der Filme MARIA IIONA (1939) und KÖNIGIN LUISE (1956)." *Frauen und Film* 38 (1985): 47–57.

———. "Phenomonology of Film: On Siegfried Kracauer's Writings of the 1920s." *New German Critique* 40 (Winter 1987): 97–114.

Shapiro, Susan C. "Sex, Gender and Fashion in Medieval and Early Modern Britain." *Journal of Popular Culture* 20, no.4 (Spring 1987): 113–128.

Silverman, Kaja. *The Subject of Semiotics.* New York: Oxford University Press, 1983.

———. "Fragments of a Fashionable Discourse." In *Studies in Entertainment,* edited by Tania Modleski. Bloomington: Indiana University Press, 1986.

Simmel, Georg. "Fashion." In *On Individuality and Social Forms,* edited by Donald N. Levine. Chicago: University of Chicago Press, 1971.

Snitow, Ann, Christine Stansell and Sharon Thompson, eds. *Powers of Desire: The Politics of Sexuality.* New York: Monthly Review Press, 1983.

Spivak, Gayatri Chakravorty. "Displacement and the Discourse of Woman." In *Displacement: Derrida and After,* edited by Mark Krupnick. Bloomington: Indiana University Press, 1983.

Stacey, Jackie. "Desperately Seeking Difference." In *The Female Gaze: Women as Viewers of Popular Culture,* edited by Lorraine Gamman and Margaret Marshment. London: The Women's Press, 1988.

Stansell, Christine. *City of Women: Sex and Class in New York, 1789–1860.* New York: Knopf, 1986.

Steven, Peter. "Body Politics: Some Notes on the Stealing and Selling of Non-Verbal Communication." *Film Reader* 5 (1982): 203–215.

Straayer, Arny Christine. "Sexual Subjects: Signification, Viewership, and Pleasure in Film and Video." Ph.D. diss., Northwestern University, 1989.

Studlar, Gaylyn. *In the Realm of Pleasure: Von Sternberg, Dietrich, and the Masochistic Aesthetic.* Urbana and Chicago: University of Illinois Press, 1988.

Suleiman, Susan Rubin, ed. *The Female Body in Western Culture: Contemporary Perspectives.* Cambridge, Mass.: Harvard University Press, 1986.

Tickner, Lisa. " . . . and they sewed fig leaves together . . . " *Spare Rib* no. 45 (April 1976): 14–16.

———. "Fashionable Bondage." *Spare Rib* no. 47 (June 1976): 12–14.

———. "Allen Jones in Retrospect: A Serpentine Review." *Block* 1 (1979): 39–46.

———. "Why Not Slip into Something a Little More Comfortable?" In *Spare Rib Reader,* edited by Marsha Rose. London: Penguin, 1982.

Turim, Maureen. "Gentlemen Consume Blondes." *Wide Angle* 1 (1979): 52–59. Reprinted in *Movies and Methods II,* edited by Bill Nichols. Berkeley: University of California Press: 1985.

———. "Fashion Shapes: Film, the Fashion Industry and the Image of Women." *Socialist Review* 71 (1983): 83–95.

———. "What is Sexual Difference?" *Afterimage* 12 (1985): 4–5.

Vance, Carole S., ed. *Pleasure and Danger: Exploring Female Sexuality.* Boston: Routledge & Kegan Paul, 1984.

Waldman, Diane. "Critical Theory and Film: Adorno and 'The Culture Industry' Revisited." *New German Critique* 12 (Fall 1977): 39–59.

———. "What's Wrong with Positive Images?" *Jump Cut* no. 18 (August 1978): 31–32. Reprinted in *Jump Cut: Hollywood, Politics, and Counter-Cinema,* edited by Peter Steven. New York: Praeger, 1985.

———. "From Midnight Shows to Marriage Vows: Women Exploitation, and Exhibition." *Wide Angle* 6, no. 2 (1984): 40–48.

Warner, Marina. *Monuments and Maidens: The Allegory of the Female Form.* London: Picador, 1985.

Whitaker, Claire. "Hollywood Transformed: Interviews with Lesbian Viewers." In *Jump Cut: Hollywood, Politics and Counter-Cinema,* edited by Peter Steven. New York: Praeger, 1985.

Williams, Linda. "Film Body: An Implantation of Perversions." *Ciñe-tracts* 3, no. 4

(Winter 1981): 19–35. Reprinted in *Narrative, Apparatus, Ideology: A Film Theory Reader,* edited by Philip Rosen. New York: Columbia University Press, 1986.

Williamson, Judith. "Images of 'Woman.' " *Screen* 24, no. 6 (November-December 1983): 102–106. Reprinted in Judith Williamson. *Consuming Passions: The Dynamics of Popular Culture.* London: Marion Boyars, 1986.

———. *Consuming Passions: The Dynamics of Popular Culture.* London: Marion Boyars, 1986.

Willis, Ellen. "Consumerism and Women." *Socialist Review* 3 (1970): 76–82.

Willis, Susan. *A Primer for Daily Life.* New York and London: Routledge, forthcoming.

———. "Work(ing) Out." *Cultural Studies,* forthcoming.

Wilson, Elizabeth. "How Much is it Worth?" *Red Rag* 10 (1976): 6–9.

———. *Adorned in Dreams: Fashion and Modernity.* London: Virago, 1985.

Winship, Janice. *Inside Women's Magazines.* London: Pandora, 1987.

Wohlfarth, Irving. "Re-fusing Theology. Some First Responses to Walter Benjamin's Arcades Project." *New German Critique* 39 (Fall 1986): 3–24.

Wollen, Peter. "Fashion/Orientalism/The Body." *New Formations* 1 (Spring 1987): 5–34.

Wood, Robin. "Sternberg's Empress: The Play of Light and Shade." *Film Comment* 11 (March-April 1975): 6–10.

———. "Venus de Marlene." *Film Comment* 14 (March-April 1978): 58–63.

Yeck, Joanne Louise. "The Woman's Film at Warner Brothers, 1935–1950." Ph.D. diss., University of Southern California, 1982.

List of Contributors

JEANNE THOMAS ALLEN is an Associate Professor in the Department of Radio Television and Film at Temple University.

SERAFINA K. BATHRICK is an Associate Professor in the Communications Department at Hunter College.

CHARLES ECKERT was an Associate Professor in the English Department at Indiana University when he died in 1976.

JANE M. GAINES is an Assistant Professor in the English Department at Duke University.

CHARLOTTE HERZOG is an Associate Professor in the Art Department at William Rainey Harper College.

ANGELA MCROBBIE is a lecturer in Sociology at Ealing College of Higher Education, London.

ELIZABETH NIELSEN is an Assistant Professor in the Communications Department at Florida Atlantic University.

LAURIE SCHULZE is an Assistant Professor in the Department of Mass Communications at the University of Denver.

GAYLYN STUDLAR is an Assistant Professor in the Department of Theater and Film at Emory University.

MAUREEN TURIM is an Associate Professor in the Cinema Department at the State University of New York at Binghamton.

ELIZABETH WILSON is a Senior Lecturer in the Department of Applied Social Studies at Polytechnic of North London.

AFI Film Readers, published in cooperation with the American Film Institute, focus on important issues and themes in film and video scholarship. Series editors: **Edward Branigan** and **Charles Wolfe**, Film Studies Program, University of California, Santa Barbara.

Women consume, women observe, women indulge in an opulent and spectacular consumer culture—and they pay a price. They are both the target and the raw material of the culture of the body. **Fabrications** interrogates the construction of the female body, from turn-of-the-century colossal statuary to 1950s Sweetheart fashions to contemporary body-building.

Fabrications begins with a single germ in feminist film theory—the "to-be-looked-at" aesthetic described by Laura Mulvey—and pushes it further, considering the pleasures women derive from consumer culture against the social costs they have paid as wife, mother, and worker. Here, American feminist film theory converges with British cultural studies; critics from both sides of the Atlantic survey the connections between the female consumer and the female viewer, the motion picture industry and the ready wear industry, the fashion in critical theory and the fashion in clothes. Bringing together theories of representation, narrative and readership theory, audience ethnography, and other fields, **Fabrications** offers an intriguing perspective on the female body in contemporary culture.

Contributors: Jeanne Allen, Sarafina K. Bathrick, Charles Eckert, Jane M. Gaines, Charlotte Herzog, Angela McRobbie, Betsy Holdsworth Nielson, Laurie Schulze, Gaye Studlar, Maureen Turim, Elizabeth Wilson.

Jane M. Gaines is Assistant Professor of English at Duke University. **Charlotte Herzog** is Associate Professor in the Art Department at William Rainey Harper College.